Monographs in Computer Science

Editors

David Gries
Fred B. Schneider

W0080069

Springer Science+Business Media, LLC

Monographs in Computer Science

Andrew Herbert
Karen Spärck Jones
Editors

Computer Systems

Theory, Technology,
and Applications

A Tribute to Roger Needham

With 110 Illustrations

Springer

Andrew Herbert
Microsoft Research Ltd.
Roger Needham Building
7 JJ Thomson Avenue
Cambridge CB3 0FB
UK

Karen Spärck Jones
Computer Laboratory
University of Cambridge
JJ Thomson Avenue
Cambridge CB3 0FD
UK

Series Editors:
David Gries
Department of Computer Science
The University of Georgia
415 Boyd Graduate Studies
  Research Center
Athens, GA 30602-7404
USA

Fred B. Schneider
Department of Computer Science
Cornell University
4115C Upson Hall
Ithaca, NY 14853-7501
USA

Library of Congress Cataloging-in-Publication Data
Herbert, A.J. (Andrew J.), 1954–
    Computer systems: theory, technology, and applications/[edited by] Andrew J. Herbert,
Karen I.B. Spärck Jones
    p. cm. — (Monographs in computer science)
    Includes bibliographical references.
    ISBN 978-1-4757-8075-8   ISBN 978-0-387-21821-2 (eBook)
    DOI 10.1007/978-0-387-21821-2

    1. System design.   2. Computer science.   I. Spärck Jones, Karen I.B.   II. Needham,
R.M. (Roger Michael)   III. Title.   IV. Series.

QA276.9.S88H45 2004
005.1'2—dc21   2003066215

Printed on acid-free paper.

© 2004 Springer Science+Business Media New York
Originally published by Springer-Verlag New York, Inc. in 2004.
Softcover reprint of the hardcover 1st edition 2004

9 8 7 6 5 4 3 2 1   SPIN 10944769

springeronline.com

Roger Needham
1935 – 2003

Contents

Preface

Roger learnt that he was seriously ill late in December 2002. When he heard this, Rick Rashid, Microsoft Senior Vice-President for Research, suggested that there should be some occasion to mark Roger's contribution to the field, and an associated publication.

In response, we proposed a one-day meeting with both technical talks and a more personal session about Roger, with the presentation of a volume of papers from Roger's many technical colleagues as the key element.

There was not much time to prepare the volume. So we asked for short papers on any technical topic of each contributor's choosing likely to be of interest to Roger. The papers could be on an area of current research, a conjecture about the future, or an historical reflection. They had to be delivered in four weeks. We much appreciated the rapid and enthusiastic responses to our invitation, and were delighted with the range of topics covered and their technical interest. We were also grateful, as each editor reviewed all the papers, for the positive spirit with which our comments and suggestions were received.

The meeting itself, 'Roger Needham: 50 and 5,' marking Roger's fifty years in Cambridge and five at Microsoft Research, took place on February 17th, 2003. The programme is given, for reference, following this Preface. The entire proceedings were recorded, publicly available at:

        http://www.research.microsoft.com/needhambook

We would like to thank all those who wrote for the volume, and those who spoke at the meeting.

We know that Roger was very touched by how many came to the meeting, some from far away, by how many wrote for the volume and in doing so responded to his interests, by the references to his work in the technical talks, and by the accounts of his roles and contributions in the presentation session. At the end of the meeting he said:

> The first thing to say is thank you very much—which is sort of obvious.

> The next thing I want to say is one or two words about what I've done and what my subject is. In many sorts of engineering the theoretical background is obvious: it's continuous mathematics which comes from the 18th century. In computing there is a theoretical background and it's not obvious but it had to be invented, and people in the theoretical part of our subject have devoted themselves to inventing it—which is fine because you can't expect it to happen by itself and you can't go and build computer systems with any complexity at all without some formalised understanding to fall back on.

It is an odd thing that in my career I have contributed one or two bits to that, but that's basically not what I'm about.

I have the greatest respect for the people who build the theoretical underpinnings of our subject, and I wish them every success because it will enable the people who want to get on and make things to do it better and to do it more quickly and to do it with less mistakes—and all of this is good: but at the end of the day I am a engineer—

and so saying, he put on his engineer's hard hat. He died less than two weeks later, on March 1st.

Roger's last major talk was his Clifford Paterson Lecture 'Computer security?' at The Royal Society in November 2002. We have included its text, which is also posthumously published in the Society's *Philosophical Transactions*, as the last paper in the volume, along with a complete list of Roger's publications. We have used the classic Needham-Schroeder authentication protocol as the cover design.

The papers in this volume are as they originally appeared for the meeting, apart from some minor corrections and some small modifications, necessary in the circumstances, to specific references to Roger.

These papers address issues over the whole area of computer systems, from hardware through operating systems and middleware to applications, with their languages and their implementations, and from devices to global networks; also from many points of view, from designers to users, with lessons from the past or concerns for the future. Collectively, they illustrate what it means to be a computer system.

Acknowledgements

We are very grateful to Microsoft for supporting the celebration meeting itself, producing the volume in its original form, and for further supporting the preparation of the volume for formal publication.

We are also grateful to Professor Fred Schneider for facilitating the Springer publication and to Tammy Monteith for her work on formatting the material.

Andrew Herbert, Karen Spärck Jones

Roger Needham: 50 + 5
Meeting Programme

	Title	Presenter
Time		
11 am	Introduction	Andrew Herbert, Microsoft Research
	TECHNICAL TALKS	
11.05 am	Location Aware Computing	Andy Hopper, Cambridge University
11.30 am	How Software Components Grew Up and Conquered the World	Butler Lampson, Microsoft Research
12 noon	Thoughts on Network Protocol Engineering	Jonathan Smith, University of Pennsylvania
12.30 pm	*Lunch*	
1.30 pm	Online Science: Putting All Science Data Online and Putting Analysis Tools Online.	Jim Gray, Microsoft Research
2 pm	Logics and Languages for Access Control	Martin Abadi, UCSC
2.30 pm	Protocol Analysis, Composability and Computation	Ross Anderson, Cambridge University
3.00 pm	*Coffee*	
3.30 pm	Information and Classification	Karen Spärck Jones, Cambridge University
	Clumps, Clusters and Classification	Christopher Bishop, Microsoft Research
	IN HONOUR OF ROGER NEEDHAM	
4.10 pm	Early Days	Maurice Wilkes, Cambridge University
4.20 pm	Head of Department, Computer Laboratory	Ian Leslie, Cambridge University
4.30 pm	PARC/DEC-SRC Activities	Mike Schroeder, Microsoft Research
4.40 pm	Pro Vice-Chancellor, Public Service	Alec Broers, Cambridge University
4.45 pm	Microsoft Managing Director	Rick Rashid, Microsoft Research
4.55 pm	Presentation	Andrew Herbert Microsoft Research
5 pm	*Reception*	

Contributors

Martín Abadi
University of California, Santa Cruz,
CA, USA

Ross Anderson
University of Cambridge, England

Jean Bacon
University of Cambridge, England

Andrew Birrell
Microsoft Research—Silicon Valley,
CA, USA

Christopher Bishop
Microsoft Research Ltd, Cambridge,
England

Michael Bond
University of Cambridge, England

Alan Bundy
University of Edinburgh, Scotland

Mike Burrows
Google Research, Mountain View, CA,
USA

Luca Cardelli
Microsoft Research Ltd, Cambridge,
England

David Clark
MIT, Cambridge, MA, USA

John Crowcroft
University of Cambridge, England

Ewen Denney
QSS Group Inc, NASA, Moffet Field,
CA, USA

Dorothy Denning
Naval Postgraduate School, Monterey,
CA, USA

Peter Denning
Naval Postgraduate School, Monterey,
CA, USA

Sandy Fraser
Bernardsville, NJ, USA

Li Gong
Sun Microsystems, Santa Clara, CA,
USA

Jim Gray
Microsoft Research, San Francisco,
CA, USA

David Hartley
Cambridge, England

Andrew Herbert
Microsoft Research Ltd, Cambridge,
England

Tony Hoare
Microsoft Research Ltd, Cambridge,
England

Andy Hopper
University of Cambridge, England

Pierre Jansen
University of Twente, Enschede,
The Netherlands

Anita Jones
University of Virginia, Charlottesville,
VA, USA

Butler Lampson
Microsoft Research, Redmond, WA,
USA

Peter Landrock,
Århus University, Denmark

Hugh Lauer
TeraRecon, Inc., Concord, MA, USA

Paul Leach
Microsoft Corporation, Redmond, WA,
USA

Stewart Lee
Orillia, Ontario, Canada

Ian Leslie
University of Cambridge, England

Roy Levin
Microsoft Research—Silicon Valley,
CA, USA

Derek McAuley
Intel Research, Cambridge, England

Robin Milner
University of Cambridge, England

Ken Moody
University of Cambridge, England

Bob Morris
Dartmouth College, Hanover, NH,
USA

Sape Mullender
Lucent Technologies, Murray Hill, NJ,
USA

John Naughton
Open University, Milton Keynes, England

Lawrence Paulson
University of Cambridge, England

Brian Randell
University of Newcastle, England

Rick Rashid,
Microsoft Research, Redmond, WA,
USA

Stephen Robertson
Microsoft Research Ltd, Cambridge,
England

Jerome Saltzer
MIT, Cambridge, MA, USA

Mahadev Satyanarayanan
Carnegie Mellon University, Pittsburgh, PA, USA

Fred Schneider
Cornell University, Ithaca, NY, USA

Michael Schroeder
Microsoft Research—Silicon Valley,
CA, USA

Gustavus Simmons
Sandia Park, NM, USA

Jonathan Smith
University of Pennsylvania,
Philadelphia, PA, USA

Karen Spärck Jones
University of Cambridge, England

Graham Steel
University of Edinburgh, Scotland

Robert Taylor
Woodside, California, USA

David Tennenhouse
Intel Research, Santa Clara, CA, USA

Chuck Thacker
Microsoft Corporation, Redmond, WA,
USA

David Wheeler
University of Cambridge, England

John Wilkes
HP Labs, Palo Alto, CA, USA

Maurice Wilkes
University of Cambridge, England

Introduction: Roger Needham[1]

Rick Rashid
Senior Vice President, Microsoft Research

I first encountered Roger Needham almost 20 years ago while lecturing in an advanced course on distributed systems being held in Glasgow during the summer of 1983. I must admit that I felt just a bit out of place lecturing alongside the likes of Gerald Le Lann, Jim Mitchell and Roger Needham. Roger had become head of Cambridge University's fabled Computer Laboratory just three years earlier, about the same time I had received my Ph.D.

When I heard Roger lecture for the first time, I was taken aback by his remarkable and very unusual speaking style. I've since seen it described in the press as "deliberate and thoughtful," and it is all of that. Listening to a lecture in computer science can sometimes make you feel as though you are chasing after the words trying to piece together the speaker's meaning. When Roger spoke I found myself hanging on each word, wondering with great anticipation what would come next. The wait was usually worthwhile. That summer in 1983 I discovered to my delight Roger's keen insight, dry wit and ability to turn the English language into his personal plaything:

> An improvement is something your program will not work with and a bug fix
> is something it will not work without.

Looking back, I still find it hard to believe that 20 years later I would be running a large research organization for Microsoft and would have the privilege of working with Roger on a daily basis as Managing Director of our Cambridge research laboratory. It has been quite a journey.

Early career

I've heard the story told that while studying for his Ph.D., Roger lived in a caravan with his wife Karen Spärck Jones, with whom he also collaborated on sev-

---

1 This text is as written before Roger's death, except for changes in the last paragraph.

eral papers. The reason for their unorthodox living arrangements was that while completing his Ph.D., Roger and Karen also undertook the building of their own house. Despite this rather strenuous side occupation, Roger completed his Ph.D., at Cambridge in 1961. This was on automatic classification and information retrieval, exciting, new and interdisciplinary areas. At the time, Roger was working with the Cambridge Language Research Unit, which was investigating machine translation, automated retrieval, and the like. He joined the University's Mathematical Laboratory—what is now known as the Computer Laboratory—in 1962, as a Senior Assistant in Research.

Although his Ph.D. was on an applications topic, Roger's career has been that of a classic—almost prototypical—"systems" computer scientist. It is hard to pin him down to a single area. Roger has made significant contributions to areas such as operating systems, networking, distributed systems, computer security and multimedia. In an interview for SIGSoft's Software Engineering Notes published in January 2001, Roger is quoted as saying:

> I regard myself as a systems person, not an OS person, nor a communications systems person. I think all three systems require the same kind of skills.

During his career Roger has had a knack for apparently being at the right place at the right time, working with the right collaborators and hitting on the right idea. Roger is fond of saying,

> Serendipity is looking for a needle in a haystack and finding the farmer's daughter.

The reality is that his consistent contributions have had nothing to do with serendipity but rather his personal talents and ability to draw to himself talented people and find ways to inspire and motivate them.

The first major system Roger worked on following his Ph.D. was TITAN. The Laboratory, under Maurice Wilkes, was providing the software for hardware built by Ferranti (subsequently ICT/ICL). TITAN was the earliest computer system to employ cache memory, and its operating system was the first multi-access system written outside the US to go into public use. Roger first worked with David Wheeler on design automation, and then became involved in building the operating system. One of Roger's enduring innovations was the use of a one-way function to protect its password file—something virtually every modern computer system does today. The TITAN file system also introduced the notion of full backup and restore and the ability to do incremental backups.

Computing in the 1960s and early 1970s was a "full contact sport." In keeping with his "systems" image, Roger was not above doing anything that might be required to keep his operating system running. In addition to developing TITAN's software, he enjoys telling the story of the miserable day he sat in an air conditioning unit pouring water from a bucket over a pile of bricks to cool the system and keep it running for users.

As a member of staff, Roger also began to teach, initially for the Diploma and later, when Cambridge accepted Computer Science as a degree subject, to undergraduates; and he began to take Ph.D. students, now to be met round the world.

CAP, Rings and the Cambridge Model Distributed System

Building on lessons learned from TITAN, in the late 1960s Roger began to concentrate on protection—providing fine-grained access control to resources between users, between users and the operating system, and between operating system modules. From the early 1970s he worked with Maurice Wilkes and David Wheeler on the design and construction of the CAP computer, an experimental machine with memory protection based on capabilities implemented in hardware. Once the machine was running in 1975, Roger then led the development of the machine's operating system and was responsible for many innovations in computer security. The CAP project received a British Computer Society Technical Award in 1977. As the Internet moves toward adoption of a common web services infrastructure, there is renewed interest in capability based access control today.

Working with Maurice Wilkes, David Wheeler, Andy Hopper and others, Roger was also involved in the construction of the Cambridge Ring (1974) and its successor the Cambridge Fast Ring (1980). The 10-megabit-per-second Cambridge Ring put the Computer Laboratory at the forefront of high-speed local-area networking and distributed computing research. The Cambridge Fast Ring ran at 100 megabits per second—still the typical speed of local computer networks more than 20 years later—and helped to inspire the creation of the ATM switching networks in use today.

The software developed to run on top of the Cambridge Ring was no less remarkable than the hardware. The Cambridge Model Distributed System on which Roger worked with Andrew Herbert and others was an innovative distributed software environment exploiting the Ring. It included computing components such as a Processor Bank, File Server, Authentication Server, Boot Server, etc., and was an early model for what we would today call "thin client computing."

This line of work on distributed systems was taken further in the 1980s in work with Ian Leslie, David Tennenhouse and others on the Universe and Unison projects, where independent Cambridge Rings that sat at several UK sites were interconnected by satellite (Universe) and high-speed point-to-point links (Unison) to demonstrate wide-area distributed computing. Both rings were used to do real-time voice and video applications (the Cambridge "Island" project)—another "first."

There were several commercial and academic deployments of Cambridge Rings spun out from the Computer Laboratory. It is believed that a derivative of the Cambridge Ring still runs part of the railway signalling system at London's Liverpool Street Station!

Head of Department, Computer Laboratory

Roger had been promoted to Reader in Computer Systems in 1973, and was made Professor in 1981. When Maurice Wilkes retired in 1980, Roger became Head of Department. In addition to his personal scientific achievements, Roger oversaw the growth and maturation of Cambridge University's Computer Laboratory during an important part of its history. When he took over as Head of Department, the Laboratory had a teaching and research staff of 10 and just over 40 Ph.D. students. Ten years later, in 1990, the teaching and research staff had grown to 27, and the number of Ph.D. students had more than doubled. Roger is quoted as referring to this as the Laboratory's

> "halcyon days"—an expanding Laboratory and no external interference.

Though the Laboratory's strength was in systems, and Roger himself was a "systems" scientist, he encouraged new areas to develop, for example, formal methods, and language and information processing. One topic of research Roger particularly promoted at Cambridge was the intersection of multimedia systems and networking. As a result, Cambridge became one of the first research laboratories in the world where teleconferencing and video mail became regular tools for research.

Roger continued in the 1980s and 90s to be interested in all aspects of computer systems, but was especially concerned with security. He participated in every one of the ACM Symposia on Operating Systems Principles, and is believed to be the only person to have achieved a 100% attendance record. With Ross Anderson and others he significantly developed and expanded Cambridge research into computer security. He took an active role in creating a security programme at the Newton Institute and hosting an annual Security Protocols Workshop, which he continues to do from Microsoft. He has recently combined his intellectual and (left wing) political interests as a Trustee of the Foundation for Information Policy Research. He has also emphasised, in a related spirit, in his 2002 Saul Gorn Lecture at the University of Pennsylvania and Clifford Paterson Lecture at the Royal Society, that doing system security properly is as much about people as about machines.

Referring to Roger's impact on the Computer Laboratory on the occasion of his Honorary Doctorate from the University of Twente in 1996, Sape Mullender wrote:

> Needham works as a catalyst. When he is around, systems research gets more focus and more vision. He brings out the best in the people around him. This helps to explain why, for as long as I can remember, the Cambridge Univer-

sity Computer Laboratory has been among the best systems research laboratories in the world. This is recognized even by Americans, although their national pride doesn't always allow them to admit that MIT, Stanford, Berkeley, Cornell, and the rest of them, have something to learn abroad, in Cambridge.

Public service

Roger began his public service career in the 1960s as a member of the Science Research Council's Computing Science Committee. His public service activities ramified in the 80s and 90s, extending into all kinds of government and other boards and committees. He has said he found some of them fun—the Alvey Committee, for example, had the opportunity to drive a large national computing research programme; some were interesting, like the Research Councils' Individual Merit Promotion Panel; and some were keeping a particular show on the road. He has felt the obligation to do these things; he has also enjoyed learning and deploying the skills required to do them effectively. His most recent challenge has been chairing a Royal Society Working Party on intellectual property.

Roger was able to exploit these skills, and what he had learnt about the University while Head of Department, as Pro Vice-Chancellor from 1996–1998, with a remit on the research side of the University's operations. This had all kinds of interesting side-effects, like chairing Electors to Chairs across the University and so getting snapshots of what's hot in pharmacology, or economic history, or Spanish.

The list of awards and honors Roger has received for both his personal achievements and his contributions to Cambridge and to the field is impressive, including being named Fellow of the British Computer Society, Fellow of the Royal Society, Fellow of the Royal Academy of Engineering and Fellow of the ACM. Roger was also awarded the CBE (Commander of the Order of the British Empire) for his services to Computer Science in 2001.

Working with industry

One constant of Roger's career has been his consistent connection to industrial research and development. He was a Director of Cambridge Consultants in the 1960s, and for ten years on the Board of Computer Technology Ltd. He was a consultant to Xerox PARC from 1977 to 1984 and to Digital's System Research Center from 1984 to 1997. From 1995 to 1997 he was a member of the international advisory board for Hitachi's Advanced Research Laboratory, and on the Board of UKERNA from its inception until 1998.

Spin-offs from the Computer Laboratory had begun in the 1970s, contributing to the "Cambridge Phenomenon." When Roger was Head of Department, he fostered these connections, welcoming the idea of a Laboratory Supporters Club and becoming one of the "Godfathers" for Cambridge entrepreneurs.

Some of Roger's most famous papers were conceived during consulting trips and sabbaticals working at industrial research laboratories. The secure authentication system he described in his 1978 paper with Mike Schroeder of Xerox PARC became the basis for systems such as Kerberos—still in use today—and represented a turning point in distributed system security research. Working with Digital Equipment's Mike Burrows and Martin Abadi, he created the first formalism for the investigation of security protocols to come into wide use (also called the BAN logic, named for its authors). Roger also made contributions to Xerox's Grapevine project and Digital's AutoNet project.

Roger valued his longstanding connections with these company research centres. He was also able to observe the business of running a research centre—how, and also how not, to—at first hand.

In 1995 Roger was asked in an interview how he viewed the relationship between academic work and industrial work in computer science:

> If there wasn't an industry concerned with making and using computers the subject wouldn't exist. It's not like physics—physics was made by God, but computer science was made by man. It's there because the industry's there.

I didn't realize it at the time, but I would soon become the beneficiary of Roger's positive attitude toward working with industry.

By the mid 90s, too, Roger was finding university life, squeezed between a rampant audit culture and a lack of money, less and less satisfying. Doing something new without either of these features, and with positive advantages of its own, looked very attractive.

Microsoft Research, Cambridge

My personal history intersected again with Roger's almost 14 years after my first meeting with him in 1983. In 1991 I left Carnegie Mellon University, where I had been teaching for 12 years, and joined Microsoft to start its basic research laboratory: Microsoft Research. From the beginning, Nathan Myhrvold, who had hired me as the first lab director, had contemplated creating a laboratory in Europe to complement the one we were building in the United States. For the first 5 years of Microsoft Research's growth our Redmond facility was small enough that our first priority was to build it up to critical mass. By 1996 we had grown to over 100 researchers, and it was time to consider expanding outside the US.

It was in the fall of 1996 as we were considering European expansion that we learned through the grapevine that Roger Needham was willing to consider taking the position of director of a new lab. When I first heard the news I was tremendously excited. I couldn't imagine a better person to anchor this new venture.

In December, Nathan Myhrvold, Chuck Thacker, Roger Needham and I all met for a day in a hotel near the San Francisco airport to talk about starting the lab, and by the end of the meeting it was clear we were moving forward. By April of 1997 the lab was announced with much fanfare, and in October of 1997 Microsoft Research Cambridge officially opened with Roger Needham as its Managing Director.

In its first temporary space in the middle of Cambridge, the Microsoft lab was close to the Computer Laboratory. Their two new buildings in west Cambridge are also close together, striking additions to the growing West Cambridge campus, and with their people interacting as Roger wanted.

In a 1999 interview for the book *Inside Out—Microsoft—in Our Own Words*, Roger talked about the new lab he had started:

> I had a complete restart of my career at age 62, when I was asked to open MSR at Cambridge. I asked Rick what he wanted me to do. He said, "Hire the best people and help them to do what they are good at." Nathan Myhrvold added, "If every project you start succeeds, you have failed."

> One of the most important rules of this research game is that unless you can get some of the best people in the field, you should not bother.

> I spent 35 years at Cambridge surrounded by brilliant people, and I rarely had sufficient money to hire them. That is why I enjoy this job so much.

Just as he was able to build the strength of the Computer Laboratory during the 1980s and 1990s, Roger did a stellar job hiring "some of the best people in the field," and in so doing turning Microsoft Research Cambridge into one of the premier institutions in Europe and a strong engine for innovation within Microsoft. Technology from Microsoft Research Cambridge is now embedded in many of Microsoft's key products, including Visual Studio, Office and Windows. Coming full circle, one of the earliest Cambridge technologies incorporated into Microsoft's products was an information retrieval engine—the field in which Roger received his Ph.D. nearly 40 years earlier.

In celebration of Roger Needham

The papers in this volume were written to celebrate Roger's 50 years at Cambridge and 5 years at Microsoft and the tremendous impact he had on so many people in our field. In them you will find a variety of work contributed by some of the top computer scientists in the world—all of whom had worked with Roger or been touched or influenced by Roger's work. These papers were a labor of love and friendship and deep admiration. Enjoy

1
On Access Control, Data Integration, and Their Languages

Martín Abadi

This paper considers the goals and features of recent languages for access control in distributed systems. In particular, it relates those languages to data integration.

Languages for access control

Access control is central to security, and in computer systems it appears in many guises and in many places. Applications, virtual machines, operating systems, and firewalls often have their own access-control machinery, with their own idiosyncrasies, bugs, and loopholes. Physical protection, at the level of doors or wires, is another form of access control.

Over the years, there have been many small and large efforts to unify models and mechanisms for access control. Beyond any tiny intellectual pleasure that such unifications might induce, these may conceivably contribute to actual security. For example, when there is a good match between the permissions in applications and those in the underlying platforms, access control mechanisms may have clearer designs, simpler implementations, and easier configurations. The benefits are, however, far from automatic   the result is sometimes more problematic than the sum of the parts   and there probably will always be cases in which access control resorts to *ad hoc* programs and scripts.

Those efforts have sometimes produced general languages for access control (e.g., [2–5, 7, 10, 11]). The languages are flexible enough for programming a wide variety of access control policies (for example, in file systems and for digital rights management). They are targeted at distributed systems in which cryptography figures prominently. They serve for expressing the assertions contained in cryptographic credentials, such as the association of a principal with a public key, the membership of a principal in a group, or the right of a principal to perform a certain operation at a specified time. They also serve for combining credentials from many sources with policies, and thus for making authorization decisions. More broadly, the languages sometimes aim to support trust management tasks.

Several of the most recent language designs rely on concepts and techniques from logic, specifically from logic programming: Li et al.'s D1LP and RT [10, 11], Jim's SD3 [7], and DeTreville's Binder [4]. These are explicitly research projects. Languages with practical aims such as XrML 2.0 include some closely related ideas, though typically with less generality and simpler logic. This note will focus on Binder.

One might question whether the use of these sophisticated languages would reduce the number of ways in which access control can be broken or circumvented. Policies in these languages might be difficult to write and to understand but perhaps no worse than policies embodied in Perl scripts and configuration files. There seem to be no hard data on this topic.

A look at Binder

Binder is a good representative of this line of work. It shares many of the goals of other languages and several of their features. It has a clean design, based directly on that of logic-programming languages.

Basically, a Binder program is a set of Prolog-style logical rules. Unlike Prolog, Binder does not include function symbols; in this respect, Binder is close to the Prolog fragment Datalog. Also, unlike Prolog, Binder has a notion of context and a distinguished relation `says`.

For instance, in Binder we can write:

```
may-access(p,o,Rd)   :- Bob says may-access(p,o,Rd)
may-access(p,o,Rd)   :- good(p)
```

These rules can be read as expressing that any principal p may access any object o in read mode (Rd) if Bob says that p may do so or if p is good.

Here only :- and `says` have built-in meanings. The other constructs have to be defined or axiomatized. As in Prolog, :- stands for reverse implication ("if"). As in previous logical treatments of access control, `says` serves to represent the statements of principals and their consequences [1]. Thus,

```
Bob says may-access(Alice,Foo.txt,Rd)
```

holds if there is a statement from Bob that contains a representation of the formula

```
may-access(Alice,Foo.txt,Rd)
```

More delicately,

```
Bob says may-access(Alice,Foo.txt,Rd)
```

also holds if there is a statement from `Bob` that contains a representation of the formula

```
may-access(Alice,Foo.txt,RdWr)
```

and another one that contains a representation of the rule

```
may-access(p,o,Rd)  :- may-access(p,o,RdWr)
```

The author of an access control policy need not be concerned with the details of how formulas are associated with piles of bits and network protocols. In particular, `says` abstracts from the details of authentication. When `C says S, C` may send `S` on a local channel via a trusted operating system within a computer, on a physically secure channel in a machine room, on a channel secured with shared-key cryptography, or in a certificate with a public-key digital signature.

Each formula is relative to a context. In our example, `Bob` is a context (a source of statements). Another context is implicit: the local context in which the formula applies. For example,

```
may-access(p,o,Rd)  :- Bob says may-access(p,o,Rd)
```

is to be interpreted in the implicit local context, and `Bob` is the name for another context from which the local context imports statements. This import relation might be construed as a form of trust.

There is no requirement that predicates mean the same in all contexts. For example, `Bob` might not even know about the predicate `may-access`, and might assert

```
peut-lire(Alice,Foo.txt)
```

instead of

```
may-access(Alice,Foo.txt,Rd)
```

In that situation, one may adopt the rule:

```
may-access(p,o,Rd)  :- Bob says peut-lire(p,o)
```

On the other hand, Binder does not provide much built-in support for local name spaces. A closer look reveals that the names of contexts have global meanings. In particular, if `Bob` exports the rule

```
may-access(p,o,Rd)  :-
        Charlie says may-access(p,o,RdWr)
```

the local context will obtain

```
Bob says may-access(p,o,Rd)  :-
        Charlie says may-access(p,o,RdWr)
```

without any provision for the possibility that `Charlie` might not be the same locally and for `Bob`. Other systems, such as SDSI/SPKI [5], include more elaborate naming mechanisms.

Distributed access control as data integration

In the database field, a classic problem is how to integrate multiple sources of data. The basic problem set-up is that there is a collection of databases, each defining some relations, and one wants to do operations (in particular queries) on all of them. The query language may be some variant of Prolog, or of its fragment Datalog. Modern versions of the problem address the case where some or all of the sources of data provide semi-structured objects   on the Web in XML, for instance. The languages vary accordingly.

Each database may expose a different interface and export its data in a different format. In systems such as Tsimmis [6, 12], wrappers translate data from each source into a common model. Mediators then give integrated views of data from multiple (wrapped) sources. For instance, the following is a mediator, written in the language MSL (Mediator Specification Language) of Tsimmis:

```
<cs_person {<name N> <relation R> Rest1 Rest2}>@med :-
    <person {<name N> <dept 'CS'> <relation R> |
        Rest1}>@whois
    AND decompose_name(N, LN, FN)
    AND <R {<first_name FN> <last_name LN> | Rest2}>@cs
```

This mediator defines an information source med in terms of two others, whois and cs. A query to med on cs_persons results in two queries, one on whois and one on cs, plus a call on the external predicate decompose_name. In expressions of the form <...>@s, s is a site: a constant or a variable that represents an information source. The details, which are unimportant for present purposes, can be found in Papakonstantinou's dissertation [12].

MSL and Binder have more in common than their proximity to Datalog. Both deal with multiple sources of data (sites or contexts). In Binder, access control policies may be regarded as mediators that integrate data from multiple contexts. Each context may define some relations (good, may-access, etc.), so we may as well regard contexts as databases. However, the databases may be implemented by certificates, rather than with big tables (so revocation and negation can be difficult). There is even a remarkable syntactic similarity between MSL and Binder, at least at the level of abstract syntax: @ in MSL is analogous to says in Binder, and we may read P@s as s says P.

These similarities suggest the possibility of exploiting ideas and methods from databases in security. For instance, we may borrow implementation techniques and some theory. We may also borrow some language design. The thought of basing access control on semi-structured data is inevitable but somewhat frightening. More conservatively, languages for access control may incorporate important query-language constructs that go beyond first-order logic and Datalog, for example for aggregating data.

While MSL and Binder have similarities in syntax and semantics, their pragmatics are quite different. In short, the two languages are used in different environments, for different purposes, and under different constraints.

- Work on data integration seems to assume a messy but benign world. This attitude may sometimes motivate pragmatic shortcuts, for example the plausible assumption that two relations with the same name in different sites might be intended to mean the same unless stated otherwise.
- In security, on the other hand, we tend to regard data from foreign contexts with a healthy dose of distrust. While users may work around mistakes in data integration, and tolerate them as ordinary bugs, mistakes in access control are vulnerabilities, often with serious consequences.

The term "views," so often used in data integration, suggests that each source of data provides part of the truth on a whole. The literature on data integration explores two possible approaches [9]:

- Global-as-view (GAV): each relation in the mediator schema is defined by a query over the data sources;
- Local-as-view (LAV): the data sources are defined by queries over the mediator schema.

Both approaches have benefits in data integration. On the other hand, Binder seems to fit only the GAV model; it is not clear how the LAV model might apply in distributed access control.

Security is primarily a property of systems, not a property of languages. The observation that some "security languages" resemble some "data integration languages" seems intriguing, and perhaps useful, but it mostly ignores the systems for which the languages were invented.

Nevertheless, distributed access control is at least partly about data integration. We may therefore hope that advances in data integration, and more broadly in databases, would eventually be of some benefit in security. We may even imagine that we will be able to dispense with much of the special machinery for access control, relying instead on systems for data integration and the like (e.g., [8]), by subsumption. Whether that outcome would be good, rather than merely interesting, remains open to debate.

Acknowledgments

I am grateful to John DeTreville, Phokion Kolaitis, Butler Lampson, Roger Needham, Dan Suciu, and Wang-Chiew Tan for discussions that contributed to this note and to Mike Burrows for comments on the presentation of a draft. This work was partly supported by the National Science Foundation under Grants CCR-0204162 and CCR-0208800.

References

1. ABADI, M., BURROWS, M., LAMPSON, B., AND PLOTKIN, G., 'A calculus for access control in distributed systems,' *ACM Trans. on Programming Languages and Systems,* vol. 15, no. 4, September 1993, pp. 706–734.
2. BLAZE, M., FEIGENBAUM, J., IOANNIDIS, J., AND. KEROMYTIS, A.D., 'The KeyNote trust-management system, version 2.' IETF RFC 2704, September 1999.
3. BLAZE, M., FEIGENBAUM, J., AND LACY, J., 'Decentralized trust management,' *Proc. 1996 IEEE Symposium on Security and Privacy,* pp. 164–173.
4. DETREVILLE, J., 'Binder, a logic-based security language,' *Proc. 2002 IEEE Symposium on Security and Privacy,* pp. 105–113.
5. ELLISON, C., FRANTZ, B., LAMPSON, B., RIVEST, R., THOMAS, B., AND YLÖNEN, T., 'SPKI certificate theory.' IETF RFC 2693, September 1999.
6. GARCIA-MOLINA, H., PAPAKONSTANTINOU, Y., QUASS, D., RAJARAMAN, A., SAGIV, Y., ULLMAN, J.D., VASSALOS, V., AND WIDOM, J., 'The TSIMMIS approach to mediation: data models and language,' *Journal of Intelligent Information Systems,* vol. 8, no. 2, 1997, pp. 117–132.
7. JIM, T., 'SD3: A trust management system with certified evaluation,' *Proc. 2001 IEEE Symposium on Security and Privacy,* pp. 106–115.
8. JIM, T., AND SUCIU, D., 'Dynamically distributed query evaluation,' *Proc. 2001 ACM Symposium on Principles of Database Systems,* pp. 28–39.
9. LENZERINI, M., Slides of the invited tutorial 'Data integration: a theoretical perspective,' given at the 21st ACM SIGMOD-SIGACT-SIGART Symposium on Principles of Database Systems, PODS 2002, available at: http://www.dis.uniroma1.it/~lenzerin/homepagine/publifile.html
10. LI, N., GROSOF, B.N., AND FEIGENBAUM, J., 'Delegation logic: a logic-based approach to distributed authorization,' *ACM Trans. on Information and System Security,* vol. 6, no. 1, February 2003, pp. 128–171.
11. LI, N., MITCHELL, J.C., AND WINSBOROUGH, W.H., 'Design of a role-based trust-management framework,' *Proc. 2002 IEEE Symposium on Security and Privacy,* pp. 114–130.
12. PAPAKONSTANTINOU, I.G., 'Query processing in heterogeneous information systems.' Doctoral Dissertation, Stanford University, 1997, available at: http://www.db.ucsd.edu/people/yannis.htm

2
Protocol Analysis, Composability and Computation

Ross Anderson, Michael Bond

Security protocols—early days

The study of security protocols has been associated with Roger Needham since 1978, when he published the seminal paper on the subject with Mike Schroeder [2].

The problem they investigated was how to distribute cryptographic keys in a network of computers. One solution is to have an authentication service with which all the principals share a key. Then if Alice wants to chat with Bob (for example) she can call the service and get two encrypted messages containing the same session key—one encrypted under the key she shares with the service so she can read it, and one encrypted under the key Bob shares with the service so Bob can read it. She can now send the second of these to Bob to establish secure communication. The mechanism that Needham and Schroeder designed for this evolved into Kerberos, which is now part of Windows and is probably the most widely used of all authentication protocols.

Security protocols are now embedded in a great many applications, but it is common to find unexpected bugs in them. For example, many banks used to encrypt each customer's PIN using a key known to their ATMs and write it on the ATM card magnetic strip. The idea was to provide limited service when the network was down. Years later, a villain discovered that the account number and the encrypted PIN were not linked: he could make up a bank card with his own encrypted PIN but someone else's account number, and loot their account. He went on to steal a lot of money, and once in prison wrote a manual telling everyone else how to do it too. The banks had to spend millions on changing their systems.

Clarifying the assumptions

Researchers started to gnaw away at the protocols described in the literature and found fault with essentially all of them. The failure to bind protocol elements was one frequent problem; another was that old messages could be replayed. In the case of the original Needham-Schroeder protocol, for example, the freshness of the key generated by the server was guaranteed to only one of the principals. This was not necessarily an attack, as its inventors only claimed to protect honest insiders from dishonest outsiders. However, it led to a debate about the assumptions underlying security protocol design. Do we protect only against outsiders, or against insiders? Against the malicious, or the merely careless? For example, if we use timestamps to guarantee protocol freshness, are we vulnerable to principals who carelessly let their clocks run slow? Do we only consider an attacker to have won if he can impersonate an authorised principal, or do we need to stop people abusing the protocol mechanisms to perform a service denial attack?

The early attacks led to a second seminal paper, which Roger wrote with Mike Burrows and Martin Abadi in 1989 [1], and which introduced a logic of authentication. This enables an analyst to formalise the assumptions and goals of a security protocol, and to attempt to prove its correctness. When a proof cannot be found, the place at which one gets stuck often shows where an attack can be mounted. This style of analysis turned out to be very powerful, and a large literature quickly developed in which the "BAN Logic" and other formal tools were developed and extended to tackle a range of problems in protocol design.

One of the remarkable things about security protocols is that they have not become a solved problem. One might think that managing the objects associated with authenticating users over a network—passwords, keys and the like—was a fairly compact problem which would have been done to death within a few years. However, the more we dig, the more we find.

Between 1992 and 2002, Roger hosted a protocols workshop every Easter. Early events dwelt on matters of authentication and logic, but by the mid-90s, the growing interest in electronic commerce was yielding papers on mechanisms for micropayments, bets, streaming media, mobile communications and electronic voting. Later years brought work on PKI, trust management and copyright enforcement. More and more problems come along as more and more businesses reinvent themselves online; threat models have also become more realistic, with dishonest insiders displacing the mythical 'evil hacker on the Internet'.

Dishonest insiders, and the composition problem

Over the last two years, we have been exploring exactly how one might re-engineer cryptography to cope with dishonest insiders. One conclusion is that the analysis of security protocols must be extended to application programming interfaces. This is because the crypto keys used in authentication and payment protocols are often kept in separate hardware security processors, or at least in cryptographic libraries, to which access can be restricted using physical or logical mechanisms. However, an interface has to be exposed to the application program, which will occasionally be suborned—whether by a corrupt insider or by malware. How much harm can be done, and how can we limit it?

Protecting protocols was hard enough, and yet the typical protocol consists of 3–5 messages exposed to manipulation. The API of a modern crypto library or hardware cryptoprocessor may contain 30–500 callable functions, many with a range of options. This provides a very rich and complex environment for mischief.

Attacks often involve using two separate mechanisms provided by the cryptoprocessor for different purposes, each of which could be innocuous by itself but which combine to cause trouble. For example, it is common to compute a customer PIN by encrypting the account number with a 'PIN derivation key': the cryptoprocessor then returns the PIN encrypted with a PIN storage key, so that the application has no access to its clear value. So far, so good. Then there is another transaction that can be used to encrypt a communications key under the terminal key loaded in an ATM. Here things start to go wrong, as the cryptoprocessor does not distinguish between a terminal key and a PIN derivation key; it considers them both to be of the same type. The upshot is that an attacker can supply the device with an account number, claiming that it is a communications key, and ask for it to be encrypted under the PIN derivation key.

Attacks like this extend protocol analysis all the way to the composition problem—the problem that connecting two systems that are secure in isolation can give a composite system that leaks. This had previously been seen as a separate issue, tackled with different conceptual tools.

Differential protocol analysis

We are now working on the second generation of API attacks, which exploit the application syntax supported by the cryptographic service. These attacks are even more powerful, and at least as interesting from the scientific point of view. PIN generation provides a neat example here too. In more detail, the standard PIN computation involves writing the result of the encryption as a hex string and decimalising it. As some banks like to let customers change their PIN to a more memorable number, there is a provision to add an offset to give the PIN that the customer actually enters:

Account number:	8807 0123 4569 1715
PIN derivation key:	FEFE FEFE FEFE FEFE
Encrypted account number:	A2CE 126C 69AE C82D
Natural (decimalised) PIN:	0224
Offset:	6565
Customer PIN:	6789

The typical implementation requires the programmer to send the cryptoprocessor the account number, a table describing the decimalisation (here, '0123 4567 8901 2345') and the offset. The processor returns the PIN, encrypted under the PIN storage key.

The designers do not seem to have realised that a crooked programmer can manipulate the decimalisation table and the offset as well as the account number. A multitude of attacks follow. For example, one can send in an account number with a decimalisation table of '1111...11' to find out the ciphertext corresponding to a clear PIN of '1111,' and then with a decimalisation table of '0111...11' to see if there is a zero in the first four digits of the encrypted account number (if so, the PIN, and thus the ciphertext output, will be different). By manipulating the decimalisation table further, he can get all the digits in the PIN, and by then playing with the offset, he can get their order. In total, the attack requires only 15–25 unprivileged cryptoprocessor transactions to discover the PIN on a single target account.

This second type of attack takes protocol analysis into yet another realm: that of differential attacks. Over the last ten years, a number of techniques have been invented for attacking cryptographic systems by bombarding them with inputs with chosen differences. For example, in differential cryptanalysis, one analyses the changes in the output of the encryption algorithm; while with differential power analysis, one measures changes in the current consumption or electromagnetic emissions of the equipment. Now we have examples of how consecutive runs of a protocol can leak information if the inputs are suitably chosen. The resulting 'differential protocol analysis' appears to be very powerful against application-level crypto.

It will take us some time to figure out the general lessons to be drawn from attacks like this, the robustness principles that designers should use to avoid them, and the analysis techniques that might assure us of a particular design's soundness. The randomisation of all protocols (another feature of Roger's work) is likely to be important.

Quantitative analysis and multiparty computation

Various researchers have speculated about whether there might one day be a quantitative analysis of protocol security. This might be feasible for PIN processing applications as we can measure the information leakage per transaction in terms of the reduction of entropy in the unknown PIN. This leads in turn to a possible real-world attack previously considered theoretical.

Gus Simmons wrote extensively on covert channels in protocols. One such channel that is always present is the 'balking channel'—when one of the principals in a protocol signals something by halting and refusing to continue. This is normally considered unimportant, as its information capacity is only a third of a bit per transaction. But with systems designed to cope with large transaction volumes, this need no longer hold. For example, a Trojanned cryptoprocessor could balk when it sees a predetermined PIN. If the PIN length were eight digits, this would be unlikely to hinder normal operation, but at a thousand transactions a second, a programmer could quickly find a number in a typical nine-digit account-number range with just this PIN, and open an account for it. Once this kind of problem is appreciated, one can start to look for attacks that involve inducing rare error conditions that cause the cryptoprocessor to abort a transaction. (They exist.)

A third emerging link is between protocol analysis and secure multiparty computation. In application-level crypto we may have several inputs to a computation, some of them coming from an untrusted source, and we have to stop users manipulating the computation to get outputs useful for bad purposes. In the PIN decimalisation example above, one might try to solve the problem by blocking tables such as '1111...11.' Yet an attacker can get by with scarcely more work by using two normal-looking tables that differ slightly (another kind of differential attack). We might therefore think that if we can't sanitize the inputs to the computation, perhaps we can authenticate them, and use only those tables that real banks actually use. But building every bank in the world into our trust base is what we were trying to avoid by using cryptography!

Conclusion

The protocol work that started off a quarter of a century ago may have seemed at the time like a minor detail within the larger project of designing robust distributed systems. Yet it has already grown into the main unifying theme of security engineering. Application-level protocols, and especially those from which an attacker can harvest data over many runs, open up new problems. The resulting analysis techniques are set to invade the world of composable security and the world of multiparty computation. The influence and consequences of Roger's contribution just keep on growing.

References

1. BURROWS, M., ABADI, M., AND NEEDHAM, R.M., 'A logic of authentication,' *ACM Trans. on Computer Systems*, vol. 8, no. 1, pp. 18–36, 1990.
2. NEEDHAM, R.M., AND SCHROEDER, R.M., 'Using encryption for authentication in large networks of computers.' *Comm. ACM*, vol. 21, no. 12, pp. 993–999, 1978.

3

Access Control in Distributed Systems

Jean Bacon, Ken Moody

We trace the evolution of access-control-policy expression and implementation from centralised operating systems, through locally distributed, LAN-based systems, to large-scale, widely distributed systems with independently developed components. Current approaches to the latter favour role-based access control enforced through encryption-protected certificates that have their roots in capability mechanisms.

Access-control policy and mechanism

Access control is a crucial aspect of most computerised systems. Access-control policy is the specification of the rights of principals to access objects or use services. Access-control mechanisms implement the policies at runtime. There is a tension between expressiveness of policy and efficiency and functionality of mechanism. We trace the evolution of policy and mechanism from early centralised systems to current, large-scale, widely distributed systems.

From the earliest operating system (OS) designs, discretionary schemes have been supported. Here, policy on service use is implicit, and an object's owner specifies its access permissions. An access-control list (ACL) associated with an object has been the most usual form of policy specification; implementation is by checking the list on object access. ACLs can be expressive, most generally containing any combination of groups (with nesting) and principals. As systems grow and groups contain increasing numbers of members, the implementation becomes unacceptably slow, as shown for Grapevine [7].

For this reason the alternative of issuing authorised principals with capabilities has been investigated. Capabilities are efficient to check, but how to manage and revoke them has exercised the research community over many years. Signed authorisation certificates are the most recent manifestation of capabilities.

Capabilities in centralised and distributed systems

The CAP operating system [11, 12, 13] was the culmination of capability-based OS design. The CAP project explored how a general-protection-domain structure (as opposed to nested rings) might be enforced and used to implement minimum necessary privilege both in the use of services and in access to objects. But hardware support for protection is expensive compared with off-the-shelf processors, and before the CAP project ended, the emerging local-area-network technology was making distributed systems feasible and changing the research focus.

Many distributed system designs—such as the Cambridge Distributed Computing System (CDCS) [14], Amoeba, Mach and Chorus— have been based on capabilities. In CDCS, capabilities were issued to authenticated principals to allow subsequent use of system services. The CDCS file system (CFS) [6] was also capability-based, providing a universal storage service on which any number of OS directory services could be built. The MSSA (multi-service storage architecture) project [1, 10] extended this design approach to provide a hierarchy of services above the lowest flat-file level. Specialised continuous media services were supported, as well as structured objects such as OS directories, indexes, mail objects and general database objects.

Issues for capability-based access control

A capability contains an object name and some access rights. The necessary properties of a capability are as follows:

1. *Integrity.* It is essential to protect capabilities from illegal construction, tampering and theft. A principal must not be able to create a capability for itself. The possessor of a capability must not be able to increase its access rights. It should not be possible for a network eavesdropper to pick up and use a capability.
2. *Propagation.* The transfer of capabilities should be controlled. For example, should it be possible for a principal with a capability to pass a copy to some other principal? It may be that this should be allowed only under system control; that is, a principal should ask the system to create a capability containing specified rights for some other principal. A mechanism is needed to enforce such a policy.
3. *Delegation.* A specific example of the use of the capability transfer mechanism is for a principal to delegate a subset of its rights to an object to another principal. This may be for a specific purpose for a limited time. For example, one may wish to delegate to a printing service the right to *read* a file only for the time it takes to print that file.
4. *Revocation.* Capabilities are held by principals, or their agents, rather than residing with objects. It may therefore be difficult for a system to keep track of all the capabilities that exist for an object. Some may have

been issued directly to principals by the system; some may have been passed from one principal to another. If the access-control policy for an object is changed, then some capabilities may need to be revoked. Ideally, individual revocation should be possible. The alternative is to revoke all the capabilities for an object, thus forcing all principals to request new capabilities; the new access-control policy will determine which ones will succeed. This is simple to implement but imposes avoidable overhead on the valid principals each time the access-control policy for an object is changed.

Capability generation and checking in distributed systems

In a distributed system, capabilities may be used to prove a principal's right to use a service or access an object. If capabilities are to be transferred around a distributed system, it is no longer sufficient to protect them by hardware in the memory of individual nodes of the system. Encryption techniques must be used instead. One scheme is as follows: when an object is created, a *secret* (random number) is generated and stored with the object. An encryption function, such as a one-way function, is available to the object manager. When a capability is issued, the object name, rights and the secret are put through the encryption function and the result is stored in the capability as check digits. When the capability is presented with a request to use the object, the object name and rights from the capability and the stored secret are put through the encryption function. The resulting number is compared with the check digits in the capability. If they are the same, access may go ahead. If they are different, then the capability has been tampered with and is invalid. This scheme allows the object name and rights to be represented in clear in the capability.

The four issues for capability-based access control highlighted above are only partially addressed in the approach just described. The scheme protects capabilities from tampering but not from theft. Propagation is as difficult as ever to control and capabilities may now be transferred widely throughout a distributed system. Revocation cannot be selective; a typical approach is to invalidate all existing capabilities by associating a new secret with the object. Newly generated capabilities will use the new secret, old ones will fail the encryption check, and the principal must request a new capability.

Principal-specific capabilities

A simple extension of the scheme described above is to include the name of a principal in the capability [9]. The principal's name is put through the encryption function, together with the object name and access rights, when the capability is issued and checked. We then have a mechanism to enforce that only the principal whose name is embedded in a capability for an object may access the object; a principal cannot use a capability it has acquired by eavesdropping on network communication. Principal-specific capabilities were used in two later Computer Laboratory projects, MSSA (mentioned above) and OASIS (see below); in the latter, with the additional insight that the principal ID need not be embedded in the capability, provided that it is input to the encryption function.

The principal naming mechanism is based on the system's authentication infrastructure; it assumes that the identity of the principal making the request can be ascertained correctly and that one principal cannot masquerade as another. But the IP address and port number of the presenting principal are not sufficiently secure, and some public key of the principal is likely to be needed [15].

The transfer of capabilities can now be controlled; only the object manager with access to the secret can generate capabilities. A principal must ask the object manager to generate a new capability for some other principal. Selective revocation may be supported more easily; for example, a 'hot list' of principals whose rights to access an object have been revoked by a change in access-control policy may be held with the object and checked when a capability is presented.

Certificates and integration with a PKI

Over the years this approach has grown in popularity as systems have become larger and more widely distributed. Capabilities have been implemented as standard, signed certificates, for example, as X.509 authentication certificates with access-control information in the extension fields or, more recently, as X.509 attribute certificates [8]. The presenting principal may be challenged for knowledge of the private key associated with the public key within the certificate, or public/private key encryption may be used for communication, which integrates access-control with a standard PKI (public key infrastructure).

Role-based access control (RBAC)

Managing the access rights of principals to objects becomes increasingly difficult as systems grow in size and their user communities vary. The privileges of a group or "role" are largely independent of the principals who are members, and these privileges change slowly as an organisation evolves. This is the key idea behind role-based access control (RBAC), in which access-control policy assigns privileges to roles rather than to individual principals. There are usually many fewer roles than principals in an organisation, although a large organisation may have several thousand roles. Also, the privileges associated with a particular role change less frequently than people join and leave, or move to a new role within the organisation. RBAC therefore promises to be an appropriate access-control scheme for large-scale systems. An additional requirement for managing access control in widely distributed applications is that heterogeneous, independently developed and administered systems should interwork; that is, principals managed by one system will need to use the services of others. Access to such privileges must be negotiated between the systems. For example, the services may be associated with e-government, where police, social services or health trusts may be authorised to access certain electronic records managed by another agency.

Various RBAC models have evolved over the years, most notably [16], but there are few architectures and implementations. If RBAC is to be adopted in practice, large-scale engineering issues must be addressed.

OASIS: an open architecture for secure, interworking services

The OASIS project at the Computer Laboratory draws these threads together. An overview of OASIS is given in [2, 3], details of its architecture and engineering can be found in [4], and a formal model is presented in [5].

OASIS is an access control system for open, interworking services in a distributed environment, with services being grouped into domains for the purpose of management. Services may be developed independently, but service level agreements allow their secure interoperation. OASIS is closely integrated with an active, event-based middleware infrastructure. In this way we can notify applications of any change in their environment, making it possible to ensure that security policy is satisfied at all times. A heartbeat infrastructure means that failures of nodes or communications can be detected. The receiver of an alarm, which that may (or may not) be delayed, can take appropriate action.

OASIS is role-based but has important differences from other RBAC schemes:

- Roles are service-specific; there is no notion of globally centralised administration of role naming and privilege management.
- Roles may be parameterised, as required by applications.
- Roles are activated within sessions. An OASIS session is started by strong authentication of a principal, and an initial role such as *logged_in_user* is created as a side effect of authentication. Roles may have activation conditions that require prerequisite roles, and a dependency tree of active roles is built up within a session (see Figure 1).
- All privileges are associated with roles. We use appointment instead of delegating roles or privileges; the activation conditions of roles may include appointment certificates. Persistent credentials (as opposed to session-limited role membership certificates (RMCs)) are implemented as appointment certificates, which do not confer privileges directly.

- We provide an *active security environment*. Constraints on the context can be checked during role activation; the role may be deactivated, or use of a service may be forbidden, if particular conditions subsequently become false.

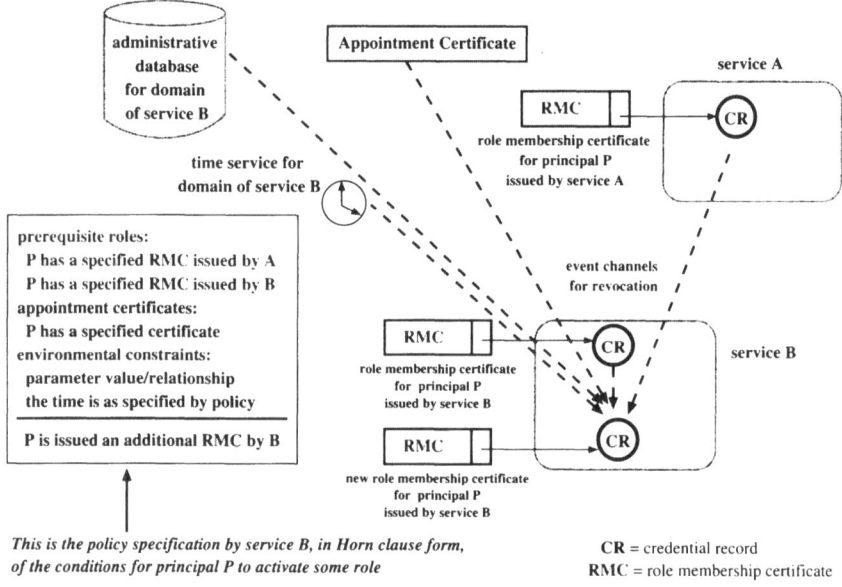

Figure 1: OASIS role activation within a session

Although the OASIS architecture overcomes many problems, the expression and management of policy for role activation and service/object use is still a major concern. Policy may derive from multiple sources such as national legislation and local management. Consistency must be ensured and evolution must be controlled. Our current work is concerned with these issues, and a web-based implementation is a basis for our investigations.

Summary

Research on capabilities as an access-control mechanism in centralised, then distributed, systems has led directly to current, widely used, certificate standards. Roger Needham's work has been key at every stage in this development.

The need for large-scale, widely distributed systems comprising separately-developed, independent, administrative domains leads to many new problems. These include how access control policy can be negotiated, expressed and managed when principals' work spans several such domains. At present members of our group are working in two specific application areas. In complex applications the privileges of a number of users change as progress is made towards achieving one or more real-world tasks, possibly described by a workflow. Access-control policy must be integrated with the workflow specification, with the enforcement mechanism responding as workflow subtasks are completed. More speculatively, how mutually unknown principals and services might establish sufficient trust to interwork is a challenging problem. We would have enjoyed Roger's insight on all of these topics.

References

1.   BACON, J. M., HAYTON, R. J., LO, S. L., AND MOODY, K., 'Access control for a modular, extensible storage service,' *Proc. IEEE SDNE, Services in Distributed Network Environments*, Prague, June 1994, pp. 108–114.

2.   BACON, J., MOODY, K., BATES, J., HAYTON, R., MA, C., MCNEIL, A., SEIDEL, O., AND SPITERI, M., 'Generic support for distributed applications,' *IEEE Computer*, vol. 33, no. 3, March 2000, pp. 68–76.

3.   BACON, J., AND MOODY, K., 'Towards open, secure, widely distributed services,' *Comm. ACM*, vol. 43, no. 6, June 2002, pp. 59–63.

4.   BACON, J., MOODY, K., AND YAO, W., 'Access control and trust in the use of widely distributed services,' in *Middleware 2001*, ed. R. Guerraoui, Lecture Notes in Computer Science 2218, Springer 2001, pp. 295–310.

5.   BACON, J., MOODY, K., AND YAO, W., 'A model of OASIS role-based access control and its support for active security,' *ACM Trans. on Information and System Security*, vol. 5, no. 4, November 2002, pp. 492–540.

6.   BIRRELL, A.D., AND NEEDHAM, R.M., 'A universal file server,' *IEEE Trans on Software Engineering*, vol. SE-6, no. 5, May 1980, pp. 450–453.

7.   BIRRELL, A.D., LEVIN, R., NEEDHAM, R.M., AND SCHROEDER, M.D., 'Grapevine: an exercise in distributed computing,' *Comm. ACM*, vol. 25, no. 4, April 1982, pp. 260–274.

8.   FARRELL, S., AND HOUSLEY, R., 'An Internet attribute certificate profile for authorization,' RFC 3281, IETF, April 2002. Available at: ftp://ftp.rfc-editor.org/in-notes/rfc3281.txt

9.   GONG, L., 'A secure, identity-based capability system,' *Proc. IEEE Symposium on Security and Privacy*, Oakland, California, May 1989, pp. 56–63.

10. LO, S.L., 'A modular and extensible network storage architecture,' Ph.D. thesis, University of Cambridge, 1994 and Technical Report TR 326. Published by Cambridge University Press as a Distinguished Dissertation, ISBN 0-521-55115-3, 1995.

11. NEEDHAM, R.M., AND WALKER, R.D.H., 'The Cambridge CAP computer and its protection system,' *Proc. 6th Symposium on Operating Systems Principles*, November 1977, West Lafayette, Indiana, United States, pp. 1–10.

12. NEEDHAM, R.M., AND BIRRELL, A.D., 'The Cap filing system,' *Proc. 6th Symposium on Operating Systems Principles*, November 1977, West Lafayette, Indiana, United States, pp. 11–16.

13. NEEDHAM, R.M., 'The CAP project—an interim evaluation,' *Proc. 6th Symposium on Operating Systems Principles*, November 1977, West Lafayette, Indiana, United States, pp. 17–22.

14. NEEDHAM, R.M., AND HERBERT, A.J., *The Cambridge distributed computing system*, Addison Wesley, 1982.

15. NEEDHAM, R.M., AND SCHROEDER, R.M., 'Using encryption for authentication in large networks of computers,' *Comm. ACM*, vol. 21, no. 12, December 1978, pp. 993–999.

16. SANDHU, R.S., COYNE, E.J., FEINSTEIN, H.L., AND YOUMAN, C.E., 'Role-based access control models,' *Computer*, vol. 29, no. 2, February 1996, pp. 38–47.

4
Implementing Condition Variables with Semaphores

Andrew D. Birrell

Introduction

All of today's popular systems for programming with multiple threads use designs based around three data types:

- "Thread," with operations Fork and Join
- "Lock" with operations Acquire and Release
- "Condition Variable" with operations Wait, Signal and Broadcast

This is true of PThreads, Java, and C#. It's also true of their predecessors: Modula-3, Modula-2+ and Mesa.

In 1984 a group of us at DEC SRC were implementing a new multi-processor operating system: the system was Taos, the machine was Firefly and the language, which we created, was Modula-2+. As part of that effort we implemented these data types. In doing so we observed that the semantics of Acquire and Release were identical to those of a binary semaphore.[1] Also, the semantics of Wait and Signal are tantalizingly similar to those of a binary semaphore. So we thought we could provide a single abstraction in the kernel and present it as locks and condition variables in the language support layer. This paper is the tale of what happened then.

The system we were building used what would nowadays be called a micro-kernel architecture (the term hadn't been invented then). The lead programmer for the kernel was Roy Levin, and I was doing the user-mode thread support code (and the RPC system). We were ably assisted in building the threads facility by a large and highly qualified cast of other SRC employees, consultants, and passers-by, including Butler Lampson, Paul Rovner, Roger Needham, Jerry Saltzer and Dave Clark.

---

[1] Modula-2+ did not support the notion of re-entrant mutexes. If a thread holding m tried to acquire m again, the thread would deadlock. This still seems like a good idea. Implementing locks with semaphores is messier if for some reason you want to allow re-entrant locking, but it's still not difficult.

Ground rules

I'm not going to give formal semantics for the threads operations here. You can read the ones we wrote for Modula-2+ [1], or you can read the reasonably good description in Chapter 17 of the Java Language Specification [3] (ignoring the stuff about re-entrant mutexes). It's worth reading those specifications sometime, but the following summary should be enough for appreciating this paper.

- A condition variable, c, is associated with a specific lock, m. Calling c.Wait() enqueues the current thread on c (suspending its execution) and unlocks m, as a single atomic action. When this thread resumes execution, it re-locks m.
- c.Signal() examines c, and if there is at least one thread queued on c, then one such thread is dequeued and allowed to resume execution; this entire operation is a single atomic action.
- c.Broadcast() examines c, and if there are any threads queued on c, then all such threads are allowed to resume execution. Again, this entire operation is a single atomic action: the threads to be awoken are exactly those that had called c.Wait() before this call of c.Broadcast(). Of course, the awoken threads have to wait in line to acquire the lock m.

Note that these are the Mesa (and Modula, PThreads, Java and C#) semantics. Tony Hoare's original condition variable design [4] had the Signal operation transfer the lock to the thread being awoken and had no Broadcast.

See Dijkstra's 1967 paper [2] for a precise description of semaphore semantics. In summary:

- A semaphore sem has an integer state (sem.count) and two operations, "P" and "V".
- sem.P() suspends the current thread until sem.count > 0, then decrements sem.count and allows the thread to resume execution. The action of verifying that sem.count > 0 and decrementing it is atomic.
- sem.V() increments sem.count atomically. For the special case of a binary semaphore, the increment is omitted if sem.count is already 1 (this is done by setting sem.limit to 1).

It's quite easy to implement semaphores very efficiently using a hardware test-and-set instruction, or more modern interlocked memory accesses (such as the load-locked and store-conditional features of the MIPS and Alpha architectures, or the analogous features of modern Intel processors).

To give this historical tale a modern flavour, I'm going to use C# for the programming examples (Java would be almost identical). In reality the implementations for the Firefly were written in Modula-2+, and the actual data representation was somewhat different than given here. I'm also going to ignore exceptions completely, to avoid cluttering the code with try ... finally statements.

Getting started

A semaphore is ideal for implementing a lock with the Modula or Mesa semantics. We represent the lock directly as a semaphore, with its integer restricted to the range [0..1], initially 1. The Acquire operation is exactly P and Release is exactly V:

```
class Lock {
        Semaphore sm;
        public Lock() {                    // constructor
                sm = new Semaphore(); sm.count =1; sm.limit = 1;
        }
        public void Acquire() { sm.P(); }
        public void Release() { sm.V(); }
}
```

You can come quite close to implementing a condition variable in a similar way:

```
class CV {
        Semaphore s;
        Lock m;
        public CV(Lock m) { // Constructor
                this.m = m;
                s = new Semaphore(); s.count = 0; s.limit = 1;
        }
        public void Wait() { // Pre-condition: this thread holds "m"
                m.Release();
(1)             s.P();
                m.Acquire();
        }
        public void Signal() {
                s.V();
        }
}
```

Most of this is obvious. The condition variable is associated with a Lock m. Enqueueing a thread on a condition variable is implemented by the s.P() operation. The only issues occur in the area around (1). Recall that the semantics say that c.Wait should *atomically* release the lock and enqueue the thread on c, which this code blatantly doesn't do.

The critical case is where there is no thread currently enqueued on c, and some thread A has called c.Wait() and has reached (1). Then thread B calls c.Signal(). This calls s.V(), which sets s.count to 1. When thread A eventually gets around to calling s.P(), it finds that s.count is 1, and so decrements it and continues executing. This is the correct behaviour. The effect was christened "the wake-up waiting race" by Jerry Saltzer [5], and using a binary semaphore ensures that A will not get stranded enqueued incorrectly on s.

However, this does have a side-effect: if a thread calls c.Signal() when no thread is inside c.Wait(), then s.count will be left at 1. This mean that the next thread to call c.Wait() will just decrement s.count and drop through, which isn't really what the semantics said. Fortunately, we were experienced enough to notice this problem immediately. You can fix it by counting the calls of c.Wait() and the matching calls of c.Signal(). The counter also gives us a plausible implementation of c.Broadcast.

Of course, you need a lock to protect this counter. For the purposes of the current description I'll use another semaphore x in each condition variable. In a real implementation you'd probably optimize to some form of spin-lock, perhaps combined with a private agreement with the thread scheduler. Java and C# avoid this extra lock by requiring that the caller of Signal or Broadcast holds c.m; we didn't want this restriction in Modula-2+.

```
class CV {
        Semaphore s, x;
        Lock m;
        int waiters = 0;
        public CV(Lock m) { // Constructor
                this.m = m;
                s = new Semaphore(); s.count = 0; s.limit = 1;
                x = new Semaphore(); x.count = 1; x.limit = 1;
        }
        public void Wait() { // Pre-condition: this thread holds "m"
                x.P(); {
                        waiters++;
                } x.V();
                m.Release();
    (1)         s.P();
                m.Acquire();
        }
        public void Signal() {
                x.P(); {
                        if (waiters > 0) { waiters--; s.V(); }
                } x.V();
        }
        public void Broadcast() {
                x.P(); {
                        while (waiters > 0) { waiters--; s.V(); }
                } x.V();
        }
}
```

This looks pretty good and we were happy with it for several weeks. But actually, it rates only as a "good try." It took us a while to notice.

Fixing things up

The problem with the above implementation of condition variables again lies at position (1), and there are actually two bugs there.

The first one we noticed is that there might be arbitrarily many threads suspended inside c.Wait at (1). Although a call of c.Broadcast() would call s.V() the correct number of times, the fact that it's a binary semaphore means that s.count stops at 1. So all but one of the threads at (1) would end up stranded, enqueued on s. We noticed this one day when Dave Clark was visiting. The obvious fix is to declare that s is a general counting semaphore, with unbounded s.count. That ensures the correct number of threads will drop through in c.Wait.

Unfortunately, they might not be the correct threads. If 7 threads have called c.Wait and are all at (1) when c.Broadcast is called, we will call s.V() 7 times and bump s.count to 7. If the threads that are at (1) were to continue, all would be fine. But what if before that some other thread were to call c.Wait()? Then that thread would decrement s.count and drop through, and one of the 7 threads would end up enqueued on s. This most definitely violates the specified semantics. Notice that c.Signal has the same problem.

So our next attempt was to use some form of handshake to arrange that the correct threads drop through. We do this by introducing yet another semaphore h, a general counting semaphore. This lets the signaller block until the appropriate number of threads have got past the call of s.P() in Wait. The thread in c.Signal waits on h.P() until a thread has made a matching call of h.V() inside c.Wait().

```
class CV {
    Semaphore s, x;
    Lock m;
    int waiters = 0;
    Semaphore h;
    public CV(Lock m) { // Constructor
        this.m = m;
        s = new Semaphore(); s.count = 0; s.limit = 999999;
        x = new Semaphore(); x.count = 1; x.limit = 1;
        h = new Semaphore(); h.count = 0; h.limit = 999999;
    }
    public void Wait() { // Pre-condition: this thread holds "m"
        x.P(); {
                waiters++;
        } x.V();
        m.Release();
```

```
(1)                    s.P();
                       h.V();
                       m.Acquire();
             }
             public void Signal() {
                       x.P(); {
                                  if (waiters > 0) { waiters--; s.V(); h.P(); }
                       } x.V();
             }
             public void Broadcast() {
                       x.P(); {
                                  for (int i = 0; i < waiters; i++) s.V();
                                  while (waiters > 0) { waiters--; h.P(); }
                       } x.V();
             }
   }
```

By this time you're probably thinking that this implementation is getting a bit heavyweight. You're probably right. But it's worse than that.

I think that the above version of CV is formally correct, in that it implements the correct semantics. However, it has a fundamental performance problem: there are necessarily two context switches in each call of Signal, because the signalling thread must wait for the signalled thread to call h.V() before the signalling thread can continue. We noticed this and worried about it. There are a lot of similar designs you can construct, but as far as we could tell in 1984, all of them either give the wrong answer or have unacceptable performance problems.

So eventually we gave up on the idea that we should build locks and condition variables out of semaphores. Roy took the semantics of condition variables and implemented them directly in the kernel. There it's not difficult to do them: we built the atomicity of Wait as part of the scheduler implementation, using the hardware test-and-set instructions to get atomicity with spin-locks, and building the requisite queues through the thread control blocks.

The sequel—NT and PThreads

Microsoft released Windows NT to the world in 1993. At SRC we observed that this was a high-quality kernel running on widely available hardware, and we decided it would be good to port our Modula-3 development environment to NT. As part of this I volunteered to implement Modula-3 threads on top of the Win32 API provided by NT. On the face of it, this seemed like it should be easy. It turned out to be easy in the same way that building condition variables out of semaphores was easy.

Even in 1993 the Win32 API provided lots of potentially useful features for concurrent programming. There was a satisfactory design for multiple threads in an address space, and a lot of synchronization primitives (events, mutexes, semaphores and critical sections). Unfortunately, none of them was exactly what was needed for condition variables. In particular, there was no operation that atomically released some object and blocked on another one. I went through much the same sequence of bad solutions as we went through in 1984 (our memories were short). In this case, though, we couldn't give up and modify the kernel primitives. Fortunately, there is another solution, as follows.

You can indeed build condition variables out of semaphores, but the only way I know of that is correct and adequately efficient is to use an explicit queue. If I have an object for each thread, I can implement Wait by running a queue through the thread object, with the head being in the condition variable object. Here's an outline (to keep it simple, the queue in this outline is LIFO; it should of course be roughly FIFO, allowing for thread priorities).

```
class Thread {
        public static Semaphore x;  // Global lock; initially
                                    // x.count = 1; x.limit = 1;
        public Thread next = null;
        public Semaphore s = new Semaphore(); // Initially
                                    // s.count = 0; s.limit = 1;
        public static Thread Self() { ... }
}
class CV {
        Lock m;
        Thread waiters = null;

        public CV(Lock m) {  // Constructor
                this.m = m;
        }

        public void Wait() {  // Pre-condition: this thread holds "m"
                Thread self = Thread.Self();
                Thread.x.P(); {
                        self.next = waiters;
                        waiters = self;
                } Thread.x.V();
                m.Release();
                self.s.P();
(2)             m.Acquire();
        }
}
```

```
public void Signal() {
        Thread.x.P(); {
                if (waiters != null) {
                        waiters.s.V();
                        waiters = waiters.next;
                }
        } Thread.x.V();
}
public void Broadcast() {
        Thread.x.P(); {
                while (waiters != null) {
                        waiters.s.V();
                        waiters = waiters.next;
                }
        } Thread.x.V();
}
}
```

Mike Burrows encountered this problem one more time when implementing Posix Threads (PThreads) for the DEC Tru64 operating system. Once again, the kernel primitives didn't include a suitable operation to let him build condition variables in an obvious way, so once again he implemented them by running an explicit queue through per-thread control blocks.

Optimising signal and broadcast

Since we're considering this level of the threads implementation, I should point out one last performance problem, and what to do about it. If Signal is called with the lock m held, and if you're running on a multi-processor, the newly awoken thread is quite likely to start running immediately. This will cause it to block again a few instructions later at (2) when it wants to lock m. If you want to avoid these extra reschedules, you need to arrange to transfer the thread directly from the condition variable queue to the queue of threads waiting for m. This is especially important in Java or C#, which both require that m is held when calling Signal or Broadcast.

Conclusions

Well, history doesn't really have conclusions. But it does have a tendency to repeat. It will be nice if reading this anecdote prevents someone from repeating our mistakes, though I wouldn't bet on it.

Implementing condition variables out of a simple primitive like semaphores is surprisingly tricky. The tricky part arises because of the binary atomic operation in Wait, where the lock is released and the thread is enqueued on the condition variable. If you don't have a suitable binary operation available and you attempt to construct one by clever use of something like a semaphore, you'll probably end up with an incorrect implementation. You should either do the queuing yourself or lobby your kernel implementer to provide a suitable primitive.

Eager readers of the Win32 API will have noticed that NT version 4.0 and later provides such a binary operation (SignalObjectAndWait). This is probably sufficient to do a simple implementation of condition variables, but I'm not going to write it here. Using SignalObjectAndWait does have the down-side that the object being released has to be an NT kernel object, for example a kernel mutex or kernel semaphore. This makes it trickier to use if you want to implement locks with the more efficient Win32 "critical section" operations.

Finally, I should admit that this is an area where a small investment in formal methods would help. With a formal specification of the underlying primitives and a formal specification of the desired condition variable semantics, it should not be difficult to see at least the correctness flaws in the buggy designs. Current formal methods would do less well in detecting unacceptable performance penalties.

References

1. BIRRELL, A., GUTTAG, J., HORNING, J., AND LEVIN, R., 'Synchronization primitives for a multiprocessor: a formal specification,' In Proc. 11th Symposium on Operating System Principles (Nov. 1987), 94–102.

2. DIJKSTRA, E.W., 'The structure of the T.H.E. multiprogramming system,' *Comm. ACM*, vol. 11, no. 5, May 1968, 341–346.

3. GOSLING, G., JOY, B., STEELE, G., AND BRACHA, G., The Java Language Specification, Second Edition, Sun Microsystems, 2000, 429–447.

4. HOARE, C.A.R., 'Monitors: an operating system structuring concept,' *Comm. ACM* vol. 17, no. 10, Oct.1974, 549–557.

5. SALTZER, J., 'Traffic control in a multiplexed computer system,' Ph.D. Thesis., Technical Report MAC-TR-30, MIT, Cambridge, Mass., July 1966.

5
Clumps, Clusters and Classification

Christopher M. Bishop

Introduction

The clustering problem has been widely studied in many fields, including information retrieval, machine learning and statistics, and it remains an active area of research. Its goal is to take a set of observations, or data points, and to partition them into groups such that, in some appropriate sense, the similarity of points lying within a group is greater than the similarity of points lying in different groups. The number of such groups is generally not known in advance.

Clustering may be performed as a step towards data compression, as a preprocessing stage for pattern recognition algorithms, as a way of identifying natural groupings in the data, and for many other applications. Historically, the clustering problem was often referred to as classification [5]. Today, in the machine-learning community at least, the term classification refers to the problem of assigning observations to one of a number of predefined classes. This is typically achieved by constructing a model using a 'training set' of examples, each of which has been labelled (possibly by hand) with the desired class or category. I will not discuss classification in this categorisation sense here.

In order to define an operational procedure for clustering it is necessary to quantify the notion of similarity. It is clear that many definitions are possible, and that the choice will necessarily be application dependent. In speech recognition for instance, training data may be clustered based on Euclidean distance in the space of Mel Cepstral coefficients. However, Euclidean distance need not always be an appropriate similarity metric, and indeed even the triangle inequality may be inapplicable. Consider a problem involving word clustering based on the frequency with which two words occur within 3 words of each other in the Encyclopaedia Britannica. We might discover, for instance, that the word "bank" is similar to "overdraft" and is also similar to "river," even though "river" and "overdraft" may be strongly dissimilar. For simplicity, however, we shall focus here on the use of Euclidean distance as a measure of similarity.

The definition of a similarity metric alone, however, is insufficient to determine the clusters within the data. We also need to prescribe how the similarity measure will be used. For instance, Needham [6] defines a *B-clump* as follows:

> A set *S* is B-clump if no member has a resemblance greater than a threshold θ to any non-member, and each member of *S* has a resemblance greater than θ to some other member.

Many clustering algorithms aim to minimize a cost function which that depends on the values of the pairwise similarities of points in the data set, and the choice of this cost function can have an important impact in determining the resulting set of clusters. However, other approaches are also possible, for instance, those based on geometrical properties of the cluster boundaries.

An additional requirement is to be able to find numerical solutions within reasonable computational time for the problems of interest, and this can easily rule out some otherwise appealing strategies [6]. Even where it is computationally feasible to minimize a cost function, it may be non-convex, and the solution found by iterative strategies can depend upon the initialization because of the presence of multiple local optima.

Example: *K*-means

One widely known clustering technique is the *K-means algorithm*, which aims to partition the data set into *K* clusters, each of which is summarized by a single prototype vector which acts as a representative of all the data points assigned to that cluster. The prototype vectors are first initialised (for instance by setting them equal to *K* randomly chosen points from the data set), and then the algorithm proceeds iteratively, where each iteration comprises two successive phases. In the first phase the prototype vectors are held fixed and each data point is assigned to the cluster whose prototype vector is closest. For the second phase, the cluster assignments are fixed, and the prototype vectors are recomputed to be the means of the corresponding clusters of data vectors. The *K*-means algorithm is simply minimizing a cost function given by the sum of squares of the Euclidean distances between each data point and its corresponding prototype vector, in which the two phases correspond to alternate minimization with respect to the class assignments and with respect to the prototypes. In fact, the algorithm must necessarily converge in a finite number of steps, since there is only a finite number of possible partitions of the data. An example of the *K*-means clustering algorithm applied to the "Old Faithful" data set is shown in Figure 1.

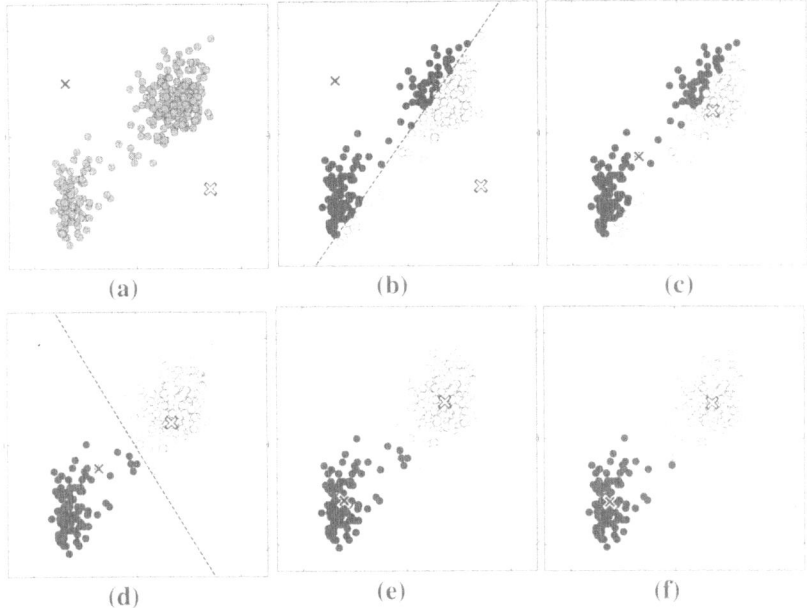

Figure 1. Illustration of the K-means clustering algorithm for two clusters ($K = 2$) using the "Old Faithful" data set, which comprises a plot of time between eruptions (vertical axis) versus eruption duration (horizontal axis) for the Old Faithful geyser in Yellowstone National Park. These axes have been rescaled such that each has zero mean and unit standard deviation over the data set. (a) The data points, together with the initial prototype vectors shown as white and black crosses. (b) In the first phase the data points are assigned to the nearest cluster prototype. The dashed line indicates the 'decision boundary' between the two clusters. (c) In the second phase the assignments are held fixed and the prototype vectors are re-calculated by moving them to the mean of the corresponding cluster of data points. This completes one iteration of the K-means algorithm. (d) In the next iteration the data points are re-assigned to the clusters using the new decision boundary. (e) The new assignments are then used to re-calculate the prototype vectors by setting them to the means of the corresponding clusters. (f) After two further complete iterations the algorithm has converged, since re-calculation of the data point assignments leaves them unchanged.

We can illustrate the use of clustering in a simple data compression scenario by applying the K-means algorithm to the compression of images, as shown in Figure 2.

$K = 2$ $K = 3$

$K = 10$ Original image

Figure 2. Illustration of the K-means clustering algorithm applied to a simple image compression problem. Here each pixel of an image is associated with a grey-level intensity value. The set of pixel values is then clustered using the K-means algorithm for various values of K. In each case we illustrate the result by replacing the actual pixel intensity by the prototype value of the cluster to which it is assigned (a process known as vector quantization).

From clusters to probabilities

One rather unsatisfying aspect of the K-means approach involves the 'hard' assignment of data points to clusters. Consider two data points A and B, and suppose that, at some point in the algorithm, A is much closer to prototype m than to any other, while B is only slightly closer to prototype m than to the next nearest prototype. Nevertheless, both *A* and *B* will be assigned exclusively to the proto-type *m*. We might expect some benefit to be had by taking account of what may be interpreted as the different degree of certainty associated with the assign-ments, and indeed this proves to be the case, as we shall see shortly. Further-more, there are strong reasons to believe that probability theory provides the most appropriate framework for quantifying such uncertainty [1].

In fact the probabilistic version of *K*-means turns out to be another well-known clustering model called a Gaussian mixture. This is simply a model for the probability distribution of the data comprising a linear superposition of Gaussian components, in which the coefficients in the superposition (known as mixing coefficients) themselves have a probabilistic interpretation. We can fit such a model to the data by optimizing the parameters of the model (the centres, covariances and mixing coefficients) so as to maximise the probability of the observed data. This approach is called maximum likelihood.

While we could solve the maximum likelihood problem using standard non-linear optimization strategies such as conjugate gradients, there exists a very elegant and general approach to tackling such problems known as the *EM (ex-pectation-maximization) algorithm*. This is an iterative algorithm in which each step comprises two successive phases. In the E phase, the parameters are held fixed and for each data point the posterior probability of assigning that data point to each of the clusters is computed. These probabilities (which are sometimes also called *responsibilities,* since they reflect the responsibility which each clus-ter takes for 'explaining' that data point) are non-negative numbers which sum to one. They represent 'soft' cluster assignments, in contrast to the hard assign-ments of *K*-means. In the M phase the probabilities are held fixed and the pa-rameters re-estimated. Each EM step is guaranteed to increase the likelihood function (unless the model is already at a local maximum). Rather than giving the mathematical formulation of this algorithm, we provide a graphical illustra-tion in Figure 3, using the same data set as in Figure 1.

If we consider a mixture of Gaussians whose covariance matrices are all given by ε times the unit matrix and we consider the limit ε 0, then the EM algorithm becomes the *K*-means algorithm [2]. In this limit, the means of the Gaussian components become the prototype vectors, and the probabilities (which tend to 0 or 1) become the hard cluster assignments. The E step then becomes the assignment phase, while the M step becomes the re-calculation step for the prototype vectors.

One of the many powerful aspects of the probabilistic approach is immedi-ately apparent, since we can easily obtain a whole raft of generalizations of *K*-means by considering, for example, diagonal covariance matrices, common co-variance matrices for all components, mixtures of non-Gaussian distributions and so on, and then taking an appropriate deterministic limit.

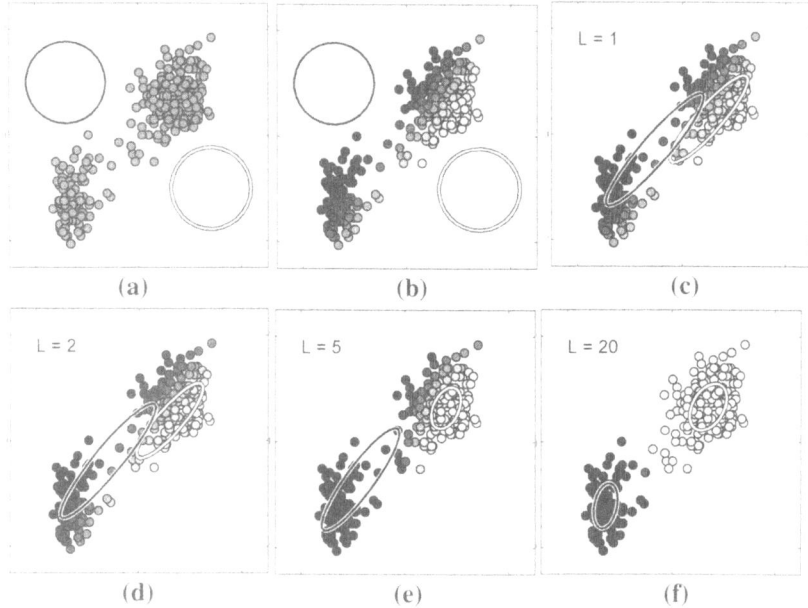

Figure 3. Illustration of the EM algorithm for fitting a mixture of Gaussians, applied to the same data set as used in Figure 1. (a) The data points are shown in grey, and the white and black circles represent the initial 1-standard-deviation contours of the two Gaussian components. (b) After the first E step each data point has been assigned a probability of belonging to each of the white and black components. This is illustrated graphically by shading each data point according to the probability associated with each cluster. Thus, if a data point has a probability p of belonging to the black cluster, and hence probability $(1 - p)$ of belonging to the white cluster, then we can think of the point as having been rendered using a proportion p of black ink and a proportion $(1 - p)$ of white ink, giving the appropriate shade of grey. (c) In the M step the parameters (means and covariances) of the Gaussian components are re-calculated, which simply involves fitting each component to the mean and covariance of the corresponding distribution of black or white ink. The mixing coefficients (not shown) are also re-calculated in the M step. (d) The situation after 2 complete iterations of EM. (e) The situation after 5 complete iterations of EM. (f) After 20 iterations of the EM algorithm, the model is now close to convergence.

Model complexity

There remains the interesting problem of deciding on the appropriate number of clusters. If our algorithm is based on the minimization of a cost function, we might naively think of comparing a range of models having different numbers of clusters and then choosing the model having the smallest (converged) value of the cost function. This approach, however, suffers from a major flaw called over-fitting, which favours overly complex models. In K-means, for instance, this would lead us to choose a model with one prototype vector per data point, since the cost function can then be reduced to zero. One pragmatic approach is to measure the value of the cost function using new data which was not used to fit the model (so called 'hold out' data). This approach avoids the over-fitting problem but is wasteful of possibly expensive data, and in many cases can prove computationally expensive.

How then should we decide on the number of clusters? One clue comes from the predictive power of a proposed partitioning, as Needham [6] points out:

> In a good classification, a lot follows from a statement of class membership, so that in a particular application the predictive power of any classification that we propose is a good test of its suitability.

This intuition can be formalised through the framework of lossless data compression. Imagine each data point is expressed (for simplicity, we consider the case of finite precision) by a bit string of given length. Instead of transmitting the raw data, we might hope to achieve a lower data rate by first clustering the data set. Then we transmit the (relatively small number of) prototype vectors followed, for each data point, by the identity of the nearest prototype together with the error between the prototype and the data point. It is not difficult to see that, if the data comprise tightly packed clusters, this can lead to a significant reduction in the total number of bits which need to be transmitted. Now if our model has many clusters, then a lot of bits are needed to specify the cluster identity, whereas if there are few clusters, then the discrepancy between individual data points and the cluster representatives can become large, again requiring many bits. We see that there is a natural trade-off favouring models having some intermediate number of clusters. Indeed, choosing the model which leads to the shortest message length thus provides a principled approach to selecting the number of prototype vectors.

This *minimum-description-length framework* [8] in fact has a deep relationship to the probabilistic viewpoint since the number of bits needed to code an observation $\mathbf{x}$ under a distribution $p(\mathbf{x})$ is related to $-\log p(\mathbf{x})$ [9]. The overall message length corresponds to the *marginal* probability of the data given the model, in which the model parameters (means, covariances and mixing coefficients in the case of a mixture of Gaussians) have been integrated out with respect to appropriate prior distributions. The optimal number of clusters, under the given probabilistic model, then corresponds to the maximum of the marginal probability of the data.

It may not be immediately clear why the maximum of the marginal probability corresponds to the required solution. For instance, we might expect that the more complex the model, in other words the greater the number of clusters, the better the model could fit the data, and hence the higher the probability of the data under the model. We can gain some intuition as to why the marginal probability prefers a model of intermediate complexity (having neither too few nor too many clusters) from the schematic illustration in Figure 4.

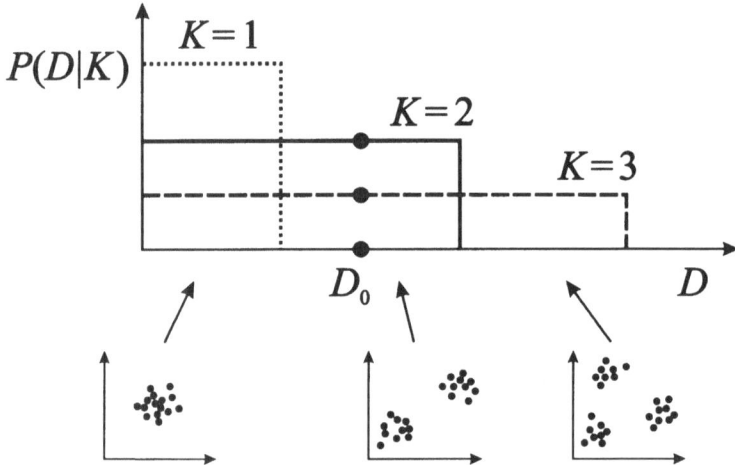

Figure 4. An illustration of why the marginal probability can be largest for models of intermediate complexity. The graph shows schematically the marginal probability $p(D|K)$ of the data given some number K of components in the mixture model plotted against the space of all possible data sets D. Here we imagine the data sets have been ordered so that simpler data sets (having fewer clusters) are to the left of the horizontal axis, while more complex data sets are to the right. The marginal probability distribution for a 'mixture' model comprising one component is shown schematically by the dotted line. This only assigns significant probability to simple data sets. Conversely, a more complex model having three components has the marginal probability distribution shown by the dashed line. This is able to provide a good fit to data sets comprising one, two or three clusters. The distribution shown by the solid line represents a model of intermediate complexity having two components. Since these distributions are normalized, the broader the distribution, the smaller is its typical value. If we observe a particular data set D_0, we see that the highest marginal probability (corresponding to the highest of the three dots) arises from the model having intermediate complexity, corresponding to two clusters.

Unfortunately, the integrations required to evaluate the marginal probability are analytically intractable. Although they could be computed numerically using Monte Carlo techniques, in recent years powerful new deterministic approximation schemes based on variational methods [4] have been developed which provide a practical alternative to numerical integration.

In fact we can take this approach a stage further and use variational methods to evaluate the marginal probability as a function of the mixing coefficients and then optimize with respect to those coefficients [3]. The result is that surplus components in the mixture model are automatically pruned out by virtue of having their mixing coefficients driven to zero. This leads to an algorithm for clustering which simultaneously performs soft clustering of the data while determining the appropriate number of clusters (illustrated in Figure 5).

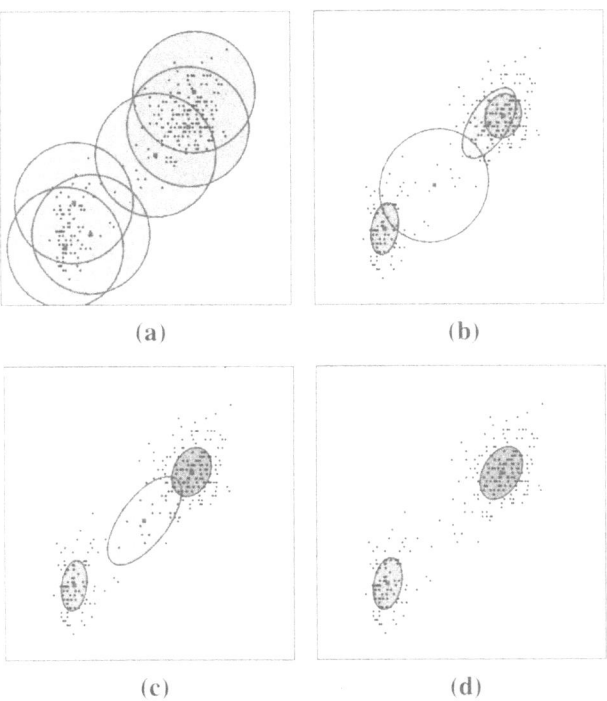

Figure 5. Illustration of the use of variational methods to fit a mixture of Gaussians in which the number of components is determined automatically, again using the Old Faithful data set. The model is initialized using six components with means given by a random subset of the data points and covariance matrices set to a multiple of the unit matrix. (a) The ellipses show the initial 1 standard deviation contours for each of the six components. (b) After 32 iterations two of the six components have had their mixing coefficients driven to zero and no longer play a role. (c) After 58 iterations a further component has been pruned out. (d) After 120 iterations, only two components remain and the algorithm has converged.

It should be noted that this approach determines an optimal number of clusters from a data-representation perspective. However, in a particular application, for example information retrieval, there will be some overall system performance measure for which the optimal number of clusters may be different.

Current research directions

Clustering techniques such as mixtures of Gaussians make strong assumptions about the cluster structure which may not always be appropriate. For this reason the last few years have seen considerable interest in spectral methods based on the eigenspectrum of the 'affinity' matrix **A** of inter-point similarities. Needham [6] recognised this possibility but considered it to be computationally impractical using the technology of the day (which in part still relied on punched paper tape and cards).

> There is clearly some relation between clumps and the eigenvectors of **A**. ...
> In matrices of the order likely to arise in classification problems, the solution
> of the eigenproblem would almost be a research problem in itself.

Figure 6 shows an example of the spectral approach based on the recent algorithm of Perona and Freeman [7]. Data clustering has come a long way in the last forty years. Nevertheless, there are still many open problems, and insights developed in the 1960s remain equally valid today.

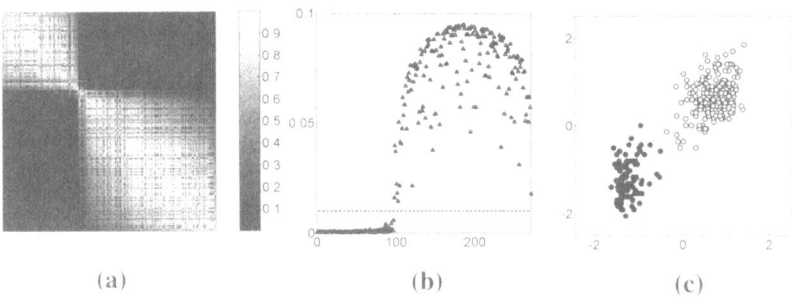

(a)   (b)   (c)

Figure 6. Example of the spectral approach to clustering, for the Old Faithful data set. (a) Plot of the affinity matrix **A** whose elements are defined by $A_{ij} = \exp(-d^2_{ij}/2\sigma^2)$, where d_{ij} is the distance between points i and j, and σ is a length scale. For clarity, the data points have been sorted according to the value of the eruption duration. (b) Plot of the components of the first eigenvector of the affinity matrix corresponding to each of the 272 points in the data set. The horizontal line shows the threshold used to partition the data into two clusters. (c) Assignments of data points to the two clusters, in which points above the threshold in (b) are shown in white and those below are shown in black.

References

1. BERNARDO, J.M., AND SMITH, A.F.M., *Bayesian theory*, Wiley, 1994.
2. BISHOP, C.M., *Neural networks for pattern recognition*, Oxford University Press. 1995.
3. CORDUNEANU, A., AND BISHOP, C.M., 'Variational bayesian model selection for mixture distributions,' in *Proc. of the 8th International Conference on Artificial Intelligence and Statistics, 2001*, T. Richardson and T. Jaakkola (eds.), Morgan Kaufmann, pp. 27–34.
4. JORDAN, M.I., GHAHRAMANI, Z., JAAKKOLA, T.S., AND SAUL, L.K., 'An Introduction to Variational Methods for Graphical Models,' in *Learning in Graphical Models*, M. I. Jordan (ed.), MIT Press, 1999.
5. NEEDHAM, R.M., 'Automatic classification: models and problems,' in *Mathematics and Computer Science in Biology and Medicine*, The Medical Research Council, London, 1965, pp. 111–114.
6. NEEDHAM, R.M., 'Applications of the theory of clumps,' *Mechanical Translation*, vol. 8, 1965, pp. 113–127.
7. PERONA, P., AND FREEMAN, W.T., 'A factorization approach to grouping,' in *Proc. Of the 5th European Conference on Computer Vision*, 1998, H. Burkardt and B. Neumann (eds.), pp. 655–670.
8. RISSANEN, J., 'Modelling by shortest data description,' *Automatica*, vol. 14, 1978, pp. 465–471.
9. SHANNON, C., 'A mathematical theory of communication,' *Bell System Technical Journal*, vol. 27, pp. 379–423 and 623–656.

6
How to Implement Unnecessary Mutexes

Mike Burrows

Introduction

In languages like Modula, Java, and C#, it is common to write reusable modules. In order to allow for multithreading, programmers typically protect the invariants of their modules with mutexes (i.e., binary semaphores). These are used via language constructs like synchronized in Java, or lock in C#.

Often, only one thread touches a particular object. An example is Java's StringBuffer class. Typically, a thread creates a StringBuffer, uses it to create a new String, and then discards the StringBuffer. All of the methods of StringBuffer acquire a mutex to allow potential concurrent use from multiple threads, even though this almost never occurs.

When a mutex is used by only one thread, the mutex is unnecessary and could be removed. Removal is desirable, because mutex operations typically involve hardware-atomic instructions that are considerably more expensive than normal memory accesses. We measured mutex acquisition at between 50 and 70 cycles on various Alpha systems, whereas incrementing a memory location only takes four or five cycles. As a result, applications can waste several percent of their CPU time on unnecessary synchronization. However, one would not wish to allow programmers to specify whether they need to use mutexes, because they may make mistakes, and even correct decisions may become wrong in the future.

Various people have investigated static analysis techniques to identify unnecessary mutexes and to translate compiled modules automatically so that unnecessary mutexes are omitted [1]. An annoyance here is that the analysis can take some time and is necessarily conservative.

Hardware-atomic instructions have been avoided on uniprocessors by preventing context switches during code sequences that should be atomic [2, 3]. But these techniques do not help with multiprocessors and require support from the scheduler.

It is also possible to enable hardware-atomic sequences only when the second thread is created. The strategy fails in complex run-time systems, such as Java's, which create multiple threads in every application.

Goal

Our goal is to optimize mutexes for the case where they are not needed. That is, we optimize for mutexes that are used by only one thread of control, yet we hope not to lose significant performance when multiple threads access the mutex. It is a requirement that the mutexes must function correctly with multiple threads, that the technique work on both uniprocessors and multiprocessors, and that no un-usual operating-system support be needed. We assume that loads and stores of individual words are atomic.

The technique

This section initially describes the technique, which seems slow at first sight. Optimizations and refinements follow in later paragraphs. In the description, we assume that mutexes normally occupy a machine word, and are re-entrant, so each mutex contains a lock nesting count. Re-entrant mutexes are odious, but are now almost universal; they allow locked regions to be nested, and hence make it easier for the writer of an object method to call another method without dead-locking, and without maintaining that pesky monitor invariant.

The representation of each mutex M is modified to contain the thread identi-fier M.assoc of some thread that has been *associated* with the mutex. The asso-ciated thread is typically the last thread to have used the mutex. Initially, M.assoc is either null or identifies the thread that created the mutex.

A thread T wishing to use the mutex proceeds as follows:
>T loads the word for M
>T checks whether (T == M.assoc)
>If so, T updates the lock nesting count and stores the mutex back into its word.
>Otherwise, T takes the slow path.

This is the *fast acquire/release sequence*. Notice that the fast path requires no memory barriers and no hardware-atomic operations.

When T is using the mutex, any other thread T' will fail to verify that (T' == M.assoc). In this case, T' must obtain exclusive access to the mutex word. This is done at great cost, but later refinements will guarantee that it is done infre-quently.

T' must stop two classes of threads from touching M:

a.   the associated thread, M.assoc

b.   all other threads

We deal with case (b) first. With each mutex M, there is a *supervisor* mutex S(M) that operates on normal principles—that is, it does not use the present technique. There could be one supervisor mutex for all mutexes in the address space, or one supervisor mutex for each mutex, or anything in between.

T' acquires the supervisor mutex S(M). Since all threads operating on M other than M.assoc will attempt to acquire S(M), we can assume that once T' has acquired S(M), only T' and M.assoc will operate on M.

T' now suspends the thread M.assoc (assuming M.assoc is non-null). The *thread_suspend* operation is required by many garbage collectors, so no operating-system changes should be required provided that the suspend operation is reference-counted. T' must now verify that the thread M.assoc is not in a fast acquire/release sequence on M, and if it is, it must dislodge M.assoc. There are at least three ways to determine whether M.assoc is in a fast acquire/release sequence:

1.   If the sequence cannot be inlined, T' can compare the program counter of M.assoc with the known address of the acquire/release sequence(s).

2.   T' can look at the pattern of instructions around the M.assoc program counter to determine whether it could possibly be an acquire/release sequence.

3.   The acquire/release sequence can be augmented to force each thread to set a per-thread variable on entry to the sequence, and to reset it on leaving the sequence. T' may then check this variable. This may slow down the acquire/release sequence somewhat, but it works even when a thread's program counter cannot be obtained by another thread.

All of these techniques have been tried and can be made to work. In addition, T' may be able to determine that M.assoc is not operating on M by checking that the address of M is not in the appropriate register(s).

There is an extra complication on systems that allow asynchronous userspace trap handlers (e.g., UNIX signal handlers, or VMS ASTs). The handler return sequence (the "trampoline code") must test whether it is about to return into the middle of an acquire/release sequence.

If M.assoc is in an acquire/release sequence for M, it must be dislodged. This can be done in any of three ways:

1.   T' can resume M.assoc and suspend it anew, then test again to see whether it is in a fast acquire/release sequence.

2.   If the sequence is restartable, T' can move the program counter of M.assoc back to the start of the sequence so that when awoken, M.assoc will re-execute the sequence.

3.   T' can interpret the state of M.assoc forward until it is out of the sequence. This requires a machine-code interpreter.

All of these techniques have been tried and can be made to work.

T' must now check M once more to ensure that the value of M.assoc did not change while it was in the process of acquiring S(M) and suspending M.assoc. If M.assoc changed, T' releases S(M), resumes the thread it stopped, and tries again.

If M.assoc is unchanged, T' now has exclusive access to M. It may now do one of two things:

1. set M.assoc to T', so that T' becomes the associated thread, or
2. set a bit in M indicating that all further operations on M must use hardware-atomic sequences.

In case (2), the format of the mutex word may be changed arbitrarily, provided that one bit allows the associated thread format to be distinguished from the hardware-atomic format. Thus, if the technique described here is merged with an existing mutex implementation, only one spare bit need be found in the existing mutex word. The fast acquire/release sequence must be modified to test this bit. The atomicity of loads and stores guarantees that other threads will see either that the bit has been set, or that it has not been set and M.assoc is not the thread's identifier. The memory barrier in *thread_resume* ensures that a thread that was once the associated thread will no longer observe its thread ID in M.assoc.

Different designs may choose different approaches for choosing between (1) and (2). A simple implementation may choose to revert to hardware-atomic operations if M.assoc is non-null—this works reasonably well. A slightly more sophisticated implementation can use a small (8 or 9 bit) saturating counter M.counter in the mutex. Each time the associated thread acquires M on the fast path, it increments M.counter. Each time a thread suspends the associated thread, it decrements M.counter by some constant K. If M.counter underflows, T' chooses (2), and otherwise chooses (1). K is calculated according to the speeds of the various operations so that M.counter will underflow when the optimization is not paying off. If T_{fast} is the time taken to acquire and release the mutex by the fast path, T_{atomic} is the time taken to acquire and release the mutex using hardware-atomic instruction, and $T_{suspend}$ is the time taken to suspend and resume the associated thread, we want the time for K fast operations plus one suspend/resume to equal the time for K operations using hardware-atomic sequences:

$$K \times T_{fast} + T_{suspend} = K \times T_{atomic},$$

so:

$$K = T_{suspend} / (T_{atomic} - T_{fast}).$$

Typically T_{atomic} is much bigger than T_{fast}, so

$$K = T_{suspend} / T_{atomic}.$$

We used $K = 200$ in one implementation and $K =$ in another. ($K =$ means convert the mutex as soon as the second thread touches it.)

If K is chosen well, mutexes that do not benefit from the optimization will be converted quickly to use the hardware-atomic sequences, and performance should not suffer. One could conceive of applications that create new mutexes, use them just long enough to force them to be converted and then discard them, causing the application to be slowed down. We have found no such applications among the Java spec benchmarks and C server applications we tried. If this were a serious concern, one could arrange to detect this dynamically. When it occurs, new mutexes may be created so that they always use hardware-atomic instructions.

One could imagine converting mutexes back, depending on the usage pattern, but we have not implemented this, and it seems unlikely to be of practical value.

Memory barriers are not needed in the fast-path sequences, because the operating system thread suspend/resume must perform the necessary memory barriers when communicating with whatever processor is running the target thread.

Reducing the cost of finding a thread's identifier

In the preceding section, each thread operating on mutex M is required to test whether the thread identifier in the mutex, M.assoc, is equal to the thread's own identifier. In one of our implementations, where we controlled the code generator and had a large number of integer registers, we were able to store the thread identifier in a general purpose register. This makes the test quite cheap.

When the code generator cannot be changed, or when the processor has too few integer registers, it may take a significant number of cycles to obtain the thread ID. In one of our implementations, it required a seven-cycle operation, which significantly exceeded the time for the rest of the fast acquire/release sequence.

In order to optimize this case, we chose to store not the thread ID, but the high-order bits of the stack pointer. When these match the current thread's stack pointer, we can be sure that it is the associated thread. When the bits do not match, the thread reads its stack bounds and checks them. If the value in the mutex is within bounds, the value can be updated to match the current stack pointer value. We found that this optimization worked well and produced a fast-path sequence of 5 cycles.

In a system with a page size of 2^P bytes and where at least one guard page separates each pair of stacks, two threads will differ in the high-order bits of their stacks even if the bottom $(P + 1)$ bits are ignored. Thus, these $(P + 1)$ bits can be used for M.counter, a bit to indicate which representation is in use, and two or three bits for a small lock-nesting count. In the rare case where the lock-nesting count overflows, the mutex can be converted to the hardware-atomic style.

A disadvantage of using stack pointers to identify threads is that they must be mapped back to thread identifiers in order to allow the corresponding thread to be suspended or resumed. The requirement is for a mapping from a stack page to a thread identifier, which is best done with a balanced binary tree or a skiplist.

We implemented this scheme in a system where the client could choose where to put each thread's stack. In this case, we were forced to turn off the optimization if the client chose to use stacks not separated by at least one page.

Results

We found that no real applications were measurably slowed down by using this technique. Many applications show no change in performance—this is because most applications are not limited by the speed at which mutex acquisition and release occur. Some applications show a few-percent speedup, and a few applications show more significant speedups, as high as around 10%. Contrived examples can show speedups of a factor of three.

Almost all of the gain is obtained when K is set to infinity, that is, by choosing to convert the mutex to use hardware-atomic instructions as soon as it is touched by the second thread. However, we did observe some interesting beneficial effects with $K = 200$. In particular, we had assumed that a mutex with extremely high contention would not benefit from this technique and would quickly be converted to use the previous scheme. However, if the contention is high enough, this does not happen. Consider this code:

```
for (;;) {
    acquire (M);
    x++;
    release (M);
}
```

If multiple threads are running this code on a uniprocessor, the thread that has the current time slice will saturate M.counter. At the next context switch, M.counter will be decremented by K once, but this will not cause it to underflow. The thread running in the next time slice will then saturate M.counter once more. This is, of course, a contrived example, but in cases where locks protect fast operations, a similar effect may occur in real applications.

We felt sure that the effect described in the previous paragraph could not pay off on a multiprocessor. But on small-scale multiprocessors we found that the (contrived) loop above did benefit from the technique. We found that threads took so long to wake up (that is, the scheduler path was so long), that the associated thread had time to saturate the counter before the previous associated thread could suspend it. We were unable to confirm that this occurred in any real application.

Summary

We have constructed a mutex that is optimized for the case where only one thread uses it. We achieved this by allowing only a designated thread to access the mutex until another thread displaces it through the use of thread suspend and resume operations. This technique provides a modest, but possibly valuable, gain in performance in situations where code is written to work with multiple threads, but often is used by just one. It also provides a gratifying increase in complexity that will entertain programmers for many happy hours.

Acknowledgements

This work was done by Mike Burrows, Sanjay Ghemawat, and Mark Vandevoorde at Compaq SRC. The technique is now used in Tru64 Alpha systems.

References

1. ALDRICH, J., CHAMBERS, C., SIRER, E.G., AND EGGERS, S., 'Eliminating unnecessary synchronization from Java programs,' in *Proc. of the Static Analyses Symposium*, Venice, Italy, September 1999, pp. 19–38.
2. MOSS, J., AND KOHLER, W., 'Concurrency features for the Trellis/Owl language,' *Proc. European Conference on Object-Oriented Programming*, LNCS, vol. 276, Springer, pp.171–180.
3. BERSHAD, B.N., REDELL, D.D., AND ELLIS, J.R., 'Fast mutual exclusion for uniprocessors,' *5th Symp. on Architectural Support for Programming Languages and Operating Systems (ASPLOS V)*, October 1992, pp. 223–233.

7
Bioware Languages

Luca Cardelli

Preface

I have not operated, technically, in the research areas of direct interest to Roger Needham, and therefore have not worked with him. However, I have enjoyed at least one of the research environments that he was instrumental in setting up and running. I will try here to give a (possibly extreme) example of the kind of free research spirit that he has encouraged. Incidentally, a basic technical notion in this note is the 'pure names' that Roger pioneered in a slightly different context [4].

Introduction

This work can be seen as example of an emerging class of languages for describing, and possibly programming, biological systems (bioware). A living cell is, to a rather surprising extent, an information-processing device [1]. One can envision describing precisely such complex biological systems, and then deriving simulation and analysis from such descriptions. One can even imagine one day "compiling" bioware languages into real biological systems, just like silicon chips are today compiled from hardware languages.

Biological systems, far from being unstructured chemical soups, employ membranes to organize and isolate chemical reactions and their products. Hierarchies of membranes are a necessary component of any description of such systems. The π-calculus [3] has been used to model chemical reactions [6]. As an extension [7], the ambient calculus [2], which is based on a dynamic hierarchy of containers, can be used to model biological interactions. (Stochastic aspects can be handled, but are not discussed here [5].)

We represent biological systems with a graphical (rather than textual) notation; this is somewhat natural because of the aspect and hierarchical structure of many such systems. It is also possible to provide a formal textual notation and related semantics, using standard techniques from process calculi. Moreover, it is possible to provide a formal graphical notation and related semantics, as a special case of Milner's BiGraphs. But here we just present a (formalizable) graphical notation: the graphical language of *biographs*.

Biographs

A biograph represents a biological system via three primitive constructions and eight basic reactions. (The number of reactions could be reduced, but it then becomes harder to program 'instantaneous' reactions.)

Membranes. For our purposes, a *membrane* is simply a boundary that confines reactions to its interior, unless these are reactions that explicitly interact with a membrane, as discussed below. Graphically, a membrane may contain reagents or other membranes. Membranes are nameless, but it useful to attach *comments* to them (e.g., "cell membrane" or "virus capsid").

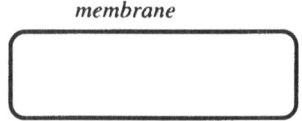

Reagents. A *reagent* represents a biological (or chemical) entity that is ready to interact with some other biological entity. Reagents typically represent protein complexes that are ready to bind to each other and transform each other as a result. Rather than considering the countless protein structures that exists in reality, we take a fixed set of primitive reagents, enumerated later, that can be used to express a large class of interactions (the formalism is, in fact, Turing-complete). Each reagent is parameterized by a number of *binding sites*. These binding sites are named by *pure names* [4] $n_1 \ldots n_k$, that is, names that have no structure other than their identity. Graphically, a reagent encloses the future product of its activation inside a dotted line.

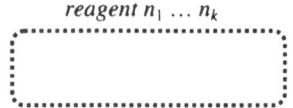

Binding. The binding of, e.g., a protein to a ligand, can be represented as a binding site (a pure name) n that is privately shared by two reagents. A *binding box* represents a region where a pure name n is privately shared. Unlike membranes, which have physical existence, binding boxes are more of a bookkeeping device. A binding box for n can graphically expand, contract, and cross other membranes and binding boxes, as long as this process does not lead to revealing n or to confusing it with some other n.

Named subsystems. This is meta-notation for subsystems, used when expressing general interaction rules (named subsystems do not occur in specific system instances). The notation below represents a subsystem (the dashed boundary) that is named P so we can refer to it. Sometimes we need to apply a name replacement {*m/n*} (replacing *m* with *n*) to a still undetermined subsystem; the name replacement then sits on the boundary, until later when the subsystem is determined and the replacement can be applied.

{*m/n*}

P

Membrane reactions

We start by describing reagents that affect membranes. These reagents typically represent protein complexes that sit on or across a membrane, and cause membranes to interact with each other. Graphically, these reagents are drawn inside the membrane that they actually sit on or across, so that they are transported along with the membrane.

On the left of the reaction arrow we have the situation before the interaction, and on the right we have the situation after the interaction.

The first reaction describes a membrane that enters another contiguous membrane, through the interaction of two specific reagents, *enter* and *accept*, that have a common binding site *n*. Here P and Q represent the residuals of the interacting reagents (which could be void), while R and S represent whatever else is initially contained in the membranes. The following two reactions describe the effects of reagents that cause membranes to exit each other (*exit* and *expel*) or to merge (*merge+* and *merge−*), each based on a common interaction site *n*.

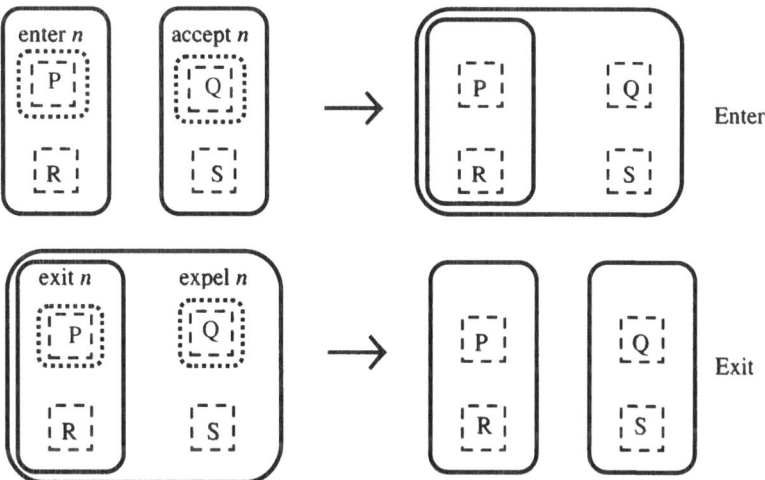

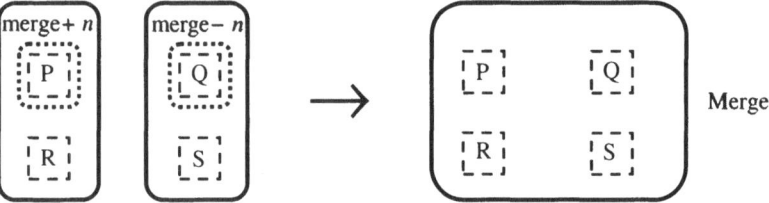

Merge

Site reactions

The next group of reactions do not affect membranes (although membranes may be involved), but affect only reagents. In these reactions, reagents interact on a binding site n, and can also exchange tokens m. These tokens can represent further binding sites, or other entities that get passed along in reactions (e.g., electrons or small molecules).

The first site reaction represents a pure chemical reaction: two molecules interact and produce two other molecules, within the confines of some common solution (the two molecules must be inside the same membrane, if any). The two complementary molecules are indicated by $n!$ and $n?$. The common name n means that they can interact, and the !,? pair determines the direction of the interaction. In full, $n!\{m\}(P)$ means that this is a molecule that, when interacting, provides a token m to the other molecule and transforms itself into P. On the other hand, $n?\{p\}(Q)$ means that this other molecule receives some token m, and transforms itself into $Q\{m/p\}$. Here p is really a formal input parameter, and $Q\{m/p\}$ is Q where the formal p is replaced by the actual m.

$n!\{m\}$ $n?\{p\}$ $\{m/p\}$ Local

$\boxed{P}$ $\boxed{Q}$ $\rightarrow$ $\boxed{P}$ $\boxed{Q}$

The next two reactions are similar, but the interaction between reagents happens across a membrane. The exchanged token m flows either down through a membrane (indicated by '_') or up through a membrane (indicated by '^').

$n\_!\{m\}$ $n^?\{p\}$ $\{m/p\}$ To child

$\boxed{P}$ $\boxed{\begin{array}{c} Q \\ S \end{array}}$ $\rightarrow$ $\boxed{P}$ $\boxed{\begin{array}{c} Q \\ S \end{array}}$

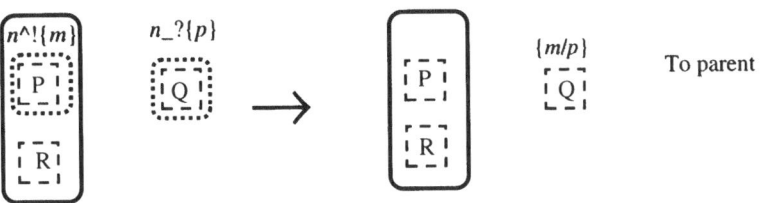

To parent

Finally, we have a reaction where the token m flows through two sibling membranes (indicated by '#').

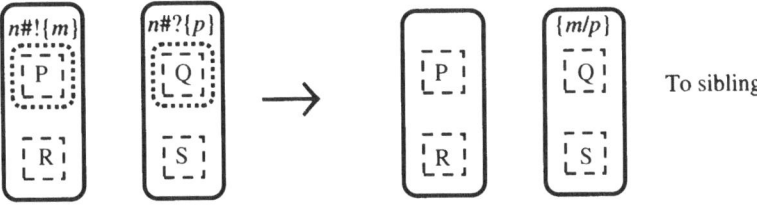

To sibling

Repeat reaction and some abbreviations

A "repeat" reagent creates new copies of a given reagent or subsystem. This models, abstractly, unbounded resources and processes.

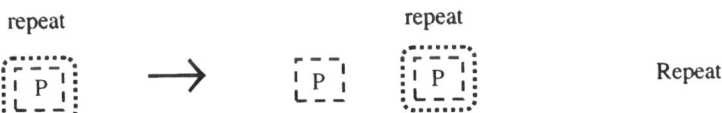

Repeat

Moreover, we use some graphical abbreviations to simplify drawings:

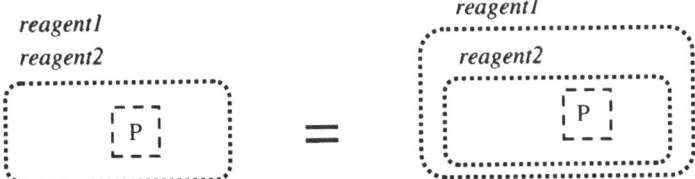

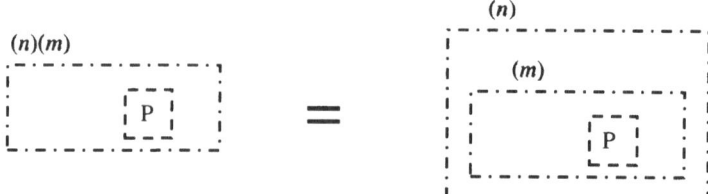

Example: symporter

A *symporter* is a molecular channel. It binds two specific proteins, here called protein-P and protein-Q, from outside the cell in either order, and then simultaneously transports them inside the cell.

The symporter subsystem can repeat its behavior indefinitely (given sufficient energy, which is not modeled), and persists within the cell. It is first written separately, and then indicated by name in the larger system below. Two interaction sites, bind-P and bind-Q, represent the binding sites of the symporter with any instance of protein-P and protein-Q respectively. Each repeated interaction uses a fresh pair of distinct tokens p, q, which represent bindings with specific protein instances. After an instance of a protein is bound, nothing can then interfere with that binding because nothing else knows the freshly created pure names p, q. We write a symporter thus:

symporter =

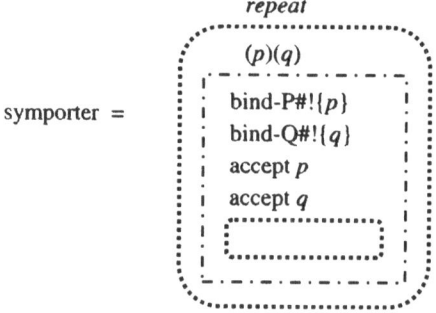

The whole system then looks like the picture below. Initially, a cell contains a symporter and whatever else, and is contiguous (that is, within the same surrounding membrane, if any) with instances of protein-P and protein-Q. Note that the proteins are themselves modeled as membranes: this is common because protein complexes can have a complicated structure.

After a sequence of reactions, during which the proteins are bound in either order, the proteins are both transported inside the cell membrane. Each reaction in the sequence is an instance of one of the reactions explained previously.

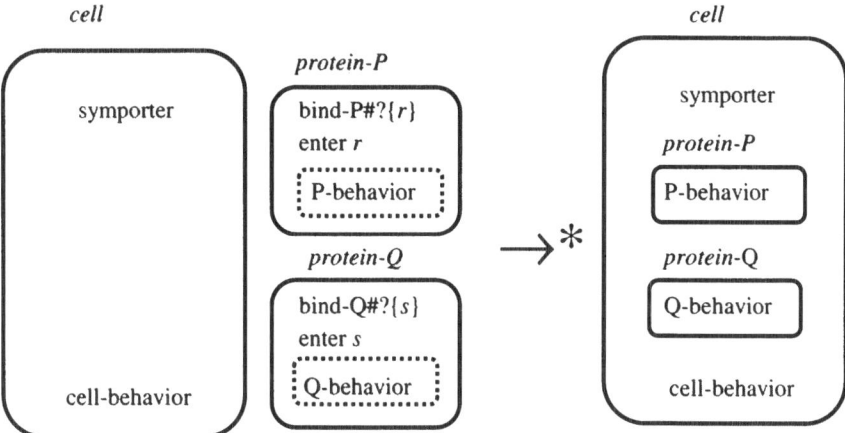

Although this protocol works under 'ordinary conditions,' it is not perfect, and one can study ways in which it can be subverted. In fact, this is an important reason for modeling biological systems in all their complexity: many drugs and natural defences work by subverting natural pathways. We need to model biological systems in order to understand them, but also to study how they can or cannot be tampered with at any level of abstraction.

References

1. ALBERTS, B., BRAY, D., LEWIS, J., RAFF, M., ROBERTS, K., AND WATSON, J.D., *Molecular biology of the cell*, Garland Publishing, 1994.
2. CARDELLI, L., AND GORDON, A.D., 'Mobile ambients,' *Theoretical Computer Science*, vol. 240, no. 1, June 2000, pp. 177–213.
3. MILNER, R. *Communicating and mobile systems: the Pi-Calculus*, Cambridge University Press, 1999.
4. NEEDHAM, R.M., 'Names,' in S. Mullender, (ed.), *Distributed systems*, pp. 89–101. Addison-Wesley, 1989.
5. PRIAMI, C., REGEV, A., SILVERMAN, W., AND SHAPIRO, E., 'Application of stochastic process algebras to bioinformatics of molecular processes,' *Information Processing Letters*, vol. 80, 2001, pp. 25–31.
6. REGEV, A., SILVERMAN, W., AND SHAPIRO, E. 'Representation and simulation of biochemical processes using the pi-calculus process algebra,' *Proc. Pacific Symposium of Biocomputing 2001 (PSB2001)*, vol. 6, pp. 459–470.
7. REGEV, A., Ph.D. Thesis, to appear.

8
The Economics of Open Systems

David D. Clark

Computer system designers have a set of principles and techniques they use in their trade: modularity and interfaces, layering and dependency relationships. Breaking a large system into parts so that they can be separately designed and built is among the most basic of techniques to tame size and complexity.

However, systems are not just designed and built, they are operated in the real world, and modularity matters here too. This paper is concerned with distributed systems that are operated by multiple commercial providers in a profit-seeking context, such as the telephone system and more recently the Internet. The central observation of this paper is that in systems such as the Internet, modularity and interfaces shape not only the technical design but the industry structure, and system designers would do well to consider the desirability and viability of the industry structure that their modularity induces.

The obvious starting point

How can I make money? That is the question that almost everyone asks when they think about a commercial undertaking. But the system designer should ask a more sophisticated set of questions. For a system to work, all the parts have to fit together, so the questions have to address all the parts:
- What are the industry sectors defined by the interfaces?
- How does each of them make money?
- What sectors may not make (enough) money?
- Does the system fit together economically?

This is not a design space that most technical engineers are familiar with.

Some examples

The industry structure of the Internet offers many illustrations of interfaces and industry structure. One of the earliest examples is the interface between routers—the protocols that exchange control and routing information. The creators of the first routers argued that there was so much complexity and uncertainty in these router interfaces that it would not be practical to standardize them. They needed to be kept proprietary, so that they could be upgraded or replaced quickly. But this approach would have prevented the emergence of a competitive market in router vendors, and the Internet designers strongly resisted the call to leave those interfaces as closed, engineering interfaces. Without these interfaces, companies like Cisco could never have come into existence.

Cisco, of course, is an equipment manufacturer, not a service provider. The open interfaces that permit routers from different companies to interoperate also permit different Internet service providers (ISPs) to interoperate. (The business arrangement behind the standards-based connection is another matter, of course.) We have now lived with commercial ISPs for almost a decade, and the industry structure seems natural. It is important to remember that there is no fundamental reason why it had to come out the way it did: the number of and interrelation between the providers, and the degree of vertical integration in the marketplace, is a result of the particular protocols and interfaces. For example, a redesign of the Internet routing protocols was undertaken in the 1980s specifically to allow multiple competitive wide-area ISPs, as opposed to the prior structure of NSFNet as the single wide-area service provider.

There are many other examples that can be found in the Internet. Internet routers both forward packets and compute routes. The interface between these two functions is not standardized, but is left as a proprietary interface, almost always an internal software interface inside the router. So there is no separate set of companies that sell systems to compute routes. One can debate if this alternative structure would have advantages, but it cannot come into existence because the interfaces don't allow it.

Consequences of economic modularity

The design rules for breaking a system into parts for technical reasons are fairly well known. It is recognized that getting the modularity of a system right is a hard design problem that requires skill and judgment. Good modularity is subjective, and a bit of an art. In a system where the modules represent distinct business entities, the design questions are expanded. It is still the case that the answers (and the resulting modularity) will be subjective.

The first question is, How will the business entity representing each module make money? Again, the communications industry provides a useful example. In the telephone system, there is no business interface between the part of the telephone company that provides the actual wires and the part of the company that provides the telephone "service."[1] The money raised from selling the service covers the cost of the wires, and this value transfer was inside the business module represented by the telephone company. In the Internet, there is an open interface between the basic network service (provided by the Internet protocol with its packet transport capability) and the higher level services such as email, the Web, content in general, and so on. This open interface makes it easy (indeed, it was the goal) for different players to provide the basic Internet service and the higher level services on top. So each sector must separately have a strategy for making money.

In this structure, how do the ISPs make money? ISPs charge fees to the parties that attach to them, roughly in proportion to the size of the access link they use. What ISPs cannot do today is charge more for carrying "more valuable bits." Competition drives prices toward marginal cost, and squeezes out the options for value pricing. Some services, like television, require orders of magnitude more bits than others, like Internet telephony. Looking at the typical monthly consumer expenditure for television and telephone, even a rough calculation suggests that to capture an equivalent share of what the consumer is willing to pay, a provider must charge a lot more for a "telephone call" bit than a "television show" bit. This sort of value pricing does not work in the Internet today. ISPs are forced to be commodity carriers of undifferentiated bits.

There is an analogy to the well-know history of the railroads. Railroads used to charge more to haul a ton of valuable product than a ton of rock. But when trucking and other forms of competition entered the market and skimmed off these valuable products, the railroads were left with only the bulk, low-value cargo unless they converted to a fee based only on weight. Economic disruption followed. And that is what has happened with the Internet. The "old" telephone companies were vertically integrated and provided both the wires and the service. The revenue structure did not require them to "price the bits," but only the "telephone service." As soon as an open interface was inserted into the industry structure, those who looked ahead and saw the consequences realized that anyone who had to "charge for the bits" as the only way to make money would make no money from telephony, because there were so few bits to carry it as compared to other services.

The fact that there are physical facilities at the base of the Internet companies that actually install and operate fibers, wires, and so on, signals another economic reality. Owners of facilities are in a "sunk cost" industry. They spend money up front to install these communication links, and then try to recover these costs from subsequent utilization or resale. Industries with major sunk costs have to deal with the economic reality that competition tends to drive prices toward marginal or incremental cost of providing service, and prices based on incremental costs may not recover the capital initially invested. If in-

---

1   An interesting topic not explored in this paper is that recent regulatory tactics try to create such an interface.

dustries with major sunk costs become highly competitive, there is a risk that all the players go out of business. (In practical terms, what happens is that the weaker ones go out of business or are acquired by the stronger players, until the competition is not so demanding.)

So the open interface in the Internet architecture implies two painful facts for the ISPs and the facilities providers on which they depend (if ISPs don't own their own facilities). First, the open interface has deprived them of an important opportunity for value pricing, and second, it has imposed competition on a sector with major sunk costs. Both of these signal economic stress. While it was not reasonable to expect an observer in the mid-90s to predict the full trajectory of the industry—with over-exuberant investment in facilities, followed by bankruptcy, an oversupply of long-distance fiber that owners cannot even afford to light, components of old-line telephone companies fighting for their economic life, and major industry consolidation raising anti-trust concerns—all of these consequences are consistent with the economic constraints imposed by slicing a competitive open interface through the middle of what had been a stable, vertically integrated industry.

The withering of openness

The pressures of commodity bit-carriage and covering sunk costs may in fact drive toward industry consolidation at the lower levels of the Internet industry—the ISPs and the facilities providers that support them. What might this imply for the Internet interfaces?

The Internet interface, at the present time, seems to remain open. But if one ISP achieved significant market power, it might be to its advantage to offer a "modified" or "enhanced" or "just different" interface, and try to get a number of higher-level service providers to adopt this interface instead. By doing so, they shut other ISPs and other higher-level service providers out of the market. So an erosion of competition among ISPs might not just cause higher prices for Internet access, but might cause erosion in the entire Internet model. It is for this reason that the possible lack of competition among broadband ISPs is being so closely watched.

The paper started with a simple question, How do I make money? It continued by observing that the more important (and sophisticated) question is, How does every sector make money? We can now see the full import of this question. If an open interface is seen as desirable to shape the market structure but the sector on one side of this interface is not in a market situation that can sustain competition, consolidation among players may well lead to the consequence that this open interface is driven from the marketplace by the actions of the dominant player. So thinking about how to ensure that all the sectors can make money is a key to ensuring that the open architecture itself survives.

Facing the design challenge

When we think about interfaces as a problem in economic design, what should our design principles be? Experts in economics and business may have many suggestions, but a few principles emerge from the discussion to this point.

Competition is a tool to impose discipline on the market

This discipline is a two-edged sword. It can motivate players to invest and innovate; it can drive them out of business. An example is *end-point controlled routing*, which is not a part of the Internet today. There is no way for a consumer to route his traffic over one ISP rather than another. If this feature were added, it might increase the total competitive pressures and actually make things worse for the ISPs. On the other hand, it would allow a provider with a new idea for a service enhancement to bring it to market and attract (and charge) users. Consumers might be persuaded to pay more, in exchange for real innovation in value that they cannot obtain today.

Price discrimination may be better than monopoly

Few would argue for a return to the good old days of vertical integration, high margins and regulated monopoly. But if the pressures on the facilities providers lead to consolidation and market exit by enough of the ISPs, that might be the result. The alternative is to let the providers make a little more money, with the hope that more competitors survive. Our instinct as consumers is to build a system that appropriates all the excess utility to us. We may need to build mechanisms that deliberately give up some of that to the providers. Allowing the sectors of the industry with sunk costs to recover more of the value associated with consumer utility may be the best compromise to insure a stable industry.

For example, the telephone system has the concept of a "normal" and "800" long-distance call. The idea is that different ends of the call can pay, depending (presumably) on which end attaches more value to the call. The Internet has no such mechanism. Should Internet packets have "Which way is the value flowing?" tags? Quality of service (QOS) is the term in the Internet to describe the concept that some customers can obtain better service (presumably by paying for it). This is an obvious starting point for pricing tiers.

A debate of engineering and religion

By and large, Internet tools for price discrimination were resisted, and still are resisted, because of the fear that incorporating them into the network would create uncontrollable opportunities for the ISPs to impose new costs even on users who did not want them. If there is a high value-tier, one way to make it preferable is to degrade the low value tier, and so on. This resistance, which is almost of religious quality in some network architects, puts at a disadvantage those customers who would actually be willing to pay more for better service. But the risk is real. The force that will resist abuse here is competition. So designers face a dangerous gamble. If putting in these tools is sufficient to sustain competition, then adding them is a good thing. But if competition fails anyway, adding them may make monopoly pricing worse.

Creative market entrants are finding clever ways to bypass the architectural limitations of the basic interfaces and impose price discrimination. Leaving a feature out of an interface does not make it go away. It drives it under the covers, outside the architecture, but not out of existence. We see ISPs today seeking ways to introduce value stratification, and they will do this whether the building blocks are in the architecture or not. This raises the question of whether this after-the-fact evolution is the right approach to achieve economically motivated innovation, or whether we would have been better served to have designed these sorts of value-building blocks into the original open interfaces, so that the facilities providers could have had more direct access to them.

We as system designers should make a conscious choice whether to design these sorts of mechanisms and interfaces, or let them happen after we lose control.

9
From Universe to Global Internet

Jon Crowcroft

The Universe project was a seminal research program that aimed at deploying the Cambridge Distributed System (CDS) over a wide area. In retrospect, the goals were similar to many of the now common test-bed projects in the world: to build from existing ideas, and learn the key problems, and some tentative solutions, for future systems.

Universe sites ran a variety of operating systems and applications that were connected together by 10 Mbps (million bits per second) local and wide area links. At this stage, at the start of the 1980s, when the project spanned several institutions, academic and industrial, such capacity was more than two orders of magnitude greater than that enjoyed by the early Internet researchers. We are still learning from the results over 20 years later.

Research as you mean to develop

A feature of the Universe project was that the system was used by the participants. Many research projects before (and after) entailed two systems: one for development, one for research. In Universe, the operating systems, networks and applications under test were the systems of choice. This is culturally common-place now in the computer science research community, but in those days, and in a large system where failures could disable every day work in catastrophic ways, this was a high-risk, but high-payoff decision.

A number of features of the CDS were notable, and we look at these next.

Naming, addressing and routing

The CDS architecture was notable for a clear separation of concerns. Unsurprisingly, given the strong links maintained between Cambridge distributed-computing researchers and counterparts in laboratories such as those run by

Xerox and the Digital Equipment Corporation (DEC), the network architecture was much more elegant than the Internet Protocols, which had evolved in a narrower manner from research at Bolt, Beranek and Neumann (BBN, a US research company responsible for much of the early Internet development), centred around the problems of survivable routing. It is clear from the first that Universe had a clean design for names, and name-servers operated 5 years before the Internet Domain Name System (DNS); it had an addressing system that kept apart system identifiers and path identifiers; and it had a routing system which seamlessly allowed the community to scale from a single university to many.

Protocols

The protocols in the Universe project are of historic interest, since they include aspects of the Internet Datagram Protocol, but also of the Broadband ISDN communications approach of cell switching.

At the lowest level, at least on the site LANs, the mini-cell structure of a ring was a given. In its full generality, this was a major advantage when it comes to fine-grain resource allocation on the network, including experiments with mixed data and voice (20 years before Voice-over-IP!).

Above this structure, both locally and in the wide area, there were several choices. The Universe project was "agnostic" with regard to network state versus end-to-end state, and thus provided both.

For client-server applications employing Remote Procedure Call (RPC), there was the Single Shot Protocol (SSP, a bit like the Internet's User Datagram Protocol, UDP, commonly used for RPC, albeit with a response; perhaps more like Transaction-Transmission Control Protocol, T-TCP, whose author worked at a Universe partner site at this time). For long-lived flows, there was the Byte Stream Protocol (BSP), which was semantically similar enough to the Internet's Transmission Control Protocol (TCP) that transport-level relaying between them was implemented successfully.

Both SSP and BSP were capable of using state in the intermediate network: the ring-ring bridges that connected local area networks together (a misnomer, for surely they implemented routing functions) assisted in the setup of the return path.

To enable the Internet protocol to run over the Universe infrastructure, a *native* framing protocol known as the Universe Datagram was developed. This was really a concession to a less well designed protocol suite, but a pragmatic one, since native internet applications could then run over the Universe infrastructure, albeit without the advantages of resource management.

Resource management and policy

In Universe, the network was a distributed system no different than the processor farms, storage servers, name servers, boot servers and so on. Ring-ring bridges booted from the same place as file-servers. Thus it was natural to manage resources and policy for management in the same way as for any type of resource. Access to network routes, file permissions, process capabilities are all unified. When built in this way, why would one consider any of these components differently?

Similarly, when it came to looking at quantitative resources (network, storage, processor capacity) and associated policies, it was clear that there are no especial reasons to manage these in different ways.

Now and then—universal expectations

In the last two and a half decades, we have seen the components of computing and communications approximately double in performance every year in every dimension, be it processor speed (in line with Moore's Law), memory, stable storage or communications speed (and displays). The Internet was as important as the personal computer because it connected all the users, information storage and processing together. The Universe project pre-empted the performance in terms of numbers of users, services and devices by 15 years.

	1970s	1980s	1990s	21st Century
Processor	Kilo-instructions per second (KIPS)	MIPS	GIPS	TIPS
Storage	Kilobytes (Kbps)	MBytes	Gbytes	Tbytes
Networks	Kilobits per second (Kbps)	Mbps	Gbps	Tbps
Number of devices	Tens	Hundreds	Millions	Billions (US)

Table 1: Performance trends of every dimension

Other aspects of networking were presaged in more fundamental ways. At the physical layer, most local area networks in the world today use twisted pairs of wire, as did the Cambridge Ring.

The transmission substrate for most networks for the 1990s was Asynchronous Transfer Mode (ATM), a cell switched system whose units of transfer allowed for fine-grain control of delay, as did the Cambridge Ring[1]. This meant that voice and data integration on the same communications resource (and processing environment) was straightforward and natural. We have yet to regain this capability in the Internet of the 21st century!

Before the Universe Project (and for some time afterwards) a great many researchers treated wide-area-network systems (geographically distributed over multiple organisations) as if there was some important difference between them and local-area networks. This was especially true of the telecommunications and broadcast networks that evolved from the telephone system and analogue TV and radio. In contrast, at the time in a most revolutionary way, the Universe project had what we now call a "Control Plane," which was as much a part of the distributed system as the management of any other facility. This is now the standard approach to building signalling systems that control network resources.

What more can we rediscover?

The US Academy of Science published a report recently entitled "Looking over the fence at network research." There were two goals, one to see what computer scientists in other areas could learn from the successes of networking and distributed-systems research, and vice versa. It was clear that there was more of the former than the latter. The National Science Foundation recently published a report of a meeting to discuss network test beds, which reaffirmed most of the principles which were exemplary in the Universe project.

The EPSRC recently held an International Review of UK Computer Science, and this review regarded systems (implicitly operating systems, security networks and distributed systems) as notable.

To summarise, we could say that the lessons were these:

> *Be realistic, to get real results*: you learn more from the practice of theory than from the theory of practice.

> *Nothing scales an experiment like scale*: the bigger we test a better idea, the better we learn about how much better it is bigger.

> *Network control is a distributed application*: if the idea doesn't apply to itself, it ain't computer science.

---

1   Albeit a very small cell, known as a mini-packet, of only 16 bits!

10
Needham-Schroeder Goes to Court

Dorothy E. Denning

In 1978, Roger Needham of the University of Cambridge Computer Laboratory and Michael Schroeder of the Xerox Palo Alto Research Center published a seminal paper on protocols for remote key distribution. Their paper
was titled 'Using Encryption and Authentication in Large Networks of Computers' and appeared in the December issue of the Communications of the
ACM. It provoked considerable excitement in computing circles and was
widely read.

Needham and Schroeder addressed the problem of how entities in a computer network could establish a data-encrypting key (called a conversation
key in their paper) when they did not already share a secret key-encrypting
key. To solve the problem, Needham and Schroeder introduced a trusted Authentication Server (AS). Each entity has a private key-encrypting key that is
shared with the AS. The AS generates the conversation key and sends it to
one entity enciphered under its private key-encrypting key together with copies of the conversation key enciphered under the private keys of the other entities. The first entity can then forward the enciphered key to the other parties
with the encrypted message. Alternatively, it can provide the key in advance.
Needham and Schroeder showed how this could be done in the context of
both one-way (e.g. electronic mail) and two-way communications.

As a young assistant professor of computer science at Purdue University, I immediately recognized the significance of the paper and made it required reading
in my computer security class. One of my students, Giovanni Sacco, found a
security weakness in one of the methods described in the paper. This led to our
jointly writing a paper called "Timestamps in Key Distribution Protocols," which
showed how timestamps could be added to the Needham-Schroeder protocol to
enhance its security. This paper was submitted to the *Communications of the
ACM* in November 1979 and published in August 1981.

About the same time I also co-authored a paper with Fred Schneider of Cornell University that built on the Needham-Schroeder protocol. Titled "Personal
Keys, Group Keys, and Master Keys," and later "The Master Key Problem," the

paper showed how group keys could be generated and managed in order to allow for secure group communications in broadcast networks.

While the entire security community recognized the value of Needham-Schroeder to secure communications and, as the Internet evolved, to e-commerce and the future of the Internet itself, it was considered a scientific and technical matter. It was not something to discuss with colleagues and friends in other disciplines. They would be able to communicate securely without concern for exactly how it was done. Even though the public now appreciates the need for Internet security, few are interested in the details of cryptographic algorithms and protocols.

Imagine my surprise then when about two years ago, lawyers called me to talk about Needham-Schroeder and various other cryptographic protocols, including my own. Not only did they know about this highly technical work—they had delved into its inner workings.

It turned out that Needham-Schroeder would become a significant piece of prior art in a patent litigation case. The plaintiff in the case was arguing that patents of theirs dating back to the early 1980s had been infringed. I was contacted by the lawyers for the defense and eventually agreed to serve as an expert witness.

My initial reading of the claims in the patents was "How could they get a patent for this—it had all been done!" I would quickly learn that proving this was not a simple matter. After learning more about patent law than I ever thought I would need to know, I wrote a report explaining why I thought the patents were not valid in the first place. In particular, I showed that the patents' claims were disclosed in prior art (and hence not novel) or were obvious.

My report describes Needham-Schroeder and various other protocols for key establishment. The opening two paragraphs of this paper are quoted almost verbatim from that report.

The case went to trial, and I was impressed with the judge's understanding of the technology and issues. I looked forward to testifying, but the two parties agreed on a settlement just minutes before I was to be called to the witness stand.

In the end, I think the lawyers for the plaintiff realized the patents were on shaky ground. The prior art was just too compelling. Had the case gone to completion and the judge ruled the patents invalid, they would not have been in a good position for future litigation involving those patents. I doubt the plaintiff was pleased with the settlement, but rather viewed it as a better alternative to losing. We, on the other hand, went out and celebrated.

In 1978, Needham and Schroeder recognized the value of their work for network communications. Little did they know that one day their work would also help defeat a lawsuit.

11
The Design of Reliable Operating Systems

Peter Denning

Back in the summer of 1975, Dorothy Denning and I, then still newlyweds, spent a month at Cambridge. During that time Roger Needham and I met daily to discuss topics in the design of operating systems. We were searching for fundamental principles for reliable systems. I recorded many of my conclusions in my paper, "Fault tolerant operating systems," in ACM *Computing Surveys*, December 1976 [1]. Two topics of our discussions have stuck in my mind for all these years because the principles were sound and remain relevant to real systems. They are interrupts and capability addressing.

Interrupts

Roger and I were concerned about the considerable variation in the interpretations of the purpose and operation of interrupt systems, which had been a part of operating systems since the Atlas Project at University of Manchester in the late 1950s. We saw no clear consensus on their design principles. The Atlas team called them *interrupts* because they were used to interrupt normal processing to allow calls to operating system functions. Other operating systems called them *traps*—a metaphorical reference to a mousetrap springing in response to a preset condition. In describing the Burroughs and Multics operating systems, Elliot Organick called them *unexpected procedure calls*. In their seminal paper "Programming semantics for multiprocess computations" [2], Jack Dennis and Earl Van Horn (DVH) called them *exceptional conditions* and linked them to the protected entry of any routine providing a function for a class of objects. IBM referred to interrupts as *exceptions*. By 1975 several leading language designers believed that every procedure call, whether to the OS or not, should provide both a normal return and an exception return. The common features of these interpretations were that interrupts gave safe access to supervisory functions of the operating system, stopped programs that encountered error conditions, enabled the operating system to divert to high-priority functions, and relied on the procedure calling mechanism. Roger and I were specifically interested in a uniform interpretation of interrupt systems that accommodated these common features and gave clear guidance on how the interrupt hardware and software should be designed for reliability of the whole operating system.

In a nutshell, our conclusions were these:

- An interrupt system is at a low kernel level, just above the procedure mechanism.

- The interrupt vector, which points to the handler routines for each type of exception, should encode not only the handler entry points, but their proper supervisor state and interrupt mask settings. The procedure mechanism should, on call, replace the current supervisor state and masks with those encoded and, on return, restore them.

- Hardware condition detectors notify the interrupt dispatcher of faults and external device signals. The detectors for faults could generally be synchronized with the system clock, but the detectors for external conditions could not.

- Failure to realize that external-condition signals could occur simultaneously led to interrupt dispatchers prone to arbitration failures.

Now some explanations. The interrupt system itself consisted of detectors, a dispatcher, a mask, and a vector (list) of interrupt handler routines. The detectors were hardware devices that monitored for pre-set conditions and raised a signal when one occurred. The dispatcher, a combination of hardware and microcode, selected one of the unmasked, raised conditions and invoked a procedure call on the corresponding handler. The mask told which signals to respond to. The vector listed the interrupt-handler routines.

One of the open questions concerned the placement of the interrupt system in the functional hierarchy of the operating system. Following the principle of layering, which was gaining popularity since Edsger Dijkstra used it successfully in the THE system, we concluded that the interrupt system belonged in the kernel just above the procedure mechanism, which was itself just above the instruction set. The interrupt system had to be higher than the procedure mechanism since the dispatcher calls procedures. It had to be lower than everything else, since all other OS functions could define exceptional conditions.

Another open question was how to get the dispatcher to safely put the CPU into supervisor mode when it invoked an interrupt handler, and restore user mode upon return. Entry into the supervisor state had to be coupled tightly to interrupt dispatching lest a separate mechanism become a back door for intruders. We borrowed from the DVH capability idea to describe a clean way to do this. The entries in the interrupt vector would encode the entry point address, the target supervisor mode, and the target interrupt mask. Procedure call would load the instruction pointer, mode, and mask registers simultaneously from these data. Procedure return would restore the former values.

Still another open question was what kinds of conditions should be handled by the interrupt system. Real systems recognized two categories of conditions: faults and external signals. A fault condition meant that the running program could not continue until the detected error was corrected; examples were memory parity, arithmetic, addressing, protection, illegal instructions. An external signal meant that a peripheral device (such as disk) needed an OS action before a deadline; examples were disk completion, receipt of network packet, clock interruption. We did not see any good mechanism for separating these two kinds of conditions. Yet there was a crucial difference between them. Errors could be detected in the CPU between instruction cycles; therefore, the dispatcher always saw a stable set of error-condition signals. In contrast, external signals were unconstrained by the CPU clock; therefore, the dispatcher could witness simultaneously arriving device signals and suffer arbitration failures. Arbitration failures are a serious threat to reliability.

David Wheeler and other colleagues had documented arbitration failures that occur when the dispatch circuit is unable to select, within a clock cycle, exactly one of several simultaneously occurring incoming signals. Wheeler argued persuasively that, although the probability of an arbitration failure might appear small (e.g., 1 in 100,000), it is only a matter of a few days before enough interrupts have been processed that a failure is nearly certain. When the failure occurs, the CPU mysteriously hangs up, losing data and requiring a complete cold-restart. Wheeler designed a threshold flipflop (TFF) for the interrupt system that would pause the CPU clock until the TFF indicated it had reached a decision. This averted arbitration failure in exchange for an occasional delay of more than one clock cycle until the TFF correctly registered an interrupt.

Capability addressing

Roger and I also discussed capability addressing and the structure of capability-based operating systems. Invented by Dennis and Van Horn in 1966 [2], capabilities were long, protected, globally unique addresses for objects. Robert Fabry built a prototype capability machine two years later. Within a few more years the Plessey Company built the System 250, a telephone switching computer that used capability addressing; they reported ultra-high reliability, security, and resistance to software errors. In 1975, Roger and his colleagues were undertaking a project to build CAP, a general-purpose capability machine and operating system. Their own preliminary experiments had suggested that such a system would be extremely reliable because errors could not spread outside the local address space in which they occurred.

Roger was extremely worried about the complexity of the CAP operating system. It appeared that the requirement that capabilities be hardware protected from alteration could only be met by partitioning the memory of the machine into separate data and capability parts, which then precipitated a similar partition of the operating system and its data structures into separate data and capability parts. There was a significant problem of maintaining consistency between data and their corresponding capabilities. The complexity was further aggravated by the rigid interpretation of capabilities as "access tickets" for objects. File owners seemed to find it more natural to control access to their files with access control lists than to set up a daemon process to hand out capabilities on request to qualified users. Roger and I discussed possible ways to reduce the complexity to be competitive with other operating systems.

We concluded that the principle of hardware-protected capabilities was the source of much complexity. If we could relax that principle, we could preserve the good features of capability addressing without the cost of special memory or of partitioning. One way to do this would be to use type-checking in compilers to verify that capability arguments passed to system routines were in fact capabilities. The integrity of capabilities could be guaranteed if the set of OS programs that used capabilities (all layers up through the directory level) were all part of a trusted set assembled and verified by experienced programmers. This might not prevent a determined hacker from penetrating the kernel and modifying capabilities, but it would guarantee the proper use of capabilities for all normal users. Unfortunately, the CAP hardware was already committed to memory partitioning, and the OS design was too far along for this to be a realistic option. Besides, compiler technology had not evolved to the point where the required type-checking could be trusted.

We also developed a hybrid access-control method that would combine features of access control lists and access tickets. We observed that an access control list is permanent and persists as long as the file exists. In contrast, a capability list can be a temporary structure that survives only as long as the associated computational process. After a process is created, its capability list can be loaded (on demand) with capabilities dynamically constructed from the access lists attached to the files holding the objects addressed by the process. This hybrid generalized the standard virtual memory: the mapping tables contain capabilities constructed on the fly from access control lists attached to files. This hybrid was of great interest both to Roger and to Maurice Wilkes. But again, the CAP project was too far along to retrofit this.

In their 1979 follow-on book about the CAP operating system [3], Roger and Maurice lamented that they were unable to reduce the complexity of the system enough to make it competitive with more conventional operating systems. The main benefit, reliable and secure object addressing and sharing, had too large a cost.

Was that the end for these ideas? Was it futile to pursue operating systems with the reliability of capabilities and at conventional costs? Far from it. These ideas are the backbone of modern object-oriented programming systems. The compilers use "handles" to refer to objects—handles are software capabilities—and type checking to assure that handles are passed only to functions authorized to receive them. Objects can be dynamically loaded from external files, to which conventional access lists control access. Although these ideas did not make it in

CAP, Roger can nonetheless take pleasure in seeing the technology he helped to develop become a mainstay in computing.

References

1. P.J. DENNING, 'Fault tolerant operating systems,' *ACM Computing Surveys*, vol. 8 no. 4, 1976, pp. 359–390.
2. J.B. DENNIS AND E.C. VAN HORN, 'Programming semantics for multiprogrammed computations,' *Comm. ACM*, vol. 9 no. 3, 1966, pp. 143–155.
3. M.V. WILKES AND R.M. NEEDHAM, *The Cambridge CAP Computer and Its Operating System*, Elsevier North Holland, New York, 1979.

12
An Historical Connection between Time-Sharing and Virtual Circuits

Sandy Fraser

I left Ferranti for Cambridge University in 1966 after having spent six years inventing and then developing Nebula, a language and compiler for commercial data processing. At Cambridge, Maurice Wilkes was Professor and Head of the Mathematical Laboratory, home of EDSAC I and EDSAC II, and in 1966 home of the Atlas computer known as Titan. Sir Maurice, as he is today, had been inspired by CTSS [2] to create a time-sharing system for the Titan, and had assembled a team which included Roger Needham, David Hartley and Barry Landy. I was very grateful to these gentlemen for accepting into their midst a programmer and engineer without anything more than a BSc in Aeronautical Engineering.

The Titan, constructed in Cambridge under the leadership of David Wheeler, had recently become operational when I arrived. Peter Swinnerton-Dyer had astonished everyone by creating a usable operating system, seemingly overnight after a period of much thought and no contact with the machine. Peter's operating system allowed the Titan to provide a computing service for the University. That service quickly acquired customers, including physicists and chemists, some of whom at the time were engaged in the personality-testing task of performing long computations of great scientific importance on a machine that was not quite convinced that it wanted full-time employment. But Maurice wanted time-sharing and I was at once inducted into the team.

I do not recall anyone explaining to me that there was a management structure for the Titan operating-system project, other than Maurice's leadership of the laboratory. Roger, David and Barry had tables (substitutes for desks) clustered in one room, and I was assigned a table in an adjacent room. We all seemed to know what part of the operating-system we were responsible for. My task was to create a file system.

The basic architecture for the Titan operating system was already established. There was to be a small kernel responsible for resource management, process creation and scheduling, operation of peripherals, and administration of data transfers to and from disk. The Atlas under Tom Kilburn's guidance, it will be recalled, had pioneered virtual memory, and it was the operating system's task to manage it. Each process had its own address space, and the machine distinguished between user-mode (virtual addressing) and kernel-mode (absolute addressing). It had already been decided that the file system would be implemented as a trusted suite of user-level programs with a system call interface to the kernel. The File Master was the central component. It provided file directories, managed disk space, coordinated access to files and administered a permissions control system. Other programs in the suite were responsible for long-term file integrity, file backup and file archiving on magnetic tape.

Two aspects of the file system were perhaps notable. The permissions control system was unusually general. It allowed a user's authority to be computed on the basis of simple functional expressions stored as independent entries in a file directory. Whereas today a file directory might contain a file descriptor or a symbolic link to a file, in the Titan system a directory entry might be a 'privacy arrangement.' For example, there was one function type which, when decoded, meant: if the name of the program currently executing is 'x' then activity 'y' is authorized. The union of all such authorizations contained in a user's directory enabled file access or allowed the use of certain restricted system functions.

The other unusual feature concerned the file backup and archiving system. As is now common, an incremental backup system copied files to tape, and through a less frequent process all 'known' files were copied onto archive tapes. A known file was one that had a directory entry. If a user deleted the directory entry, the archive copy eventually disappeared from the archive. A file title included a 'class' identifier as the last component of its name. Three classes were defined: permanent (P), temporary (T) and archive (A). A file designated as class A would disappear from disk after two copies of the file had been made on archive tape. When the class was changed from A to P the file would automatically (with the invisible help of a computer operator) be restored to disk.

I will not elaborate further on the Titan file system. If interested, one can refer to Maurice Wilkes' book and other publications [1, 5, 6, 7]. By 1968 it was running well enough that the new operating system was launched into service. That itself was not an easy task when one considers that we were working with what amounted to being prototype hardware, including David Wheeler's tunnel diode cache memory, prototype software, which implemented 'time-sharing,' at the time a new concept for British computing, and a large user population that spanned the university and had a heavy workload for the machine. We scrambled, and Maurice held the critics at bay.

My future in research was much influenced by the fact that the file system was a separate program, that data transfers were separated completely from the administration of files, and the fact that it was so much of a struggle to construct and maintain such a 'mammoth machine' as the Atlas. Would it not be possible to assemble an interconnected collection of smaller machines along with a separate machine for storing files, and operate on the whole a time-sharing service for a large user community? I made some informal measurements of traffic volumes and transfer rates to convince myself that this was a plausible and interesting idea if a suitable interconnection method could be devised.

At some point in 1967–68 Roger and I were invited to participate in the very British sport of educating and berating the government in the princely surroundings of a London club. Those who would now be considered to be the Chief Information Officers of some of England's largest corporations paid for the meals and on each occasion invited to dinner a senior politician or civil servant. The goal was to persuade the Post Office, which at that time was the government arm that operated the telephone system, to take time-sharing seriously and to provide a data communication service for its customers. In this era, data communications meant allowing modems on the phone network. While I cannot say how successful the Real Time Club was, for that became its name, I can say that these discussions of using the telephone network for data communication had a big impact on me. It was the possibility that there might one day be a national communications service devoted to computer communications that attracted my attention and curiosity.

In May 1969 I moved to the United States. My interest in computing and file systems was now expanding rapidly to include communications. Surely, computing and communications would become one, and computers would become as widespread as telephones. Where better to go for an education in communications than Bell Laboratories. However, when I arrived there I was surprised and disappointed to find that Bell Labs, the research laboratory for world-wide communications, at the time had no data network and only the smallest program of research on the topic. Andy Hall, my host during those early days in America, encouraged my interest in computer communications, and we talked of a network that would link together the many mini-computers that were then to be found at Bell Labs. Clearly, my ambition to build a network-based file system would have to wait while I figured out how to network those mini-computers.

Henry McDonald became my mentor for a rapid education in the logic and science of the telephone system. At this time there were three ongoing research interests that Bell Labs had in data networking. Ed Newhall and Wayne Farmer were working on what would soon be demonstrated as a token ring. Wes Chu (at the time just departed from Bell Labs) had spawned an interest in stochastic models for statistically multiplexed traffic between asynchronous terminals and a time-sharing system. Dave Weller and Carl Christianson were working on a ring bus to connect peripherals with their mini-computer. I was excited by the vision of a world-wide network that could carry telephony and data, and eventually video. One need spend but a moment in Bell Laboratories to acquire a sense of grandeur and possibilities. The telephone network was going digital, Bell Labs had tested a video telephone on its network, digital switching was in the throes of being born, microprocessors were on the horizon, and in this one research laboratory there was all the expertise that it would take to create a single network that could bring an integrated communications service for voice, video and data to every home and business throughout the land.

By the Fall of 1969 I had learned enough of digital switching and wide area networking to conceive of a switching machine and network access arrangement that might eventually scale to large proportions with the performance and quality of service which was husbanded so dearly by the operators of the Bell System [3, 4]. Thus, there were born that year notions of virtual circuit switching, asynchronous time-division multiplexing of cells, window flow control, and the slotted ring. A network, called Spider, was in due course constructed with connections to twelve computers, including one that served as a print server and another as a file server. For the latter, which was based on Unix, we re-implemented the Titan method of incrementally dumping files on magnetic tape. The original goal had been to logically recreate the Titan file system, not as part of some new large machine but as the networked hub of many small machines. To a limited degree that goal had been reached. It was successful because some of the mini-computers had weak operating systems and very limited storage. However, several years would pass before network performance would be sufficient that distributed computing with shared file storage would be seen as a competitive option.

I would like to conclude by thanking Roger and Maurice for their part in shaping my career. By giving me the opportunity to be part of the Titan team, to benefit from the rich environment that is Cambridge, and to join in the discussions of The Real Time Club, they started my career down an ever widening path that, over the years, has brought great pleasure and professional satisfaction.

References

1. BARRON, D.W., ET AL., 'File handling at Cambridge University,' *AFIPS Conf. Proc.*, vol. 30 (SJCC 1967), pp. 163–167.
2. CORBATO, F.J., ET AL., The Compatible Time-Sharing System: A Programmer's Guide, MIT Press, Cambridge, Mass., 1963.
3. FRASER, A.G., 'Early experiments with asynchronous time division networks,' *IEEE Network Magazine*, January 1993, pp. 12–26.
4. FRASER, A.G., 'The Origins of ATM,' video tape, University Video Communications, Stanford, California, January, 1994.
5. FRASER, A.G., 'File integrity in a disc-based multi-access system,' in *Operating Systems Techniques*, C.A.R. Hoare and R.H. Perrott, eds., Academic Press, New York, 1972, pp. 227–248. Also in *Classic Operating Systems*, P.B. Hansen, ed., Springer, New York, 2001, pp. 167–194.
6. HARTLEY, D.F., 'The Cambridge multiple-access system user's reference manual,' Cambridge University Mathematical Laboratory, 1968.
7. WILKES, M.V., *Time-Sharing Computer Systems*, Macdonald, London, 1968.

13
On Cross-Platform Security

Li Gong

Why cross-platform security?

Today in any IT system installation of a non-negligible size, heterogeneity is a given. From hardware platforms, to operating systems, to networking protocols, to applications, one is bound to discover a variety of technologies for every layer of the system stack. Heterogeneity has its advantages: it fosters innovation, competition, and even has the potential to improve security and reliability in that one may hope that the same error or security hole does not exist in all of the different designs.

Heterogeneity also brings a number of problems for implementing security requirements. For example, system administrators with different knowledge and skills are needed to manage different systems. In addition, these different systems may offer vastly different sets of security properties so that interoperability becomes difficult if not impractical.

The most important problem, though, is how to provide security support for application developers. In other words, when developing an application that must run on a number of different platforms (think about web services, for example), how does the developer ensure that the required security properties can be correctly implemented and deployed across the different platforms.

The primitive way to deal with heterogeneity is to find out the collection of the target deployment platforms a priori and design a solution that works on this set of platforms. However, a solution obtained this way does not apply to a new environment. It also needs to change, usually with great difficulty, when a new target platform is added into the mix. What is desirable is a systematic approach to cross-platform security.

Approaches to cross-platform security

The obvious idea towards cross-platform security is to find common ground among the diverse systems that is sufficiently broad to implement needed security requirements. Let us consider, bottom up, a number of common grounds from the system stack.

The one thing that is common to all systems, especially in today's world of the Internet, is a set of communication protocols such as TCP/IP. These protocols, however, are too low-level to represent basic system and security concepts such as files and file security. Moreover, some devices may be equipped with 802.11 or Bluetooth, but not TCP/IP.

Next up, all systems have operating systems. The difficulty here is that there are multiple systems that are widely used (Unix and Microsoft Windows, for example), which all have unique characteristics. Moreover, just Unix alone has a number of different flavors, notably Solaris from Sun Microsystems and HP/UX. Even Windows has incompatibilities among its own versions, Win95, Win98, NT, and XP. What's worse, more operating systems are popping up and gaining widespread use, such as Linux and embedded Linux, Palm OS for PDAs, and systems for mobile phones and other emerging devices. In other words, there is not a lot of common ground to find at the OS level.

The most promising area for interoperability seems to be programming languages and APIs. After all, implementing a language on different platforms is not too difficult a task. Traditionally, we have had BASIC, Fortran, COBOL, and the more popular, C and C++. However, none of these languages offers a security model. Java is perhaps the first widely deployed programming language that has cross-platform operation and security declared as its two primary design goals. What also helps Java tremendously is the associated set of APIs that can be used to implement just about any application, independent of the underlying operating systems. If everyone adopted Java, cross-platform security would have been a problem largely solved. For a while, this was indeed the dream of many practitioners. Eventually, the harsh reality of commercial competition dictates that the dream remains a dream. Support for Java on MS Windows—the platform with the largest number of seats—cannot be guaranteed or expected. The same fate awaits C#, the Microsoft competitor to Java, which is unlikely to become standard on all major platforms.

Failing all the above, many folks are pushing so-called web services as the conceptual layer for interoperability, where technologies like HTML and its variants are the basis for interoperation. This approach is still evolving, so it is too early to write its obituary. But the early-warning signs are already here: ASCII-based exchanges have severe limitations. To be powerfully expressive, flexible, and extendable, exchanging text messages alone is not enough. One must either exchange commands to be executed by the end systems (here we must not replicate the shortcomings of CORBA) or communicate programs that can run directly on the end systems, both of which lead us back to the problems we started with.

What now?

Recently, a new interoperability approach has emerged as an open source community effort, JXTA, at jxta.org. JXTA attempts to describe entire systems completely within a set of protocols. The basic elements are peers and messages. Through discovery, peers can form groups, communicate with each other, share contents, and so on. Everything stored or communicated is in the form of a message. JXTA is designed to be independent of networking protocols, operating systems, and programming languages. In other words, it is truly cross-platform.

In this environment, we can think of peers and messages as subjects and objects in the traditional security model. Messages can have types, such as advertisements, which can then be subdivided into advertisements for peers or for content. Content can be code or data; they are no different in JXTA and are all of the type "CODAT." Messages can be encrypted for secrecy and/or integrity. Typical authentication and authorization systems can be used. Access control policies can be embedded or encoded into the messages. Cryptographic techniques can be deployed to enforce access controls.

Although promising, JXTA is still very new. Its security design is not yet complete. (Solving the cross-platform security problem is not what JXTA was started for.) It is too early to predict whether this approach will work out at the end. Even if it works, it be non-threatening enough so that it can be adopted on all major platforms? Will commercial competition stand in the way yet again?

References

1. GONG, L., *Inside Java 2 Platform Security*, Addison-Wesley, Reading, Massachusetts, 1999.
2. LAUER, H.C., NEEDHAM, R.M., 'On the Duality of Operating System Structures,' *Operating Systems Review*, vol. 13, no. 2, 1979, pp. 3–19.
3. OAKS, S., TRAVERSAT, B., AND GONG, L., *JXTA in a Nutshell*, O'Reilly & Associates, Sebastopol, California, 2002.

14
Distributed Computing Economics

Jim Gray

Computing economics are changing. Today there is rough price parity between 1 database access, 10 bytes of network traffic, 100,000 instructions, 10 bytes of disk storage, and a megabyte of disk bandwidth. This has implications for how one structures Internet-scale distributed computing: one puts computing as close to the data as possible in order to avoid expensive network traffic.

The cost of computing

Computing is free. The world's most powerful computer is free (SETI@Home is a 54 teraflops machine).[1] Google freely provides a trillion searches per year to the world's largest online database (2 petabytes). Hotmail freely carries a trillion email messages per year. Amazon.com offers a free book search tool. Many sites offer free news and other free content. Movies, sports events, concerts, and entertainment are freely available via television.

Actually, it's not free, but most computing is now so inexpensive that advertising can pay for it. The content is not really free; it is paid for by advertising. Advertisers routinely pay more than a dollar per thousand impressions (CPM). If Google or Hotmail can collect a dollar per CPM, the resulting billion dollars per year will more than pay for their development and operating expenses. If they

---

1 This paper makes broad statements about the economics of computing. The numbers are fluid—costs change every day. They are approximate to within a factor of 3. For this specific fact: SETI@Home averaged 54 teraflops (floating point operations per second) on 26th January 2003, handily beating the sum of the combined peak performance of the top four of the TOP500 supercomputers registered at http://www.top500.org/ on that day.

can deliver a search or a mail message for a few micro-dollars, the advertising pays them a few milli-dollars for the incidental "eyeballs." So these services are not free—advertising pays for them.

Computing costs hundreds of billions of dollars per year. IBM, HP, Dell, Unisys, NEC, and Sun each sell billions of dollars of computers each year. Software companies like Microsoft, IBM, Oracle, and Computer Associates sell billions of dollars of software per year. *So, computing is obviously not free.*

Total cost of ownership (TCO) is more than a trillion dollars per year. Operations costs far exceed capital costs. Hardware and software are minor parts of the total cost of ownership. Hardware comprises less than half the total cost; some claim less than 10% of the cost of a computing service. So the real cost of computing is measured in trillions of dollars per year.

Megaservices like Yahoo!, Google, and Hotmail have relatively low operations-staff costs. These megaservices have discovered ways to deliver content for less that the milli-dollar that advertising will fund. For example, in 2002 Google had an operations staff of 25 who managed its two petabyte (2^{15} bytes) database and 10,000 servers spread across several sites. Hotmail and Yahoo! cite similar numbers—small staffs manage ~300 terabytes of storage and more than 10,000 servers.

Most applications do not benefit from megaservice economies of scale. Other companies report that they need an administrator per terabyte, an administrator per 100 servers, and an administrator per gigabit of network bandwidth. That would imply an operations staff of more than 2,000 people to operate Google—nearly ten times the size of the company.

Outsourcing is seen as a way for smaller services to benefit from megaservice efficiencies. The outsourcing business evolved from service bureaus through timesharing and is now having a renaissance. The premise is that an outsourcing megaservice can offer routine services much more efficiently than an in-house service. Today, companies routinely outsource applications like payroll, insurance, web presence, and email.

Outsourcing has often proved to be a shell game—moving costs from one place to another. Loud Cloud and Exodus trumpeted the benefits of outsourcing. Now Exodus is bankrupt and Loud Cloud is gone. Neither company had a significant competitive advantage over in-house operations. Outsourcing works when it is a service business where computing is central to operating an application and supporting the customer—a high-tech low-touch business. It is difficult to achieve economies-of-scale unless the application is nearly identical across most companies—like payroll or email. Some companies, notably IBM, Salesforce.com, Oracle.com, and others, are touting outsourcing, labeled *On Demand Comput-*

ing, as an innovative way to reduce costs. There are some successes, but many more failures. So far there are few outsourced megaservices—payroll and email are the exception rather than the rule.

SETI@Home sidesteps operational costs and is not funded by advertising. SETI@Home is a novel kind of outsourcing. It harvests some of the free (unused) computing available in the world. SETI@Home "pays" for computing by providing a screen saver, by appealing to people's interest in finding extraterrestrial intelligence, and by creating competition among teams that want to demonstrate the performance of their systems. This currency bought 1.3 *million* years of computing; it bought 1.3 thousand years of computing on 3 February 2003. Indeed, some SETI@Home results have been auctioned at eBay. Others are emulating this model for their compute-centric applications (e.g., Protein@Home and ZetaGrid.net).

Grid computing hopes to harvest and share Internet resources. Most computers are idle most of the time, disks are ½ full on average, and most network links are under utilized. Like the SETI@Home model, Grid computing seeks to harness and share these idle resources by providing an infrastructure that allows idle resources to participate in Internet-scale computations [4].

Web services

Microsoft and IBM tout web services as a new computing mode—Internet-scale distributed computing. They observe that the HTTP Internet is designed for people interacting with computers. Traffic on the future Internet will be dominated by computer-to-computer interactions. Building Internet-scale distributed computations requires many things, but at its core it requires a common object model augmented with a naming and security model. Other services can be layered atop these core services. Web services are the evolution of the RPC, DCE, DCOM, CORBA, RMI, standards of the 1990's. The main innovation is an XML base that facilitates interoperability among implementations.

Neither grid computing nor web services have an outsourcing or advertising business model. Both are plumbing that enable companies to build applications. Both are designed for computer-to-computer interactions and so have no advertising model—because there are no eyeballs involved in the interactions. It is up the companies to invent business models that can leverage the Web services plumbing.

Web services reduce the costs of publishing and receiving information. Today, many services offer information as HTML pages on the Internet. This is convenient for people, but programs must resort to screen-scraping to extract the information from the display. If an application wants to send information to another application, it is very convenient to have an information structuring model, an object model, that allows the sender to point to an object (an array, a structure, or a more complex class) and simply send it. The object then "appears" in the address space of the destination application. All the gunk of packaging (serializing) the object, transporting it, and then unpacking it is hidden from sender and receiver. Web services provide this *send-an-object/get-an-object* model. These tools dramatically reduce the programming and management costs of publishing and receiving information.

So web services are an enabling technology to reduce data interchange costs. Electronic Data Interchange (EDI) services have been built from the very primitive base of ASM.1. With XML and web services, EDI message formats and protocols can be defined in much more concise languages like XML, C#, or Java. Once defined, these interfaces are automatically implemented on all platforms. This dramatically reduces transaction costs. Service providers like Google, Inktomi, Yahoo!, and Hotmail can provide a web service interface that others can integrate or aggregate into a personalized digital dashboard and earn revenue from this very convenient and inexpensive service. Many organizations want to publish their information. The World Wide Telescope is one example,[2] but the example is repeated in biology, the social sciences, and the arts. Web services and intelligent user tools are a big advance over publishing a file with no schema (e.g., using FTP).

Application economics

Grid computing and computing on demand enable applications that are mobile and that can be provisioned on demand. What tasks are mobile and can be dynamically provisioned? Any purely computation task is mobile if it is written in a portable language and uses only portable interfaces—*write once run anywhere* (WORA). Cobol and Java promise WORA. Cobol and Java users can attest that WORA is difficult to achieve, but for the purposes of this discussion, let's assume that this problem is solved. Then, the question is,

What are the economic issues of moving a task from one computer to another or from one place to another?

A computation task has four characteristic demands:
- *Networking*—delivering questions and answers
- *Computation*—transforming information to produce new information

---

2   See http://SkyQuery.net/ and http://TerrraService.net/. These two websites each act as a portal to several SOAP web services.

- *Database access*—access to reference information needed by the computation
- *Database storage*—long term storage of information (needed for later access)

The ratios among these quantities and their relative costs are pivotal. It is fine to send a gigabyte over the network if it saves years of computation—but it is not economic to send a kilobyte question if the answer could be computed locally in a second.

To make the economics tangible, take the following baseline hardware parameters:[3]

2	GHz cpu with 2GB ram (cabinet and networking)	$2,000
200	GB disk with 100 accesses/second and 50 MB/s transfer	$200
1	Gbps Ethernet port-pair	$200
1	Mbps WAN link	$100/month

From this we conclude that one dollar equates as follows:

1	$
1	GB sent over the WAN
10	Tops (tera cpu operations)
8	hours of cpu time
1	GB disk space
10	M database accesses
10	TB of disk bandwidth
10	TB of LAN bandwidth

The ideal mobile task is stateless (no database or database access), has a tiny network input and output, and has huge computational demand. For example, a cryptographic search problem: given the encrypted text, the clear text, and a key search range. This kind of problem has a few kilobytes input and output, is stateless, and can compute for days. Computing zeros of the zeta function is a good example.[3] Monte Carlo simulation for portfolio risk analysis is another good example. And, of course, SETI@Home is a good example: it computes for 12 hours on half a megabyte of input.

Using the parameters above, SETI@Home performed a multi-billion dollar computation for a million dollars—a very good deal! SETI@Home harvested more than a million cpu years worth more than a billion dollars. It sent out a billion jobs of ½ MB each. This petabyte of network bandwidth cost about a mil-

---

3   The hardware prices are typical of web prices, the WAN price is typical of rates paid by large (many Gbps/month) Internet service providers. Hardware is depreciated over 3 years.

lion dollars. The SETI@Home peers donated a billion dollars of "free" cpu time and also donated 10^{12} watt-hours, which is about 100 million dollars of electricity. The key property of SETI@Home is that the compute-cost:network-cost ratio is 10,000:1. It is very cpu-intensive.

Most web and data processing applications are network or state intensive and are not economically viable as mobile applications. An FTP server, an HTML web server, a mail server, and an online transaction processing (OLTP) server represent a spectrum of services with increasing database state and data access. A 100 MB FTP task costs 10 cents, and is 99% network cost. An HTML web access costs 10 microdollars and is 88% network cost. A Hotmail transaction costs 10 microdollars and is more cpu intensive so that networking and cpu are approximately balanced. None of these applications fits the cpu-intensive stateless requirement.

Data loading and data scanning are cpu-intensive, but they are also data intensive, and therefore not economically viable as mobile applications. Some applications related to database systems are quite cpu intensive: for example, data loading takes about 1,000 instructions per byte. The "vision" component of the Sloan Digital Sky Survey that detects stars and galaxies and builds the astronomy catalogs from the pixels is about 10,000 instructions per byte. So they are break-even candidates: 10,000 instructions per byte is the break-even point according to the economic model above (10 Tops of computing and 1 GB of networking both cost a dollar). It seems the computation should be at least 30,000 instructions per byte (a 3:1 cost benefit ratio) before the outsourcing model becomes really attractive.

The break-even point is 10,000 instructions per byte of network traffic or about a minute of computation per MB of network traffic. Few computations exceed that threshold; most are better matched to a Beowulf cluster. Computational fluid dynamics (CFD) is very cpu intensive, but again, CFD generates a continuous and voluminous output stream. To give an example of an adaptive mesh simulation, the Cornell Theory Center has a Beowulf-class MPI job that simulates crack propagation in a mechanical object [5]. It has about 100 MB of input, 10GB of output, and runs for more than 7 cpu-years. The computation operates at over one million instructions per byte, and so is a good candidate for export to the WAN computational grid. But the computation's bisection bandwidth requires that it be executed in a tightly connected cluster. These applications require inexpensive bandwidth available to a Beowulf cluster [7]. In a Beowulf cluster networking is ten thousand times less expensive than WAN networking—which makes it seem nearly free by comparison.

Still, there are some computationally intensive jobs that can use Grid computing. Render-farms for making animated movies seem to be a good candidate for Grid computing. Rendering a frame can take many cpu hours, so a Grid-scale render farm begins to make sense. For example, Pixar's *Toy Story 2* images are very cpu intensive—a 200 MB image can take several cpu hours to render. The instruction density was 200 k to 600 k instructions per byte [2]. This could be structured as a grid computation—sending a 50 MB task to a server that computes for ten hours and returns a 200 MB image.

BLAST, FASTA, and Smith-Waterman are an interesting case in point—they are mobile in the rare case of a 40 cpu-day computation. These computations match a DNA sequence against a database like GenBank or SwissProt. The databases are about 50 GB today. The algorithms are quite cpu intensive, but they scan large parts of the database. Servers typically store the database in RAM. BLAST is a heuristic that is ten times faster than Smith-Waterman, which gives exact results [1, 6]. Most BLAST computations can run in a few minutes of cpu time, but there are computations that can take a cpu month on BLAST and a cpu year on Smith Waterman. So it would be economical to send SwisProt (40GB) to a server if it were to perform a 7,720 hour computation for free. Typically, it does not make sense to provision a SwissProt database on demand; rather, it makes sense to set up dedicated servers (much like Google) that use inexpensive processors and memory to provide such searches. A commodity 40 GB SMP server would cost less than 20,000 dollars and could deliver a complex one cpu-hour search for less than a dollar—the typical one minute search would be a few millidollars.

Conclusions

Put the computation near the data. The recurrent theme of this analysis is that "on demand" computing is only economical for very cpu-intensive applications (100,000 instructions per byte or a cpu-day per gigabyte of network traffic). Preprovisioned computing is likely to be more economical for most applications—especially data-intensive ones.

How do you combine data from multiple sites? Many applications need to integrate data from multiple sites into a combined answer. The arguments above suggest that one should push as much of the processing to the data sources as possible in order to filter the data early (database query optimizers call this "pushing predicates down the query tree"). There are many techniques for doing this, but fundamentally it dovetails with the notion that each data source is a web service with a high-level object-oriented interface.

Caveats

Beowulf clusters have completely different networking economics. Render farms, materials simulation, and CFD fit beautifully on Beowulf clusters because there the cost of networking is very inexpensive: a GBps Ethernet fabric costs about $200/port and delivers 50 MBps, so Beowulf networking costs are comparable to disk bandwidth costs—10,000 times less than the price of Internet transports. That is why rendering farms and BLAST search engines are routinely built using Beowulf clusters. Beowulf clusters should not be confused with Internet-scale Grid computations.

If telecom prices drop faster than Moore's law, the analysis fails. If telecom prices drop slower than Moore's law, the analysis becomes stronger. Most of the argument in this paper pivots on the relatively high price of telecommunications. Over the last 40 years telecom prices have fallen much more slowly than any other information technology. If this situation changed, it could completely alter the arguments here. But there is no obvious sign of that occurring.

Acknowledgements

Many people have helped me gather this information and present the results. Gordon Bell, Charlie Catmull, Pat Hanrahan, Gerd Heber, George Spix, Alex Szalay, and Dan Worthheimer helped me characterize various computations. Ian Foster and Andrew Herbert helped me present the argument more clearly. This paper has also appeared on the IEEE Task Force on Cluster Computing web site and the Genesis Forum strategy web site, see:

>   http://www.clustercomputing.org/content/tfcc-5-1-gray.html
>   http://www.xsp-strategy.com/modules.php?op=modload&name=News
>   &file=article&sid=318&mode=thread&order=0&thold=0

References

1. ALTSCHUL, S., GISH, W., MILLER, W., MYERS E., LIPMAN, D., 'Basic local alignment search tool.' *J. Molecular Biology*, vol. 215, 1990, pp. 403–410.
    See http://www.ncbi.nlm.nih.gov/BLAST/ and also http://www.sun.com/products-n-olutions/edu/commofinterest/compbio/pdf/parcel_blast.pdf for a large BLAST task.
2. CATMULL, E., Pixar, Private communication, 2 April 2003.
3. FERREIRA, L. ET. AL., Introduction to Grid computing with Globus, IBM Redbook series, 2002, available at:
    http://ibm.com/redbooks.
4. FOSTER, I., AND KESSELMAN, C. (EDS.), The Grid: blueprint for a new computing infrastructure. Morgan Kaufmann, San Francisco, 1999, ISBN 1558604758.

5. HEBER, G., Cornel Theory Center, Private communication, 12 January 2003.
6. SMITH, T.F., WATERMAN, M.S., 'Identification of common molecular subsequences,' *J. Molecular Biology*, vol. 147, 1981, pp. 195–197.
7. STERLING, T., SALMON, J., BECKER, D., AND SAVARESE, D., *How to build a Beowulf: a guide to the implementation and application of PC clusters*, MIT Press, Cambridge, 1998

15
The Titan Influence

David Hartley

The Titan project was the major focus of research and development in the Cambridge Mathematical Laboratory for most of the 1960s. The objective, as with the EDSAC 1 and EDSAC 2 before, was to pioneer a computer system (hardware and software) exploiting the latest technology to produce a next-generation system to meet and stimulate the computational needs of the University of Cambridge.

To say that Titan was the last such major development in the laboratory might appear to deny many substantial and successful system development projects since then, but it certainly was from my perspective as one who worked in the project and, in 1970, became responsible for the computing service.

Tradition and objectives

Having built two pioneering systems by the end of the 1950s, the laboratory could claim to have established a tradition. If these first two systems were ground breaking and pushed forward the state of the art, then any third system was bound to follow the same ambitions. Further, the first two systems were in regular use by a growing community of scientists and others breaking new ground in their research, and we had created a demand for more.

The main objectives were efficiency, utility, and advancement. Efficiency to get as much as possible out of very limited hardware; optimization was very much the name of the game. Utility came in two senses: the system had to be simple to use for simple tasks, and at the same time provide a comprehensive range of facilities. Advancement, because there was clearly much scope for pushing forward the state of the art.

Not entirely home-made

The basic central-processor design of Titan was not something we developed ourselves. Manchester University, in collaboration with Ferranti, were developing the Atlas, and on the face of it the Laboratory might have settled for one of those. But Atlas was far too expensive, and it was decided that Cambridge would develop with Ferranti a much-reduced version. Indeed, Titan became the prototype of the Ferranti Atlas 2, although its commercial success was no more than its big brother's. Including the prototypes, only three machines of each type were ever built.

Apart from the basic central processing unit, Titan was so different from Atlas that a new operating system had to be developed. Atlas had a one-level store, with hardware paging and a high-speed drum, while Titan originally had a simple relocation register, a limited amount of main memory, and a magnetic tape backing store. We did, however, adopt the same design philosophy, and learnt much from studying the work of our Manchester colleagues.

Operating systems for all seasons

Titan being the prototype Atlas 2, the operating-system project from the outset was a collaboration with Ferranti (later ICT and eventually ICL). We began with common motives, namely to develop a multiprogramming system, optimising mainframe processor use while enabling a mix of jobs of various sizes, shapes and priorities to make their way smoothly through the system.

With a Cambridge team of about five and at least twice that number in Ferranti, we laid the foundations for the operating system. A notable achievement was the design, mainly by the leader of the Ferranti team, Chris Spooner, of a highly sophisticated input/output buffer using a dynamically variable number of magnetic tape drives. Several of us found it difficult to believe it would work, but eventually work it did, although not on Titan itself.

Our aims and objectives began to diverge when Cambridge tradition and objectives began to clash with the conservatism of marketing executives. Ferranti found difficulty selling the concepts of multiprogramming to potential customers, who could see little value in an operating system unless it exhibited the features of the Fortran Monitor System, popular in those days on IBM mainframes. When we set our sights on time-sharing, this was too much for the collaboration to continue. So before any version of the operating system had been completed, Cambridge and Ferranti agreed to go their separate ways, each in the end developing different, but very successful, systems built on the same hardware and software technologies.

Maurice Wilkes discovered CTSS on a visit to MIT in about 1965, and returned to Cambridge to convince the rest of us that time-sharing was the way forward. This didn't take much doing, although to add terminals and interactive working to a partly completed job system was something of a challenge. It was essential to maintain our tradition and policies of an efficient and useable system.

Inevitably, we had a desire *to do better*, but more important was the need *to do differently*. David Wheeler came to our help by adding a second memory relocation register so we could, for example, place a program in one part of memory and its working data in a different part. This rather rudimentary kind of segmentation enabled us to create a workable system for on-line interactive working. The alternative of an investment in high-speed secondary storage for memory swapping was quite out of the question.

A generous gift from Ferranti did, however, produce a disc unit to hold a file store. The filing system was designed chiefly by Sandy Fraser, and in due time developed by Mike Guy into a highly practical system embodying sophisticated access controls, and comprehensive back-up and archive facilities.

One innovation, which to us was an obvious requirement, was compatibility between off-line jobs and terminal access. Whether you used Titan by submitting a background job or by running a program at a terminal, the commands to edit and manipulate files, to compile programs, and to handle input and output called the same system modules and were therefore the same commands. This was in contrast with other developments of the time, where system designers saw time-sharing as fundamentally different from previous ways of using computers. This approach was followed when the Computing Service later developed Phoenix on IBM's 370 mainframe operating system, with considerable success.

Programming language excursions

One of the less well known, and indeed less successful, elements of the Titan project was CPL. The world discovered high-level programming languages with the advent of Algol in the early 1960s, when computers had become sufficiently powerful for the languages not to have to exhibit quirky features of the underlying hardware. In spite of this, it still seemed natural to want a new language to go with our new computer. Collaborating with University of London colleagues, we set out to develop a language that would be complete and sufficient for all applications.

CPL made many strides forward in establishing new and regular language concepts. But the objectives were too ambitious, and the approach too theoretical, so we were forced to put aside the pragmatic requirement of a complete and implementable system. A user circular, rashly produced in the early days, declared that CPL would be the language for all applications on Titan, and no other language, not even assembly language, would either be needed or available. This came home to roost a few years later, when a research student was hastily commissioned to write a Fortran compiler.

In the context of Titan, CPL failed to follow the tradition of efficiency and utility. But it did have its influences. Martin Richards developed a simpler version, known as BCPL, designed for writing systems programs, which was implemented in a readily portable manner and lived long beyond not only Titan but also Cambridge. BCPL was to influence Bell Laboratories to develop their own language, first as B and later as C.

A quart from a pint pot

Providing facilities to satisfy the needs of upwards of 1,000 academic users was a challenge that called for some ingenious techniques of resource allocation and control, and also a little marketing. To provide a fully interactive system in which all users could interact on-line with any and every program, be it a text editor, a compiler or their own application, was out of the question because of the lack of any kind of one-level store.

Instead, we found the following pragmatic and efficient solution. Certain tightly written programs, such as the text editor, were permitted to operate interactively, communicating directly with the user's terminal. All other programs, be they compilers or users' applications, could be called at the terminal, but were permitted to communicate only with the file store. Once such a program had completed execution, its output file would then be automatically printed at the terminal.

The effect to the user was a form of command level interaction that largely satisfied their needs. At the same time, by restricting interaction in this way, memory swapping to disc was avoided, and Titan supported far more simultaneous users than otherwise.

Other techniques for sharing the severely limited resources of the system were developed. File space was at a premium; the amount available for the average user was tiny when compared with a modern PC. We had to find a way of ensuring that only the most immediately required files were kept on disc, with the remainder archived on magnetic tape.

It was wisely decided *not* to develop an intelligent system to purge files automatically to tape, our pragmatic approach telling us that, given the right incentives, the human user had the best intelligence to do this. Incentive came from an accounting system that not only limited total disc use, but also controlled average use over time, so that minimising disc space accumulated credit to use more later. It worked like a treat.

We had discovered the principle that a wasting asset is best regulated by controlling the rate of its use, rather than just its maximum use. It worked well and the technique was re-used on the later Phoenix system, not just for file storage, but for controlling computer time as well.

Avoiding new releases

Titan was, for most of its existence, a unique one-off system. Apart from the Atlas 2 installed at the CAD Centre, other Atlas computers had substantially different operating systems. This virtual singularity provided the opportunity to solve one of the major software engineering problems of large complex systems, namely the control of repairs and enhancements.

We had discovered the problem associated with the management of new software releases, where bug fixes, patches, and new features are first introduced into a development version and saved until sufficient to endure the trauma of inflicting a new release on users. It is well known that new software releases can introduce more problems than they resolve. Barry Landy developed tools to install changes, whether repairs or new features, on an incremental and almost daily basis. Changes could be made almost on the fly and, just as important, removed if and when they caused problems, all with minimal disruption to the operational service.

Of course, the problem is more difficult when there are many instances of the system out in the field, but the advent of the Internet has at last enabled some suppliers to provide incremental upgrades and fewer major new releases.

A secure and trusted environment

Given incremental development, we adopted a policy that any bug, security exposure, or other loophole was fixed immediately after it was discovered. In consequence, the Titan system became highly secure, and was relatively impervious to user errors, whether accidental or otherwise. Obviously there was no guarantee of complete security, but if systems today were as secure as Titan, the hacking menace of the Internet would be vastly diminished.

Those who served

Almost everyone in the Laboratory in the 1960s, from Maurice Wilkes downwards, was involved in the Titan project, and for some of us it consumed our formative years.

Bill Elliott joined the Laboratory to act as project leader and to bring the joint efforts of the Ferranti and Cambridge teams to the stage of hardware being designed, delivered, installed, and commissioned. David Wheeler commanded the logical design efforts, and Roger Needham, having just completed his PhD, was engaged to do pioneering design automation. Our trusty team of engineers and technicians put it all together and kept working what, by today's standards, was a very unreliable piece of equipment.

On the software side, the operating-system team was initially led by David Barron and later by Roger Needham, and included David Hartley, Barry Landy, and Mike Guy, with Sandy Fraser coming from Ferranti in the later stages. David Barron and David Hartley started the CPL project, joined in due course by Christopher Strachey.

Contributions were made by other laboratory staff and research students, as well as by the wider user population. It is worth mentioning that Steve Bourne worked on text editors as a research student, before taking his Titan experiences to Bell Laboratories to influence the development of UNIX.

That Titan was highly successful there is no doubt. It broke new ground in providing computing facilities to a large, diverse user population, was well engineered, and in the end highly stable. Its legacy stretched into later computer science research activities in Cambridge and the wider world, while it set standards for future service systems within Cambridge. Indeed, the quality of today's University Computing Service, although totally transformed by advancing technology, can be traced back to those pioneering days of the 1960s.

Titan followed the tradition and policies of an efficient and useable system. We were driven to make a real system that advanced the state of the art while providing a service for very demanding university users. EDSAC 1 and EDSAC 2 had user populations of around 50 and 200 respectively. Titan's user population rose to nearly 1,000, and almost all of them used time-sharing facilities—no mean feat on a machine with the power of 0.25 MIP, about 0.75 Mbytes of memory, and 128 Mbytes of on-line file storage.

At the celebrations for the 50th anniversary of the EDSAC held in 1999, Roger Needham, who certainly contributed as much to the project than anyone else, gave a presentation on the Titan. He summed up the achievements of Titan with the following:

> If you are in our trade, nothing gives you more charge than having put together a system which nobody else can match.

16
Middleware? Muddleware!

Andrew Herbert

From 1978 to 1985 I worked with Roger Needham and others in the Computer Laboratory on the Cambridge Model Distributed System (CMDS) [9]. CMDS admirably demonstrated the benefits of local area networks and distributed computing. My role was to develop several of the management services and protocols that glued the CMDS processor bank and associated servers together. The work caught the attention of industry, and I was invited to become Chief Architect of the Alvey Advanced Networked Systems Architecture (ANSA) Project [1]—an industrial collaboration to research, develop, and standardize what came to be known as "middleware."

Now I find myself back working with Roger once more, but no longer studying middleware, since it is firmly out of the "doing research with a shovel" phase. In this paper I explore how middleware evolved, what succeeded, and what fell by the wayside.

Beginnings

Much of the CMDS environment was built using simple microprocessor-based systems, each dedicated to a single function and networked together to form an integrated system. The foundation for this was a very simple packet-level request-reply "single-shot" protocol (SSP). A software library was provided to applications for assembling the request packet, following agreed layout and format conventions, transmitting it, waiting for the reply, and extracting the results. Developers were carefully told about the possibility of packets being lost and the need to design idempotent operations. With these uncomplicated facilities we created dynamic naming services, user-authentication services, distributed-resource-management services, boot servers, automatic wire-wrapping machine controllers, amongst others. The services were documented in one or two sides of simple English text each.

Evolution: remote procedure call

Very quickly the systems community spotted the relationship between protocols like SSP and procedure calls in programming languages, and hence "remote procedure calls (RPC)" [3] were invented. The driving force for RPC was "transparency": that is, hiding the nitty gritty of distributed computing behind familiar programmatic syntax.

Unfortunately, transparency was found to be too demanding a mistress, in respect of differences in failure models, parameter-passing mechanisms, and type systems between the local and remote case.

Failure models

Procedure calls are atomic. In contrast, a request-reply exchange across a network might fail, leaving the caller unsure whether or not the operation had been executed at the server. Many argued for "exactly-once" RPC execution, since this matched local procedure calls. However, this could leave orphan executions stranded on a server. "Orphan extermination" techniques were investigated but were found to be a slippery slope towards multi-phase commitment protocols, and clearly overkill. Idempotency ("at least once" semantics) was held to be too limiting, so the consensus settled on "at most once," with sequence numbering of request and reply packets, and a simple state machine to manage the retransmission of lost data.

Parameter passing

Parameters passed by reference present problems in the remote case, since client and server are in separate address spaces. Some argued for a distributed shared memory to underpin RPC, others for various forms of copying. This was a particularly serious issue for languages like C, where only a single result parameter is permitted. The normal pattern of returning complex data structures by updating a variable through a reference argument didn't work.

Type system

Potentially client and server in an RPC system are written in different programming languages with different type systems. Consequently, a key component of early RPC systems were Interface Definition Languages (IDLs), providing syntax for describing request and reply interactions, characteristically in terms of "in" parameters (arguments) and "out" parameters (results). Client and server "stub code" to marshal data in and out of packets was generated automatically from IDL specifications, removing one source of potential programming errors.

Programmers had to learn how IDL concepts mapped onto their programming language of choice, and also obscure conventions for managing the heap memory used to marshal arguments and results in and out of packets. Arguments reigned about IDL syntax: many held it should be language-neutral, both for clarity and to emphasize the potential for working between different languages. To reduce the burden on the user, others wanted IDLs to be close to a specific language (or a subset of it, for example, object type specifications in languages like C++). Several systems, such as Sun RPC [11], managed without an IDL, relying instead on a standard encoding and supporting libraries.

RPC performance

In the early days of RPC research groups competed to demonstrate how their implementation was faster than anyone else's—whatever it took, including burying the protocol inside the operating system [10, 12]. This was driven not only by competition between researchers, but in the belief that RPC was a tool for constructing specialized application protocols, displacing "general" protocols such as TCP.

Evolution: network objects

The later stages of RPC development coincided with the emergence of object-oriented programming into the mainstream, in the form of the C++ programming language. Many groups, including ANSA, extended their RPC systems into "network object" systems [4]. The basic idea was that the client held a "network pointer" or "object reference," and an operation was invoked using a network pointer to identify which object should respond. Objects moved the computational model for distributed computing from remote "procedure call" to remote "method invocation" and introduced the concept of a "service": a set of methods (operations) over a shared state. With RPC, the relationship between procedures and state had been left implicit, dependent upon implementation details and operating-system structure. With an object model, a server could support multiple services as independently named entities, including, for example, multiple instances of the same service bound to different state variables. The paradigm example was of a "bank server," which embodied individual bank accounts as separate objects. Network pointers became capabilities, as envisioned in an early paper by Needham [8].

Network pointers resolved many of the problems with reference parameters that had arisen with RPC systems, since objects provided a way to wrap up complex data structures and network pointers provided a way to reference objects on one machine from another. Nothing is for free, however, and now such issues arose as how long-lived network pointers should be, how tightly bound they are to object instances, and how a server might garbage-collect objects that are no longer referenced by its clients.

Object model variations

The network object model developed along two paths. Some systems emphasized programming language independence and working between operating systems and runtime environments. Others looked for more complete integration with a single language and operating system: the attraction of doing so being that little new syntax was required.

Network objects and databases

In the academic research community the emphasis was on RPC as a system-building tool for general distributed computations. In contrast, in the rapidly growing market for PC applications the focus was on interactive desktop client applications making use of database servers through "database connectivity" protocols such as ODBC [7].

Network objects and a flurry of interest in object-orientated databases brought these strands together. For example, in the Guide system [2], the database server was treated as a repository of "passive objects" to be "activated" when a database operation touched them. Depending upon the particular system architecture, the activation was either local to the server or by copying the state to the client. The latter was attractive if database objects were small, rarely shared, and frequently accessed—they were effectively cached at the client for the duration of a transaction. However, if the object was heavily shared, distributed locking and cache consistency had to be introduced. Some systems did this by introducing transactional capabilities, others by using a distributed virtual memory. A further challenge in these systems was the need to ensure that clients had the correct "object manager" code available—which opened another can of worms having to do with implementation repositories, security, and code versioning.

The final evolution of the network object model was its extension to include "mobile objects" [5], often linked to notions of "(intelligent) agents" [13]. This permitted objects to migrate from computer to computer automatically in response to operation invocation, or explicitly in response to application instructions to the infrastructure that an object be relocated, or because the object itself decides to migrate to a different location.

Evolution: application servers

Around 1993, from a research perspective network objects were done—they were being standardized by the Object Management Group though its portfolio of CORBA specifications. At this time the World Wide Web[1] exploded and e-commerce was invented. Very quickly people saw the attraction of offering web front-ends to CORBA applications, and network objects evolved into "web objects." These were the first steps towards the emergence of application servers supporting the now classic three-tier model of 1) web-browser based "thin" client, 2) application objects representing dynamic state (typically electronic shopping carts), executing on an application server 3) back-end databases queried and updated in response to transactions issued by the application objects, all three tiers interconnected using RPC.

Evolution: reflective middleware

The CORBA specifications tried to span all the various flavours of network object systems. This turned out to be a complex task, and made implementations of CORBA object request brokers cumbersome. People asked if it would be possible to build customized brokers using re-usable middleware components and, if so, how much common architecture there could be across them. This spawned research into "reflective middleware" which continues to this day. Network objects have become introspective (you can find out from an object what operations it supports, and what infrastructure it requires). Object request brokers have become reflective (you can intercept internal data paths, and dynamically add and replace components). Java, the dominant programming language used in this research, fortunately has the necessary language facilities. The result has been highly flexible systems such as the author's "FlexiNet" system [6], developed in 1996-8, which at last achieved the goal of "selective transparency" that had been the ANSA project's holy grail since the outset in 1984.

This strand of research was given a great deal of impetus by interest from the telecommunications industry looking to apply the ideas of network objects to distributed control of Asynchronous Transfer Mode (ATM) networks, as part of their attempt to deliver integrated data and real-time communication services, and to reclaim the Internet. It led to extended interaction models to allow network objects to consume streamed traffic, and to operate in the context of real-time control.

---

1   Itself an RPC system but with none of the baggage of IDLs, fussy failure models or network objects.

Evolution: web services

At the time of writing, we are in the fourth generation of middleware, called "web services" [14]. Web services are promoted as the means to integrate applications across the Internet and develop "virtual businesses."

In web services, interfaces are defined using an XML based IDL called the "Web Services Description Language" (WSDL) and requests are transported using the SOAP protocol ("Simple Object Access Protocol") RPC layered above HTTP.

Curiously, in many respects web services have taken us back to a simpler model which is perhaps closer to the SSP of the Cambridge Model Distributed System, than to contemporary reflective middleware:

- *Distributed systems are composed of services*: The unit of specification and binding in web services is "the service," a collection of inter-related operations encapsulating data and applications. The service is not strongly tied to any specific language or object-request-broker concept of "object." In this respect it is implementation neutral.
- *Services are defined semantically*: WSDL is based on XML, which is a general notation for describing data. It is not tied to programming language views on the structure of concrete data types.
- *Services are stateless*: Web services don't have a notion of network pointer. Because they are intended to be used over the global Internet, there is an expectation that requests will fail, and therefore using idempotent operations is a good thing. State (e.g., an electronic shopping cart) is stored by the Web service, fetched by the client when needed, and pushed when changed. If there is a conflict, the client is invited to retry. Thorny issues, like garbage collection, that are hard to make work at the Internet scale have been side-stepped.

Hindsight

Looking back over the evolution of middleware, we can see there were many false paths and perhaps lessons for the future:

- *Moore's Law solves performance problems*: Performance is not the first priority in web services. A SOAP-level-request reply may itself be mapped onto lower-level reliable message passing. XML is not an efficient coding. That doesn't matter: we have CPU cycles and network bandwidth to burn. What does matter is that we can't assume the speed of light will double, and so latency (round-trip times) is an issue, but with the standard distributed computing techniques of caching and parallel and speculative execution, we can often conceal this.
- *RPC is not a tool for building optimized application protocols*: TCP rules in this respect. It has been honed to handle both interactive re-

quest-reply traffic and bulk flows. The global Internet is optimized for TCP. TCP is optimized to use network resources fairly, and because of this TCP is often the only protocol that is widely available and supported.

- *Component-oriented middleware isn't a user feature*: While vendors may construct their middleware using component-oriented software engineering, this isn't something they expose to users, except in very simple ways—for example, selecting between different profiles for local versus wide-area networking. Probably in part this is to protect the vendor's ability to ship different product variants and control evolution of their products. Moreover, conservative users (which most are) generally stick to standard profiles recommended by the vendor.

- *Distributed control of telecommunications networks missed the boat*: A lot of the reflective middleware research was driven by an interest in "telecomms object request brokers" This didn't happen: ATM disappeared into the backbone and the telecommunications industry has spent all its money for the foreseeable future.

- *Network objects are too general*: Web services are not network objects. Distributed object systems and mobile object systems are mostly relegated to academic interest. This comes about because many of the programming-language concepts that crept into distributed computing, such as garbage collection, don't work at the Internet scale. However, there are some applications of distributed-object platforms found in tightly coupled cluster-based computing, and database connectivity protocols have continued to evolve and remain important. For example, Microsoft.Net provides a facility called "Active Data Objects"—which allows a federation of databases to stream query results to a client and take in updates.

In summary, with hindsight, Roger and his colleagues, when designing the Cambridge Model Distributed System and its single-shot protocol, mostly got it right: services were defined semantically, they were stateless, entanglement with programming-language concepts was avoided, and no attempt was made to use SSP as a protocol-building tool—other system services, such as the file server, had their own custom protocols designed from the ground up and optimized for the task in hand.[2]

---

2   There were conventions about the location of addressing information to help gateways and network monitors, but fortunately, since protocol layering hadn't reached Cambridge in 1979, we refrained from overdoing it.

References[3]

1. ANSA Project Archive, available at http://www.ansa.co.uk
2. BALTER, R. ET AL, 'Architecture and implementation of Guide, an object-oriented distributed system,' *Computing Systems*, vol. 4, no. 1, April 1991, pp. 31-67.
3. BIRRELL, A.D. AND NELSON, B.J., 'Implementing remote procedure calls,' ACM Trans. On Computer Systems, vol. 2, no. 1, February 1984, pp. 39-59.
4. BIRRELL, A., NELSON, G., OWICKI, S. AND WOBBER, E.,. 'Network objects,' *Proc. 14th Symposium on Operating Systems Principles*, Asheville, NC (USA), December 1993, pp 217-230.
5. CAUGHEY S. AND SHRIVASTAVA, S.K., 'Architectural support for mobile objects in large-scale distributed systems.' In L.-F. Cabrera and M. Theimer, (eds.), *Proc. Fourth Int'l Workshop on Object Orientation in Operating Systems*, Lund, Sweden, Aug. 1995, pp. 38-47.
6. HAYTON, R., HERBERT, A. AND DONALDSON, D., 'FlexiNet: a flexible component-oriented middleware system,' *Proc. 8th ACM SIGOPS European Workshop on Support for Composing Distributed Applications*, Sintra, Portugal, Sept. 1998.
7. MICROSOFT CORPORATION, The ODBC Programmer's Reference, MSDN online library: available at
   http://msdn.microsoft.com/library/default.asp?url=
   /library/en-us/odbc/htm/dasdkodbcoverview.asp
8. NEEDHAM, R.M., 'Adding capability access to conventional file servers,' *Operating Systems Review*, vol. 13 no. 1, 1979, pp. 3-4.
9. NEEDHAM, R.M. AND HERBERT, A.J., The Cambridge distributed computing system, Addison-Wesley, Reading, Mass., 1982.
10. SCHROEDER. M.D. AND BURROWS, M., 'Performance of Firefly RPC,' *ACM Trans. On Computer Systems*, vol. 8, no. 1, February 1990, pp. 1-17.
11. SUN MICROSYSTEMS INC, 'XDR: External Data Representation Standard,' Internet RFC 1014, June 1987.
12. TANENBAUM, A.S., VAN RENESSE, R., VAN STAVEREN, H., SHARP, G.J., MULLENDER, S.J., JANSEN J. AND VAN ROSSUM, G., 'Experiences with the Amoeba operating systems,' *Comm. ACM*, vol. 33, no. 12, December 1990, pp. 46-63.
13. WOOLDRIDGE, M. AND JENNINGS, N., 'Intelligent agents: theory and practice,' *Knowledge Engineering Reviews*, vol. 10, no. 2, 1995, pp. 115-152.
14. WORLD WIDE WEB CONSORTIUM, Web services activity, available at:
    http://www.w3.org/2002/ws

---

3   Note that these references are by no means a full bibliography for "middleware"; they are simply a representative set to support points made in the paper.

17
Grand Challenges for Computing Research

Tony Hoare

The Microsoft Research Laboratory at Cambridge provides a wonderful environment for pursuit of pure and applied research. It is the policy of the Company to promote research according to the traditional pattern that has contributed so much to the progress of science in the past. Researchers are free to pursue their interests in exciting directions, and there is no prior target set for the first application of the results of research in industrial products. Open publication is the norm, and contact and collaboration with researchers in universities is encouraged.

Ironically, the policy that has directed much university research in recent years throughout the world is in stark contrast with Microsoft's research policy. The current administrative procedures for funding bodies for academic research favour short-term industrial goals that will lead to competitive advantage for the community that provides the funds. One reason that I took up Roger's offer of a job in Cambridge was because I strongly believed in Microsoft research policy, which he so successfully implemented. More than that: I wanted to encourage my former colleagues in universities to raise their eyes to longer term goals and take control of the general scientific agenda. I also hoped to use my influence (if any) to rectify the imbalance in current funding policies in UK.

When Roger promoted an initiative to set up a UK Computing Research Council (UKCRC), I felt that my membership of this body would offer me a good opportunity. And when the Council sponsored a Workshop entitled Grand Challenges for Computing Research, I volunteered to serve as co-organiser. In the call for proposals, I drafted a list of criteria relevant for evaluation of a research proposal as a grand challenge. These criteria emphasised the long-term contribution to science itself that can arise from pursuit of an ambitious long-term challenge on an international scale, and this complements the kind of research initiative that pursues shorter-term local goals. In order to test the formalisation of the criteria, I applied them to my own favourite challenge, the old challenge of constructing a verifying compiler.

The call for proposals attracted over a hundred excellent submissions. The workshop took place on 24–26 November 2002 in the highly suitable environment of the National e-Science Centre in Edinburgh. There were over fifty participants, including representatives from abroad. The attending scientists were very enthusiastic at the prospect of formulating and pursuing a grand challenge generated by scientific curiosity or engineering ambition. Many of the participants are still engaged in refinement and more detailed planning of a small selection of proposals that inspire support among the scientists best qualified to contribute to them. I have also been developing my own challenge proposal for a verifying compiler, both because it is dear to my heart and to show an example that may be useful to others.

What follows is my latest draft of criteria for maturity of a grand challenge, followed by a sample from a report on the Verifying Compiler. The original list of criteria was sent out in the call for submissions for the Edinburgh Workshop; it was adopted by participants at the workshop as the basis for evaluation of proposals, and it is was applied in the detailed proposals that were submitted to the UKCRC in June 2003.

Criteria for a grand challenge

The primary purpose of the formulation and promulgation of a grand challenge is to contribute to the advancement of some branch of science or engineering. A grand challenge represents a commitment by a significant section of the research community to work together towards a common goal, agreed to be valuable and achievable by a team effort within a predicted timescale. The challenge is formulated by the researchers themselves as a focus for the research that they wish to pursue in any case, and which they believe can be pursued more effectively by advance planning and co-ordination. Unlike other common kinds of research initiative, a grand challenge should not be triggered by hope of short-term economic, commercial, medical, military, or social benefits; and its initiation should not wait for political promotion or for prior allocation of special funding. The goals of the challenge should be the purely scientific goals of the advancement of skill and of knowledge. It should appeal not only to the curiosity of scientists and to the ambition of engineers, but also to the imagination of the general public. It may thereby enlarge the general understanding and appreciation of science, and attract new entrants to a rewarding career in scientific research.

An opportunity for a grand challenge arises only rarely in the history of any particular branch of science. It occurs when that branch of study first reaches an adequate level of maturity to predict the long-term direction of its future progress and to plan a project to pursue that direction on an international scale. Much of the work required to achieve the challenge may be of a routine nature. Many scientists will prefer not to be involved in the co-operation and co-ordination involved in a grand challenge. They realize that most scientific advances, and nearly all break-throughs, are accomplished by individuals or small teams, working competitively and in relative isolation. They value their privilege of pursuing bright ideas in new directions at short notice. It is for these reasons that a grand challenge should always be a minority interest among scientists, and that the greater part of the research effort in any branch of science should remain free of involvement in grand challenges.

A grand challenge may involve as much as a thousand man-years of research effort, drawn from many countries and spread over ten years or more. The research skill, experience, motivation, and originality that it will absorb are qualities even scarcer and more valuable than the funds that may be allocated to it. For this reason, a proposed grand challenge should be subjected to assessment by the most rigorous criteria before its general promotion and wide-spread adoption. These criteria include all those proposed by Jim Gray in his Turing address [1] as desirable attributes of a long-range research goal. The additional criteria that are proposed here relate to the maturity of the scientific discipline and the feasibility of the project. In the following list, the earlier criteria emphasize the significance of the goals, and the later criteria relate to the feasibility of the project and the maturity of the state of the art.

- *Fundamental.* It arises from scientific curiosity about the foundation, the nature, and the limits of an entire scientific discipline, or a significant branch of it.
- *Astonishing.* It gives scope for engineering ambition to build something useful that was earlier thought impractical, thus turning science fiction to science fact.
- *Testable.* It has a clear measure of success or failure at the end of the project; ideally, there should be criteria to assess progress at intermediate stages too.
- *Inspiring.* It has enthusiastic support from (almost) the entire research community, even those who do not participate in it and do not benefit from it.
- *Understandable.* It is generally comprehensible and captures the imagination of the general public, as well as the esteem of scientists in other disciplines.
- *Useful.* The understanding and knowledge gained in completion of the project bring scientific or other benefits; some of these should be attainable, even if the project as a whole fails in its primary goal.
- *Historical.* The prestigious challenges are those which were formulated long ago; without concerted effort, they would be likely to stand for many years to come.
- *International.* It has international scope, exploiting the skills and experience of the best research groups in the world. The cost and the prestige of the project is shared among many nations, and the benefits are shared among all.

- *Revolutionary*. Success of the project will lead to radical paradigm shift in scientific research or engineering practice. It offers a rare opportunity to break free from the dead hand of legacy.
- *Research-directed*. The project can be forwarded by the reasonably well understood methods of academic research. It tackles goals that will not be achieved solely by commercially motivated evolution of existing products.
- *Challenging*. It goes beyond what is known initially to be possible, and requires development of understanding, techniques, and tools unknown at the start.
- *Feasible*. The reasons for previous failure to meet the challenge are well understood and there are good reasons to believe that they can now be overcome.
- *Incremental*. It decomposes into identified intermediate research goals, which can be shared among many separate teams over a long time-scale.
- *Co-operative*. It calls for planned co-operation among identified research teams and research communities with differing specialized skills.
- *Competitive*. It encourages and benefits from competition among individuals and teams pursuing alternative lines of enquiry; there should be clear criteria announced in advance to decide who is winning, or who has won.
- *Effective*. Its promulgation changes the attitudes and activities of research scientists and engineers.
- *Risk-managed*. The risks of failure are identified, symptoms of failure are recognized early, and strategies for cancellation or recovery are in place.

The tradition of grand challenges is familiar in many branches of science. If you want to know whether a challenge qualifies for the title 'grand,' compare it with the following:

- Prove Fermat's last theorem   (accomplished)
- Put a man on the moon within ten years (accomplished)
- Cure cancer within ten years   (failed in 1970s)
- Map the Human Genome   (accomplished)
- Map the Human Proteome   (too difficult for now)
- Find the Higgs Boson   (under investigation)
- Find gravity waves   (under investigation)
- Unify the four forces of physics   (under investigation)
- Hilbert's programme for mathematical foundations
                                          (abandoned in the 1930s)

All of these challenges satisfy many of the criteria listed above in varying degrees, though no individual challenge could be expected to satisfy all the criteria.

The first in the list was the oldest and in some ways the grandest challenge, but being a mathematical challenge, my suggested criteria are considerably less relevant to it.

In computer science, the following examples may be familiar from the past. That is the reason why they are listed here, *not as recommendations*, but just as examples:

- Prove that P is not equal to NP   (open)
- The Turing test   (outstanding)
- The verifying compiler   (abandoned in the 1970s)
- A championship chess program   (completed)
- A GO program at professional standard (too difficult)
- Literature translation from English to Russian
-                                      (failed in the 1960s).

The first of these challenges is mathematical. It may seem quite easy to extend this list with new challenges. The difficult part is to find a challenge that passes the requirements for maturity and feasibility. That was the task of the Workshop on Grand Challenges for Computing Research, and the work still continues.

The verifying compiler: implementation and application

A verifying compiler uses automated mathematical and logical reasoning methods to check the correctness of the programs that it compiles. The criterion of correctness is specified by types, assertions, and other redundant annotations that are associated with the code of the program, often inferred automatically, and increasingly often supplied by the original programmer. The compiler will work in combination with other program development and testing tools to achieve any desired degree of confidence in the structural soundness of the system and the total correctness of its more critical components. The only limit to its use will be set by an evaluation of the cost and benefits of accurate and complete formalization of the criterion of correctness for the software.

An important and integral part of the project proposal is to evaluate the capabilities and performance of the verifying compiler by application to a representative selection of legacy code, chiefly from open sources. This will give confidence that the engineering compromises that are necessary in such an ambitious project have not damaged its ability to deal with real programs written by real programmers. It is only after this demonstration of capability that programmers working on new projects will gain the confidence to exploit verification technology in new projects.

I found that the most difficult criteria to satisfy were those for testability, feasibility, and effectiveness. These are my latest thoughts on just these points.

Testable. If the project is successful, a verifying compiler will be available as a standard tool in some widely used programming productivity toolset. It will have been tested in verification of structural integrity and security and other desirable properties of millions of lines of open-source software, and in more substantial verification of critical parts of it. This will lead to removal of thousands of errors, risks, insecurities, and anomalies in widely used code. Proofs will be subjected to check by rival proof tools. The major internal and external interfaces in the software will be documented by assertions, to make existing components safer to use and easier to reuse. The benefits will extend also to the evolution and enhancement of legacy code, as well as the design and development of new code. Eventually programmers will prefer to confine their use of their programming language to those features and structured-design patterns which facilitate automatic checks of correctness.

Feasible. Most of the factors which have inhibited progress on practical program verification are no longer as severe as they were.

1.   Experience has been gained in specification and verification of moderately scaled systems, chiefly in the area of safety-critical and mission-critical software, but so far the proofs have been mainly manual.

2.   The corpus of open-source software is now universally available and used by millions, thus justifying almost any effort expended on improvement of its quality and robustness. Although it is subject to continuous improvement, the pace of change is reasonably predictable. It is an important part of this challenge to cater to software evolution.

3.   Advances in unifying theories of programming suggest that many aspects of correctness of concurrent and object-oriented programs can be expressed by assertions, supplemented by automatic or machine-assisted insertion of instrumentation in the form of ghost (model) variables and assignments to them.

4.   Many of the global program analyses which are needed to underpin correctness proofs for systems involving concurrency and pointer manipulation have now been developed for use in optimizing compilers.

5.   Theorem-proving technology has made great strides in many directions. Model checking is widely understood and used, particularly in hardware design. Decision procedures are beginning to be applied to software. Proof search engines are now well populated with libraries of application-dependent theorems and tactics. Finally, satisfiability checking promises a step-function increase in the power of proof tools. A major remaining challenge is to find effective ways of combining this wide range of component technologies into a small number of tools, to meet the needs of program verification.

6.   Program analysis tools are now available that use a variety of techniques to discover relevant invariants and abstractions. It is hoped that

7.   that these will formalize at least the program properties relevant to its structural integrity, with a minimum of human intervention.

8. Theories relevant for the concurrency correctness are well established, and theories for object orientation and pointer manipulation are under development.

Effective. The promulgation of this challenge is intended to cause a shift in the motivations and activities of scientists and engineers in all the relevant research communities. They will be pioneers in the collaborative implementation and use of a single large experimental device, following a tradition that is well established in astronomy and physics but not yet in computer science.

1. Researchers in programming theory will accept the challenge of extending proof technology for programs written in complex and uncongenial legacy languages. They will need to design program-analysis algorithms to test whether actual legacy programs observe the constraints that make each theoretical proof technique valid.

2. Builders of programming tools will carry out experimental implementation of the hypotheses originated by theorists. Following practice in experimental branches of science, they seek to explore the range of application of the theory to real code.

3. Sympathetic software users will allow newly inserted assertions to be checked dynamically in production runs, even before the tools are available to verify them.

4. Empirical computer scientists will apply tools developed by others to the analysis and verification of representative large-scale examples of open code.

5. Compiler writers will support the proof goals by adapting and extending the program analyses currently used for optimization of code; later they may even exploit, for purposes of further optimization, the additional redundant information provided with a verified program.

6. Providers of proof tools will regard the project as a fruitful source of low-level conjectures needing verification, and will evolve their algorithms and libraries of theories to meet the needs of actual legacy software and its users.

7. Teachers and students of the foundations of software engineering will be encouraged to set student projects that annotate and verify a small part of a large code base, thus contributing to the success of a worldwide project.

Reference

1. GRAY, J., 'What next? A dozen information-technology research goals,' ACM Turing Award Lecture, published as Microsoft Research Technical Report MSR-TR-99-50, available at:
http://research.microsoft.com/scripts/pubs/view.asp?TR_ID=MSR-TR-99-50

18
Sentient Computing[1]

Andy Hopper

Sentient computing is the proposition that applications can be made more responsive and useful by observing and reacting to the physical world. It is particularly attractive in a world of mobile users and computers.

Location sensing

Cheap sensors make it possible for computer systems to react to the physical environment. Sensors giving location information are probably the easiest to construct and deploy. Use of such location information makes it possible for user interfaces to be based on space itself. Such context-aware, or sentient, interfaces and applications have been constructed and used for a number of years.

Infra-Red Location

      15 metre range
      diffuse
      room-scale accuracy
          95% of time
      containment location

Figure 1: Containment—active badge

1   This is an abridged and updated version of the Royal Society Clifford Paterson Lecture, 1999. The original paper was published in *Phil. Trans. R. Soc. Lond.*, vol. 358, pp. 2349–2358, Royal Society, August 2000.

Sensors tell us about the location or position of things. To reflect the requirements of different applications, we take three different approaches to categorising the concept of location. First, *containment* is where we say that an object is within this container, e.g., a room. Second, *proximity* is where we register that we are close to something. Finally, *co-ordinate* systems provide a point location in space, subject to some error value. These categories are not hard and fast and can blend together. Small containers are very similar to a co-ordinate system, and proximity has much in common with the concept of containment.

Our first experience of developing a sensor specifically to provide spatial information originated in the late 1980s in the form of the Active Badge (Figure 1). Personnel and equipment could be tagged using the Badge, which transmitted a unique infrared signal every few seconds. The transmissions were diffuse, and receivers in a room picked up the signal, giving room-scale containment. It told us who and what was in which room. The Active Badge was the inspiration that started us on this whole line of enquiry.

In the case of proximity, promising commercial systems are starting to appear. The radio-based Bluetooth system gives accuracy of about 10 metres using the received-signal-strength indication (RSSI). This will improve to about 50 centimetres in future implementations by using specialised on-board ranging circuitry. Similarly, RSSI information from Wavelan (802.11) systems, together with heuristics about the movement of people, can be used to provide in-building location information.

Outside, one can use the Global Positioning System (GPS), which has given rise to a large number of applications. GPS is accurate to around 30 metres most of the time, although greater precision can be achieved, and is one example of a co-ordinate based system.

In order to test the impact of fine-grain location information, we have developed a co-ordinate system for indoors. This uses a tag, which incorporates ultrasonic transmitters, and an array of ceiling-mounted detectors. A detector on the far side of the room will register a pulse later than a detector directly above an object. Using this differential timing information, we can calculate the position of objects to within a few centimetres almost all the time (Figure 2). If two transmitters are attached to a rigid object, it is possible to compute its orientation. The Active Bat technology is likely to remain the basis of the most precise indoor location systems for the foreseeable future. There will be many applications that do not require this level of precision and refinement. However, as a research tool, it is providing us with valuable information on what can be done with very precise positional data.

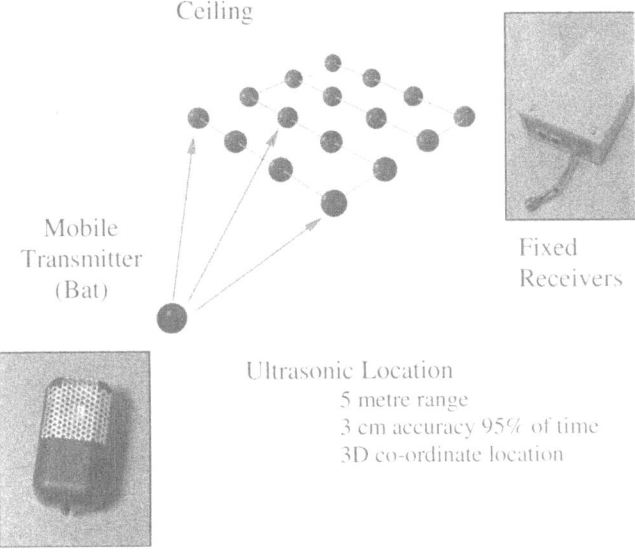

Figure 2: Co-ordinate system—Active Bat

The Active Bat system requires a substantial amount of infrastructure, particularly in ceilings. A new technology, which may provide similar location information, is ultra-wideband radio. This emits very short pulses of several picoseconds duration, from which we can measure propagation delays accurately at the receiver from transmitters spaced up to 20 metres apart. A large spectrum is used, for example, from 3 GHz to 10 GHz, but the power levels are low, so that interference to other users is minimised. Ultra-wideband transmissions may be less susceptible to interference in particular parts of the band, and thus instrumenting buildings may prove much easier than with the Active Bat system. However, it is likely that the precision will be some 10 times worse than the ultrasonic Active Bat, with a location accuracy of about 30 centimetres most of the time. It also remains to be seen what the local effect of monitors and other metallic objects is on precision.

Spatial monitoring

Our sensors provide raw spatial facts about objects. They tell us where an object is, and possibly the direction in which an object is pointing. Location-aware applications need more than raw spatial data, they need to be notified of spatial relationships between objects that are significant for the execution of the application. But how do we decide whether a spatial relationship is significant? The approach we have adopted operates on the basis of zones of containment surrounding objects. In Figure 3(a) X represents a person and K a keyboard. Now suppose we have an application that needs to be notified when person X is in a position to use keyboard K, when X is possibly "holding" K. If the zone of confinement of K overlaps the zone of confinement of X, then X is said to hold K, and the application receives the appropriate space-location event. The situation in Figure 3(b) indicates how this principle could be applied to support a multi-camera video conferencing system, giving participants the freedom to look in different directions while talking, or even walking around their offices.

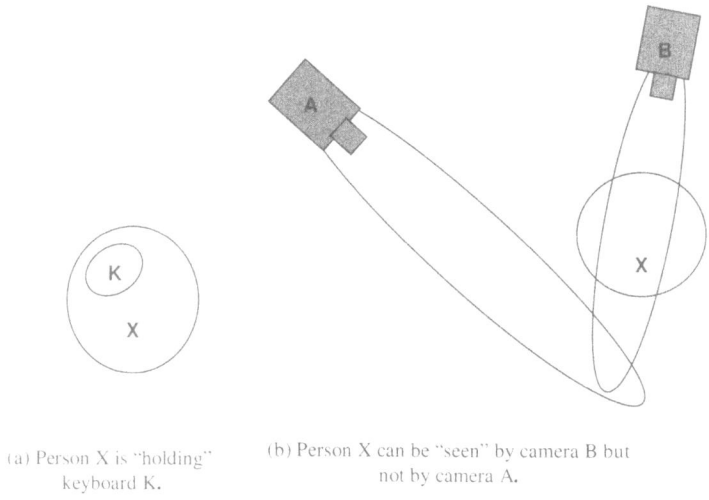

(a) Person X is "holding" keyboard K.

(b) Person X can be "seen" by camera B but not by camera A.

Figure 3: Evaluating spatial facts

The principle of turning raw spatial data into application-significant events through geometric containment and overlapping is reasonably straightforward. Scalability can be addressed by applications indicating the interest and precision required. The computations are then only performed to the required level, and the computational task scales linearly with the number of overlapping spaces. This approach can be thought of as the mouse/desktop metaphor mapped onto the physical world in real time.

The operational system that has been built uses a variety of sensors. It allows space representations to change quickly, provides the means to express event-driven control logic, uses caches and proxies to handle large volumes of data quickly, and executes in real-time to satisfy a human in the loop.

Note that Figure 3 is a 2D representation of what in reality would be a 3D environment. This simplification can be made because, in general, people and objects tend to remain relatively fixed in the vertical plane. At the heart of such spatial monitoring systems we need to define a world model that is easily understood by the user yet computable by the system. Is 3D important or is 2D satisfactory for most office and home applications? What is the precision of location information required? How can the spatial metaphor be made obvious to the user?

Data distribution

Publishing sensor data that relates to the position of people and objects is one end application. Beyond this we consider the automatic control of the digital environment with reactive and possibly predictive features. An attractive application for a user in a networked environment is the ability for the personal desktop to follow the user to any nearby device. In order to achieve this, in addition to location information we need a platform for connecting and displaying information on all these devices in a ubiquitous way.

One way to do this is to tunnel connections to all devices using a simple device-independent protocol. We have devised one such ubiquitous platform called the Virtual Network Computer (VNC). In our approach the viewer, at the receiving end of the connection, has no state and simply displays information graphically. The connection from viewer to server is also stateless, just keystrokes and pointer clicks. Our viewer is a particularly simple version of the so-called thin client (Figure 4), with all application state and processing centralised on a server.

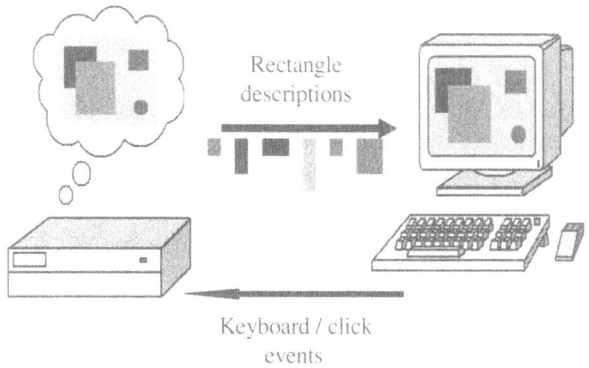

Figure 4: VNC—the platform

The absence of application state at the viewer eliminates any requirement for re-synchronisation, and the appearance is of user-interface mobility. In order to achieve this we have traded bandwidth, or more precisely we have relied on ubiquitous connectivity and low latency end-to-end.

The low-level nature of the protocol is the key to device independence, providing a platform that supports the connection of any device to anything. The connections can be one-to-one (fixed or mobile), and the streams can be split, giving one-to-many, many-to-one, and many-to-many.

The performance of the VNC system has turned out much better than expected. By using a variety of compression schemes and caching, it has been possible to operate useably across links with capacities of only 10's of Kbps and latencies of up to 40 milliseconds. Therefore, incorporating the simplest devices with wireless connectivity within this framework now appears plausible.

Applications

Location information appears to be a powerful tool in constructing new applications. Opening and closing doors automatically is an obvious example. In my ten or more years of being immersed in such systems, some of the most enduring applications have been those where raw location data is processed in a simple way and made available ubiquitously. A textual indication of where someone is, how fast they are moving, how long they have been there, has proved the most popular. Showing the local context, including who and what else is nearby, is also attractive. Publishing such information to the local (trusted) peer group saves time; if someone is not observed by the location system, they are not available, whatever the reason. Graphical representations and in particular maps appear attractive but can become cumbersome in what is a familiar physical environment. So simple sensing and simple logic appear to work, and applications using these stand the test of time. The containment location information provided by the Active Badge is quite sufficient for this purpose.

Personalisation by teleporting VNC desktops has also proved popular. The teleport can be triggered without using location data, but having a personal tag with a button, which acts as a personal ubiquitous controller, is neat. More precise coordinate location information as provided by the Active Bat becomes important for its ability to select the correct workstation or other device. Another use that takes advantage of the more precise location information associates a control function with any 3 centimetres cube of space. Typically this is done on the surface of a wall or other planar object and is normally a control trigger of some type. This use appears to have some merit and the walls of our laboratory are sprouting a number of such "active posters." For this specific application a local proximity RFID tag can provide the same location information in a simpler way.

Specialist applications, for example, surveillance where the selection of a particular camera is based on spatial data, can provide opportunities. However, there is always scope for such bespoke solutions.

Observations

So what are the results of over a decade of research, and what is the prognosis for the future? The research area is now very popular and is variously labelled ubiquitous, pervasive, ambient, calm, as well as sentient. In this paper I have permitted myself to give users attributes such as "holding," "seen," and have even suggested the notion of prediction. Is this realistic?

We have learnt many aspects of how to construct such systems. Sensor information can be generated on a reasonable scale and presented to users in various ways. It seems the more direct the presentation the more attractive (or perhaps less irritating) the application. Some simple logic to interpret the data can be useful. Occasionally, a domain-specific agent operates as envisaged.

Our attempts at automatic control without user intervention have not proved enduring. For example, automatically teleporting to the nearest screen throughout the laboratory did not stand the test of time. Similarly, automatic routing of phone calls had sufficiently serious flaws that the human operator remained as the interpreter of location data. User profiles were attempted but quickly became confusing themselves. Applications where predictions of user preference or intent are required have so far not been successful at all.

So anything beyond promulgation and simple interpretation seems problematic. Once more than a simple inference is attempted, we seem to hit a brick wall. We realised this with the Badge system a decade ago. Interpreting the sighting of three or more badges in a single space was presented as a "meeting." However, even in an office environment there are many reasons for three or more sightings at one place (meeting, tea time, passing in corridor). And that is before we extend to home or other environments.

One potential research direction is to provide much more feedback to the user. When we move a cursor on a screen, it is clear where it is and what is likely to happen when we click. When walking through space, it is much less obvious what the options are and how to control them. So visual and aural feedback with perhaps every nearby wall being used as a display may be one approach. The user might then be able to keep up as the context keeps changing. If proxy decisions are being made, the reasoning can now be presented more easily. The user can interact in a much more informed way and help guide any decision-making process.

Perhaps a way to make progress beyond the engineering level is to imagine a "perfect" sensing system with full coverage of the environment. How would we define the context (world knowledge), semantics of queries, and user intent? How would the user interact to resolve ambiguities? Are statistical techniques likely to make useful predictions or are there too many plausible choices at each point? Could a series of functional tests be devised which would give us the foundations to build on? It seems we are a long way from finding answers, and only by moving away from unrealistic ambitions will we prevent the research area being discredited in due course.

19
Cyber Security in Open Systems

Anita Jones

In the early days of computer systems, the 60s through the 80s, software systems were *closed*, that is, a single operating system owned and doled out the computation and storage resources. Each computer system stood alone, and operated solo. Security properties, if any, were integral to and enforced by the operating system architecture. Today, multitudes of computers are interconnected, communicating via messages. Operating systems still manage the same resources for one or a few computers and their attachments, as of old. But typically only software with limited function has cognizance of the overall interconnected software and hardware. The interconnected parts can be called an *open* system. It is open just as human society is open; individuals each operate with some degree of autonomy. Cyber security has been a *casualty* of the transition from closed to open systems.

In closed systems sufficient protection of one user from another could be assured by designing a single, preferably elegant (!), mechanism that was integral to the operating system. Roger Needham and his colleagues, and my colleagues and I, helped advance a protection mechanism called capabilities. Access-control mechanisms likewise served well. Both continue to be useful in limited contexts. Both of these protection mechanisms incorporate an assumption that the single mechanism is sufficient for its correct functioning, and that no software can get around the mechanism and obviate the protection that it provides. That assumption is unfounded in open systems, and sometimes in closed systems.

As the transition from closed to open occurred, the security-research community adopted a paradigm of *perimeter defense*. The notion was to continue to trust the protection mechanisms within the closed system, and to check all information flowing across the perimeter into the closed system to ensure that it was "acceptable." Firewalls are one example of perimeter guards. The perimeter-defense paradigm permitted the preservation of the "one-mechanism" closed-system approach to security.

But the perimeter-defense paradigm is fatally flawed. First, it assumes that the "thing" that we need to protect is "inside" the system and that we need to keep "outside" attackers from penetrating our defenses and gaining access to the inside. The perimeter-defense paradigm is like the French Maginot Line. It is fragile. In WWII, France fell in 35 days because of its reliance on this model. No matter how formidable the defenses, an attacker can make an end run, and once inside, can compromise the entire system. Second, the paradigm fails to account for the reality that many security flaws are "designed in." Security may be compromised while the system is performing exactly as specified. In 1993, the Naval Research Laboratory performed an analysis of some 50 security flaws and found that nearly half of them (22) were designed into the requirements or the specifications for *correct* system behavior! Third, perimeter defenses face outward, and are typically useless against an inside attack. Lastly, there exist attacks, such as distributed denial-of-service attacks, which do not rely on penetration. They create a flood of false requests for service. The closed system cannot discern the difference between legitimate and false requests and squanders resources servicing false requests. The perimeter-defense paradigm cannot work for sound theoretical reasons. Other approaches are needed.

Open systems are distinguished by the fact that they have heterogeneous components, some of which may come and go without warning. There is no single architecture, no single set of behavioral attributes except at the most primitive of levels. Unlike in a closed system, there is no single mechanism through which all access flows. Many open systems of interest are integral to human processes and procedures, e.g., information systems involved in health care administration or (just in time) inventory delivery to a chain of supermarkets.

We need a new model of cyber security to accommodate open systems. Indeed, the fundamental security properties of privacy, integrity of information, and denial of service that are implemented in part today are insufficient. We need a model that permits tailoring of security properties to what is important for the real-world situation in which an information system is embedded. Factors such as the timing or the temporal order of actions need to be considered. Likewise correlation of operations on related entities are essential for real-world security. The new model of cyber security should be appropriate to the context of the user's application. This is far from the notion of perimeter defense.

This new model of security may require software that, in effect, detects and reacts to the emergent "overall" behavior of the open system. Today, system administrators "stick their fingers in the dike" to stem "leaks" of many kinds as they attempt to configure and upgrade software to assure security. In a recent attack, called "Slammer," the company whose software had holes that made the attack possible had announced those holes and some associated fixes. However, even that company had not protected all of its own systems. That illustrates how difficult it is for system administrators to keep up with the myriad patches, fixes, and reconfiguration changes they must apply to close security holes, not to mention dealing with a spate of false alarms. Their systems have little self-awareness, little ability to self-configure or self-sustain.

In the absence of open systems being able to "police" themselves, and in the absence of the research community finding a new approach to security, it is not surprising that increasingly society is beginning to rely on traditional societal mechanisms to assure well-behavedness—courts, government regulation, and law enforcement.

Most societal approaches to assuring socially acceptable behavior involve "after the fact" enforcement involving a detective force, arrest, trial, and incarceration.

Unless an alternative model for securing cyberspace is found, society will use its physical-world approaches, whether they fit well with cyberspace or not. We see this playing out in the music industry in the United States today. Application of these traditional (re)actions may trample and destroy some of the attributes that open information systems deliver, such as a release from associating all actions and all actors to a geographical "place."

Conclusion

Cyber security concerns and the inadequacy of current systems stem from the transition from closed to open systems and to the integration of those systems into the very processes of society. Improving security of today's systems is greatly impeded by our current inability to design, develop, and maintain large and complex software systems. The inability of a system to recognize its own emergent behavior as it unfolds and of systems to self-adapt in the face of that observed behavior makes progress toward more secure and more reliable systems difficult.

We need entirely new models of information security that go beyond notions of privacy, integrity, and assurance of service quality. Security of an information system that is integral to a physical, human activity needs to reflect the specific, possibly unique, needs of that activity. Today's models and mechanisms are not up to the task. As a result, society is moving along the path toward using traditional approaches to assuring well-behavedness. The window in which it might be possible to formulate new notions of security and well-behavedness that do not reflect today's "place-based" laws and jurisdictions is closing rapidly.

20
Software Components: Only the Giants Survive[1]

Butler W. Lampson

For many years programmers have dreamed of building systems from a library of reusable software components together with a little new code. The closest we've come is Unix commands connected by pipes. This paper discusses the fundamental reasons why software components of this kind have not worked in the past and are unlikely to work in the future. Then it explains how the dream has come true in spite of this failure, and why most people haven't noticed.

Introduction

People have been complaining about the "software crisis" at least since the early 1960's. The famous NATO software engineering conference in 1968 brought the issue into focus, and introduced the term "software engineering." Many people predicted that software development would grind to a halt because of our inability to handle the increasing complexity; of course this has not happened.

What is often overlooked is that the software crisis will always be with us (so that it shouldn't be called a "crisis"). There are three reasons for this:

- As computing hardware becomes 100 times more powerful every decade (because of Moore's law), new applications become feasible, and they require new software. In other branches of engineering the pace of change is much slower.
- Although it's difficult to handle complexity in software, it's much easier to handle it there than elsewhere in a system. A good engineer therefore moves as much complexity as possible into software.
- External forces such as physical laws impose few limits on the application of computers. Usually the only limit is our inability to write the programs. Without a theory of software complexity, the only way to

---

1   This paper is based on a keynote address given at the 21st International Conference on Software Engineering, 1999.

find this limit is trial and error, so we are bound to over-reach fairly often. As Browning said "A man's reach should exceed his grasp, or what's a heaven for."

At the 1968 NATO conference, Doug McIlroy proposed that a library of software components would make programming much easier [7]. Since then, many people have advocated and worked on this idea; often it's called "reusable software," though this term has other meanings as well. Most recently, the PITAC report [9] proposed a major research initiative in software components. This paper explains why these ideas won't work.

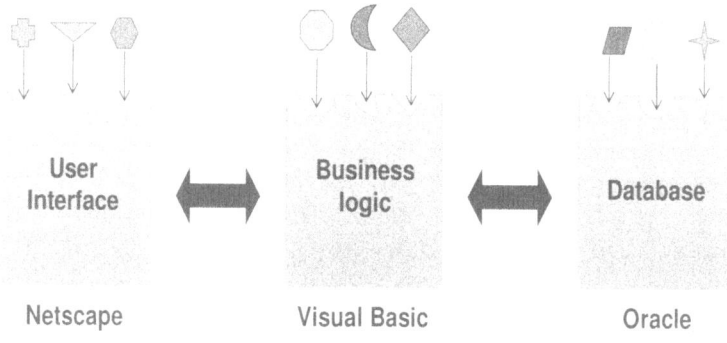

Figure 1: A typical business application

How much progress has there been in software in the last 40 years? Either a little or a lot: the answer depends on what kind of software you mean.

A little if you are writing a self-contained program from scratch or modifying an existing self-contained program. The things that help the most are type-safe languages such as Pascal and Java, and modules with clean interfaces [8]; both have been around for 30 years. Program analysis tools help with modifications, and they have been improving steadily [3].

A lot if you are doing a typical business computing application. You build your application on top of a few very large components: an operating system (Linux or Windows), a browser (Netscape or Internet Explorer), a relational database and transaction processor (DB2, Oracle, or SQL Server), and a rapid application development system (Visual Basic or Java); see Figure 1. You use only a small fraction of the features of each component, and your program consumes 10 or 100 times the hardware resources of a fully custom program, but you write 10% or 1% of the code you would have written 30 years ago. Certain kinds of domain-specific programs are also dramatically easier. If a spreadsheet, SQL, Matlab, Mathematica, or HTML is a good match for your problem, again you can write your program 10 or 100 times more easily.

The component library: dream and reality

McIlroy's idea was a large library of tested, documented components. To build your system, you take down a couple of dozen components from the shelves and glue them together with a modest amount of your own code.

The outstanding success of this model is the Unix commands designed to be connected by pipes: `cat`, `sort`, `sed`, and their friends [6]. There are quite a few of these, and you can do a lot by putting them together with a small amount of glue, usually written in the shell language. McIlroy [1] gives a striking example. It works because the components have a very simple interface (a character stream, perhaps parsed into lines or words) and because most of them were written by a single tightly-knit group. Not many components have been added by others.

Another apparent success is the PC hardware industry. PC's are built from (hardware) components: processor and chipset, DRAM SIMM, hard disk, monitor, graphics card and driver, etc. Manufacturers really do slap these components together to make systems. Reality is uglier than appearance, though. Only a few components really work well, the ones that can be tested adequately by running Windows on them for a few days. Others cause lots of problems, as anyone knows who has tried to build a PC. And Microsoft is responsible for the integrity of the PC ecosystem.

For the most part, component libraries have been a failure, in spite of much talk and a number of attempts. There are three major reasons for this:
- There's no business model.
- It costs a client too much to understand and use a component.
- Components have conflicting world views.

No business model

Design is expensive, and reusable designs are very expensive. It costs between ½ and 2 times as much to build a module with a clean interface that is well-designed for your system as to just write some code, depending on how lucky you are. But a reusable component costs 3 to 5 times as much as a good module. The extra money pays for the following:

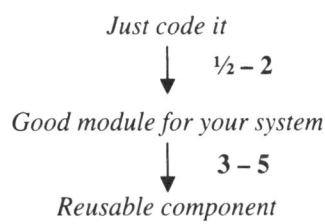

Just code it

↓ **½ – 2**

Good module for your system

↓ **3 – 5**

Reusable component

- Generality: A reusable module must meet the needs of a fairly wide range of 'foreign' clients, not just of people working on the same project. Figuring out what those needs are is hard, and designing an implementation that can meet them efficiently enough is often hard as well.

- Simplicity: Foreign clients must be able to understand the interface to a module fairly easily, or it's no use to them. If it only needs to work in a single system, a complicated interface is all right, because the client has much more context.
- Customization: To make the module general enough, it probably must be customizable, either with some well-chosen parameters or with some kind of programmability, which often takes the form of a special-purpose programming language.
- Testing: Foreign clients have higher expectations for the quality of a module, and they use it in more different ways. The generality and customization must be tested as well.
- Documentation: Foreign clients need more documentation, since they can't come over to your office.
- Stability: Foreign clients are not tied to the release cycle of a system. For them, a module's behaviour must remain unchanged (or upward compatible) for years, probably for the lifetime of their system.

Regardless of whether a reusable component is a good investment, it's nearly impossible to fund this kind of development. It's not necessary for building today's systems, and there's no assurance that it will pay off.

It's also very difficult to market such components:

- There are many of them, so each one gets lost in the crowd.
- Each client needs a number of them, so they can't be very expensive.
- Each one is rather specialized, so it's hard to find potential customers.

Cost to understand

To use a component, the client must understand its behaviour. This is not just the functional specification, but also the resource consumption, the exceptions it raises, its customization facilities, its bugs, and what workarounds to use when it doesn't behave as expected or desired. One measure of this cost is the ratio of the size of a complete specification (which of course seldom exists) to the size of the code. For a modest-sized component, this ratio is usually surprisingly large.

Furthermore, because the written spec is almost always quite inadequate, there is uncertainty about the cost to discover the things that aren't in the spec, and about the cost to deal with the surprises that turn up. If the module has been around for a while and has many satisfied users, these risks are of course smaller, but it's difficult to reach this happy state.

The client's alternative is to recode the module. Usually this is more predictable, and problems that turn up can often be handled by changing the module rather than by working around them. This is probably feasible if the module is built as part of the same project, but impossible if it's a reusable component.

Conflicting world views

The interface to a component embodies a view of the world: data types, resource consumption, memory allocation, exception handling, etc. If you take 10 components off the shelf, you are putting 10 world views together, and the result will be a mess. No one is responsible for design integrity, and only the poor client is responsible for the whole thing working together. There can easily be n^2 interactions among n components.

Good things that aren't reusable components

People often ask "What about Corba and COM; aren't they successful?" Perhaps they are, but they are ways to run components, not components themselves. They play the role of a linker and a calling convention for distributed computing.

The "components" that you can get for Visual Basic, Java, Microsoft Office, and browsers are not reusable components either. You can use a couple of them in your system, but if you use 10 of them things will fall apart, because they are not sufficiently robust or well-isolated. If you don't believe this, try it for yourself.

Nor is a module with a clean interface a reusable component, for all the reasons discussed above. A clean interface is a very good thing, and it's certainly necessary for a reusable component, but it's not sufficient.

Platforms

The next to last section showed why a public library of software components is not possible. Some less ambitious things have worked, however. Most of them are variations on the idea of a *platform*, which is a collection of components on top of which many people can build programs, usually application programs. Windows, Linux, Java, DB2, Microsoft Office, OpenGL, the IMSL numerical library, and PC hardware are examples of platforms. So, on a smaller scale, are the Unix shell and text processing commands discussed in the introduction.

The essential property of a platform is that someone takes responsibility for its coherence and stability. Often this is a vendor, motivated by the fact that having lots of application expands the market for the platform. It can also be a community, as in the case of Linux or OpenGL, in which component builders are motivated by status in the community or by the fact that they are also clients. A platform needs a shared context that everyone understands and a common world view that everyone accepts; this means that its community must include both the component builders and many of the clients. A shared context is much easier when the domain is narrow and there's a clean mathematical model, as with graphics or numerical libraries.

Sometimes people try to build lots of components on a common and hospitable platform, such as Visual Basic or Java. This can work if the components come from (or pass through) a single source that takes responsibility for their coherence. Otherwise, the problems of too little generality, cost to understand, and conflicting world views make it impossible to use more than two or three of them in a system.

Big components

As we saw in the introduction, big components like browsers and database systems do work, even though a library cannot. They are five million lines of code and up, so huge that you only use three or four of them: Linux or Windows, Netscape or Internet Explorer, Oracle or DB2, Visual Basic or Java. How do they overcome the problems with component libraries?

Business model: there's a market for such big things. Lots of people need each one, there are only a few of them, and the client only has to buy a couple of them, so marketing is feasible. Building your own, on the other hand, is not feasible, even if you only use 1% of the features: 1% of 20 million lines is still 200,000 lines of code to write, and that's a low estimate of the amount of code for 1% of the features.

Cost to understand: the specification may be large and complicated, but it is much smaller than the code. Because the market is large, vendors can afford to invest in documentation; in fact, every such component has a mini-industry of books about it. They can also afford to invest in customization: operating systems have applications and scripting languages, browsers have scripts, Java, plug-ins, and dynamic HTML, and database systems have SQL.

Conflicting world views: if you use three of them, there are only three pairwise interactions, and only two if they are layered. The vendor provides design integrity inside each big component.

In fact, big components, along with transaction processing, spreadsheets, SQL, and HTML, are one of the great successes of software in the last 20 years.

People often complain about big components because they are wasteful. A business application built on a browser and a database system can easily consume 100 times the resources of one that is carefully tailored to the job at hand. This is not waste, however, but good engineering. There are plenty of hardware resources; what's in short supply are programmers and time to market, and customers care much more about flexibility and total cost of ownership than about raw hardware costs.

Another way to look at this is that today's PC is about 10,000 times bigger and faster than the Xerox Alto [10], which it otherwise closely resembles. It certainly doesn't do 10,000 times as much, or do it 10,000 times faster. Where did the cycles go? Most of them went into delivering lots of features quickly, which means that you can't have first-class design everywhere. Software developers trade hardware resources for time to market. A lot of them also went into integration (for example, universal character sets and typography, drag and drop, embedding spreadsheets in text documents) and into compatibility with lots of hardware and with lots of old systems. And a factor of 10 did go into faster responses to the user's actions.

What else could work?

If components can't help us much to build software, what can? Two approaches are promising: declarative programming and specifications with teeth.

Declarative programming

"Declarative programming" is not a precise concept, but the idea is that the program is close to the specification, perhaps even the same. For example, in a simple spreadsheet the program is just the formulas; if there is no higher structure, the formulas express the user's intent as simply as possible. Of course, if the user's intent was "a capital gains worksheet with data from my brokerage account," the raw spreadsheet has a lot of extra detail. On the other hand, when equipped with suitable templates, Excel can come fairly close to that intent.

Other examples of declarative programming are the query language of SQL, a parser generator like YACC, a system for symbolic mathematics like Mathematica, and a stub generator for calling remote procedures. What they have in common is that what you have to tell the system is closer to your intent than an ordinary program. This makes programming faster and more reliable. It also opens up opportunities for analysis and optimization; parallel implementations of SQL are a good example of this.

Specifications with teeth

Specifications are useful as documentation, but they have the same problem as all documentation: they are often wrong. A spec is more valuable if it has teeth, that is, if you can count on its description of the program's behaviour. Such specs are much more likely to pass Parnas' coffee-stain test: the value of a spec is proportional to the number of coffee-stains on the implementers' copies. A type declaration is an example of a spec with teeth.

Teeth mean tools: the computer must check that the spec is satisfied. There are two kinds of teeth: statically checked and dynamically enforced by encapsulation. A type-safe language, for example, usually is mostly statically checked, but has dynamic checking of some casts. Static checks are better if you can get them, since they guarantee that the program won't crash in Peoria. We are slowly learning how to check more things statically.

Encapsulation takes many forms. The simplest and most familiar is the sand-boxing provided by operating system processes or Java security permissions. Much more powerful is the automatic concurrency, crash recovery, and load balancing that a transaction monitor provides for simple sequential application programs [5]. Another example is the automatic Byzantine fault-tolerance that a replicated state machine can provide for any deterministic program [4].

Conclusion

A general library of software components has been a long-standing dream, but it's unlikely to work, because there's no business model for it, it costs the client too much to understand a component, and components have conflicting world views. In spite of this discouraging conclusion, very large components do work very well, because they have lots of clients and you use only three of them.

Two other approaches can make software easier to write: declarative programming and specifications with teeth. The latter guarantee something about the behaviour of a module. The enforcement can be done statically, as with a type checker, or dynamically, as with transaction processing.

References

1. BENTLEY, J., KNUTH, D., AND MCILROY, M.D., 'A literate program,' *Comm. ACM*, vol. 29, no. 6, June 1986, pp. 471–483.
2. BROOKS, F., 'No silver bullet,' *IEEE Computer*, vol. 20, no. 4, April 1987, pp. 10–19. Reprinted in Brooks, *The mythical man-month*, 2nd ed., Addison-Wesley, 1995.
3. BUSH, W., PINCUS, J., AND SIELAFF, D., 'A static analyzer for finding dynamic programming errors,' *Software—Practice and Experience*, vol. 30, no. 7, June 2000, pp. 775–802.
4. CASTRO, M., AND LISKOV, B., 'Practical Byzantine fault tolerance and proactive recovery,' *ACM Trans. Computer Systems*, vol. 20, no. 4, October 2002, pp. 398–461.
5. GRAY, J., AND REUTER, A., Transaction processing, Morgan Kaufman, 1993.
6. KERNIGHAN, B., AND PIKE, R., *The Unix programming environment*, Prentice-Hall, 1984.
7. MCILROY, M.D., 'Mass produced software components,' in P. Naur and B. Randell, eds., *Software engineering, Report on a conference sponsored by the NATO Science Committee, Garmisch, Germany, October 1968*, Scientific Affairs Division, NATO, Brussels, 1969, pp. 138–155., available at:
   http://www.cs.dartmouth.edu/~doug/components.txt
8. PARNAS, D., 'On the criteria to be used in decomposing systems into modules,' *Comm. ACM*, vol. 15, no. 12, December 1971, pp. 1053–1058.
9. President's Information Technology Advisory Committee, *Information technology research: investing in our future*, February 1999, available at:
   http://www.hpcc.gov/pitac/report/

10. THACKER, C., 'Personal distributed computing; The Alto and Ethernet hardware,' in A. Goldberg, ed., *A history of personal workstations*, Addison-Wesley, 1988, pp. 267–290.

21
Security Protocols:
Who Knows What Exactly?

Peter Landrock

All security protocols have a number of players, typically each with distinct information available. Security protocols are very difficult to design. It is an art rather than just good craftsmanship to develop a secure yet useful and practical protocol. The potential pitfalls are plentiful but, thanks to work by Roger Needham and many others who have collaborated with him (see, e.g., [1, 2]), we have a pretty good understanding today of the challenge—at least of how not to do it!

Common to most such protocols are the following ingredients:

1. A neat mathematical trick which forms the basis of the protocol
2. The use of various keys given to various players (which in the following we will call "classified information"
3. The most treacherous part: to fit the protocol into a scenario, or a real application where it does not fall apart because of the fact that e.g. one of several principles described so well in [1, 2] were not taken into account.

In this note I will focus on the following pieces of advice taken from these references:

Principle 4: Account for all the bits: how many provide equivocation, redundancy, computational complexity, and so on. Make sure that the redundancy you need is based on mechanisms which are robust in the application context, and that any extra bits cannot be used against you in some way [2].

Principle 11: The protocol designer should know which trust relations his protocol depends on, and why the dependency is necessary. The reasons for particular trust relations should be explicit, even though they will be founded on judgment and policy rather than logic [1].

"Classified information"

I am interested in protocols using public key techniques. Given a public key pair (P, S), P is the public information, S the private. Here we are, of course, already making substantial assumptions which fundamentally are based only on trust: we assume that even though we publish P, we can keep S secret. However, it is generally agreed that this is a reasonable assumption, and in any event this is not an issue we want to pursue further in the discussion here. We will just assume that we have some means at hand of well defined magnitude, such as computational power, time, etc. We will also assume similarly that it is not possible to calculate S from P.

The first issue I would like to address is the following: does there exist some "degree" of classified information between the class of S and the class of P (i.e., all information that may be derived from P using S with the means we have at our disposal)?

Ultimately, as already pointed out, this is a question of trust, and we have to keep Principle 11 above very much in mind. For instance, do we believe there exists a "semi-private" key M such that

a.   M cannot be calculated from P,
b.   M can be calculated from S, but S cannot be calculated from M,
c.   no digital signature can be calculated from P and M,
d.   it is possible in an interactive protocol to prove possession of M to any verifier who knows P?

Note that (c) implies that M cannot merely be a signature.

Surprisingly, perhaps, the answer sometimes appears to be affirmative, even though it would be difficult, if not impossible, to support this with an extension of the complexity usually employed to justify the concept of public keys (e.g., if P = NP, the public key concept as such does not have any theoretical foundation).

Note that "secret sharing" schemes would not satisfy our assumptions. This concept was first introduced by A. Shamir: a polynomial of degree $k - 1$ with a secret number (such as a private RSA key) a as the constant term is constructed. Choose n "shares" as n random points on the defined curve, where n k. Then any k of these determines the curve and hence a may be derived from these shares.

But each individual share is useless as such, and the owner will not be able to determine if he has a genuine share, i.e., (d) above does not apply. But more to the point, unless the polynomial was to be introduced as a function of the secret key, (b) above is not satisfied either.

Others have introduced solutions where the user may verify that indeed he does have a share. But the user is unable to prove to a third party that he has a share (see [3]).

Quite some time ago, a new concept in identification protocols was introduced, namely that of zero-knowledge identification—or proof—schemes. Out of this grew a number of interesting practical protocols, such as the Fiat-Shamir scheme. This is based on one particular family of digital signature schemes, namely Rabin/RSA, but produces signatures of its own, which are weaker in a sense than signatures produced by the underlying Rabin/RSA pair. The underlying zero-knowledge scheme proves possession of the digital signatures on, say, k publicly known messages.

However, as we have carefully added condition (c) above, these schemes would not fit either.

An example

In the following, "$a \quad b$" mod k means a and b have the same residue modulo k. In [5] we introduced the concept of "computational delegation," which is an example of what we are after.

P. Fermat observed that if p is a prime, then
(1) $p \quad 1$ mod 4 iff there exist a, b with $p = a^2 + b^2$
i.e., p factors to $(a + ib)(a - ib)$ in the Gaussian ring $\mathbf{Z}[i]$ (with a unique factorization domain). This beautiful result is mentioned in T.H. Hardy's "A Mathematician's Apology" as an example of a delightful mathematical theorem.

An equivalent statement is that
(2) $p \quad 1$ mod 4 iff -1 is a square root modulo p.

Now, let $n = pq$ be an RSA modulus, where p and q are primes which both are 1 mod 4.

Let $p = a^2 + b^2$ and $q = c^2 + d^2$.

Then (also known by Fermat)
(3) $n = (a^2 + b^2)(c^2 + d^2)$, and so, expanding out:
$$n = (ac + bd)^2 + (ad - bc)^2 = (ac - bd)^2 + (ad + bc)^2$$

Thus n can be written as a sum of 2 squares in (exactly) 2 different ways.

Let
(4) $= (ac + bd)(ad - bc)^{-1}$ mod n
(5) $= (ac - bd)(ad + bc)^{-1}$ mod n

Then obviously $\quad^2 \quad^2 \quad -1$ mod n.

As may be seen from our discussion in [5],   and both satisfy (a), (b), (c), and (d) above, unless someone is able to solve the problem of Fermat primes:

Conjecture: Let s be a power 2^n of 2. Then a number of the form $2^s + 1$ is a prime iff and n 4.

That (a), (b), and (c) above are satisfied is clear. For completeness, we prove that (d) is satisfied as well.

Assumptions
Prover knows a square root   of -1 mod n.
Verifier knows Prover's public key.

Protocol (cut and choose)
Prover chooses r at random and sends r^2 mod n to Verifier.
Verifier may choose to receive either r or r mod n.
Verifier receives x and verifies that either $x^2 = r^2$ mod n or $x^2 = -r^2$ mod n.
If successful, this is repeated k times for a suitable security parameter k.

Having accomplished this, I thought of the following as one of the best ideas I've had so far in my career—for a while (and for exploitation)!

Theorem
Same notation as above, i.e. $^2 = -1$ mod n, where n is the product of 2 primes, each equal to 1 mod 4.

Let m be a random number.

Then there exist r, s with $m = r^2 + s^2$ mod n.

Proof
Choose a random and calculate b to satisfy $ab = m$ mod n.

Set $r := (a +   b)/2$, $s := (a + b)/2$.

Then $r^2 + s^2 = (a^2 - b^2 + 2   ab - a^2 + b^2 + 2   ab)/4 =   ab$ mod n.

So why does this look as a good idea? Because it suggests a new digital signature:

For m a message, let the pair (r,s) be the digital signature. All that is required to calculate it is about 2 modular exponentiations, and verification is equally easy.

This of course would be nothing short of a sensation—so how does one break it? Find a number x such that $y = x^2 m$ mod n is a prime which is 1 mod 4. This is relatively easy using say the Rabin primality test.

Use Cornacchia's algorithm to find a, b with $y = a^2 + b^2$

Then $m = (x^{-1}a)^2 + (x^{-1}b)^2$ mod n, and we have broken the scheme. In fact in doing so, we generalised our theorem. You do not even need the assumption that n be the product of two primes equivalent to 1 mod 4 to write m as a sum of two squares modulo n!

So I did not manage to introduce a new signature scheme, but I believe I managed to introduce a security protocol which satisfies all principles of [2] as well as [1] including Principle 11 of [1], which was my focus.

How to blackmail a Certification Authority

I end our discussion with a protocol which does not really fit into any traditional scheme. Indeed, this is a protocol where the verifier pretends to know more than he really does! How can he pull this off? It is all explained in Principle 4 of [2]. Here is the scenario:

- A well-known Certification Authority, CA, announces a nation-wide PKI scheme based on RSA, 1024 bits, public exponent 3.
- Message received week 1 at CA from unknown source: "I know your private key! I am going to publish the 1st upper byte of your secret exponent, unless you send me 2 €!"
- CA ignores.
- Message received week 2 by CA: "Here is the 1st byte 11011010. I am going to publish the 2nd upper byte of your private key, unless you send me 4 €!"
- CA is puzzled. The blackmailer is right about the first byte! Could he be guessing, or maybe the first byte is not so difficult?
- Message received week 3 by CA: "Here is the 2nd byte 00011001. I am going to publish the 3rd upper byte of your secret key, unless you send me 8 €!"
- The CA hires a security specialist. The problem is that it will cost 100,000 € to switch to a different key pair!
- This continues.
- Message received week 52 by CA: "Here is the 51st byte 01111101. I am going to publish the 52nd upper byte of your secret key, unless you send me 2^{52} €!"
- Conclusion of the specialist: offer him 25,000 € now!

Did the "unknown source" break RSA?

Well, 1024 bits is 128 bytes. He can only do what he does up to the first 64 bytes. Here is how he does it:

1. Subtract 1 from the modulus n.
2. Divide by 3 and multiply by 2.
3. The upper half of this number is the upper half of your private exponent.

CA: What about the lower half? Only the CA knows! The system is secure. It is all mathematics.

The point is that the secret exponent d is calculated to satisfy
(6) $3d - x(p - 1)(q - 1) = 1$ for x a natural number.

But as $d < n$, this implies that x 2! And, as the public exponent is 3, $p - 1$ and $q - 1$ are prime to 3, i.e., p and q cannot be 1 mod 3. Hence they must be 2 modulo 3, and reading (6) modulo 3, it follows that x is congruent to 2. Hence:
(7) $d = (1 + 2(p - 1)(q - 1))/3$

Now, even though we do not know $(p - 1)(q - 1) = pq - p - q - 1$, we know the upper half basically, as p and q are always chosen to be of about the same size. Indeed, this is just the upper half of pq, the public key! Obviously the CA should have thought of Principle 4 of [4]!

This has been observed independently by Mike Wiener [6].

References

1. ABADI, M., AND NEEDHAM, R.M., 'Prudent engineering practice for cryptographic protocols,' DEC SRC Research Report 125, June 1994.
2. ANDERSON, R., AND NEEDHAM, R.M., 'Robustness principles for public key protocols,' *Advances in Cryptology—Crypto 95*, Springer, LNCS, vol. 963, 1995, pp. 236–247.
3. BELLARE, M., AND GOLDWASSER, S., 'Verifiable partial key escrow,' *Proc. 4th ACM Conf. On Computer & Communications Security*, 1997, pp. 78–91.
4. BURROWS, M., ABADI, M., NEEDHAM, R.M., 'A logic of authentication,' in *Proceedings of the Royal Society of London*, series A, vol. 426, 1989, pp. 233–271; earlier version published as DEC SRC Research Report 39.
5. LANDROCK, P., 'A new concept in protocols: verifiable computational delegation,' *Security Protocols*, Springer, LNCS, vol. 1550, 1998, pp. 137–145.
6. WIENER, M., private communication.

22
Volume Rendering by Ray-Casting in Shear-Image Order

Hugh C. Lauer, Yin Wu, Vishal Bhatia, Larry Seiler

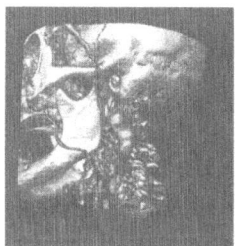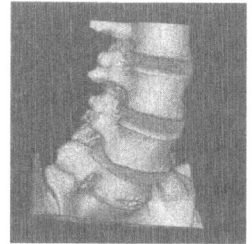

Figure 1: Shear-image gallery—various volumes with lighting effects or embedded geometry

Roger and I arrived at Xerox Palo Alto Research Center on the same day in May 1977 and immediately jumped into issues of operating system design for desktop computers. A debate was raging in the field at that time over whether it was better to design an operating system around a small, relatively static set of heavyweight processes with explicit message passing or a large number of rapidly changing, lightweight processes (nowadays called *threads*) and a synchronization mechanism based on shared data. We quickly realized that the two approaches are duals of each other in design and performance and that the choice depends mostly upon the underlying mechanisms available for the implementation. We published this "duality hypothesis" in [1], which eventually settled the issue.

For the past seven years or so, I have been involved in real-time volume imaging, a field that combines the challenges of system design, high-performance semiconductor design, and computer graphics. I hoped Roger would enjoy reading about this.

Introduction

Real-time volume rendering is a technique for creating interactive images of objects and phenomena represented as sampled data in three or more dimensions. It is becoming increasingly important in medical imaging, oil and gas exploration, and scientific visualization, and it has potential applications in industrial inspection, non-destructive testing, airline security, and any area where it is important to see the internal or hidden structures of the objects under study. While volume rendering algorithms have been known for years, there are three principal challenges to achieving useful, interactive visualization: amassing enough computational power to render images at multiple frames per second; moving huge amounts of data from memory to the processing power; and providing high-quality, visually meaningful images.

This paper describes *shear-image order*, a method of ray casting that preserves the data handling efficiency of *shear-warp*, the fastest known volume rendering algorithm, but that eliminates its intermediate image and final warp step. Shear-image order produces high-quality images by casting rays through the centers of pixels of the image plane. It is computationally efficient, requiring four interpolations per sample vs. seven interpolations per sample for full-image order. Shear-image order supports the accurate embedding of polygon and other objects, and it enables direct rendering of anisotropic and sheared data sets without the need for resampling. The shear-image-order method is implemented in VolumePro™ 1000, a second-generation real-time volume rendering engine developed by the author and colleagues at Mitsubishi Electric Research Laboratories in Cambridge, Massachusetts. This paper is an abbreviated version of [4], which describes shear-image order in more detail.

Background

Shear-warp order

One of the fastest classic algorithms for volume rendering is *shear-warp* [2]. In shear-warp, the 3D viewing matrix is factored into "a 3D shear parallel to slices of the volume data, a projection to form a distorted intermediate image, and a 2D warp to produce the final image." Shear-warp has the advantage of retrieving volume data from memory in a coherent manner, thereby maximizing the utilization of memory bandwidth. It has the disadvantages of requiring a 2D warp step and difficulty in accurately embedding polygons and images of other objects.

Figure 2 illustrates the shear-warp factorization. Voxel positions are shown as dots at the intersections of the grid. In shear-warp, the volume data is resampled into slices parallel to one of the faces of the volume. Within each slice, the sample points are arranged in a rectangular grid with axes parallel to the axes of the volume. Each sample point denotes where a ray intersects its slice.

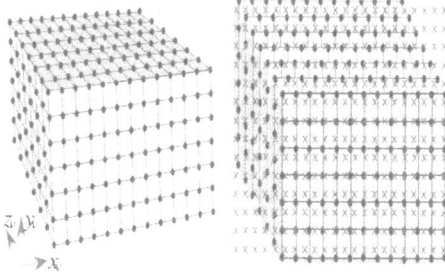

Figure 2: Volume data set (left) and shear-warp slices

This is equivalent to shearing the stack of slices with respect to each other, as shown in the right side of Figure 2. The × characters denote both sample points on each of the slices and also the pixels on a *base plane*, i.e., an intermediate image plane that is co-planar with a face of the volume. The value of each pixel is formed from the projection of the corresponding sample points of all slices.

The resulting image on the base plane is distorted and must be resampled in two dimensions to produce the final image of the volume. This resampling is called the *warp* step. It is possible to achieve high image quality using shear-warp. However, doing so requires over-sampling the volume data set and high-precision calculation to reduce error propagation. These requirements impact performance.

Because of the alignment of the grid of sample points with the grid of voxels, linear interpolation operations can be shared between adjacent points in each dimension. Tri-linear interpolation therefore requires only three multiplication operations rather than the usual seven. However, the alignment of rays with pixels on the base plane rather than the image plane makes it impractical to embed objects generated with traditional polygon graphics.

Full image order

Another class of ray-casting methods is called *full-image order*. In full-image order, rays are cast directly through the centers of pixels of the image plane and thus are not necessarily aligned with the grid of voxels in any dimension (left side of Figure 3). In addition, samples are organized into slices parallel to the image plane (Figure 3 right side). These methods eliminate the need for the warp step of shear-warp, and they can produce high-quality images without over-sampling the volume. However, the cost is increased complexity in data handling and buffering and the loss of coherent memory access.

Interpolations in full- image order cannot, in general, be shared between adjacent samples, so seven multiplication operations are needed for tri-linear interpolation: four in the first interpolation dimension, two in the second dimension,

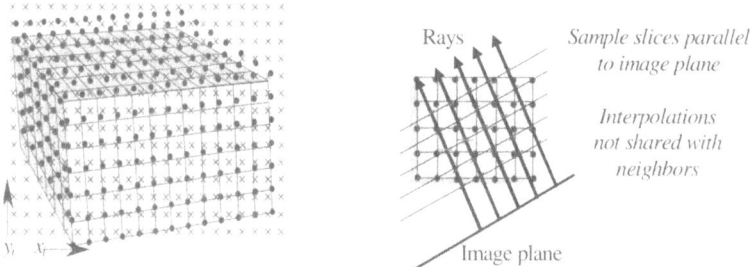

Rays   *Sample slices parallel to image plane*

Interpolations not shared with neighbors

Image plane

Figure 3: Full Image Order

and one in the third dimension. As a result, full-image-order methods are not yet competitive in performance with shear-warp methods. The shear-image method will have the same screen view as full-image order to achieve high image quality efficiently.

Image quality

In volume rendering, images of interior structures are generated by assigning different opacities to different types of tissue or materials. The interfaces between different opacity levels create the appearance of surfaces and 3D shapes. In our experience, the two most important factors in achieving high-quality, visually meaningful images are the *ability to cast rays through the centers of the pixels* of the image plane and *a good illumination function*. Ray-per-pixel rendering avoids the artifacts and degradation that result from repeated resampling. Illumination appeals to the fundamental capability of the human eye to recognize three-dimensional shapes from the way their surfaces are lighted. Figure 4 is a dramatic illustration of this. The illumination of the blood vessels of the brain highlights their positions and relationships in a way that no flat or unilluminated image can.

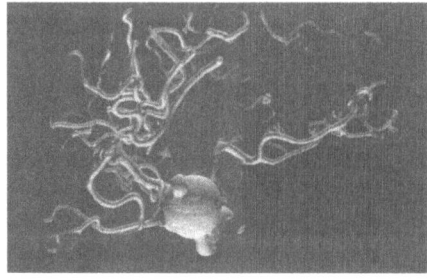

Figure 4: Image of a cerebral aneurysm

Traditional Phong illumination requires a surface normal at each sample point. In volume rendering, these surface normals are estimated from the gradients derived from voxel data. In shear-warp, gradients are easy to calculate on the fly because the volume data is read and buffered in a coherent way [3]. A convolution kernel can be applied to adjacent slices to derive the rates of change of voxel values in each of the three dimensions. These rates of change then form gradients that can be interpolated to estimate the surface normal vectors at sample points. VolumePro uses central differences, the simplest of gradient-estimation convolution kernels.

Shear-image order

Shear-image order preserves the shear-warp organization of sample points in slices parallel to the slices of the volume but casts rays directly through the centers of pixels of the image plane, as in full-image order. It thereby eliminates the intermediate image and 2D warp step of shear-warp. It is similar to 2D texture methods but substantially more efficient. Shear-image order decomposes the 3D viewing transformation into two parts: a transformation from *voxel space* to an intermediate *sample space* that defines the positions of each sample point, and a *depth warp* to characterize the distance from each sample point to the image plane. This decomposition has four beneficial features: (1) sample space is spatially coherent with the image plane and with slices of the original volume; (2) each sample of sample space is projected directly onto a pixel of the image plane, requiring no additional resampling; (3) the depth warp enables the embedding of polygons; and (4) flexible control is retained over super-sampling factors, allowing equal sample spacing in three dimensions for any view angle.

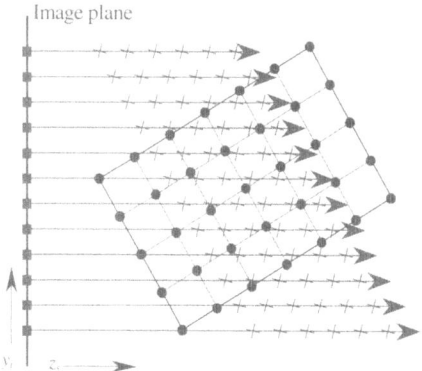

Figure 5: Side view of shear-image order ray casting

This is illustrated in Figure 5, which depicts a cross section of a volume and an image plane—for example, a vertical slice perpendicular to the page through the left figure of Figure 3. The voxels are arranged in a rectilinear array and represented by dots; voxel spacing is exaggerated for clarity. At the left of Figure 5 is an edge view of the image plane, with the pixels represented as squares. Parallel rays are cast through the centers of the pixels toward the volume, as indicated by the arrows. Sample points are represented by × characters. It can be seen that the sample points are organized into slices parallel to slices of the volume itself. Each pixel is the composition of the sample points defined by where its ray intersects each slice. As in Figure 3, the projection of the grid of voxels bears no relationship to the grid of pixels on the image plane.

Shear-image order has the same memory coherence as shear-warp. That is, voxels can be read from memory in an order related to their storage. This makes it possible to exploit the burst mode capabilities of modern synchronous-dynamic-random-access memory. The fundamental difference between shear-warp and shear-image order is that shear-image-order rendering allows rotation and shear of the sampling plane onto which rays are projected.

The shear-image algorithm operates in two parts. The first part steps through volume memory one slice of voxels at a time, like shear-warp. Gradients are estimated at each voxel point by determining the spatial rate of change of the voxel values. Then the voxel values and their associated gradients from two adjacent slices are interpolated to derive a "virtual" slice of what we call *z-interpolated samples*. This virtual slice, a sampled representation of a cross section of the volume, is parallel to slices of voxels but not necessarily aligned with any particular voxel slice, and it includes a gradient at each point. The sample points within these *z*-interpolated slices are organized in grids parallel to the *x*- and *y*-dimensions of the volume, as in shear-warp.

The second part of the algorithm steps through each slice of *z*-interpolated samples in the *x*- and *y*-dimensions *of the image plane*. Sample points are located at the intersections of rays with the virtual slice. Color and opacity values are assigned to the sample points and accumulated along their respective rays, thereby producing an image of the volume directly on the image plane. In addition, a *depth value* is associated with each sample point to measure the distance from the eye, image plane, or some other reference. These depth values correspond to the *z*-values of traditional polygon graphics and make it possible to embed polygons in the rendered image.

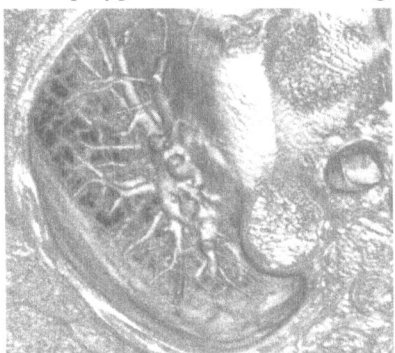 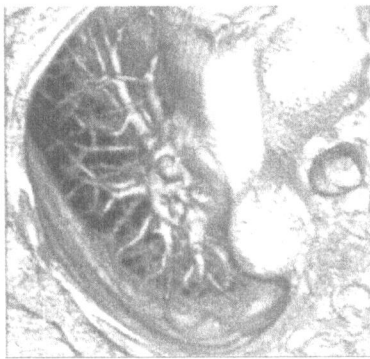

Figure 6: Comparison of shear-warp (left, rendered by VolumePro 500) and shear-image order (right, rendered by VolumePro 1000)

Figure 6 shows a comparison of shear-warp and shear-image order. Both images were rendered from the same data set and view, at the same scale, and with the same lighting, transfer function, and other parameters. It can be seen that shear-image order produces a higher-resolution image.

Anisotropic data sets—in which voxels are spaced differently in each dimension—are the rule rather than the exception in medical and geophysical imaging. In computed tomography (CT scans), for example, the spacing of slices in the longitudinal axis of the patient is determined by the speed of the table, whereas the spacing within a slice is determined by the geometry of the scanner. Also common are sheared data sets in which the axes are not at right angles to each other. For example, the gantry of a CT scanner may be tilted with respect to the axis of the patient. Most of the images in this paper are rendered from anisotropic data.

The mathematics of shear-image order automatically compensates for anisotropy and shear. In these cases, the shear image algorithm steps by different increments in each of the three dimensions. The net effect is to keep the ray spacing and sample spacing constant with respect to the image plane, regardless of the view direction and the spacing of voxels in that direction.

Embedding polygons

Volume visualization applications often need to render volume and polygon data together. For example, a surgical planning application might create a model of prosthesis in a CAD environment, render it using conventional polygon graphics, and then embed that device into a volume-rendered image of the patient's body. Figure 7 illustrates an example of a simple polygon object passing through the cranial cavity of a human head as rendered from a CT scan of a living person. It can be seen that the object lies in front of some parts of the volume (e.g., blood vessels and bone) and behind other parts.

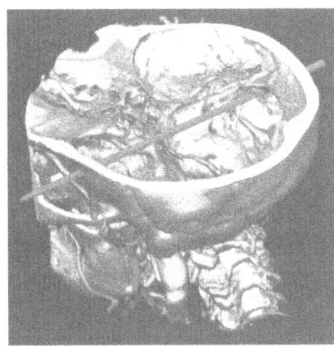

Figure 7: A polygon object embedded in a volume

Various techniques have been used in the past to combine volume and polygon data into the same image. In methods where volumes are converted to polygons, it is a simple matter to sort all of the polygons and render them using a conventional 3D-graphics engine. Another technique is to *voxelize* the polygon objects, that is, to convert them to voxels, then write them into the volume data set.

Shear-image order makes it easy to use fast commodity-graphics engines to render polygons and embed them into volumes. The polygons are rendered in the graphics environment using the same Model, View, Projection, and Viewport transformations as the volume itself. When all of the polygons have been rendered, the depth and color buffers are captured and are used in the following process:

- In the first pass, rays are initialized to the foreground color and then are cast through the volume starting at the foreground and ending at the captured depth buffer. This renders the portion of the volume in front of the polygons.

- The previously captured color buffer is then blended behind the image plane resulting from the first pass, placing the image of the polygons in the volume.
- In the second pass, rays are initialized with the result of the blend operation and then cast from the captured depth buffer to the background. This creates the image of the part of the volume behind the polygons.
- The result is a correctly located image of the polygonal objects embedded within the volume. If the polygons are opaque, only the first render is necessary.

Using two depth buffers, the process can be generalized to arbitrary translucent geometry and images of other objects, if they can be expressed as an ordered sequence of layers. By carefully managing the depth and color buffers, each polygon object can be inserted pixel-by-pixel between the samples along the rays. Obviously, the process must be repeated for each change in view direction, model transformation, and other parameter. The method can also be extended to embed images of non-polygon objects. More details are explained in [4].

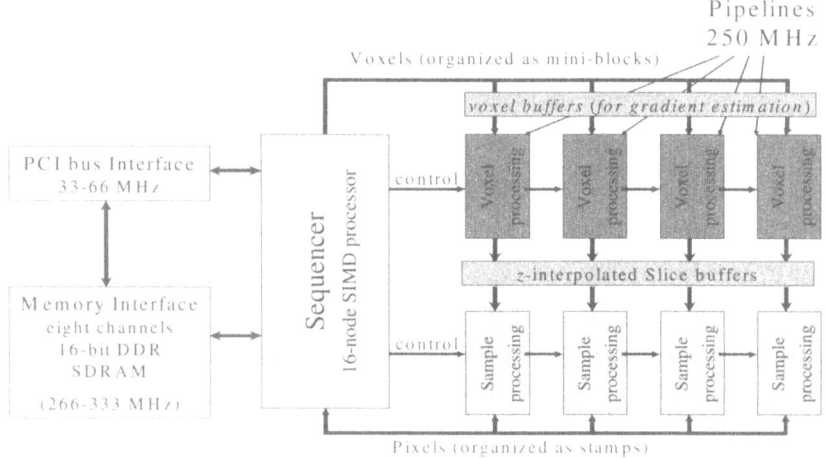

Figure 8: Block diagram of VolumePro 1000

Implementation

VolumePro 1000 implements the shear-image-order method and is a second-generation volume-rendering system developed as a successor to the VolumePro 500. It comprises an ASIC (Application-Specific Integrated Circuit) and up to 2 gigabytes of high-performance memory on a board to be plugged into the PCI bus of a personal computer, and a library of supporting software.

A simplified block diagram of the VolumePro 1000 ASIC is shown in Figure 8. It includes a sequencer, four processing pipelines, a memory controller, a PCI bus interface, and on-chip buffers for voxels and z-interpolated samples. The sequencer and processing pipelines operate at 250 MHz, so the ASIC can render 10^9 samples per second. Memory is organized so that 3D objects are stored as mini-blocks of $2 \times 2 \times 2$ voxel values, and 2D objects are stored as 2×2 stamps of pixel values. This allows sequences of related data values to be read or written in burst mode. The memory subsystem itself comprises eight channels of 16-bit Double Data Rate SDRAM operating at a data transfer rate of 266–333 MHz. Eight 16-bit voxels or four 32-bit pixels can be fetched or written per memory cycle.

Each pipeline is partitioned into two parts, decoupled by a set of buffers. Voxels are read two slices at a time into the voxel buffers at the top of the figure. The *voxel processing* part estimates gradient from the data in the buffers and, optionally, maps voxel values to color and opacity (RGB) values. Then adjacent slices of voxels and gradients are interpolated in the dimension most nearly parallel to the rays and are stored in the z-interpolated slice buffers between the two pipeline parts. The *sample processing* part of each pipeline reads from the z-interpolated slice buffer in an order unrelated to voxel order, interpolates in the remaining two dimensions to obtain sample values and gradients, maps the resulting values to RGB (if this was not already done by the voxel-processing part), then does illumination and filtering before compositing the samples into a frame buffer to form the final image.

Voxels may have up to four fields, programmable by the application as to size, position, and format. Each field is associated with its own lookup table for mapping field values to color and opacity values. These can be combined by a hierarchy of arithmetic-logic units as described in [3]. The interpolator is linear in the z-dimension and bi-linear in the x- and y-dimensions, thereby requiring four multiplications per sample. There are seven interpolation channels, one for each voxel field or color-opacity component plus one for each gradient component.

Illumination is done in the sample processing part of each pipeline and is a reflectance-map implementation of the Phong lighting model. This pro-

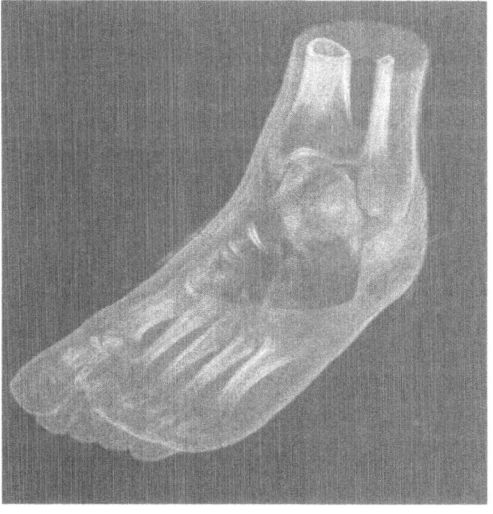

Figure 9: A CT Scan of a foot, with bone surfaces highlighted by gradient-magnitude modulation

vides emissive, diffuse, and specular lighting from an arbitrary number of light sources. It also provides a modulation function based on the magnitude of the gradient. This makes it possible to highlight surfaces in a translucent manner so that both the surface and the interior structure of the object can be seen. An example is shown in Figure 9.

VolumePro 1000 tries very hard to skip over invisible samples. The sequencer keeps track of samples that are cut, cropped, clipped, or that fail depth tests, and it jumps over them when it is useful to do so. This kind of space leaping is called *geometry-based* space leaping because it depends only upon the position of a sample, not its value. A second kind of space leaping—*content-based* space leaping that jumps over samples that are invisible by virtue of opacity assignment or filtering—is not provided in VolumePro 1000.

One of the most important factors in the design of the ASIC was the amount of buffer memory needed on the chip. The shear-warp algorithm and shear-image order both require one or more full slices of voxel values to be buffered in on-chip memory. This is far more than could be accommodate by modern semiconductor processes. VolumePro addresses this issue by partitioning the volume to be rendered into *sections* and rendering one section at a time. The amount of on-chip memory is thus limited to that needed for the number of voxels and/or samples per section, but at the cost of re-reading voxels near the boundaries of sections more than once.

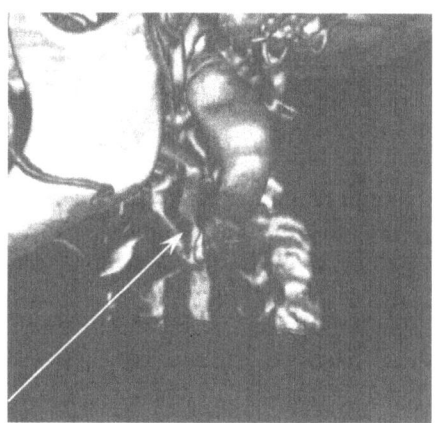

Figure 10: CT Scan showing bones and blood vessels of the head

The final example image, Figure 10, shows a zoomed view of the CT scan of the human head from the left of Figure 1. The arrow, superimposed on the figure by the author, clearly shows a blockage of the left medial carotid artery.

Acknowledgements

This work began at Mitsubishi Electric Research Laboratories (MERL) of Cambridge and Concord, Massachusetts. The author collaborated with Yin Wu, Vishal Bhatia, and Larry Seiler in the development of the algorithm and the VolumePro 1000 architecture. The ASIC implementation was done by Andy Adams, Bill Booth, Steve Burgess, Kenneth Correll, James Knittel, Jeff Lussier, Bill Peet, and Jay Wilkinson. Thanks are also due to Jan "Yon" Hardenbergh, Lisa S. Avila, James Foley, Sarah Frisken (Gibson), Hanspeter Pfister, Vikram

Simha, Andy Vesper, and T. C. Zhao for their insight into the issues of real-time volume rendering.

References

1. LAUER, H.C., AND NEEDHAM, R.M., 'On the duality of operating system structures,' in *Proceedings of Second International Symp. on Operating Systems,* IRIA, France, October 1978, reprinted in *Operating Systems Review,* vol. 13, no. 2, April 1979, pp. 3–19.
2. LACROUTE, P., AND LEVOY, M., 'Fast volume rendering using a shear-warp factorization of the viewing transformation,' *Proceedings of SIGGRAPH 94,* Orlando, Florida, ACM Press, July 1994, pp. 409–412.
3. PFISTER, H., HARDENBERGH, J., KNITTEL, J., LAUER, H.C., AND SEILER, L., 'The VolumePro real-time ray-casting system.' *Proceedings of SIGGRAPH 99,* Los Angeles, California, ACM Press, August 1999, pp. 251–260.
4. WU, Y., BHATIA, V., LAUER, H., SEILER, L., 'Shear-image ray casting volume rendering,' *Proc. ACM SIGGraph 2003 Symposium on Interactive 3D Graphics,* Monterey, California, ACM Press, April 2003, pp. 152–162.

23
A Conceptual Authorization Model for Web Services

Paul J. Leach, Blair Dillaway, Praerit Garg, Chris Kaler,
Brian LaMacchia, Butler Lampson, John Manferdelli,
Rick Rashid, John Shewchuk, Dan Simon, Richard Ward

This paper describes a conceptual authorization model for web services. It is an adaptation of those of Taos [2] and SDSI [3] with terms changed to correspond more closely to those introduced with the WS-Security model [1]. In contrast to the more formal and mathematical presentation used for Taos and SDSI, this presentation is conceptual and informal, which hopefully may provide more intuition for some readers; it also might provide an outline for the class hierarchy of an object-oriented implementation.

In addition, this model abstracts away from issues of distribution and network security such as authentication [4] and encryption (for example, by assuming that messages include the unforgeable identity of the sender and are private and tamperproof) so as to focus on authorization, but it does deal with the extensibility and composability of security services, and partial trust. It also abstracts away from issues of syntax and encoding (for example, ASN.1, proprietary binary formats, and XML) and focuses on semantics.

Figure 1 illustrates many of the elements of this model that will be described in this paper.

Basic computational model

Computations are done by running *programs* in *processes,* which contain one or more parallel *threads* of execution. Processes have separate address spaces and are isolated from unwanted interactions with other processes. A program may use an interprocess communication facility to send *requests* to other programs; or to receive requests from other programs, process them, and return results in a *response*. A program sending requests is called a *client*; one receiving them is called a *service*; a program may be both a client and a service.

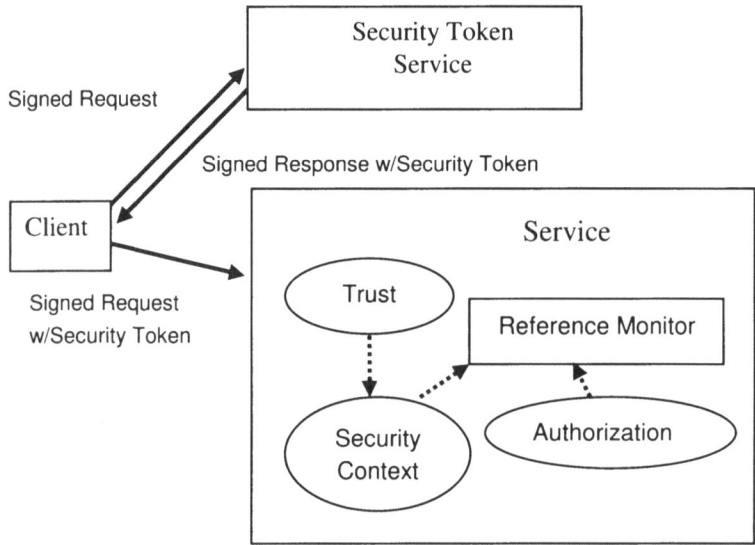

Figure 1: Elements of an authorization model.

There are many providers of services, not just the system. In particular, many security services are provided by non-system entities, and they may be not fully trusted.

We use an object oriented model: clients use requests to ask services to perform some *operation* on an *object* that the service implements.[1] Services in turn invoke other services to perform the requested operation. Ultimately, they invoke *drivers* to write pixels to the screen, bits to the disks, packets to the network, etc.

Basic security model

Computations run on behalf of *principals*; principals may be users or services (and other kinds, to be defined below, but these two are the basic ones). A system service can start an initial process and program on behalf of a user after verifying the user's identity and his permission to use the system.

---

1   Another frequently used term for object is *resource*. In this context, they mean the same thing. A service may implement only a single object, or it may implement many. If many, they may all be of the same kind, or they may be of different kinds.

Requests can be in many forms; typical examples are messages sent over a network or interprocess communication mechanism, or application program interfaces (APIs) that call into the operating system.[2]

Services are responsible for securing themselves; i.e., making sure that only authorized principals will have their requests executed. When a service receives a request, it forms the *security context* for that request, uses its *trust policy* to validate all the information in the security context, and then uses the information to evaluate its *authorization policy* to decide if the request should be honored.[3] The next few sections expand on this process.

Model components

A *statement* is a collection of data created by a principal; statements can contain other statements. A *claim* is a statement consisting of security-relevant information about a principal; a *security token* is statement containing one or more claims. An important type of claim is the *attribute-value (AV) claim*, stating that a principal has certain attributes; such a claim might be that a user has a certain identity, is a member of a specific group, or has a certain credit limit. A security token might be a list of group memberships for a user.

A *signed statement* is a statement for which an AV claim attesting to the identity of the principal making the statement can be requested from the system; they are particularly interesting when the statement is a security token. The system guarantees that signed statements are tamperproof and the principal's identity is unforgeable.[4]

Requests and responses are statements, and they too may be signed.[5] Whenever necessary, the system can guarantee that signed requests and responses are private; i.e., the contents are not accessible to any process except the intended recipient.

A security context is a collection of claims related to a particular request. It can be initialized with the AV claim identifying the sender of a signed request, or by a security token. Security tokens may be received in requests, or returned in responses to requests made to other services; a service whose primary purpose is to do the latter is called a *security-token service* (STS). Multiple security con-

---

2   The request identifies the operation and the object on which it is to be performed (if it's not implicit) and contains any other data needed to perform the operation.

3   The analogy is to the standard model of interpretation: the policy contains free variables that are bound with reference to the context.

4   To simplify exposition, we have simply posited that the system can do this, but it should be noted that in Taos both identity and authorization are verified in a uniform way using (its analog to) claims and the trust validation we outline in this paper. That is, user identity is just an AV claim.

5   We allow unsigned requests for cases where anonymity is allowed or desired.

texts may be merged to form a new security context just by taking the union of all their claims.

Trust model

The claims in the security context are validated against the service's *trust policy*. The trust policy for a service defines which of a security token service's claims will be used when evaluating its authorization policy; the service will trust a claim if it deems the service (often an STS) that made the claim authoritative for that claim. Any given STS may (and usually will) be considered by any given service to be authoritative for only a subset of all principals, and, for any principal, for only a subset of the possible kinds of AV claims that can apply to that principal; we call this its *authorization scope* with respect to that service. For example, the human resources service for a division of a corporation may be authoritative for AV claims about salaries of division employees, while the division IT department's group membership service is authoritative for AV claims about its group memberships.

There is a kind of claim, which we call a *trust claim*, which defines an authorization scope for a particular STS. The trust policy for a service is a collection of such claims. In addition, authorization scope claims can be in the security context and will be trusted if they were made by an STS that is trusted (i.e., authoritative for them). Note that trust claims are themselves a kind of AV claim: they specify a set of claims for which a service is authoritative and is therefore trusted to make.

Trust policy, in the form of a security token containing trust claims, can be an argument to a request, and is also validated against the service's trust policy. Trust claims that pass validation may be added to the service's trust policy. Trust policies can be combined to create a new trust policy just by taking the union of all their claims.

More complex principals

Principals can be organized into *groups*: a group is a set of users or groups. A group is a kind of principal: a group member is authorized to do anything that the group is authorized to do.

Principals can also be organized into *roles*. A role is a kind of principal: a role member is authorized to do anything the role is authorized to do. A role differs from a group in that its membership is tied to an object type and a scope—see the next section.

A principal may be formed from a set of other principals, making an *access token*:[6] a token is authorized to do anything that any principal in the token is authorized to do. Tokens can also be *restricted* by specifying a second set of principals; a restricted token is authorized to do anything that both sets of principals are allowed to do. These constructs allow taking the "or" and "and" of principals (respectively).

Authorization policy

A service may associate with each operation of the service a *permission* that authorizes the operation;[7] the operation is said to *require* the permission.[8] Associated with each object in a service is its *authorization policy*.[9] An authorization claim for an object specifies a set of principals, and the permission(s) *granted* to that set.[10] The set of principals can be specified by a Boolean expression which evaluates to true for all members of the set, where the free variables in the expression are bound to the values of attributes in AV claims in the security context. The authorization policy for an object is a set of such claims.

Objects in a service can be organized into *scopes*: all objects of the same type in the same scope have the same assignment of principals to roles.[11] Assigning scopes simplifies authorization management by removing the need to manage authorization policy for each object.

One kind of authorization policy is *role-based*: all objects in the service of the same type have the same authorization policy, and the only principals in the authorization policy are roles. With role-based authorization, the authorization policy is fixed by the implementation of the service, which "hard codes" the assignment of permissions to roles; authorization is managed by changing the assignment of principals to roles and objects to scopes.

Authorization policy, in the form of a security token containing authorization claims, can be an argument to a request, and also is validated against the service's trust policy. Authorization claims that pass validation may be added to the service's authorization policy. Authorization policies can be combined to create a new authorization policy just by taking the union of all their claims.

---

6   Often referred to simply as a "token" when the context is clear.

7   More than one operation may be associated with a given permission.

8   It is possible, but not encouraged, for an operation to require more than one permission.

9   More than one object may be associated with a given authorization policy.

10 Note that the set of principals with a given permission essentially defines a group.

11 For purposes of this paper, it suffices to define objects as having the same type when they implement the same operations.

Authorization verification

To secure itself, a service utilizes a *reference monitor*: for each request, it asks the reference monitor to decide whether it should grant the request. The reference monitor bases its decision on the security context for the request, the operation requested, the service's trust policy, and the service's authorization policy. (For example, a basic kind of authorization policy could simply specify which principals can perform what operations on its objects; one way to express this is with access-control lists on the objects.) Essentially, the trust policy is used to create a *trusted security context* that has only trusted claims. Then the authorization policy is treated like a program to be executed, with the free variables in it assigned values from the trusted security context. If the reference monitor OKs the request, then the service executes the operation, using its own identity to make the requests on any other services or drivers needed to do so.

The model above leads to the following flow for verifying that the authorization policy is satisfied when a service processes a request:

```
Get the operation specified in the request.
Combine all the security tokens to create the security context.
Create the trusted security context by using the trust policy to
remove untrusted claims.
Get authorization policy:
    If only one policy for the service, just return it; else:
        determine the object being referenced by the request;
        determine the object's scope;
        determine the object's type;
        get authorization policy for that type in that scope.
Determine if the requesting principal is given the required per-
missions by the authorization policy:
    If the principal is an access token, take the union of the
    permissions associated with each principal in the access to-
    ken.
    If the principal is a restricted token, take the intersec-
    tion of the permissions associated with each principal in
    the restricted token.
If the permissions do not include the one required for the re-
quested operation, return an access-denied error, else return
OK.
```

Note that if a service does not have need for flexible configuration of authorization policy and wants the ultimate in efficiency, then it can associate a role with each operation, and have the implementation of each operation simply check whether the requesting principal is that role (or an access token that contains that role).

Conclusions

We have briefly described a conceptual model for authorizing web services. If one contrasts it with "more traditional" models, the more interesting differences include:

- authorization based not just on user identity and group memberships but also on attributes of users,
- support for partial trust on attributes as well as user identity and group memberships,
- trust and authorization policy that can be arguments to requests from untrusted clients, as long as they originate with parties trusted to set such policy.

Finally, this model isn't really tied to web services—it could be used in other distributed-systems contexts that need the features that differentiate it from the more traditional model, just as web services need them.

Acknowledgements

We would like to acknowledge the support given to the work that led to this paper by Dave Aucsmith, Doug Bayer, Peter Biddle, Blair Dillaway, Mike Nash, David Treadwell, and Robert Wahbe.

References

1. IBM, MICROSOFT, 'Security in a web services world: a proposed architecture and roadmap, 2002,' available at:
    http://msdn.microsoft.com/library/en-us/dnwssecur/html/securitywhitepaper.asp
2. LAMPSON, B., ABADI, M., BURROWS, M., AND WOBBER, E., 'Authentication in distributed systems: theory and practice,' *ACM Trans. Computer Systems,* vol. 10, no. 4, November 1992, pp. 265–310.
3. LAMPSON, B., AND RIVEST, R., 'SDSI—a simple distributed security infrastructure, 1996,' available at: http://theory.lcs.mit.edu/~cis/sdsi.html
4. NEEDHAM, R., AND SCHROEDER, M., 'Using encryption for authentication in large networks of computers,' *Comm. ACM,* vol. 21, no. 12, December 1978, pp. 993–999.

24
The Trouble with Standards

E. Stewart Lee

Standards, as they used to be used, are great. Railways usually run on tracks of the same gauge. Railway cars can easily hitch together regardless of which company owns the car. One can tell the value and tolerance of a resistor independently of who manufactures it. The colour coding that contains this information is universally used and became a standard. Electrical apparatus can be plugged into a socket with little worry about the voltage or the frequency of the supply, at least within a single country. All these examples and many more allow the products of different manufacturers to interoperate with the consumer having little to worry about.

This is because these standards evolved over many years and represent a useful compromise between effectiveness, usefulness, and economy. Some manufacturers took a bath, but the consumer barely noticed.

An interesting example of great expense being incurred by a manufacturer concerns the frequency of electrical power generation. The original AC power generated at Niagara Falls was at 25 hertz; in the late 1950s Ontario Hydro had to spend some $2 billion (circa 1958 currency) to convert the power to 60 hertz, including the replacement of all household devices that were frequency sensitive.[1] This benefited the consumer and ultimately the power generator.

However, the information-technology industry has gone a different route. In IT, what happens all too often is that a consortium of manufacturers agrees to prescribe a so-called standard before anybody has built any component. It has been stated that this is being done to allow interoperability. A cynic, however, can often support the thesis that such consortia are a plan to dominate a given market before a product is offered for sale and often before it is even conceived as a design. Manufacturers want to build to a standard in order to protect their investment. Rarely does a manufacturer produce something that he considers a cutting edge product without joining a consortium to spread the risk.

---

1 DC had been generated for some years before the switch to AC, which was done to facilitate power transmission.

Fortunately for the consumer, market forces often intervene. Thus, the consortium that specified Bluetooth delayed in finalizing their standard, and several competing systems came to exist; some of them are in many respects as effective as Bluetooth. Various efforts to protect the intellectual property of recorded or broadcast information have been proposed, but as far as I know, either they are not very effective or they require the consumer to invest in expensive equipment that has only one purpose, the protection of the intellectual property of the owner of the information that the consumer wishes to access. Surely, the IP owner should pay for his own IP protection.

These consortia often resemble a cartel[2] in that they restrict the use of their standard to those organisations that contributed to it. Newcomers are often expected to pay a substantial usage fee. For this to work, the standard must be certified and protected by an influential body that is prepared to fight against its adoption by organisations that did not contribute to it. Regrettably, some standards bodies cooperate with such consortia.

Some, however, deal primarily with national standards organisations. The International Organization for Standardization is such a body.[3] It has no fewer than 225 technical committees that deal with areas as diverse as information technology; tyres, rims, and valves; gas cylinders; and nuclear energy. The IT Technical Committee covers 1696 standards directly related to IT, of which 565 are under the direct responsibility of the ISO. There are 18 subcommittees covering the field.

The ISO defines standards thus:

> Standards are documented agreements containing technical specifications or other precise criteria to be used consistently as rules, guidelines, or definitions of characteristics, to ensure that materials, products, processes and services are fit for their purpose.

> For example, the format of the credit cards, phone cards, and 'smart' cards that have become commonplace is derived from an ISO International Standard. Adhering to the standard, which defines such features as an optimal thickness (0,76 mm), means that the cards can be used worldwide.

This quote is not consistent with many of the so-called industry standards that are continually being conceived. Industry standards often exist for more commercial reasons. It would be pleasant to believe that some mechanism could be invented that would allow the desirable features of international standards to apply to industry standards. I believe it to be unlikely that such a mechanism will be forthcoming in the near future. It seems to me to be evident that the consor-

---

2 *American Heritage Dictionary*, 4th ed., 2000: "A combination of independent business organizations formed to regulate production, pricing, and marketing of goods by the members."

3 http://www.iso.org/

tium-of-manufacturers approach is going to continue, with all its downsides. Presumably, therefore, we just have to hope that with a worldwide and continually growing industry, we will be able to rely enough on market forces of one sort or another (where perhaps one such force is the kind of anti-market market force that open source represents) to provide some countervailing pressures.

25
Novelty in the Nemesis Operating System

Ian Leslie

Background

The opportunity to develop an operating system from scratch, even in a research environment, does not arise very often. One needs the inclination, a motivating proposition, and the resources to carry the development through. However, the results can be very rewarding; starting with a blank sheet of paper encourages novelty and allows conventional wisdom to be challenged.

In the early 1990's the Systems Research Group at the Cambridge Computer Laboratory began a project to develop an operating system to support the processing of continuous media. The team wanted to investigate the provision of guarantees of predictable performance for a dynamic mix of applications generating, playing, and/or processing audio and video information. The work was carried out within two serial EU funded projects.[1]

Providing predictable performance to applications entails giving them the resources they need at the time they need them. If one concentrates simply on the processor(s) as a resource, then it is tempting to think of this problem simply as a scheduling problem. While scheduling is key, it is not the only issue. It was recognised that uncontrolled resource interference between applications—denoted as *resource crosstalk*—could arise as a result of the structure of the operating system over which the applications ran.

An operating system, computer scientists are told from a very early point in their immersion in the subject, is a program (or set of programs) that controls the resources of a computer system, protects users from one another and provides services above the mere hardware of the system. They are also told about hard

---

1 The other partners were the University of Twente, Glasgow University, the Swedish Institute of Computer Science and APM (later Citrix). Their main involvement was in the production of components such as tools to support development or applications which used the operating system, rather than operating system itself.

ware support for protection, and are shown how this can be used to prevent, among other things, the operating system from being circumvented by users. Just how much of the operating system belongs inside special protection domains, or indeed how many different types of protection domain there should be, has been a topic for discussion and reinvention as long as there have been operating systems.

The goals of Nemesis gave its designers the academic luxury of exploring this issue at an extreme end of the spectrum. If, as Roger Needham often suggested, systems research is about sticking a pin in at an interesting point in a design space and then thoroughly examining the implications through implementation, then this was systems research.

Rather than a complete description of the system, we describe below a number of interesting developments made within Nemesis as a result of exploring this extreme point on the spectrum. Some of these can be seen as logical implications of initial choices, while others arose simply because of the clean sheet of paper we had.

Vertical structure and the separation of control and data paths

A significant amount of application processing is usually performed directly by the processes and threads created specifically for the application. In this case, resource contention amongst application processes is controlled by the system scheduler implementing a resource allocation policy. However, applications invariably make use of operating system services, either within the kernel or through an operating system process (server) used by other applications. Obvious examples of such services are network protocol processing, filing systems, memory management, and window systems. Within any component performing a task for multiple client applications, there is the potential for performance interference between applications. Given the design goal of controlling such interference, two obvious approaches present themselves:

- Control the interference amongst applications within shared operating system servers and the kernel. (*Be careful when you're there.*)
- Minimise processing performed by the kernel or shared operating system servers on behalf of applications. (*Don't go there.*)

The designers of Scout, at the University of Arizona and later Princeton, opted for the first of these approaches [5]. The Nemesis designers opted for the second. This decision was embraced wholeheartedly: the question arose as to what the minimum functionality was that had to be provided within a kernel or shared server.

The answer was to some extent influenced by the context in which Nemesis was developed. The playing, processing, and generation of continuous media were seen as key drivers. Traditional applications—that is, everything else— had tolerated application crosstalk. Continuous media applications can be partitioned into control path execution and data path execution, with data path execution expected to take the vast bulk of processing time. The initial solution, then, mandated that data path execution take place inside application domains, while (infrequent) control path execution would, where necessary, take place in shared servers. As an added bonus, this division corresponded well with the thinking about network control within the research group.

To use an alternate but compatible formulation: applications should be isolated from each other's behaviour, should be exposed directly to the capabilities of the underlying hardware, and should be responsible (in an accounting sense) for the actions performed on their behalf.

The organisation of the operating system which emerged [1, 4] was termed *vertically structured;* each application executed the bulk of what would traditionally be operating system code within its own process, called a *domain*. In fact it was still operating system code, but provided through shared libraries rather than shared servers. Much the same organisation was arrived at in the Exokernel system developed at MIT during the same period [2], but in that case the motivation was simply to allow applications to provide their own abstractions where those provided by the operating system were inappropriate.

Nemesis supervisor

The Nemesis "kernel" became simply a scheduler and a small set of simple trap handlers and device stubs. The word "kernel" was deprecated within Nemesis, and the temptation to talk in terms of "nano" or "pico" kernels was avoided.[2] There were no threads in the supervisor; rather, application threads could invoke a trap which would either execute a handful of instructions and return, or deschedule the domain and enter the scheduler.

The most commonly used scheduler provided a domain with a guaranteed slice, s, of processor time within a specified period, p. This gave each domain a notional share of the processor (viz., s/p), but also specified the granularity of time over which that share should be delivered. Domains could also indicate that they wished to use any available slack time, over and above their guarantee. To support multiplexing within domains, each was expected to have its own user-level thread scheduler. Special support for these schedulers was provided; for example, a domain could dynamically choose between being transparently resumed from where it was last descheduled, or alternatively having its scheduler entry point invoked.

Trap handlers were primarily concerned with the descheduling of an application, and we implemented an event delivery mechanism over which an event

---

2   However, we did not avoid the temptation to call the supervisor the Nemesis Trusted Supervisor Code (NTSC).

count and sequencer package used for interdomain communication. While the delivery mechanism was within the privileged code, the event count and sequencing system was implemented in shared library code executing within each domain.

Device organisation: control and data paths

The handling of devices was a particularly interesting aspect of Nemesis. Again, the desire was for application domains to perform as much of the application's device processing as possible. The separation into control and data paths became more formalised, with each device having two recognisable interfaces. The control interface was necessarily implemented by a shared server. Ideally the control interface simply provided a means by which a client could configure its access to the device. The device itself, possibly aided by the memory protection system, only needed to police correct access to devices. The notion of a model device was developed, although it was recognised that few hardware devices adhered to this model. The graphics frame buffer was a good example of nonadherence.

Conventionally, window systems are implemented by a shared server which "owns" the graphics frame buffer. In Nemesis this was undesirable; an application can cause some window systems to engage in vast amounts of processing. If the window system is running within each application domain, as would be the Nemesis ideal, excessive processing on behalf on one domain does not create a problem, since that domain will have the processing performed charged to its account. However, the window system does eventually have to write pixels into a frame buffer, and one can hardly classify this as a control function. We desired a frame buffer optimised for Nemesis having the property that various address space portions could be allocated to different application domains, and allow only pixels allocated to a domain to be written to by that domain. The pragmatic implementation was to have a device stub within privileged code that provided precisely that functionality, that is, checking that domains were attempting to write only the pixels they "owned" and then writing them. There was no loss of accounting accuracy, since the client domain was not descheduled when executing the privileged code.

Similar considerations with other devices led to follow-on work in placing "Nemesis ideal" functionality into the device in a way that can be exploited by traditional operating systems.

Memory management: self-paging

The memory management system in Nemesis was interesting because it was designed somewhat *post hoc*. Much of the operating system's structure and design philosophy had been determined: handling memory access exceptions had been envisaged as a control problem, not a data-path-execution problem, and memory management was therefore destined for a shared server. However, the issue of how much could be done by applications for themselves was revisited during the implementation. It was clear that novel memory-management techniques had a role to play in processing continuous media, but why should one application suffer for the novel memory management used by another? The system developed, called *self paging,* made domains responsible for their own memory-fault handling [3].[3] Although a domain might make use of a standard library paging algorithm, this executed as part of the domain. A shared system domain was required to configure the memory resources of domains, but this was the only "control path" operation.

Binding and bulk I/O

Other novel features were prompted by the flexibility of the memory system and the structure which supported application domains, but perhaps most significantly, simply by the opportunity to "do it from scratch." Particularly noteworthy were the binding model used for inter-domain communication, sometimes described as "a full distributed system in a box"[4] and the bulk I/O channel organisation, which met the requirements for both traditional data and continuous media communication.[5] Full details can be found in the references in the bibliography.

Implementation and performance

The initial implementations of Nemesis were on the DEC Alpha AXP, MIPS, and ARM architectures. The Alpha AXP was the preferred architecture, which, combined with the requirement to share large amounts of code amongst different domains, led, not unreasonably, to a single-address-space system. (Although sharing a single address space, domains of course had different protection views of the address space.) The Alpha architecture had a provision for the direct manipulation of native hardware resources known as PALcode. Much of the supervisor code on the Alpha was implemented as PALcode and its performance was outstanding.

---

3   Self paging is distinct from external paging; external paging is paging within a shared server outside of a kernel, and suffers the same drawbacks as any shared server.

4   The influence of the ANSA distributed computing architecture on the research team was very pronounced.

5   Arguably, it met the requirements of each better than existing schemes designed specifically for either.

Later, an implementation of Nemesis on Intel Pentium platforms was developed. Although the primary goal of Nemesis was realised, that is, providing control of interference between applications, the amount of state, in particular protection state, which had to be updated on a context change, was significantly higher.[6] One of the research team remarked that "modern processors are a bit like American cars: very fast in a straight line but not very good at turning corners."

Resource (re-)assignment tools

While the bulk of the effort on Nemesis was about providing mechanisms to enforce allocation policy, some work was done on allowing users to define policy. The most primitive, although most widely used, tool was a simple interface which allowed the user to move resources, notably those defined by the scheduling parameters, amongst application domains. Another tool allowed applications to be monitored to determine the appropriate-resource allocation for a desired performance, while yet another allowed a user-preference profile to be specified and acted on that profile to move resources around dynamically. These made for fun demos, not a usual output of operating systems research!

A few of the novel features that came out of the Nemesis development have been touched upon. It is difficult to see how many of them would have arisen in an incremental development of an existing system. The clean sheet was of enormous value, enabling the quite remarkable team of research students and research assistants who developed Nemesis to make interesting contributions to the subject. It was, of course, far from the first time this happened in Cambridge, and has not been the last.

Acknowledgements

I would like to acknowledge those involved in the development of Nemesis: Ian Pratt, Paul Barham, Timothy Roscoe, Richard Black, Derek McAuley, Eoin Hyden, Robin Fairbairns, Dave Evers, Steven Hand, Austin Donnelly, Dickon Reed, Stephen Early, Neil Stratford, and Paul Menage. I am grateful to Steven Hand for comments on this note.

---

6   However, it was not as high as on conventional operating systems running on the same hardware.

References

1. BLACK, R., BARHAM, P., DONNELLY, A., AND STRATFORD, N., 'Protocol implementation in a vertically structured operating system,' *Proc. 22nd IEEE Conference on Local Computer Networks*, November 1997, pp. 179–188.
2. ENGLER, D., KAASHOEK, M., AND O'TOOLE, J., JR., 'Exokernel: an operating system architecture for application-level resource management,' *Proc 15th ACM Symp. on Operating Systems Principles, Operating Systems Review*, vol. 29, no. 5, December 1995, pp. 251–266.
3. HAND, S., 'Self-paging in the Nemesis operating system,' *Proc. 3rd Usenix Symposium on Operating Systems Design and Implementation*, February 1999, pp. 73–86.
4. LESLIE, I., MCAULEY, D., BLACK, R., ROSCOE, T., BARHAM, P., EVERS, D., FAIRBAIRNS, R., AND HYDEN, E., 'The Design and Implementation of an Operating System to Support Distributed Multimedia Applications,' *IEEE Journal on Selected Areas in Communications*, vol. 14, no. 7, September 1996, pp. 1280–1297.
5. MONTZ, A.B., MOSBERGER, D., O'MALLEY, S., PETERSON, L., PROEBSTING, T. AND HARTMAN, J., 'Scout: a communications oriented operating system,' *Proc. 1st Usenix Symp. on Operating Systems Design and Implementation*, November 1994, p. 200.

26
A Technology Transfer Retrospective

Roy Levin

Many have written about the challenges that industrial research organizations face in trying to transfer the technology they create to other organizations. Research pursues a long and winding road from the proof of concept of a technology in the lab to the adoption of that technology by others and its use for corporate benefit. To follow the road to its end requires persistence, determination, flexibility, and (when, as is often the case, the road ends short of the destination) good humor. In this short paper, I offer a personal recollection of a part of one such journey—one in which the destination reached wasn't the one originally sought.

The road

My story tells of the Vesta system, the eventual result of an extraordinarily long research activity that spanned more than twenty years and three companies. The focus of this research was software-configuration management, especially the problem of building large-scale software systems incrementally and reproducibly. (An *incremental* build is one in which the minimum amount of compiling and linking occurs, exploiting as much as possible the results of previous compile/link steps.) Butler Lampson sparked my initial interest in this topic in the early 1980's at Xerox PARC. At that time, the software environment in which we were working differed significantly from those in general use elsewhere, since it had been constructed around a custom programming language and operating system (both called Cedar). Nevertheless, the overall problems of system-building were largely the same as one would have encountered under Unix or any other programming environment at the time.

Many researchers had investigated tools to build software incrementally, and some commercial systems of the time included them. Perhaps the best known was **make** [1], a simple tool originally built for Unix but subsequently adapted in many other environments. **Make** provided facilities for two essential aspects of system-building: (1) a concise way to express dependencies between components of a software system, and (2) a script of rebuilding actions for each component, to be executed when a predecessor in the dependency relation was updated. **Make** was designed and worked well for systems of a few tens of thousands of source code lines, but its limited notion of dependency did not extend well beyond that. Systems at the next order of magnitude or larger typically required build tools that supported branched development and/or multiple target platforms and/or a geographically dispersed organization. Developers of such systems still wanted to build incrementally—the value of doing so was even greater with large systems—but **make** could not do so reliably. As a result, developers of larger systems had to abandon incremental building and, while they might still use **make** as the mechanism for scripting the build actions, they reverted to "scratch" building which, for large systems, was an overnight activity conducted by a "release management" organization. As Lampson observed, this was effectively a return to the 1960's, when such systems were built overnight by submitting large card decks as a batch process.[1]

This unsatisfactory state of affairs had not gone unnoticed in the research community, and many variants of **make** were developed that sought to address the problem. Mindful of Roger Needham's maxim to do research "with a shovel rather than a tweezers" and unburdened at PARC by existing build processes based on **make**, we embarked on a line of research to rethink software system building from first principles. An early result of this research was the Cedar System Modeler [3], built by Ed Satterthwaite. However, this tool focused less on the problems of scale and incremental construction than on the use of a strong type system to minimize errors in building.

Before the Cedar System Modeler could see any significant use, Lampson and others (including me) left Xerox to found the DEC Systems Research Center (SRC). This group immediately set about creating a programming environment incorporating some of the features to which we had grown accustomed in Cedar. However, while this environment had a custom operating system (Taos [5]) and programming language (Modula-2+ [6]), the software development tools came from Unix and **make** was the system builder. We thus became acquainted firsthand with **make**'s characteristics, and I soon initiated a new project to attack "the system-building problem" afresh. The project was named Vesta.[2]

The Vesta research project produced a practical system that was deployed at SRC around 1989. It used a modular, functional programming language to express the build "script" and was able to build all of Taos, the Modula-2+ compiler and tools, and hundreds of libraries and applications built on them, all incrementally and reproducibly [4]. This body of code comprised nearly 1.5 mil-

---

1   Those too young to have experienced system construction in the days of batch processing can glean a sense of it, and much more besides, from [6].

2   According to Bulfinch, "Vesta (the Hestia of the Greeks) was a deity presiding over the public and private hearth." That duty struck me as an apt characterization of the role of a configuration management tool.

lion source lines, well beyond what **make** could reliably build incrementally. It was language-independent—that is, programs written in languages other than Modula-2+ could be built by Vesta—and supported both branched and cross-platform development.

The Vesta developers were excited by this successful demonstration of the feasibility of large-scale, incremental, reliable software system building.[3] As a result, we embarked on a series of visits to DEC product organizations that we hoped would embrace the technology. DEC had two substantial programming-environment product suites, one based on VMS, one on Unix. Both used **make** or its relatives as their build engine, and we believed the demonstrable superiority of the Vesta approach would be appealing. The tools purveyed by these groups were DEC products and were also used internally by the VMS and Unix operating-system and layered product-development groups for their very large code bases.

We returned from these visits sadder but wiser. While these groups found the Vesta technology attractive, they could not adopt it. There were several show-stoppers. For expediency, we had implemented Vesta by exploiting features of the Taos operating system that made it impractical to port Vesta to other platforms. We believed this could be fixed,[4] but it nevertheless put off the potential recipients. Furthermore, the whole Vesta system was implemented in Modula-2+, a language unsupported by DEC and unknown to most of its developers. More seriously, Vesta's idiosyncratic build-scripting language, uncertain scalability beyond systems of a few million lines, and inability to support geographically dispersed development made it an inadequate replacement for the **make**-based build systems that the product development organizations had cobbled together. We were disappointed, but went back to the drawing board, and began a new project to address these shortcomings.

The result, several years later, was Vesta 2. While continuing the original research goal, Vesta 2 had different technical objectives and substantially new personnel. Goaded by Bill McKeeman, we recast the syntax of the build-scripting language to resemble C, while retaining the underlying functional semantics that were essential for Vesta's incremental building machinery.[5] We

---

3   To be fair, the initial Vesta system was not without problems. Its build language was difficult to use, the builder's performance was quirky, and the whole system's ability to scale was limited, although still much better than **make**'s. Indeed, these problems led us to conduct an internal user study to understand how Vesta might be improved, but that's another story.

4   Indeed, by that time, SRC had shifted from Taos to Unix as its research platform and some of our colleagues were encouraging us to reimplement the Taos-dependent parts of Vesta so that they could continue to use it on Unix.

5   An explanation of the language semantics would go far beyond the scope of this paper. The key idea, however, is that the function calls of interest in a Vesta build script are invocations of tools (e.g., compiler, linker). The arguments to these function calls

completely redesigned the storage system and language interpreter to accommodate systems of 10 million (or more) source lines and to support geographic distribution of their development. We implemented Vesta 2 in C++ on top of DEC's Tru64 (Unix) operating system and equipped it with Unix-like management tools. The resulting system is described in detail in [2].

By the time that Vesta 2 was completed, DEC had largely ceased to invest in software development tools as part of its product portfolio. Some of the organizations we had previously visited no longer existed, but the operating system groups did, and the Unix organization expressed some interest in Vesta 2. Ultimately, however, they decided not to use Vesta for a combination of reasons, most of which are familiar to researchers who have followed the technology transfer road. Two in particular deserve note:

- Vesta 2, while technically superior to existing build tools, represented too radical a departure from **make**. To adopt Vesta would require rethinking the entire building methodology of the Unix organization, not to mention the structure and function of its release management group. Despite Vesta 2's evident benefits, the conversion effort and retraining necessary to adopt it were simply too much to consider.

- Vesta 2 came from a research group, not another product group or external vendor. The Unix organization would need long-term assurances of support before adopting the system, and (justifiably) didn't believe that the research organization could provide that assurance.

We could not make headway against these objections. To us it seemed ironic that the operating-system organizations periodically revised their build processes, occasionally even building specialized tools to enable them to continue to build their systems from scratch overnight or over a weekend, but they would not consider a systematic rework that could have a major impact on their productivity.[6] We were about to shelve Vesta 2 when we encountered an unexpected bend in the technology transfer road.

An unexpected destination

I was sitting in Chuck Thacker's office sometime in 1997 complaining about our inability to find an outlet for the Vesta 2 technology. Chuck reminded me that

---

are all the dependencies (e.g., included files); there are no global variables and, because of the functional language, no side-effects. Consequently, the function calls can be cached, and a cache hit indicates that a tool invocation can be bypassed and the cached result (e.g., compiler or linker output) can be used instead. This is the semantic basis of incremental building in Vesta. For an in-depth discussion, see [2].

6   This syndrome was familiar to some of us from our time at Xerox, where analogous events spawned the lament: "There's never time to do it right, but there's always time to do it over."

modern hardware development had become software-intensive and that DEC of course was fundamentally a hardware company. The company was sharply reducing its formerly broad investments in software to focus on its core line of Alpha-based computers. The software involved in development of an Alpha chip was not quite on the scale of an operating system, but it was well beyond what **make** could comfortably handle. Chuck thought Vesta 2 might help.

I realized that I had been wearing blinders. As the Vesta group had considered applications of Vesta and potential organizations for technology transfer, I had always focused on enhancing a conventional C or C++ programming environment. The Vesta group, being software developers ourselves, had never really considered the applicability of our system to hardware development. Moreover, we had generally focused on transferring Vesta technology to a group that already produced software development tools, since we knew that the support of Vesta would have to be assumed by the receiving organization. We didn't expect that a receiving organization would be willing to incur the support cost (or acquire the expertise) for the Vesta system simply in order to use it. Our experience with the operating systems groups had taught us that, but we were wrong.

DEC's Alpha division had two teams, each developing a new version of the Alpha processor chip. One of these teams was finishing up its current chip and beginning to prepare for the next one, code-named Araña. The build system they had been using was based on CVS, RCS, and **make** and had significant operational problems. Matt Reilly, who had responsibility for the development tools that the chip designers would use for Araña, was looking for something better. With a colleague, Walker Anderson, he created a list of desiderata, and then Walker prepared a comparative analysis of some potential replacement tool suites, including Vesta 2. After some stress testing showed that Vesta 2 could meet Araña's needs, Matt initiated a series of exploratory meetings with us. In the course of these discussions, we revisited all the issues that had prevented the transfer of Vesta 2 to other DEC organizations. Many were significant, but none proved to be show-stoppers. What was different this time?

- Because the Araña designers were beginning a new chip, they had the opportunity to take a fresh look at their development environment and revise or revamp it. Development of a modern CPU chip is a multi-year task involving hundreds of people, so an investment in new tools that will improve the process and resulting product merits serious consideration. Thus, Vesta 2 arrived on the scene at a propitious moment.

- While some of the basic development tools carry over from one generation of chip design to the next, many need to change to reflect advances in the underlying process technology. Moreover, little of the previous design (expressed as software) carries over; there is, in effect, a new "code base" with no legacy code. This stands in sharp contrast to the situation in the operating system groups, which have an ever-growing legacy code base.

- Despite their interest in Vesta, the Araña group could not risk wholesale introduction of a new system, with the attendant training and inevitable adoption problems involved. But, in part because they were getting a fresh start, they could structure their development to introduce Vesta in a small subgroup (about 20 engineers) first, fitting the outputs of that group into those of the rest of the organization, which continued to use older build processes. Over time, as they developed confidence in Vesta 2, they could scale up its use by introducing it to additional subgroups.

- Matt Reilly found Vesta 2's functionality (incremental build, scalability, reproducibility, parallel builds, branched development) sufficiently compelling that he was prepared to lobby his organization to commit an engineer, Ken Schalk, to become their local Vesta expert. Ken understood the needs of the Araña developers far better than we did, and could both convey problems back to us and help the Araña developers to use their new system-building tool to maximum effect.[7]

- Because the Araña group committed to taking on Vesta 2 maintenance eventually, the Vesta researchers could agree to support the Araña group until they could "go it alone." By contrast, the operating system organizations were looking for a customer/vendor relationship, which a tiny research group could not provide. An atmosphere of mutual commitment between the Vesta and Araña groups was thereby established from the outset.

The transfer of Vesta 2 technology thus began. The Vesta implementers (Allan Heydon, Tim Mann, and Yuan Yu) worked closely with and through Matt and Ken to provide training and support, which was occasionally challenging because the Araña group was in Massachusetts and the Vesta group was in California. The groups took advantage of Vesta's support for geographically dispersed organizations, using it to exchange updates between their sites and with a small remote branch of the Araña group (also in California). This worked smoothly, enabling fast and orderly response by the Vesta implementers to problems the Araña group uncovered and thereby delivering on the support commitment required to make the technology transfer succeed.

Gradually, the daily involvement of the Vesta implementers decreased; within a year the Araña team had become essentially self-sufficient. By this time the user base had grown from an initial cadre of about 20 to over 130, and a large fraction of the Araña tools and code had come under Vesta 2's management. By the time Compaq (which acquired DEC in 1998) sold the Alpha business to Intel, the Araña team had come to depend on Vesta 2 and was even using

---

7   Ken became intimately familiar with the Vesta 2 implementation and eventually became the primary support engineer for the system on-site. In fact, he ultimately took overall responsibility for porting Vesta 2 to Linux and making an open-source version available. See www.vestasys.org.

it to build software outside the scope of their original plan. They obtained permission for Vesta to be released under an open-source license before they left Compaq, and the system went to Intel with them. We had reached the end of our technology-transfer road, though the destination turned out to be an unexpected one.

Lessons

Our repeated attempts to transfer Vesta technology, and our eventual success, lead me to draw the following lessons.

- Successful technology transfer depends on finding a window of opportunity. Candidate recipient organizations have development cycles and, during most of a cycle, they cannot absorb new technology. In our case, the window was the "clean point" between Alpha chip generations, across which little code and few tools are carried forward. Only when the window is open is the development organization receptive; when the window is closed, they can't hear the researchers, no matter how loudly they shout. We found the window open largely by accident. If I had it to do over again, I certainly would seek to understand the development organization's schedule well enough to respond if/when the window opens.

- Appearances matter. Researchers often look for intellectual or aesthetic purity and ignore ugly details that are conceptually straightforward to clean up.[8] By contrast, development groups want things that work, and therefore they care about the details. Those details tell them how carefully the researchers have thought about their needs, which amounts to a litmus test of the practicality of the system under consideration. So the lesson for researchers seeking to transfer a software system is: remove the twigs over which the developers will otherwise trip. In Vesta 1, the language syntax repeatedly tripped up potential adopters.[9] We resisted, essentially on aesthetic grounds, marrying C syntax with functional language semantics. When we finally did so, we removed a place to stumble. Hiding the functional semantics under C syntax enabled many

---

8   This is not a character flaw. Rather, it is an often necessary aspect of getting research done with a small team—non-essential corners should and must be cut. Nevertheless, what gets the research done faster can be an impediment to subsequent technology transfer, and researchers need to recognize the trade-off.

9   Matt Reilly confirmed that the old Vesta language syntax would have been a significant impediment, giving the Araña developers one more new thing to learn.

developers to read the standard build scripts without being immediately aware of the non-C semantics.[10]

- Having a champion within the candidate receiving organization is essential. Matt Reilly and Ken Schalk were our champions. The old adage that "you can't push on a rope" applies; without pull from the technology recipients, the transfer will fail. Some believe that successful technology transfer requires people transfer. I don't subscribe to this view—Vesta 2 is a counter-example—but I do believe that technology transfer requires a champion, who pulls on the rope. An influential champion is especially important when a methodological change is involved, as with Vesta, because that change must be embraced and promulgated by management.

- Commitment by the research group to make the transfer succeed is equally essential. As Allan Heydon put it, "While you can't push on a rope, if the other side pulls and you're not holding on, things won't go very well either." Supporting technology transfer can be very time-consuming; the Vesta 2 implementers each spent the better part of a year supporting the Araña group. (This is the alternative to people-transfer.) Therefore, both researchers and their management must believe this is time well-spent.

- When the technology transfer requires a substantial change in thinking or operation, success depends on finding a small, somewhat separable group as the point of introduction. Even the forward-thinking Araña group couldn't swallow Vesta 2 all at once; they had to adopt it incrementally. Success is contagious, and once the initial group has had a successful adoption experience, they then become champions for the new technology within the rest of their organization.

- Technology transfer must take bounded time; there must be a plan for making the recipient organization self-sufficient. This generally means that either the receiving organization or some other non-research group commits to ongoing support of the technology. In our case, it was the former, in the person of Ken Schalk.

None of these lessons is particularly earth-shaking. Some have been noted by others, and no doubt other travelers on the technology-transfer road have encountered them along the way. However, if in recording the Vesta 2 experience I have helped to straighten the road for some future researcher, I will be well satisfied.

---

10 Going even further, Ken Schalk created user-interface tools that made it possible for most Araña developers to manipulate build scripts without having to write in the scripting language at all!

References

1. FELDMAN, S.I., 'Make—a program for maintaining computer programs,' *Software Practice and Experience*, vol. 9, no. 4, 1979, pp. 255–265.
2. HEYDON, A., LEVIN, R., MANN, T., AND YU, Y., 'The Vesta Software Configuration Management System,' Research Report 177, System Research Center, Compaq Computer Corporation, January, 2002. Available as http://www.hpl.hp.com/techreports/Compaq-DEC/SRC-RR-177.html
3. LAMPSON, B.W., AND SCHMIDT, E.E., 'Practical use of a polymorphic applicative language,' *Proc. of the 10th Annual ACM Symposium on Principles of Programming Languages (POPL)*, 1983, pp. 237–255.
4. LEVIN, R., AND MCJONES, R., 'The Vesta Approach to Precise Configuration of Large Software Systems,' Research Report 105, Systems Research Center, Digital Equipment Corporation, June, 1993. Available as http://www.hpl.hp.com/techreports/Compaq-DEC/SRC-RR-105.html
5. MCJONES, P., AND SWART, G.F., 'Evolving the UNIX system interface to support multithreaded programs,' Research Report 21, Systems Research Center, Digital Equipment Corporation, September, 1987. Available as http://www.hpl.hp.com/techreports/Compaq-DEC/SRC-RR-21.html
6. ROVER, P., LEVIN, R., AND WICK, J., 'On Extending Modula-2 for building large, integrated systems,' Research Report 3, Systems Research Center, Digital Equipment Corporation, January, 1985. Available as http://www.hpl.hp.com/techreports/Compaq-DEC/SRC-RR-3.html

27
An Optical LAN

Derek McAuley

There are significant outstanding technological challenges in providing optical switching on timescales short enough to provide statistical multiplexing at a comparable granularity to that of packets; buffering, synchronization, and regeneration within the optical domain all present problems. This paper discusses some of these issues and presents an architecture for a sub-network technology that uses optical switching but avoids these issues by limiting the scalability of the system through concentrating on local, system, storage, and desk area networks.

Introduction

There is no doubt that optical networks using Wavelength Division Multiplexing (WDM) are at the core of today's communications networks. They have massive capacity—leading commercially available equipment can multiplex 160 wavelengths at 10 Gbps per channel over 5000 km without regeneration [1]. However, deployed networks are currently controlled by network management systems operating on long timescales. The arrival of Generalized Multi-Protocol Label Switching (GMPLS) [2] for the control of optical and Synchronous Digital Hierarchy (SDH) path configurations has enabled more rapid provisioning, but the timescales are still significant and statistical multiplexing gains are at best coarse grained.

To try and achieve finer grained gains in statistical multiplexing, researchers have investigated techniques such as Optical Burst Switching (OBS) [9] and Optical Packet Switching (OPS) [4]. Simulations and component demonstrators have been built, but major hurdles remain in the realization of a complete system; I consider buffering and synchronization in this paper.

Furthermore, even allowing for great leaps forward in optical technology, my view is that the realization of an end-to-end all optical network for data communications will experience the same issues in deployment as earlier proposals for end-to-end asynchronous transfer mode (ATM). At network boundaries, issues concerning security, trust, classification, quality of service (QoS), etc., will require significant computing power to conduct deep inspection of packets; and, for the foreseeable future, this computation will necessarily be electronic.

However, recently there have been dramatic improvements in the capabilities, cost, and availability of certain photonic components and transmission systems. This trend is set to continue with key developments in short haul WDM, amplifiers, and switches delivering low-cost components that are well matched to local data-communications applications.

Together these developments lead naturally to the consideration of optical data-paths for a local area sub-network technology for system, storage area, and local area networks (LANs).

There was frantic activity in the 1970s building LANs. Valuable lessons are to be learned from their design; most importantly for the new optical era, they were designed to avoid network buffering. Drawing on this experience we present a design for an optically switched local network. Taking a local area network focus

- allows acceptably high utilization in the optical data-path without the need for optical buffering,
- limits problems due to non-linearity (e.g., dispersion, etc.),
- changes the optical power and transmission requirements,
- obviates the need for in-band processing of data within the network.

This paper highlights the optical issues in transmission, buffering, and synchronization, and then presents an architecture that can live with the limitations of optical components becoming available in the near term.

Optical issues

Dispersion

A simple ray-trace model using an ideal single wavelength is often used to illustrate the difference between single-mode and multi-mode fibre. In multi-mode fibre, the core of the fibre is much larger than the wavelength of light and a ray can take multiple paths (modes) of differing lengths down the fibre, effectively spreading an optical pulse in time, whereas in single-mode fibre only a single path is allowed. This simplistic geometric argument suggests that single-mode fibre can support much higher bit rates because the photonic pulses maintain their shape as they propagate.

A more thorough analysis involves Maxwell's equations. The classic treatment of "single-mode" propagation makes a number of simplifying assumptions which need to be reviewed as we consider higher speeds and hence shorter timescales. In particular:

- The propagation is assumed independent of wavelength. However, in fact the properties of the material (silica) and the manner in which the electromagnetic wave propagates through it (the proportion in the cladding versus the core) are both dependent on wavelength. The effects of this are commonly thought of on two different scales: *material dispersion:* the different wavelengths of a WDM channel propagate at different speeds; and *chromatic dispersion*: even within a single channel, the finite frequency range of a single bit pulse spreads out in time.
- The fibre is assumed isotropic, but manufacturing produces fibres that are not perfectly circular. Even moving to an elliptical model for the fibre results in the generation of *polarization mode dispersion*—the effective refractive index of the material varies depending on the polarization of the wave. Worse still, the polarization modes intermix as they propagate, again leading to a general spread of the pulse.

With the main use of optical transmissions for wide-area connectivity, these effects are significant at speeds 10 Gbps and above; however, they become important even in shorter links as we drive the transmission rate higher.

Temperature

Changes in operating temperature have subtle effects on optical propagation. The macro-scale effects include changes in effective refractive index within the fibre itself, at splices between fibres, and through connectors. Measurements show diurnal cycles in the "length" of the fibre [8]. However, the same experiments show a massive variation in the dispersion properties on much shorter time-scales.

Optical power

A final effect worth noting is the dependence of the effective refractive index on the optical power density; that is, the propagation of the photons is affected by the density of photons—this is referred to as *non-linearity*. At high power levels, typical of long haul optical transmission, such effects must be taken into account. Importantly, high optical power in one wavelength will modify the propagation of photons in another—thus WDM is not truly an orthogonal multiplexing scheme, although it approximates one at low power.

Optical multi-wavelength coding issues

In standard WDM format an information channel over one link is entirely coded onto one wavelength. Several of these channels on different wavelengths are then launched into a fibre. This format has considerably increased the capacity of fibre optic-transmission systems, but each of the channels is considered independent.

In contrast to standard WDM, "optical bus" [7] and bit parallel WDM [3] coding have been proposed. In this format the bits forming a word are formed into pulses launched simultaneously on different wavelengths. To avoid confusion we call this *wavelength striping*. Within the optical domain considerable effort has gone into ensuring the time alignment of pulses for a given word is maintained, which makes for simple electronics; on the other hand, compensation in the electronics is straightforward and a very small addition to the total number of gates involved in a network interface card.

Moreover, recent work has demonstrated multi-wavelength soliton-like behaviour, which is in fact reliant on the non-linearity described above. Taken together, solitons and electronic compensation offer the opportunity to consider new multi-wavelength or wideband coding techniques.

Optical switches

Switching on packet timescales and with data-rates of interest at 1 Gbps and above dictates the use of devices based on electro-optical effects rather than mechanical (e.g., MEMS), thermal, or acoustic devices. Electro-optical devices are capable of switching in several nanoseconds [10], which, although quite fast, is of the order of some number of bit times at significant data rates. We must ensure that, while the switch is in transition, no packet data is lost; we either introduce gaps between packets or require sacrificial packet preambles.

Buffering

At present there are no practical optical RAM elements available from which to build even small memories; *photonic crystals* offer some possibilities, but currently remain in the photonic laboratories.

Fibre used as a delay line (FDL) offers one means of buffering. Combined with the use of multiple wavelengths, such a delay line permits multiple packets to be simultaneously buffered in the same fibre. FDL components have been demonstrated in laboratories. One matter of concern is that during the recirculation, losses accumulate, especially in the delay-line tap for insertion and removal of packets.

Using delay lines as a buffer naturally leads to the consideration of "slotted" systems: either ATM style packets with labels, or synchronous TDM. In the general case we need to deal with the variability in the slot arrival time compared to the slot switching time. Using a slot synchronizer (Figure 1) we can insert a variable delay of up to one slot time in increments of some quantum of time based on the degree of bit-level synchronization required. For example, for a 1024 bit slot with a requirement for phase match of /8, a phase synchronizer composed of a chain of FDLs, each a factor of 2 longer that the previous, requires 14 stages. This is unsatisfactory: 14 stages of loss and noise are injected even before the packet reaches the main FDL buffer.

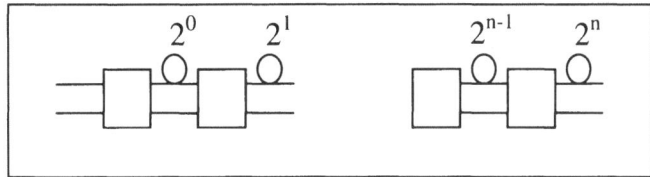

Figure 2: Chain of 2×2 elements and FDLs used as synchronizer

Wavelength conversion has often been proposed as an alternative to optical buffers: at the point of contention where two packets wish to travel on the same output link at the same time, simply ensure they are on different wavelengths. The classic Optical Burst paper by Turner [9] shows specifically the trade-off between more wavelengths and burst buffers. On the other hand, a single FDL can also hold multiple packets if they are on different wavelengths, though it requires that the tap on the FDL be able to add and remove specific wavelengths [5].

At the core of the buffering and synchronization problem is the problem that full "3R" optical regeneration, which involves reshaping and retiming pulses, as well as amplification, is not yet practical.[1] Even just with amplification alone to deal with the losses in the switch and fibre elements making up the synchronizer and buffer, noise accumulates rapidly to an unacceptable level.

Lessons from history

LANs

The original LAN technologies—Ethernet, Hubnet, Token Ring, Slotted Ring, Dual Bus, Folded bus, FDDI, etc.,—all held packets in end-systems until transmission was (believed) to have been successful. There was no buffering in the network. It is easy with today's full-switched multi-rate LANs to forget that at one point the concept of a LAN bridge, which would buffer and forward packets, was seen as a new and challenging research topic [6].

The original LANs could be categorized as either *synchronous* or *asynchronous*. In the synchronous ones, nodes in the network received a continuous signal from the communications media to which they synchronized their transmissions

---

1   3R: re-amplify, re-shape, re-time.

at the bit level, and in which was encoded the information needed to implement Media Access Control (MAC) based on *contention avoidance*. The rings and unidirectional or daisy-chained busses are examples. In the asynchronous ones, exemplified by systems such as Ethernet and Hubnet, a receiver would re-synchronize to the bit clock on a per packet basis and the MAC would implement *contention resolution*.

Wireless

Wireless networks by their very nature are "un-buffered," and there is considerable experience from wide area (ALOHA and satellite), metropolitan (mobile telephony), and local (802.11) networks to draw on. While local wireless networks often use asynchronous access techniques similar to local wired networks, experience in the wide area led to what can be categorized as *semi-synchronous* networks—that is, synchronized at a time slot level, but asynchronous at the bit level. In these networks, even when fed from a single base-station master clock, the variability in delay (jitter) introduced in radio propagation and/or mobility mean that it is simply not possible to ensure that two packets from different sources arrive at the base-station (or satellite) with the required sub-bit timing accuracy to run synchronously.

However, designing with realistic quantitative evaluations of these effects allows the imposition of a slot structure into which packets can be inserted by transmitters and be received within the defined time slot by the base-station. For example, a normal GSM "packet" is 144 bits within a time slot of 152.25 bits, allowing 8.25 bits of slack. To deal with longer-term drift as conditions change (e.g., as a cell-phone moves), the packet launch timing (skew) must be constantly re-evaluated; for the GSM example, a handset can be up to 35 Km from a base-station giving a maximum skew of approximately half a packet.

The media-access issue is orthogonal to clock synchronization and for these semi-synchronous systems has been implemented using both contention resolution and avoidance, with both fixed (TDM) and variable (demand-driven reservations) access for nodes.

Architecture

With the limitations of optical devices available in the short-term laid out and lessons from LAN and Wireless experience highlighted, the rabbit is in the hat.

Slot format

We consider a semi-synchronous optical network composed of point-to-point links and a central switch, which itself might be composed of several switching stages. Quantitative estimations for all of the effects of dispersion, temperature variation, and switch behaviour indicate that a semi-synchronous optical network can be constructed in the local area and achieve good utilization. Work continues on detailed analysis of exact materials and wavelengths, and I use illustrative numbers in the following discussion.

The switch communicates slot timing and phase information to each of the network nodes so that the transmitters can lock onto the switch slot structure. This bi-directional control channel is also used as the request/grant channel to implement Media Access Control (Figure 2). As with wireless communications, we can consider MAC layers implementing reservation and contention mechanisms. When granted access to a time slot, a node can transmit using wavelength striping on the data channels, $_{1..n}$, which are routed through the optical switch to the designated destination.

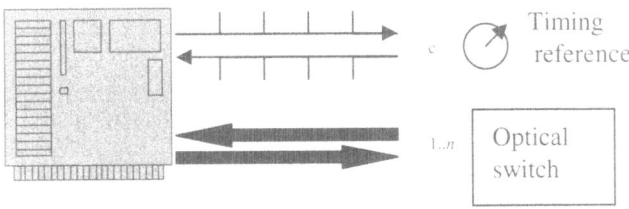

Figure 2: Timing reference supplied from switch on $_c$

Figure 3 illustrates typical values of the various timing parameters that have an impact on the design. Importantly in the small-scale network under consideration, polarization and chromatic dispersion can be neglected, while material dispersion and temperature effects are pronounced.

Assuming a commercial-grade network (rather than military grade), we might expect temperature changes of 50°C; constraining ourselves to a network of 1 km radius, we see that the most significant jitter effect is the temperature-dependent element; allowing for this jitter in both directions, we obtain a value for t_j of 6 ns. Operating within a 50 nm band around 1550, this results in a "gap" time (t_g) of 12 ns. Operating at a nominal 100 Gbps, and presuming a slot sized to take a standard Ethernet frame (12,000 bits = 120 ns), the slot time, t_p, is 132 ns—90% utilization is achieved.

Media access

The network size envisaged leads to a 5,000 ns node to switch transit time, or up to about 40 slots in flight. With a pure demand-driven reservation system, this would result in 10 s access latency. However, two further points are worth considering: some links will be significantly shorter than the full 1 km, and we envisage the number of nodes would be smaller than 64, perhaps as small as 4. Taken together, these indicate that in order to minimize latency, there will be times when it will be advantageous to implement a predictive reservation system; future work is to study the behaviour of such an adaptive scheme.

		Effect	Description
Jitter	t_o	30ps/km/C	Temperature dependant change
		80ps	Transmitter jitter
		$\ll t_s$	Switch jitter
	t_j	$t_o * 2$	Slot phase lock accuracy
Skew	t_s	5ns	Guard time for optical switch
	t	1ns/km/50nm	Chromatic dispersion at 1550nm
	t_c	80ps + few bits	Clock recovery

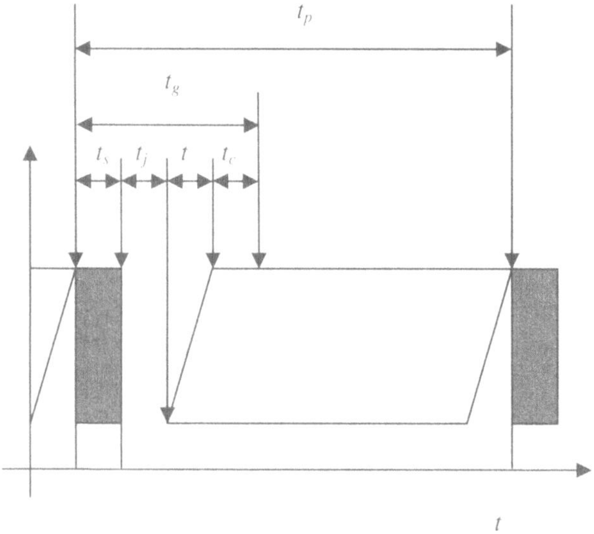

Figure 3: Timings for transmitted and received packets

Summary

Optical switches capable of switching on the timescales of packets exist, and together with low-cost short-haul WDM components enable the design of local area optical packet oriented networks. There are no practical solutions to the problems of optical buffering and the related problem of synchronization. Learning from previous LANs and wireless networks, we presented a network design, and through an illustrative example, showed that an acceptable utilization is possible.

Acknowledgments

Many thanks to Madeleine Glick for her patience in explaining the gory details of various photonics issues to me.

References

1. 'Solitons go the distance in ultra long-haul DWDM,' *Fibre Systems Europe*, January 2003.
2. 'Generalized MPLS - signaling functional description,' RFC in draft.
3. BERGMAN, L., YEH, C., AND MOROOKIAN, J., 'Advances in multichannel multiG-bytes/s bit-parallel WDM single fiber link,' *IEEE Trans. on Advanced Packaging*, vol. 24, no. 4, November 2001, p. 456–462.
4. GAMBINI, P., ET AL., 'Transparent optical packet switching: network architecture and demonstrators in the KEOPS project,' *IEEE J. Selected Areas in Communications*, vol. 15, no. 7, September 1998, pp.1245–1259.
5. GUILLEMOT C., ET AL., 'Transparent optical packet switching: the European ACTS KEOPS project approach,' *IEEE J. Lightwave Technology*, vol.16, no. 12, 1998, pp. 2117–2134.
6. LESLIE, I.M., 'Extending the local area network,' University of Cambridge Computer Laboratory Technical Report TR 43, 1983.
7. LOEB, M.R., AND STILWELL, G.R., 'High speed data transmission on an optical fiber using a byte wide WDM system,' *IEEE J. Lightwave Technology*, vol. 6, no. 8, August 1988, p. 1306–1311.
8. POOLE, C.D., TKACH, T.W., CHRAPLYVY, A.R., AND FISHMAN, D.A., 'PMD fading in lightwave systems due to polarization mode dispersion,' *IEEE Photonics Technology Letters*, vol. 3, 1991, p. 68–70.
9. TURNER, J.S., 'Terabit burst switching,' *J. of High Speed Networks*, vol. 8, no. 1, January 1999, pp. 3–16.
10. YU, S., OWEN, M., VARAZZA, R., PENTY, R.V., AND WHITE, I.H., 'Demonstration of high speed optical packet routing using vertical coupler crosspoint space switch array,' *Electron. Lett.*, vol. 36, no. 6, 2000, pp. 556–558.

28
What's in a Name?

Robin Milner

In the late eighties Roger Needham wrote a paper called 'Naming,' which is now a chapter in a leading text on distributed systems [4]. The paper highlights some subtleties of naming, and points out how these can either illuminate or confuse system design. Around the same time colleagues and I worked out the π-calculus [3], a calculus for mobile systems intended for modelling and analysis. Names are the most prominent feature in the π-calculus, and in this essay I explain in simple terms how it deploys them.

Some things about names are so buried in our linguistic habits that we hardly ever talk about them. Roger talked about one of them: the difference between pure and impure names. To paraphrase him, a *pure* name is nothing but an identifier or pointer; you can follow the pointer, but otherwise you can only test it for equality with another one. A name is *impure* to the extent that you can do other things with it. You can resolve it into parts, or you can take advantage of your knowledge about the thing that it designates; an email address like Robin.Milner@cl.cam.ac.uk illustrates both of these.

We also habitually assume that a name designates something with persistent identity. This assumption works well for us in sequential programming: a pointer designates a storage cell, and a procedure identifier designates a piece of code. It doesn't work reliably in distributed systems. Consider a call-centre; on each call you get someone different. Consider an e-mail message to Robin.Milner@cl.cam.ac.uk; it may go to me, or to an agent to which I (on holiday) have delegated the power to respond.

The π-calculus is built upon the idea that the respondent to (or referent of) a name exists no more persistently than a caller of the name. In other words, the notions of *calling* and *responding* are more basic than the notions of *caller* and *respondent*; every activity contains calls and responses, but to have a *persistent* respondent to x—one that responds similarly to every call on x—is a design choice that may be sensible but is not forced.

What follows is a taxonomy of the small range of things you can do with names in the π-calculus. At the end I speculate on whether these are enough.

Using and mentioning names

The logician W.V. Quine discussed the distinction between the use and mention of names. In natural language, a name is *used* when something is intended of the referent, *mentioned* when intended of the name itself; further, a *use* can be imperative (an invocation), or indicative (an assertion). In the π-calculus we only have imperative use, and what it intends is an act. But we distinguish between a *call* act and a *response* act, even though one cannot occur without the other. The reason to distinguish them is that, in describing any agent, we define its *potential* behaviour: what calls/responses it can make, provided that its environment makes homonymous responses/calls. Here is a *call* on x, mentioning y:

$$\bar{x}\langle y \rangle . P$$

This can be pronounced 'x, here is y; now I'll do P'. Superficially, it is like 'John, here is Stephen'; actually, it corresponds to 'John, here is (the name) "Stephen".' It is just a message with address x and content y; we can call this *quoting* y.

Here is a *response* on x, mentioning z:

$$x(z).Q$$

This can be pronounced 'x, thanks for z; now I'll do Q with it.' We can see how calls and responses are dual. Following the mathematical convention of 'co-' for a dual, we can say that the response is *co-quoting* z, because z acts as a place-holder in Q for a name quoted by a call.

In fact the only rule of action in the π-calculus is that, when a call may concur with a homonymous response, as in

$$\bar{x}\langle y \rangle . P \mid x(z).Q$$

then they are fused together; thereafter P and Q happen concurrently, with y occupying the place in Q held by z.

It is better to think of 'response on x' rather than 'respondent designated by x,' because there need be no agent identifiable as respondent. The power to *respond* on a name can be delegated or duplicated (consider the call-centre), just as the power to *call* on a name can be so. For example, in the above rule of action, if Q happens to contain a response on the place-holder z, then the call that quoted y has delegated to Q the power to respond on y.

Creating names

So far we have only talked about use and mention. But where do all the names come from? How can we represent the very specific mechanisms (e.g., timestamps) that allow a system to create names which it can safely assume to differ from all other names?

The π-calculus does this by fiat. It has a name-creator **new** that is *assumed* to create a globally distinct name. In some eyes this is cheating; in other eyes it isolates the implementer's problem of creating new names in practice from the analyst's task of explaining how a system works, *assuming* generated names are unique. Here is an example of unique name creation:

$$(\textbf{new} \quad z \; P) \; | \; Q$$

This creates z local to P. Whatever P does, this name remains different from any name occurring in Q—or in the wider environment—even if such a name is textually identical with z, and even if P mentions its new z to Q.

We can illustrate **new** with a simple example: simulating a function call. The π-calculus has no built-in notion of call-and-return, but if a process calls on x quoting y, then it can simultaneously create a private channel *res* and pack it up with y in the call; thereafter it can respond on *res* to receive the result that comes back. This call-and-return action is defined by:

$$\textbf{new} \; res \, (\, \bar{x} \langle y, res \rangle \; | \; res \, (z).Q \,)$$

(A multiple quotation, such as $\langle y, res \rangle$, can easily be coded in the π-calculus.) The creation of *res* ensures its distinction from every other return-address. This little sequence is very commonly used, so we shall abbreviate it to:

$$\bar{x} \langle y \rangle \; \Rightarrow \; (z).Q$$

Matching names

So far we have seen only one way to mention a name: quoting it in a call (or co-quoting in a response). Surprisingly, with a few control mechanisms this is enough to model all computation! Nonetheless, it does not give the direct facility to 'test a name for equality with another name'. So there is a second way to mention names: *matching*. With (only) these two kinds of mention, the π-calculus can much more directly model the handling of names in real systems.[1]

Matching in the π-calculus can done by the construction

$$[x = y] \; P \, / \, Q$$

---

[1]   In applied languages built upon the π-calculus, there can, of course, be impure names like 23, which designate known entities, operations on them like $+$ and $\times$, and variables or place-holders $a, b, c, \ldots$ for them. With appropriate type discipline, this doesn't impair the rigorous handling of pure names.

meaning 'if x and y are the same name, then do P, else do Q.' (It matches names, *not* their referents, because referents need not exist.)

In the context of π-calculus we can illustrate how directory lookup can be handled, following closely how Roger Needham illustrates it. A hierarchical directory—say the one containing the graduate students at Wolfson College, Cambridge—typically has a composite name like Wolfson/Grads. It is not a unique designator; there will be a directory with this name at Oxford too, because both Oxford and Cambridge have a Wolfson College. However, usable systems will ensure that each directory and subdirectory will also have a unique *directory identifier* (DI), which is a pure name.

If I know the DI of Cambridge University, I can access the University's main directory and then use a composite name like Wolfson/Grads—or extensions of it – to get to all its subdirectories, even if I don't have *their* DIs. For example, suppose I want to get hold of (the DI of) Smith-J at Wolfson College Cambridge. If the DI of the Cambridge University directory is #312, then I can get to where I want (without knowing any other DIs) by a composite call as follows:

$$\overline{\#312}\,\langle\text{Wolfson},\text{Grads},\text{Smith-J}\rangle \Rightarrow (di).Q$$

This call-and-return will cause the required DI to occupy the place held in Q by *di*. To make this happen, the directory itself can be defined with matching like this:

$$!\,\#312\,(college, group, person).$$

$$[college = \text{Trinity}]\quad \overline{\#427}\,\langle group, person\rangle$$

$$/\,[college = \text{Wolfson}]\quad \overline{\#203}\,\langle group, person\rangle$$

$$/\cdots/\cdots$$

Here #427 and #203 are the DIs of Trinity and Wolfson. Thus a matching occurs at each level. Notice that there is only one kind of pure name. We chose to write *college*, Trinity, and #427 differently because we treat them differently; for example, we never *use* the first two, but only *mention* them.

Finally, you may have noticed the new operator '!' in the above code for a directory. It is a *replicator*; it gives persistent identity to the respondent that it qualifies, making it a re-usable resource. So in this case the pure name #312 *does* designate a persistent agent: the Cambridge University Directory.

What else is in a name?

We have illustrated *use* (*call, response*), *mention* (*quote, co-quote, match*), and *creation* of names. That is all the π-calculus can do with them. Are there other things it might do?

I have not said anything so far about computer security, which has in fact been a main application of process calculi that use names. Another influential paper by Roger Needham and his co-authors [2] has inspired much of the recent logical work on security, authentication and associated topics, and under this heading come many approaches using process calculi that use names whose scope may be controlled (for example by **new** in the π-calculus). A leading example is the *spi calculus* of Abadi and Gordon [1], which is largely based upon the π-calculus, but uses extra features for encryption and decryption.

These extra features allow the spi calculus to represent security protocols very directly, and have led to powerful analytical studies. But there is a theoretical question that hasn't been fully answered as far as I know: in what rigorous sense do they extend the expressive power of the π-calculus? It would be illuminating to prove that the extra features *can*, or that they *cannot*, be mimicked in the π-calculus in some exact sense.

More generally, if we suspect that the π-calculus *can't* do something that *can* be done with pure names, then where could we look for the weakness? A more powerful form of *use* of names might have something to do with synchronisation. The π-calculus only ever synchronises a pair of actions, one call and one response. What about synchronising two (or more) calls with a single response? The calls could be on two distinct names x_1 and x_2, and the response on both of these names simultaneously. So our rule of action would be strengthened to synchronise these three actions:

$$\bar{x}_1 \langle y_1 \rangle . P_1 \mid \bar{x}_2 \langle y_2 \rangle . P_2 \mid x_1 x_2 (z_1 z_2) . Q$$

causing y_1 and y_2 simultaneously to occupy the places held in Q by z_1 and z_2, and then P_1, P_2, and Q to proceed concurrently. Can this be mimicked in the π-calculus? What exact meaning would 'mimicked' have here?

Such theoretical questions may seem arcane. They certainly should not distract us from applying process calculi to security (or to anything else). But they have their own charm, and the better we can answer them, the more confident we can be of finding good primitives for expressing and analysing mobile communication.

References

1. ABADI, M., AND GORDON, A.G., 'A calculus for cryptographic protocols: The spi calculus,' *Information and Computation*, vol. 148, 1999, pp .1-70.

2. BURROWS, M., ABADI, M. AND NEEDHAM, R.M., 'A logic of authentication,' *Proc. Royal Society of London*, series A, vol. 426, 1989, pp. 233–271.

3. MILNER, R., PARROW, J., AND WALKER, D., 'A calculus of mobile processes,' *Information and Computation*, vol. 100, no. 1, 1992, pp. 1–77.

4. MULLENDER, S.J., (ED.), Distributed Systems (second edition), Addison-Wesley, 1993.

29
The Cryptographic Role of the Cleaning Lady

Bob Morris

By the cleaning lady, I mean some person or entity that you believe could not possibly be part of your security or cryptographic system. I leave it to the reader to identify his or her own cleaning ladies in the remainder of this note and in real life.

Once there was an occasion when some bad guys, a man and a woman, wanted some key material (code books) from a foreign embassy. They waited until the end of the working day and managed to persuade a guard to let them into the building.

They knew that there was a guard who would show up at unpredictable times during the night and would naturally wonder what the two were doing in the building. While they were getting at the code books, they heard him coming in the front door and they had only a very short time to solve their problem. The woman rapidly took off all of her clothes and when the guard arrived in the room he seemed to understand exactly what they were planning to do—he apologized and left the room. The two intruders obtained the code books and left with them. This is a true story, but what else they did that night is not part of this story.

It is my understanding that all major countries employ cleaning ladies in this capacity.

Another sort of cleaning lady is arranged as follows. In the part of Moscow that houses foreign embassies there are two quite different fire stations. One of the fire stations responds to fires in foreign embassies, and the second responds to fires in ordinary buildings.

Would the reader please think hard about 'trusted third parties' and woman-in-the-middle attacks?

30
Real Time in a Real Operating System

Sape J. Mullender, Pierre G. Jansen

Introduction

The quality of an operating system is more a subject of religious debate than of technical merit. The Windows community is like the Catholic Church; it has the largest following, and its members are mostly laymen who do not participate much in religious debates. The community is organized on strong hierarchical lines.

The Unix community is like the mainstream Protestant Church; it has not as large a following as the Windows community, and its members define the system and run the community. Like the Protestant Church, there are many flavors of observance: Linux, FreeBSD, NetBSD, Mach; the list is as long as the list of protestant variants. Most are highly evangelical—a good Protestant trait—with Linux perhaps being the most fanatical.

The Macintosh community hangs somewhere in the lurch between Windows and Unix, the Catholics and the Protestants, a bit like the Anglican Church; they're Protestants acting like Catholics.

Plan 9 from Bell Labs is like the Quakers: distinguished by its stress on the 'Inner Light,' noted for simplicity of life, in particular for plainness of speech. Like the Quakers, Plan 9 does not proselytize.

Plan 9 is relatively little known and has but a small user community (a few thousand installations). Nevertheless, it is a complete operating system, and it is the only operating system booted by many of its users. Plan 9 is also used in several embedded environments. For instance, it is the system inside the *Viaduct*, a computer system the size of a packet of cigarettes that provides an encrypted bridge between Lucent employees' home computers and the corporate intranet. It is also beginning to find use in experimental wireless base stations.

New technologies (the printing press, organ transplants, birth control) and changing world views (the solar system, evolution) have always been upsetting to churches, causing violent debates and schisms. This is just as true in the operating system community, where new things like object-oriented programming, copyleft licensing, Ethernet vs. token ring and real-time support can cause similar violent debates and schisms.

It is the doctrine of real-time support in a general-purpose operating system that will, in this paper, be stamped with ecclesiastical authority.

We have integrated a real-time CPU scheduler in our operating system Plan 9 [7]. Although our scheduler is a new scheduler in terms of sharing the operating system resources, it has its fundaments in the EDF scheduler as first introduced by Liu and Layland [6]. Instead of only considering the CPU resource, our scheduler also considers other shared OS resources: applications indicate which resources they require (including processor use), and our scheduler determines if the set of applications can run concurrently and remain *schedulable*.

Although other operating systems may also have real-time support, we believe there are only few general-purpose operating systems with a comparable native support for real-time applications.

In many embedded systems, some applications have stringent real-time requirements, while others can be best effort. Traditionally, general-purpose operating systems have never been good at guaranteeing deadlines. Various attempts have been made to introduce real-time schedulers to general-purpose operating systems. A few systems deal with real-time applications by shutting out other applications (the general modus operandi for the Windows family of operating systems).

In the subsequent sections, we shall describe our system and the theory behind it, omitting, for lack of space, most proofs and a discussion of related work. As such, this paper has the status of an extended abstract more than a full-fledged paper. For a more formal introduction, see Jansen & Laan [4], and Jansen's forthcoming thesis.

Practicalities

Adding real-time functionality to Plan 9 as a layer below regular user programs was deemed to be undesirable. At best it would make the API for writing real-time applications a subset of the standard API; at worst, it would be completely different. We wanted to give real-time applications access to all operating system services and access to an interface to control an application's real-time behavior as well. The price one has to pay in this approach is that real-time applications may risk missing their deadline by using non-real-time services.

Although we consider this to be clumsy programming, we have no desire to forbid it. We envision that, with time, real-time versions of various operating system services will become available, e.g., a real-time file server along the lines of Nemesis' Clockwise mixed-media server [3]. Plan 9 makes extensive use of *file servers,* which, through their name space mounted in a per-process *mount table*, provides access to much more than secondary storage. The window system's interface is a file system; a *play list* file system may be associated with an audio device; mail messages present themselves as subdirectories in a mail file system, and so on. Talking to file systems is important to most applications, so it cannot be forbidden. In fact, our real-time scheduler presents itself as a file system too.

Another issue was how to deal with processes whose deadlines depend on one another. The most common example of this is a set of processes in a pipeline, for instance, a process decrypting a video stream feeding another that renders it. Scheduling theory has problems with such dependencies. We chose to allow several processes to share a single allocation of resources: one period, one deadline, and one slice of the CPU equal to the sum of the run times required by each of the member processes.

Resources are identified to the scheduler by name. A resource is shared when tasks share the name of the resource. When a resource is acquired or released, tasks inform the scheduler. This is the only involvement the scheduler has with shared resources. Resources can, therefore, be anything. One important assumption is that tasks give up any resources they hold when they give up the processor. Tasks can cause themselves to be scheduled non-preemptively with respect to each other by sharing a resource full time. When they share no resources, a task with an earlier deadline can always preempt a task with a later one.

Theory

A *task set* τ consists of a set of preemptable tasks τ_i ($i = 1 \ldots n$). Each task τ_i is specified by a *period* T_i, a *deadline* D_i, a *cost* C_i, and a *resources specification* ρ_i. It is *released* every T_i seconds and must be able to consume at most C_i seconds of CPU time before reaching its deadline D_i seconds after release ($C_i \leq D_i \leq T_i$). We use capital letters for intervals (e.g., T, D, C) and lower case for points in time: in particular, r for the next release time and d for the next deadline.

The *utilization* U of τ is defined as $U = \sum_{i=0}^{n} C_i / T_i$

For τ to be schedulable, $U \leq 1$ must hold. We define two functions, *processor demand H(t)*, introduced by Baruah et al. [2], and *workload W(t)*, introduced by Audsley et al. [1], $H(t)$ represents the total amount of CPU time that must be available between 0 and t for τ to be schedulable. $W(t)$ represents the cumulative amount of CPU time that is consumable by all task releases between time 0 and t.

Figure 1 illustrates the functions for an example task set. All tasks in τ are released simultaneously at $t = 0$. This is known as a *critical instant*, the time at which the release of tasks will produce the largest response time. If τ is schedulable from a critical instant, it is schedulable from any other starting point. A critical instant occurs in resource-free preemptive EDF scheduling when all tasks are released simultaneously. This is a well-know result, but we have also proven it for our EDF scheduler.

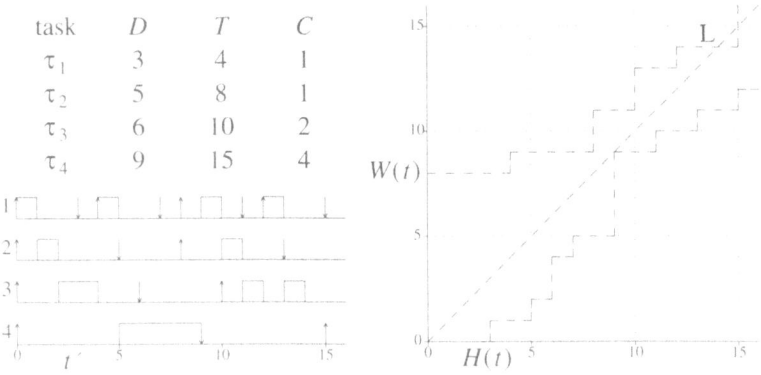

Figure 1: Example task set and its EDF schedule on the left, and the processor demand and workload functions on the right.

The right half of the figure shows the functions H and W as a function of time. It also illustrates the schedulability analysis. Note that the vertical distance between W and the diagonal in the graph represents the amount of work still to do in released tasks. At point L, there is no more work to do, and the system becomes idle. H represents the amount of work that must be finished. If H crosses the diagonal, then more work would have to be finished than there is time available. The schedulability analysis tracks W and H until either W *touches* the diagonal or H *crosses* it. If H crosses the diagonal, the task set is not schedulable. If W touches it, the task set is schedulable. The example task set is thus schedulable. Task sets can be constructed in which neither W nor H reaches the diagonal. The schedulability analysis, therefore, traces these functions for only a predetermined maximum number of steps and rejects a task set if this maximum is reached.

The scheduler manages the set of admitted tasks using two queues and a stack: The *Wait Queue* holds tasks awaiting their release. When a task gives up the processor or reaches its deadline, it is put on this queue, in release-time order, from which it will be transferred to the next queue when it is released. The *Released Queue* holds processes that have been released but have not yet run. This queue is maintained in deadline order, earliest deadline first. The *Run Stack* holds the tasks that have already run; the currently running task is at the top of the stack and pre-empted the task immediately below.

The scheduler maintains two timers. The *Release Timer* goes off when the task at the head of the Wait Queue needs to be released. Released tasks are then transferred to the Released Queue. The *Deadline Timer* goes off when the currently running task reaches its deadline. When this timer goes off, the currently running task is removed from the (top of the) stack and put back in the Wait Queue.

When a task gets to the front of the Released Queue or when a task is popped from the Run Stack, the deadlines of the task at the head of the Released Queue and the task at the top of the stack ' are compared. If $d < d$ ', it is removed from its queue and pushed onto the Run Stack. Then the Run Timer is set and the task gets the processor. If both Run Stack and Released Queue are empty, best effort processes are scheduled.

A *resource specification* is a series of zero or more quadruples *name, R, C,* { '}, where *name* names the resource, *R* indicates whether the resource is a shared-read or (in its absence) an exclusive-access resource, *C* is the *cost* of the resource (the time the resource is held), and { '} is a sub-specification which specifies nested resources, or may be absent. An example of a task set with a resource specification is:

```
D=4s  T=5s   C=1s  resources='a R 900ms { b }'
D=5s  T=8s   C=1s  resources='a R 800ms {b 200ms { c 100ms }}'
D=6s  T=10s  C=2s  resources='b R 200ms c R 1.7s { b R 1.3s }'
D=9s  T=9s   C=3s  resources='a R 1.8s { c R }'
```

When costs are omitted, they are inherited from their parent resource specification or, in the case of a top-level specification, from the task's cost *C*. Note, by the way, that the strings in this example can be written precisely as they are to the scheduler file system to specify a task's real-time parameters.

Task 1 has a period of 5 seconds, a deadline of 4 seconds (if it is released at *t*, its deadline is at $t + 4$ and its next release is at $t + 5$); it needs at most 1 second of CPU time between release and deadline. Resource *a* is shared by tasks 1, 2, and 4. In all cases it is a shared-read resource, so it imposes no restrictions on the schedulability of these tasks. Resource *b* is shared by tasks 1, 2, and 3. Task 1 needs exclusive access to it, and for the full 900 ms, it also holds resource *a*. Task 3 needs shared-read access to resource *b* for 200 ms and again for 100 ms while holding resource *c*.

The principle behind scheduling a task set with shared resources is that we keep tasks on the Released Queue until there are no tasks left in the Run Stack holding resources that the task on the Released Queue may claim. Thus, it is not possible for a task to (try to) claim a resource already held by another task. Such a task would simply not have been scheduled. Tasks never need to be preempted waiting for a resource.

Here's how we enforce this: every resource *R* is assigned an *inherited deadline* $_R = \min_{\epsilon} D \mid R \in$, the minimum of the deadlines of all tasks using *R*. Every task also receives an inherited deadline $= \min_R {}_R \mid R \in$, the minimum of the inherited deadlines of all resources used by the task. A task's thus changes as the task acquires and releases resources; is only relevant for running tasks.

Each released task is now characterized by the triple {*d, D,* }, where *d* is the current *absolute* deadline (*D* is the deadline *interval*; *d* is the absolute deadline).

Earlier, we presented the scheduling rule that the task at the head of the Released Queue would move to the top of the Run Stack if its d was less than d of the task ' on top of the Run Stack—a released task with an earliest deadline will pre-empt the currently running task. Now we modify that rule:

τ preempts τ' iff $d_\tau < d_{\tau'} \wedge D_\tau < \Delta_{\tau'}$

Figure 2 shows an example Run Stack (rectangles) and Released Queue (ellipses). At this time, the task at the head of the Released Queue may not preempt the one on top of the Run Stack ($9 < 7 \wedge 3 < 4$ is false). For every task , D and, because of the scheduling rule, for a task higher on the Run Stack than another task ', $D <$. There is, therefore, a partial ordering from D to to D, etc. up and down the Run Stack. This is indicated by the arrows.

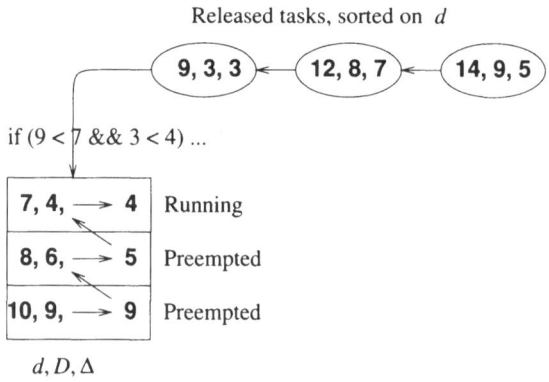

Figure 2: Example Run Stack (rectangles) and Released Queue (ellipses); the arrows indicate the partial order between the parameters.

This ordering, plus the definition of , establishes the property that the currently running task—which is at the top of the Run Stack—will not attempt to acquire any resources held by preempted tasks, which are further down in the Run Stack, because, if they held such resources, their would be less than or equal to the D of the running task, and this the scheduler does not allow.

A second property is that there is no transitive blocking, because a process that is blocked due to shared resource usage only has to wait for the blocker to release the resource. This property was already known from the Priority Ceiling protocol [8], a protocol that was the first to introduce static priority inheritance, similar to our static deadline inheritance.

The schedulability analysis is only moderately more complex with resource sharing. The processor demand and workload functions do not change, because the work that needs to be done and when it needs to be done is the same. But we do have to take into account now that one task may *block* another's access to the CPU.

This causes 'spikes' on the processor demand function. The height of the spikes encodes the time a task may have to wait for a task with a later deadline that holds a resource the task needs. A task set is inadmissible if one of the spikes crosses the diagonal. If there are no shared resources, there is no blocking (and there are no spikes), and the schedulability test reduces to the normal pre-emptive-EDF schedulability test. If there is one resource, shared full-time by all tasks, the schedulability test reduces to Jeffay's [5] non-preemptive schedulability test. Our schedulability test spans the range between the extremes of completely preemptive and completely non-preemptive scheduling.

Implementation

We implemented the scheduler in Plan 9. This was a fairly straightforward process, although we had to change the behavior of spin locks in the kernel slightly. A process is now allowed to finish its critical section before being subject to scheduling. None of the spin locks hold the CPU longer than 50 μs or so.

As explained earlier, two timers control the real-time portion of the scheduler: the Release Timer goes off when the task at the head of the Wait Queue must be released. If that task gets to the front of the Release Queue, a scheduling decision is made, otherwise, the current task continues running. When the Deadline Timer goes off, the running task has used up its quantum, and the processor is taken away from it until the next release. We also raise an exception in the process.

The interesting part about the implementation is the use of a file system to control the system. In the default mount point of /dev/realtime we find three files, clone, resources, time, and a directory: task. Existing tasks are represented by files (whose names are numbers) in the task directory. A new task is created by opening the file clone, which then behaves like the corresponding (new) file in the task directory. The main loop for a typical real-time process would look something like the following:

```
char *clonedev = "/dev/realtime/clone";
void processvideo(void){
  int fd;
  fd = open(clonedev, ORDWR);
  if (fprint(fd,
      "T=33ms D=20ms C=8ms procs=self admit") < 0)
          sysfatal("%s: admission: %r", clonedev);
  while (processframe())
          fprint(fd, "yield");
  fprint(fd, "remove");
  close(fd); }
```

This sequence creates a new task by opening /dev/realtime/clone, sets period, deadline and cost, and puts the running process into the process group of the task. It then asks the scheduler to admit the new task by running the schedulability test. If the write succeeds, the task was admitted.

The main loop processes a video frame and then gives up the processor (yield) while waiting for the next frame. When the application has finished, it removes the task from the system and exits.

Conclusion

The real time scheduler is installed in the currently distributed version of Plan 9 (obtainable through plan9.bell-labs.com). It has already been used in several applications, one of them an experimental wireless base station. But there have not been any applications that have challenged the scheduler much.

We have had some lively debates over whether it is worthwhile to have a real-time scheduler that can manage shared resources. Most of the real-time applications we considered do not have any resources that are shared. But one real-time application we built has nothing but shared resources: the Clockwise mixed-media file system has many real-time processes, with varying periods and costs, sharing disks. As it turned out, scheduling the disks was much more important than scheduling the CPU, so the Plan9 scheduler would not have been adequate for this application.

The battle about whether or not to include support for resource sharing in our real-time scheduler was won by the resource-sharing camp when the algorithms presented here emerged: the schedulability test is not overly complicated and the run-time complexity is practically $O(1)$: only the queue insertions are not constant-time operations, but the queues are invariably very short. In addition, the scheduler prevents resource contention from causing gratuitous context switches, and it is completely deadlock free. Finally, the same scheduler can trivially be used for preemptive or non-preemptive real-time EDF scheduling.

References

1. AUDSLEY, N.C., BURNS, A., RICHARDSON, M.F., AND WELLINGS, A.J., 'Hard real-time scheduling: the deadline monotonic approach,' in *Proc. 8th IEEE Workshop on Real-Time Operating Systems and Software*, Atlanta, Georgia, 1991. Available at: http://citeseer.nj.nec.com/article/audsley91hard.html

2. BARUAH, S.K., MOK, A.K., AND ROSIER, L., 'Preemptively scheduling hard-real-time sporadic tasks on one processor,' in *Proc. of the Real-Time Systems Symposium*, 1990, pp. 182–190.

3. BOSCH, P., MULLENDER, S.J., AND JANSEN, P.G., 'Clockwise: a mixed-media file system,' in *Proc. of the IEEE Intl. Conf. on Multimedia Computing and Systems (ICMCS)*, II, Firenze, Italy, 1999, pp. 277–281. Available at: http://www.cwi.nl/~peterb/papers/icmcs99.ps.gz

4. JANSEN, P. G., AND LAAN, R., 'The stack resource protocol based on real-time transactions,' in *IEEE Proc. Software*, vol. 146, no. 2, 1999, pp. 112–119.

5. JEFFAY, K., STANAT, D.F., AND MARTEL, C.U., 'On non-preemptive scheduling on periodic and sporadic tasks,' in *Proc. of the Real-Time Systems Symposium*, 1991, pp. 129–139.

6. LIU, C. L., AND LAYLAND, J. W., 'Scheduling algorithms for multiprogramming in a hard real-time environment,' *Journal of the ACM*, vol. 20, no. 1, 1973, pp. 46–61.

7. PIKE, R., PRESOTTO, D., DORWARD, S., FLANDRENA, B., THOMPSON, K., TRICKEY, H., AND WINTERBOTTOM, P., 'Plan 9 from Bell Labs,' *Computing Systems*, vol. 8, no. 3, 1995, pp. 221–225. Available at:
http://plan9.bell-labs.com/sys/doc/9.html

8. SHA, L., RAJKUMAR, R., AND LEHOCZKY, J. P., 'Priority inheritance protocols: an approach to real-time synchronization,' *IEEE Trans. on Computers*, vol. 39, no. 9, 1990, pp. 1175–1185.

31
Zen and the Art of Research Management

John Naughton, Robert W. Taylor
(with apologies to Sun Tzu)

1. HIRE ONLY THE VERY BEST PEOPLE, EVEN IF THEY ARE CUSSED. Perhaps especially if they are cussed. Your guiding principle should be to employ people who are smarter than you. One superb researcher is worth dozens of merely good ones.

2. ONCE YOU'VE GOT THEM, TRUST THEM. Do not attempt to micromanage talented people. (Remember rule #1.) Set broad goals and leave them to it. Concentrate your own efforts on strategy and nurturing the environment.

3. PROTECT YOUR RESEARCHERS FROM EXTERNAL INTERFERENCE, whether from company personnel officers, senior executives, or security personnel. Remember that your job is to create a supportive and protective space within which they can work.

4. MUCH OF WHAT YOU DO WILL FALL INTO THE CATEGORY OF ABSORBING THE UNCERTAINTY OF YOUR RESEARCHERS.

5. REMEMBER THAT YOU ARE A CONDUCTOR, NOT A SOLOIST. (Rule #1 again.) The lab is your performance.

6. DO NOT PAY TOO MUCH ATTENTION TO "RELEVANCE," "DELIVERABLES," and other concepts beloved of senior management.

7. REMEMBER THAT CREATIVE PEOPLE ARE LIKE HEARTS: they go where they are appreciated. They can be inspired or led, but not managed.

8.   KEEP THE ORGANISATION CHART SHALLOW. Never let the lab grow beyond the point where you cannot fit everyone comfortably in the same room.

9.   MAKE YOUR RESEARCHERS DEBATE WITH ONE ANOTHER REGULARLY. Let them tear one another's ideas to pieces. Ensure frank communication among them. Observe the strengths and weaknesses which emerge in the process.

10. BE NICE TO GRADUATE STUDENTS. One day they may keep you, even if only as a mascot. (Moreover, they are a lot of fun!)

11. INSTALL A WORLD-CLASS COFFEE MACHINE and provide plenty of free soft drinks.

12. BUY AERON CHAIRS. Remember that most computer science research is done sitting down.

13. INSTITUTE A "TOY" BUDGET, enabling anyone in the lab to buy anything costing less than a specified amount on their own authority. And provide a darkened recovery room for accountants shocked by the discovery of this budget.

14. PAY ATTENTION TO WHAT GOES ON IN UNIVERSITIES. Every significant breakthrough in computing in the last four decades has involved both the university and corporate sectors at some point in its evolution.

15. REMEMBER TO INITIATE AND SPONSOR CELEBRATIONS when merited.

16. WHEN IN DOUBT, ASK YOURSELF: "WHAT WOULD ROGER NEEDHAM DO IN SIMILAR CIRCUMSTANCES?"

32
The Descent of BAN

Lawrence C. Paulson
(with apologies to Charles Darwin)

The famous BAN paper [3] determined the research agenda of security-protocol verification for nearly a decade. Many others had worked on verifying security protocols, and the problem appeared to be intractable. The real-world systems were too complicated; too many different things could go wrong; the formal treatments were unusable. The BAN logic was abstract, formalizing intuitive notions directly. For example, if you receive a message containing a secret password and you know that the password is known only to you and Joe, then the message must have come from Joe. BAN proofs were short and simple, and each reasoning step could easily be rendered into plain English.

BAN certainly had some deficiencies. The paper incorrectly claimed that the Otway-Rees protocol could be simplified in a certain way. In fact, an intruder could attack this protocol, masquerading as Bob to Alice, when Bob was not even present [7]. More generally, BAN ignored all non-encrypted information, so it could "verify" any protocol that broadcast the session key in clear. Some criticisms arose from a misunderstanding of the logic's objectives. BAN assumed that the protocol would not give secrets away—a defensible assumption, since cryptanalysts already knew how to investigate such questions. BAN's strength was that it provided a precise notation and deductive mechanism for reasoning about freshness and authenticity.

Researchers introduced a great variety of other authentication logics. These were generally more complicated than BAN. Dietrich [4] published a proof of the Secure Sockets Layer (SSL) protocol using the belief logic NCP (Non-monotonic Cryptographic Protocols). This logic allowed formulae to be retracted as well as asserted, and the author accordingly had to write lengthy lists of facts holding at each step. NCP must have been more precise than BAN, but it was obviously difficult to use. Some people attempted to build automatic provers for the BAN logic, which was pointless: BAN logic proofs were easy to write, and if you wrote them yourself, you were unlikely to reach an absurd conclusion. For the more complicated authentication logics, automation became essential; Brackin [2] was a leading exponent of this approach. As do-it-yourself logics proliferated, their benefits (especially when applied using an automatic prover) were not always clear. Roger may have been right to call BAN "the original and best."

In hindsight, it is clear that all such logics must share certain limitations. Many attacks on security protocols are not clear-cut, and involve disagreements about the working assumptions. The famous attack on the Needham-Schroeder public-key protocol by Lowe [6] is a classic example. Alice opens a session with Charlie, who proceeds to attack Bob. This scenario involves a misbehaving insider, when the traditional threat model assumes that all criminals are outsiders. Only recently have researchers recognized the danger posed by corrupt insiders.

The failure possibilities of modern protocols are rather complicated. The Zhou and Gollmann non-repudiation protocol [9] is designed to be fair. Its principals are Alice and Bob, who are arranging some sort of contract, and a trusted third party, Clarence. A successful run should give both Alice and Bob sufficient evidence to prove the other's participation. It is also acceptable that neither of the pair should obtain this evidence; however, it is unfair if one of them obtains evidence and the other does not. Gürgens and Rudolph [5] recently demonstrated an attack on this protocol. Alice reuses a session identifier, retaining information from the first protocol run in order to attack a second run. She leaves enough time between the runs to ensure that Clarence will have erased all record of the first run. Alice will be left with evidence confirming Bob's participation. When Bob seeks the corresponding evidence from Clarence, it will not be available.

Formal models typically make ideal assumptions, and in this case would probably endow Clarence with unlimited storage. Alice's attack would then fail. In a more detailed model, Clarence would not be able to store all past session identifiers online, and the attack would succeed. In the real world, Clarence would probably maintain a full audit trail, though most of it would be offline. Whether this attack can succeed or not therefore depends on a detailed description of the dispute resolution mechanism. For this protocol, Gürgens and Rudolph have proposed a neat solution: let Bob contribute to the session identifier. However, we can imagine situations in which algorithms (such as the one for dispute resolution) must be formalized as part of the protocol description. In such situations, authentication logics are unlikely to be helpful, and formal models of any sort are likely to yield misleading results unless the practitioner is aware of the critical issues.

My involvement in protocol verification originated in a research project, funded by the EPSRC, which I held jointly with Roger. The project's original objective was to develop a new authentication logic based upon advanced theory. Through informal discussions (involving Kim Wagner) in Roger's office, I became familiar with the concepts of authentication protocols. I noticed that informal justifications of protocols used inductive reasoning: if X went wrong in step 4, then Y must have happened in step 3, but then Z must have happened in step 2, which is impossible by the nature of step 1. Identifying the first step at which something goes wrong is inductive reasoning, and this underlies the inductive approach to protocol verification [7].

An inductive model has much in common with the models investigated by the Oxford group of Lowe, Roscoe, and Schneider. *Principals* and *messages* are the primitive notions. Messages are recursively constructed from principal names, keys, and nonces by concatenation and encryption. The semantics of a protocol is given by the set of possible traces of *events,* such as the sending and receiving of messages. Such models are far removed from the real world, but more low-level than the BAN models. Roger encouraged this new approach, though it differed radically from his own. He offered advice of the sort that I imagine he offered his research students. He suggested, for example, that I focus attention on a specific message of the Needham-Schroeder shared-key protocol.

Roger's influence, and that of the BAN paper, ensured that my models included the necessary elements. BAN is mainly about freshness: we have received a session key, but how do we know that it is fresh? An old key may have become compromised. One of the BAN paper's most interesting analyses is that of the Yahalom protocol. Here Bob receives in separate packages a session key K (bearing no evidence of freshness) and his nonce NB, encrypted using K. Ordinarily, encryption using a potentially compromised key would yield no firm evidence. However, the Yahalom protocol keeps NB secret; an intruder in possession of K would still be unable to perform the encryption $\{NB\}_K$. Therefore, this message firmly associates NB with K, proving the latter's freshness. BAN formalizes this argument quite easily; in my inductive model of Yahalom, it was much more difficult [8].

Freshness is no less important these days, and protocol designers are careful to include the nonce challenges necessary to achieve it. Recent attacks seldom involve freshness, and many recent formal models do not represent freshness. I have been lucky to work in a research environment that is strong in both theory and computer security. (Roger can be given the credit for creating this environment.) That is how I have been able to avoid some of the mistakes made by researchers who do not work with a security group. If some authors do not understand what a nonce is for, or know that a timestamp should carry a valid time, or appreciate that a certain type of field will always have the same length in bytes, then they should spend time at the Computer Laboratory.

The BAN logic, like many other approaches to analysing security protocols, assumes perfect encryption. This assumption means, in particular, that no information can be deduced from a ciphertext without the corresponding key. Encryption is obviously not perfect, but many protocols are flawed even under this assumption.

The problem of security-protocol verification under perfect encryption is essentially solved. Numerous researchers have worked on it, and even the most complicated protocols have undergone formal scrutiny. Many of today's hard problems concern how to formalize the vulnerabilities of specific encryption methods such as Diffie-Hellman or RSA. Even exclusive-OR is difficult to model, particularly in typed formalisms, because the exclusive-OR of two bit strings can yield data of any type. Probabilistic mechanisms are also difficult to verify, although recent progress gives ground for optimism. Another difficult area concerns the composition of protocols from separately·verified components.

I have heard Roger say that the BAN logic is obsolete. How many researchers would say that about one of their most important achievements? However, even if the BAN logic is obsolete, the BAN paper is certainly not. It remains an excellent tutorial on cryptographic protocols. It describes and analyzes a variety of different protocols. With Roger's other papers, such as Abadi and Needham [1], it remains essential reading for anybody wishing to do research in this area.

References

1. ABADI, M., AND NEEDHAM, R., 'Prudent engineering practice for cryptographic protocols,' *IEEE Transactions on Software Engineering*, vol. 22, no. 1, 1996, pp. 6–15.
2. BRACKIN, S.H., 'A HOL extension of GNY for automatically analysing cryptographic protocols,' in *9th Computer Security Foundations Workshop*. IEEE Computer Society Press, 1996, pp. 62–75.
3. BURROWS, M., ABADI, M., AND NEEDHAM, R.M., 'A logic of authentication,' *Proceedings of the Royal Society of London*, vol. 426, 1989, pp. 233–271.
4. DIETRICH, S., *A formal analysis of the secure sockets layer protocol*. Ph.D. thesis, 1997, Adelphi University, Garden City, New York.
5. GÜRGENS, S., AND RUDOLPH, C., 'Security analysis of (un-)fair non-repudiation protocols.' In A. Abdallah, P. Ryan And S. Schneider, S. (eds.), *Formal aspects of security 2002*. Royal Holloway College, University of London.
6. LOWE, G., 'Breaking and fixing the Needham-Schroeder public-key protocol using CSP and FDR.' In T. Margaria and B. Steffen, (eds.), *'Tools and Algorithms for the Construction and Analysis of Systems,' Second International Workshop, TACAS '96*, Lecture Notes in Computer Science 1055, pp. 147–166., Springer, 1996.
7. PAULSON, L.C., 'The inductive approach to verifying cryptographic protocols,' *J. Computer Security*, vol. 6, 1998, pp. 85–128.
8. PAULSON, L.C., 'Relations between secrets: two formal analyses of the Yahalom protocol,' *J. Computer Security*, vol. 9, no. 3, 2001, pp. 197–216.
9. ZHOU, J., AND GOLLMANN, D., 'A fair non-repudiation protocol,' in *Proc. of the 15th IEEE Symposium on Security and Privacy*, 1996, pp 55–61., IEEE Computer Society Press.

33
Brief Encounters

Brian Randell

In compiling these personal reminiscences of Roger, I have—I must confess—mainly relied on my memory rather than consulted my files in any great detail. Given my pretensions to be somewhat of a computer historian, albeit very much part-time, it is somewhat embarrassing to reveal this lack of regard for primary evidence. However, my excuse is that I have no wish to encourage any of you to classify Roger (or me) as historical exhibits.

I cannot recall when Roger's and my paths first crossed—I'm not sure whether they did before I left the UK in 1964 to join IBM Research in Yorktown Heights. Up to this time I'd been working on compiler design for English Electric's DEUCE and then for its KDF9 computers. I had not concerned myself much with computer or operating system design, and had had little contact with Cambridge. So after I arrived at Yorktown Heights I was surprised to learn that one of the people they had contacted to check me out before head-hunting me, so to speak, was Maurice Wilkes.

At Yorktown I made a very deliberate switch from compilers to computer architecture, and this led to me operating systems and so, I presume, to my first contacts with Roger. I'm not sure now how it happened, but in 1966 I became Editor of the Operating Systems Department of the *Communications of the ACM*, a post I held for the next seven years. I have tried to find whether I could proudly claim to have accepted any papers by Roger during my seven-year editorial term. As far as I can tell he did not publish in the *CACM* until after I'd left. Luckily, I have no easy way of checking how many of his papers I rejected!

In 1967 I participated in and was editor of the proceedings of the first SOSP, the ACM Symposium on Operating System Principles. The SOSP series, which is one that Roger has had long and extensive involvement with, has in general tried hard to live up to its name and encourage papers that truly do deal with principles—though more recently I gained the impression that it had for a while become somewhat of a mere "Unix Improvements Society"—something I'm sure Roger tried very hard to prevent.

My main memories of the 1967 SOSP symposium, which was held in Gatlinburg, Tennessee, include the fact that at the time Gatlinburg was dry—all you could get within the town limits was something they called "near beer." I presume Roger was in attendance, and remembers this with even more pain than I do, though I believe that his first SOSP paper was at the 3rd Symposium, held in Palo Alto in 1971—in fact a paper entitled "Handling Difficult Faults in Operating Systems" [1].[1] This is a paper with a typically high signal-to-noise ratio, covering both principles and practice, whose introductory paragraph is, I think, worth quoting in full:

> It is commonplace to build facilities into operating systems to handle faults which occur in user-level programs. These facilities are often inadequate for their task; some faults or incidents are regarded as so bad that the user cannot be allowed to act on them and this makes it difficult or impossible to write subsystems which give proper diagnostics in all cases, or which are adequately secure, or which are adequately robust. This paper looks into why there is a need for very complete facilities and why there is a problem providing them, and provides an outline structure which could be used.

I returned to the UK in 1968 and joined the Computing Laboratory of the University of Newcastle upon Tyne. The laboratory had been created a dozen years earlier by Ewan Page. Ewan was a Cambridge man, and the laboratory he set up was, I'm sure, deliberately patterned after Cambridge's Computer Laboratory, and similarly combined the roles of academic department and university computing service, a characteristic which we proudly continued to hold and defend for many years, just as Cambridge did. I have often characterized my move from IBM Research to the University of Newcastle upon Tyne with a phrase due to John Buxton, dating from about this time. I cannot resist using an appropriate variant of Buxton's phrasing to describe Roger's rather differently directed career move, a few years ago, when what he did was abandon the sordid commercial reality of a university computing laboratory for the ivory towers of industry.

But I'm getting ahead of myself. When I arrived at Newcastle, one of the tasks I took over was the organization of the second in the series of annual Newcastle International Seminars on Computing Science. Roger was one of my choices of speaker for this 2nd Newcastle Seminar. His 1969 talk was on "Failure Recovery" [2], a fact that I must confess that I'd completely forgotten. It would be intriguing to try and determine whether this talk predated the planning we undertook at about this time, following my experiences at the now famous 1968 NATO Software Engineering Conference, that led to our first SERC-sponsored project on dependability, a topic that has been a major feature of my and Newcastle's research ever since. I have gone back and looked at the report of Roger's 1969 talk and found that it was about the problems of file system integrity and back-up in the face of unreliable hardware—it includes the nice remark "It is psychologically desirable to take greater care of users' files than they would themselves"—rather than overall system failure and recovery, so I don't

---

1   It was actually his second SOSP paper.

see any strong link to our early work, which was on techniques for providing continued service despite the presence of residual software faults.

To my surprise, in preparing these remarks, I found that Roger was not present at the 1968 NATO Conference at Garmisch in Bavaria, only at the follow-up conference held a year later in Rome. For various reasons the Rome conference was much less effective and influential than its predecessor, but Roger made some notable contributions, including one prepared during the conference itself in an intriguing instant collaboration with Joel Aron of IBM Federal Systems Division. My understanding is that Roger and Joel had never met before. Their backgrounds could hardly have been more different—Joel had been heavily involved in the awesome computing-system project that supported the Project Apollo series of moon shots, a project whose scale and style were vastly different from Roger's work on operating systems in the Cambridge Computer Laboratory. Their styles of speaking were also very different, though in each case very attractive. Joel's splendid talk on the Project Apollo Ground Support System, and each contribution he made to any discussion, always sounded as though he was giving a reading of a carefully structured and punctuated piece of elegant prose. Indeed, he did this so clearly that it was child's play to transcribe a recording of his voice and produce a fully grammatical and properly punctuated text, something that I and the others involved in producing the report of the conference much appreciated. Roger's style of delivery is, on the other hand, more notable for its wit and brevity, and thus as entertaining to transcribe as it is to listen to first hand. Yet they somehow found time during a very intense conference to reach a common viewpoint and co-author a paper, albeit a brief one, on "Software Engineering and Computer Science" [3].

At the preceding conference a disparate set of participants, ranging "from the inhabitants of ivory-towered academe to people who were right on the firing line, being involved in the direction of really large scale projects" found "commonality in a widespread belief as to the extent and seriousness of the problems facing the area of human endeavour which has, perhaps somewhat prematurely, been called 'software engineering'." However, the report on the Rome Conference, a conference which had a similarly disparate set of participants, comments that "the sense of urgency in the face of common problems was not so apparent as at Garmisch—instead, a lack of communication between different sections of the participants became ... a dominant feature" and explains that "eventually the seriousness of this communication gap, and the realization that it was but a reflection of the situation in the real world, caused the gap itself to become a major topic of discussion." The Aron-Needham paper was a thoughtful contribution to this discussion, and demonstration of the bridgeability of the communication gap, one that I enjoyed re-reading when I prepared these remarks.

Returning to the subject of Roger's contributions to the Newcastle Seminar Series, I should mention that during the thirty-four years of the series, we normally had different speakers each time. Roger is one of the very few speakers who have been invited back not just once but three times—the others being Edsger Dijkstra and Kristen Nygaard. Roger's first reappearance was in 1978. The overall subject of this seminar was Distributed Computing Systems, and Roger talked on "User-Server Distributed Computing" [4]. His two talks provided a very thoughtful analysis of the properties of local area networks such as Ethernet and the Cambridge Ring and how such networks could be exploited in order to distribute many of the tasks that traditionally were all bundled together into a large monolithic operating system across a set of much simpler specialized servers.

His next appearance was for our 25th seminar, when we used the general title "Computing Science" and deliberately chose our speakers from the by now large set of highly-renowned past speakers. In fact the other speakers at our Silver Jubilee seminar were Edsger Dijkstra, Tony Hoare, Donald Knuth, Butler Lampson, John McCarthy, Kristen Nygaard, and Michael Rabin. Almost all of the Jubilee speakers fully lived up to their reputations and gave excellent talks—Roger certainly did, with talks on "Communication System Development," and on "Reasoning about Cryptographic Protocols" [5]. This latter was, of course, largely based on his very influential and much-cited work with Michael Burrows and Martin Abadi on the BAN logic, the notation they designed for use in analyzing and verifying authentication protocols [6]. To complete the list, I should mention that Roger was a speaker at the last in the Seminar Series, in September 2001 [7]—this was a sort of benefit match for me, since it was on Dependability, and marked my (so-called) retirement. It was the first seminar in over thirty years that I had not organized—my colleague and professorial successor, Cliff Jones, was in charge—and thus for the first time ever in the series I found myself having to lecture. But who better could Cliff have chosen to speak on security than Roger?

But again I'm getting ahead of myself. Following my return to the UK, I had many opportunities to meet up with Roger. For example we served together for what seemed like many years on a whole succession of Department of Trade and Industry (DTI) advisory committees. Though at times this was an enjoyable experience—because Roger has an inimitable way of speaking to and dealing with recalcitrant civil servants, one that I find much more entertaining than they do—it was also, we both agree, an immensely frustrating experience. Though we were not so naïve as to assume that all our advice would be heeded, it is clear in retrospect that we were almost entirely wasting our time. No wonder that, as I've since learned, the department is referred to by some as the Department of Timidity and Inaction.

The one exception, the one really worthwhile experience I had with the DTI, was again one I shared with Roger. This was on a 1981 DTI mission to Japan. There is a fairly full description of this mission in the book *Alvey: Britain's Strategic Computing Initiative* by Brian Oakley and Kenneth Owen [8]. One entertaining (and all too true) passage is the following: "On arrival in Tokyo team members were fascinated to discover a completely alien culture, with strange customs, exotic behaviour, and quaint patterns of speech. And that, they recall, was just the British Embassy."

We (namely Roger, Alan Fox of RSRE Malvern as it then was called, Charles Read of the Inter-Bank Research Organization, Reay Atkinson, an uncharacteristically splendid DTI civil servant, and I) had been sent out to Japan by a minister who had come back from a visit completely entranced and highly flattered by the Japanese government's invitation to the UK to participate in the Fifth Generation Computer Project that they were planning. The Alvey book attributes to me the following subsequent assessment of the Japanese plans:

> The Japanese conference presentations were an amazingly well-orchestrated series of vague accounts of various parts of an ambitious and wide-ranging plan. . . . Everybody made respectful references, at least, to logic programming and knowledge engineering, and some of them obviously believed, and perhaps even understood, what they were saying. It came over to me as a very skilful plan which filled MITI's wish for a very ambitious goal that sounded very plausible and which could be presented to a layman in such a way as to seem socially beneficial.

However, though attributed to me, I think I detect the hand of Roger in that text—if not, it is the effect on me of an extended period of close proximity to him. The team rapidly came to the conclusion that we wished to dissuade the government from setting up a general scheme of UK-Japanese collaboration, since it was clear to us that the main beneficiaries would be Japanese industry. (We had discovered from visits we paid to various Japanese computer companies that they all were much better informed on the latest UK academic computer science research than any UK company.) Instead, we argued, what was first needed was some effective means of encouraging collaboration between UK academics and industry on a large-scale programme of information technology R&D, a programme which should not be so narrowly focussed on logic programming and knowledge engineering as the Japanese 5G plans.

After our return to the UK we were thus both heavily involved in the scheming that led to the Alvey Programme, but that is a whole story by itself, and one that has already been well documented. However, it is important to point out how central was the role that Roger played in the setting up of the Alvey Programme, not least as the sole academic allowed to join the committee of senior industrialists and civil servants, chaired by Sir John Alvey, whose report directly led to the creation of this ground-breaking programme.

The Mathematical Sciences Sub-Committee of the late lamented University Grants Committee was another arena that has provided me with happy memories of encounters with Roger. There was, for example, the sub-committee visit to a particular university (fortunately, I cannot remember which one), when, during the obligatory tour of the CS department aimed at gaining our support for additional accommodation, Roger became aware that the faces in the various laboratories we inspected were becoming familiar. This was because a crowd of students was being rushed round back corridors of the department to reappear in front of us repeatedly, rather like the chorus during the Grand March in an under-staffed performance of the opera *Aïda*. Such visits also normally involved meetings with the local Vice-Chancellor—at which Roger demonstrated a skill in the sometimes rather delicate discussions which I'm sure proved very useful when he became a Pro Vice-Chancellor himself at Cambridge some years later.

During this time, the UGC Mathematical Sciences Sub-Committee, under the able leadership of Prof. Douglas Jones, a canny Scot if ever there was one, was involved not just in a regular programme of such visits, but also in considering submissions from just about all the UK computer science departments to a whole succession of funding initiatives. We were thus able to gain detailed knowledge of the then fifty or so departments, as well as to achieve a number of significant resource enhancements for UK computer science. As a result, when we learnt that we were going to have to perform what turned out to be the first of the dreaded Research Assessment Exercises, Roger and I independently drew up, while waiting for our trains at Kings Cross Station, virtually identical and remarkably accurate predictions of the gradings that later resulted from the subsequent formal consideration of the detailed RAE submissions by the overall panel. To paraphrase a comment once made about Algol 60, this first RAE exercise was in my opinion, in regard both to the way it was carried out, and the degree of acceptance of the results by the UK computer science community, an improvement over all its successors.

Enough of committees and bureaucracy—let me end with a few further remarks on research. Roger's and my research trajectories diverged somewhat over the last thirty years. He concentrated largely on security issues—to great effect—whereas I've worked on fault tolerance, as applied to reliability and availability, though I have on occasion had fun investigating potential links between fault tolerance and security. However, in the early days Roger was equally interested in what was essentially fault tolerance even if he didn't use this term—I recall an early aphorism of his to the effect that operating systems should be designed and implemented via incremental additions to a very robust dump and restart system. I have enjoyed looking back at a number of his early papers—even if I now have some concerns as to whether I paid them as much attention at the time as they evidently deserved. Thus I can sympathize very much with the comment that Roger made in an interview in 2001: "Although for most of my career I was a practical builder of systems, the things I'm best known for are [two papers on authentication], both of a theoretical nature and both done when I was on sabbatical leave. So you can work away on a complicated system for seven years, and nobody remembers that" [9]. (Incidentally, during my little investigation of Roger's early papers, I was startled to find that he had published one in 1964 entitled "Exploitation of Redundancy in Programmes" [10]—however, this turned out to be concerned with instruction set representation, and the issues discussed were instruction storage efficiency and processor performance, not dependability!)

Regarding security, Roger's expertise regarding cryptography of course far exceeds mine—in fact, I'm sure my evident lack of knowledge of, or interest in, cryptography was of considerable benefit when I was seeking official permission to investigate Britain's highly classified wartime code-breaking machines, in particular the Colossus. But we both share a degree of scepticism about the subject of cryptography, and I very much like the comment: "Anybody who asserts that a problem is readily solved by encryption, understands neither encryption nor the problem" [11]. This comment is often attributed to Roger, by Butler Lampson among others, though I gather Roger claims it was Butler who first made it.

To have been with Roger was to enjoy, and benefit from, a whole succession of such wise and pithy remarks—it is thus a great pleasure to place on record how highly I value all the opportunities I've had of encounters with Roger from time to time over the years, and all the enjoyment and benefit I've thus gained.

References

1. NEEDHAM, R.M., 'Handling difficult faults in operating systems,' in *Proc. 3rd Symp. on Operating System Principles, Operating Systems Review*, vol. 6, nos. 1, 2, June 1972), pp. 55-57.
2. NEEDHAM, R.M., 'Failure recovery,' in On *the teaching of the design of large software systems* (Proc. Joint IBM/University of Newcastle upon Tyne Seminar, 8–12 September 1969), ed. N. S. M. Cox, 38–43, University of Newcastle upon Tyne, 1970.
3. NEEDHAM, R.M., AND J.D. ARON, 'Software engineering and computer science,' in *Software engineering techniques: report on a conference sponsored by the NATO science committee, Rome, Italy, 27–31 Oct. 1969*, ed. J. N. Buxton and B. Randell, pp. 113–114, Brussels, NATO Science Committee, 1970.
4. NEEDHAM, R.M., 'User-server distributed computing,' in *Distributed computing systems*, ed. B. Shaw, pp. 71–78, Computing Laboratory, University of Newcastle upon Tyne, 1987.
5. NEEDHAM, R.M., 'Reasoning about cryptographic protocols,' in *Computing science*, ed. B. Randell, Department of Computing Science, University of Newcastle upon Tyne, 1992.
6. BURROWS, M., ABADI, M. AND NEEDHAM, R.M., 'A logic of authentication,' *ACM Trans. on Computer Systems*, vol. 8, no. 1, pp. 18–36, 1990.
7. NEEDHAM, R.M., 'Security,' in *Dependability*, ed. C. B. Jones, Department of Computing Science, University of Newcastle upon Tyne, 2001.
8. OAKLEY, B., AND OWEN, K., *Alvey: Britain's strategic computing initiative*, pp. 33–76, Cambridge, MA, MIT Press, 1989.
9. OMITOLA, T., 'ACM Fellow Profile: Roger Needham,' *Software Engineering Notes*, vol. 26, no. 1, 2001.
10. NEEDHAM, R.M., 'Exploitation of redundancy in programmes,' in *Proc. Conf. on the Impact of Users' Needs on the Design of Data Processing Systems*, pp. 6–7, UK, IEE, 1964.
11. NEEDHAM, R.M., 'Address,' in 'The Marshall symposium—the information revolution in midstream: an Anglo-American perspective,' Rackham School of Graduate Studies, University of Michigan, 1998. Available at: http://www.si.umich.edu/marshall/docs/p201.htm

34
Retrieval System Models: What's New?

Stephen Robertson, Karen Spärck Jones

Automated retrieval systems

In the postwar development of computing, most people thought of computers as machines for numerical applications. But some saw the potential for automatic text processing tasks, notably translation and document indexing and searching, even though words seemed much messier as data than numbers. For Roger, as one of these early researchers, building systems for language processing was both intellectually challenging and practically useful, and in the late 1950s he began to work on document retrieval [5]. The specialised scientific literature was growing too fast for the existing broadly based and rigid indexing and classification schemes. This lack of appropriate retrieval tools, and the opportunities offered by computers, stimulated a critical examination of existing approaches to indexing and searching and the introduction of radically new ones.

Document (or text) retrieval systems, like libraries before them, depend on a model of the way documents should be characterised to facilitate searching, and of effective strategies for searching. Many models for retrieval systems have been proposed since the 1950s. The most innovative, attractive, and successful have been those that, unlike the earlier library models, have exploited the behaviour of the actual words used in document texts, and have facilitated flexible matching between queries and documents, leading to a ranked search output. These ground features of modern systems fit automation very well, and automation has made it possible to take advantage of the distribution of terms in documents to allow, e.g., term weighting. There are, however, different ways of modelling retrieval systems within this broad framework, and it has not been possible, until recently, to provide concrete evidence for the real value and relative merits of the competing models. It has been impracticable to conduct the necessary large-scale retrieval experiments, because performance evaluation depends on having information about which documents are relevant to a query, and getting this information is extremely expensive.

This situation has changed in a number of ways. The development of the Web and the proliferation of machine-readable text (in the broadest sense) have made the 'information layer' and its operations much more central to computing in general than they were in the 50s. 'Retrieval' is now taken to encompass a wide range of different tasks. Probably as a consequence, seriously more resources have, over the last decade or two, become available for work in the general area of text retrieval. Retrieval research since Roger worked on it in the late 1950s and early 60s has changed out of all recognition.

These changes have brought the issue of models to the forefront, and have also afforded much greater opportunities for experimental work. Both these themes are explored below.

Retrieval system evaluation and model testing

The NIST/ARPA Text REtrieval Conferences (TRECs), initiated at the beginning of the 90s and still flourishing, have made it possible to evaluate retrieval systems far more thoroughly than ever before. The scale of the data in TREC, the range of tasks, the number of participants, and the multitude of tests have all contributed to this sea change.

Much of this effort has indeed gone into exploring variations on, and developments of, familiar themes, in fact ones dating back to the beginnings of automated retrieval research. But TREC has led to more than this, in two important ways. Many (though not all) of the retrieval systems tested have an explicit theoretical underpinning, or at least implicitly assume one. The Cornell Vector Space Model (VSM) is the most commonly invoked, but the University of Massachusetts Inference Model (IM), and the London/Cambridge Probabilistic Model (PM) have also been conspicuous since TREC began in 1992.

TREC has been sufficiently rigorous to subject not only system implementations based on these models, but the models themselves, to serious stress testing. The models have benefited from the development forced on them. They have also performed very well. Newer models have appeared too. Tests with a recent and strongly-argued Non-Classical Logic Model (NCLM) have so far been limited, but what we will summarily refer to as the Language Model (LM), derived from language modelling as used in speech recognition, has been very successfully applied in TREC to the rather different retrieval task.

All of these models operate within the generic framework mentioned in the previous section, and are statistically based. They exploit occurrence and co-occurrence patterns in index terms and documents for term weighting, search-query expansion, and the like. The fact that the models perform well, and scale up, is no longer a research surprise. Nor is the fact that they perform much the same. The basic data are all the same: there are document texts, query texts, and documents judged relevant to queries; and these are all data supplying some usable information about what retrieval is really about, namely document contents, information needs, and so forth. Further, since document retrieval is essentially an approximate task being conducted in a large and partially understood conceptual space, the same general properties of the objects in the space matter for all the theories and invoke the same responses from all of them, as eventually reflected in *tf*idf* term weighting. Several of the models also share, again not surprisingly, a generic probabilistic approach to retrieval.

But the models at their most fundamental are rather different. So we may ask how one might compare these different views, or on what grounds one might choose between them. The primary issue both of comparison and of choice is usually taken to be retrieval performance. But they may be compared in other ways, particularly in the absence of a consistent and material performance differential. We may consider the richness of each approach, in the sense of the extent to which it suggests or promotes different methods or techniques. We may, in ideal scientific fashion, attempt to make and validate experimentally further predictions from the models, other than of good retrieval performance. We may also —this is the main aim of the present note—discuss how each type of model views the critical relationships between retrieval objects (documents, queries, terms).

Model characteristics

This attempt to characterise the various models by how they see the relationship between documents and queries is of necessity crude and over-simplified, if only because it is often perfectly feasible for different theorists to accept the same formal framework on the basis of very different fundamental assumptions or interpretations. However, what follows may be a useful sketch.

The VSM treats the query-document relationship simply as an object *proximity* relation in an information space. There may be other objects associated with the space, like index terms. The vectors characterising objects (or the dimensions of the space itself, as in Latent Semantic Indexing) are manipulated to bring queries and relevant documents closer together [8].

The IM views the query-document relationship as a *connectivity* one. The connections that can be made between the two, e.g., through terms, justify the inference that a document should be retrieved [10].

The NCLM takes the query document relationship as a *proof* one, with the document proving the query, e.g., through statements about the index term descriptions [6].

The PM has a *generative* relation from a query to a document, making a prediction that a document, e.g., because it has certain terms, belongs to the class of relevant documents [7].

---

1   A commonly used form of term weighting which gives more importance to a term occurring frequently in the document under consideration, and less to a term which occurs in many documents

In the LM there is also a *generative* relationship, but the other way round, from the document to the query, i.e., the query is thought of as derived from the document in the same sort of way that in speech the heard sounds are generated from a word string [1, 4].

From these broad descriptions, it may not be clear whether or not the differences are fundamental, or how important they are practically speaking. The comparison may be further confused by other similarities between them, for instance, because in the IM inference is probabilistic, or because the PM may be given a network implementation [3]. One difference which does appear fundamental lies in whether the key retrieval notion of relevance figures explicitly as a model primitive. It does this in the PM, so that the generation relation is actually from both query *and* relevance to a retrieval-worthy document. Relevance does not figure so explicitly in the VSM, or in the IM or NCLM. We have argued elsewhere [2] that the LM does not explicitly use relevance either (although it has more recently been presented with an explicit relevance variable included in the model—see Lafferty and Zhai in [2]).

But though relevance may be taken as a primitive in a model, strictly relevance is inaccessible, a hidden variable, and at a very practical level, all the models may be interpreted as saying that the stronger the proximity/connectivity/... relation between query and document is, and thus the more highly ranked a document is in the search output, the more likely it is that a user will find the document relevant to his information need. Furthermore, for all the models, the specific expression of this proximity/... notion always makes use of the same basic statistical facts.

Model implications

The point just made does not, however, imply that the models are mere notational variants of one another. They indeed all deal in the same objects, queries, documents, terms, etc., and all (in one way or another and in various versions) respond to the statistical properties of retrieval data. But they make use of notions that are individually distinctive, albeit very general. So one question is whether any of the ground notions like proximity, inference, generation, etc., is more intuitively satisfying as a (or perhaps the) key concept for a theory of retrieval. Such a question may be taken as essentially a metaphysical matter, but another question is whether thinking about retrieval systems in terms of one central notion rather than another is more productive as a base for building effective (and robust, etc.) systems.

One possible position here is that the fact that some generic model has been used for different information and language processing tasks is important, because it reflects the fact that these tasks are all, broadly speaking, discourse (text) transformation tasks with something in common. From this point of view the LM, which has been applied to translation and summarising as well as speech transcription and retrieval, has something going for it. But on inspection, the LM generative account for some of these tasks seems distinctly forced. Other model mechanisms, like vector operations or the use of Bayes' Theorem, have been very widely exploited, but these are too abstract to make substantive task links in the way that language modelling is claimed to do through the idea of generation.

However, another view is that even if there are genuine differences between the abstract models, this doesn't really matter, because it is not where the shoe pinches. Thus consider the three input contributors to a retrieval system: the formal model (F); the estimation accuracy (or training potential) of the model (E); and the implementation detail (I). As already noted, when it comes to I, the weighting formulae used, for example, are much the same. With F, on the other hand, there either are no real differences, or the only differences that count are those that affect E, since this is what is going to determine operational system effectiveness. Any system using any model, in the statistical retrieval world, has to exploit its known data to predict what documents will be valuable. It may be that the LM approach (with a variety of different applications already developed) has an advantage here, in the form of a rich range of estimation methods on which to draw.

With the evaluation data we now have, we are in a much better position to assess claims of this kind. We can hope to demonstrate whether any of the models is superior to the others, either because its key notions are more productive in leading to good ways of looking at different retrieval tasks, or because it provides better ways of dealing with the challenges of estimation, or even because it leads to better performing implementations in, say, choice of weighting formulae. The question of what a retrieval system should be like, in its essentials, was one that Roger worked on, and his work was one of the sources of a modern probabilistic system [9]. Just as we benefited from his comments in the past, so would we have welcomed his views on the present Retrieval Model Action Space.

References

1. BERGER, A., AND LAFFERTY, J., 'Information retrieval as statistical translation,' *Proc. 22nd Annual International ACM SIGIR Conference on Research and Development in Information Retrieval*, 1999, pp. 222–229.
2. CROFT, W.B., AND LAFFERTY, J., (EDS.), *Language modelling for information retrieval*, Dordrecht: Kluwer, 2003.
3. KWOK, K.L., 'A network approach to probabilistic information retrieval,' *ACM Trans. on Information Systems*, vol. 13, 1995, pp. 324–353.
4. MILLER, D.R.H., LEEK, T., AND SCHWARTZ, R.M., 'A hidden Markov model retrieval system,' *Proc. of the 22nd Annual International ACM SIGIR Conference on Research and Development in Information Retrieval*, 1999, pp. 214–221.

5. NEEDHAM, R.M., 'A method for using computers in information classification,' *Information Processing 62: Proc. IFIP Congress 1962*, ed. Popplewell, Amsterdam: North-Holland, 1963, pp. 284–287.

6. VAN RIJSBERGEN, C.J., 'A non-classical logic for information retrieval,' *The Computer Journal*, vol. 29, 1986, pp. 481–485.

7. ROBERTSON, S.E., VAN RIJSBERGEN, C.J., AND PORTER, M.F., 'Probabilistic models of indexing and searching,' in *Information retrieval research*, ed. R.N. Oddy et al., London: Butterworths, 1981, pp. 35–56.

8. SALTON, G., WONG, A., AND YANG, C.S., 'A vector space model for automatic indexing,' *Comm. ACM*, vol. 18, 1975, pp. 613–620.

9. SPÄRCK JONES, K., WALKER, S., AND ROBERTSON, S.E., 'A probabilistic model of information retrieval: development and comparative experiments. Parts 1 and 2,' *Information Processing and Management*, vol. 36, 2000, pp. 779–840.

10. TURTLE, H.R., AND CROFT, W.B., 'Inference networks for document retrieval,' *Proc. of the 13th Annual International ACM SIGIR Conference on Research and Development in Information Retrieval*, 1990, pp. 1–24.

35
Slammer: An Urgent Wake-Up Call

Jerome H. Saltzer

The Slammer worm is an unusually urgent wake-up call,[1] demonstrating as never before the remarkable ease with which an attacker might paralyze the otherwise very robust Internet. Slammer did not quite succeed, because it happened to pick on an occasionally used interface that is not essential to the core operation of the Internet. If Slammer had found a target in a really popular interface, the Internet would have locked up before anyone could do anything about it, and getting things back to even a semblance of normal operation would probably have taken a long time.

How it worked

The basic principle of operation of Slammer was stunningly simple:[2]

1. Discover an Internet port that is enabled in many network-attached computers, and for which a popular listener implementation has a buffer overflow bug that a single, short packet can trigger. IP/UDP ports are thus a target of choice. Slammer exploited a bug in Microsoft SQL Server 2000 and Microsoft Server Desktop Engine 2000, both of which enable the SQL UDP port. This port is used for database queries, and it

---

1 This paper was written in January 2003 just following a devastating attack on the Internet by the Slammer worm. A later comparison of the measurements reported here with those reported in the final version of the paper by Moore et al. [footnote 4] suggests that Internet congestion distorted our measurements enough that they should not be relied upon; the situation in all respects is probably worse (from the point of view of defenders of the Internet) than the analysis here suggests.

2 This description of the operation of Slammer is based on a preliminary report found at Internet Worm W32/SQL/Slammer.worm, *McAfee Security Virus Information Library*: http://vil.nai.com/vil/content/v_99992.htm
(URL verified 30 January 2003)

is vulnerable only on Windows computers that run one of these database packages, so it is by no means universal.

2. Send to that port a packet that overflows the buffer, captures the execution point of the processor, and runs a program contained in the packet.

3. Write that program to go into a tight loop, generating an IP address at random and sending a copy of the same packet to that address, as fast as possible. The smaller the packet, the more packets per second the program can launch. Slammer used packets that were, with headers, 404 bytes long, so a broadband-connected (1 Megabit/second) machine could launch packets at a rate of 300/second, a machine with a 10 Megabits/second path to the Internet could launch packets at a rate of 3,000/second and a high-powered server with an OC-3 (155 Megabits/second) connection might be able to launch as many as 45,000 packets/second.

Forensics

Receipt of this single packet is enough to instantly recruit the target to help propagate the attack to other vulnerable systems. Recruitment modifies no files and leaves few traces, because the worm exists only in volatile memory. If you stop a recruited machine, disconnect it from the Internet, and reboot it, you will find nothing. There may be some counters indicating that there was a lot of outbound network traffic, but no clue why. So one remarkable feature of this kind of worm is the potential difficulty of tracing its source. The only forensic information available is likely to be the payload of the intentionally tiny worm packet.

Exponential attack rate

The second thing that makes this worm significant is how rapidly it increases its aggregate rate of attack. It recruits every vulnerable computer on the Internet as both a prolific propagator and also as an intense source of Internet traffic. The original launcher need merely find one vulnerable machine anywhere in the Internet and send it a single worm packet. This newly-recruited target will immediately begin sending copies of the worm packet to other addresses chosen at random. There are about 4 billion IP addresses, and even though many of them are unassigned, sooner or later one of these worm packets will hit another machine that has the same vulnerability. The worm packet immediately recruits this second machine to help with the attack. The expected time until a worm packet hits yet another vulnerable machine is now half and the volume of attack traffic double. Soon third and fourth machines will be recruited to join the attack; the expected time to find new recruits halves again and the malevolent traffic rate doubles again. This epidemic process proceeds with exponential growth until either a shortage of new, vulnerable targets or bottlenecked network links slows it down; the worm will quickly recruit every vulnerable machine on the Internet.[3]

The exponent of growth depends on the average time it takes to recruit the next target machine, which in turn depends on two things: the number of vulnerable targets and the rate of packet generation. If we suppose that the average recruited machine can generate IP addresses and send worm packets at a rate of 1 thousand per second, it will hit any one IP address about once every 4 million seconds, or roughly 45 days. At my home, my computer advertises a single IP address, and at the peak I was receiving a worm packet every 80 seconds. Starting with that observation, we can estimate the minimum number of recruits, assuming that the IP address generation mechanism of each worm is independent and memoryless and hits every IP address with equal probability:[4]

observed arrival rate:	$1/80 = 0.0125$ packets/second/IP address
number of IP addresses:	$2^{32} = 4 \cdot 10^9$ IP addresses
aggregate rate:	$.0125 \cdot 4 \cdot 10^9 = 5 \cdot 10^7$ packets/second
assumed rate per recruit:	10^3 packets/second/recruit
number of recruits:	$5 \cdot 10^7/10^3 = 50,000$

This number is a minimum, because at the peak of the packet storm it is likely that link and router saturation in many parts of the Internet substantially reduced the observed arrival rate. These 50 thousand or more recruits would be launching at least 50 million packets per second into the Internet, and the aggregate extra load on the Internet of these 3,200-bit packets probably amounted to something over 150 Gigabits/second, but that is well below the aggregate capacity of the Internet, which is why reported disruptions were localized rather than universal. (Warning: these back-of-the-envelope calculations depend on rough

---

3 The initial rate of spread up to the point that Internet bandwidth limitations begin to cap it can be described by a well-known formula called the logistic equation, applicable to population growth and epidemics. An analysis of the application of the logistic equation to Internet worm recruitment rate can be found in:
S. STANIFORD, V. PAXSON, AND N. WEAVER, 'How to own the Internet in your spare time,' *Proceedings of the 11th USENIX Security Symposium,* San Francisco, August 5–9, 2002.
http://www.icir.org/vern/papers/cdc-usenix-sec02/
(URL verified 30 January 2003)

4 An early report by disassemblers of Slammer indicates that its pseudo-random number generator was defective, and that the equal probability assumption did not apply, at least during the initial propagation of the worm. See D, MOORE,. ET AL., 'The spread of the Sapphire/Slammer worm.'
http://www.caida.org/outreach/papers/2003/sapphire/sapphire.html
(URL verified 1 February 2003)

measurements, unconfirmed assumptions, and a speculative guess about average rate of packet generation of each recruit. With luck this estimate of the number of recruits may be in the right order of magnitude.)

With 50 thousand vulnerable ports scattered through a space of 4 billion addresses, the chance that any single packet hits a vulnerable port is 1 in 120 thousand. If the first recruit sends 1 thousand packets per second, the expected time to hit a vulnerable port would be about 2 minutes. In four minutes there would be 4 recruits. In 6 minutes, 8 recruits. In half an hour, nearly all of the 50 thousand vulnerable machines would probably be participating.[5]

Extrapolation

The real problem appears if we redo that analysis for a port to which 5 million vulnerable computers listen: the time scale drops by two orders of magnitude. With that many listeners, a second recruit would receive the worm and join the attack within 1 second, 2 more 1 second later, etc. In less than 30 seconds, most of the 5 million machines would be participating, each launching traffic onto the Internet at the fastest rate they (or their Internet connection) can sustain. This level of attack, about two orders of magnitude greater than the intensity of Slammer, would almost certainly paralyze every corner of the Internet. And it could take quite a while to untangle, because the overload of every router and link would hamper communication among people who are trying to resolve the problem. In particular, it could be very difficult for owners of vulnerable machines to learn about and download any necessary patches.

Prior art

Slammer used a port that is not widely enabled, yet its recruitment rate, which determines its exponential growth rate, was at least one and perhaps two orders

---

5   These estimates both of the speed of onset and the Slammer worm's relatively mild effect on the Internet as a whole are confirmed by published measurements that show packet loss rates averaged across many servers increasing from near zero to a peak of a little under 20% in less than 30 minutes—see Matrix Net Systems Event Advisories, Slammer Worm Attack, Weekly summary, January 24 through January 30, 2003. http://www.matrixnetsystems.com/ea/index.jsp
(URL verified 1 February 2003)
In their paper cited above, Moore, et al., report observing Slammer to have an initial recruitment rate of 7/minute, about 15 times as fast as my calculation. This observation suggests that there were actually many more vulnerable hosts than estimated here. The alternative explanation, that the generation rate of the average recruit was far higher than 1 thousand packets/second, seems unlikely, though a somewhat higher generation rate may have contributed part of the difference.

of magnitude faster than that reported for the previous generation of fast-propagating worms, Code Red and Mind.[6] Those worms attacked much more widely-enabled ports, but they took longer to propagate because they used complex multipacket protocols that took much longer to set up. Interestingly, Slammer did not use any of several propagation enhancement techniques suggested by Staniford et al. Instead, the Slammer attack demonstrates the power of brute force. By choosing a UDP port, infection can be accomplished by a single packet, so there is no need for a time-consuming protocol interchange. And the smaller the packet size, the faster a recruit can then launch packets to discover other vulnerable ports.

Another risk

The worm also revealed a risk of what in the Internet are called class A or CIDR /8 networks. At the time that my computer, which advertises a single IP address, was receiving 1 Slammer worm packet every 80 seconds, a class C network (which advertises 256 addresses) would have been receiving 3 packets per second, a class B network (which advertises 65 thousand addresses) would have been receiving 750 packets/second, and a class A network (which advertises 16 million IP addresses) would have been receiving 200 thousand packets/second, with a data rate of about 640 Megabits/second. In confirmation, incoming traffic to the M.I.T. class A network-border routers peaked at a measured rate of around 500 Megabits/second, with the 155 Megabits/second link to the public Internet saturated.[7] Being the home of 16 million IP addresses has its hazards.

Lessons

From this incident we can draw some important lessons for different Internet participants: For users, the perennial but often-ignored advice to disable unused Internet ports does more than help a single computer resist attack, it helps protect the entire Internet. For vendors, shipping an operating system that by default activates a listener for a feature that the user does not explicitly request is hazardous to the health of the Internet. For implementers, the importance of diligent

---

6   The above-cited paper by Staniford et al., reported that Code Red had an initial recruitment rate of about 2 recruits/hour. Our lower-bound estimate for Slammer of 0.5 recruits/minute is 15 times greater, and the measurement of Slammer by Moore et al. of 7/minute is 200 times greater.

7   The M.I.T. router traffic statistics were reported in an e-mail message:
From: James D. Bruce (Director of Information Systems)
To: the MIT community,
Date: 28 January 2003 09:51:51 EST
Subject: Weekend Network Outage

care in network listener implementations, especially on widely activated UDP ports, has just ratcheted up another notch or two.

Acknowledgement

This note benefited greatly from review by and ensuing discussion with Hari Balakrishnan.

36
Caching Trust Rather Than Content[1]

M. Satyanarayanan

Position statement

Caching, one of the oldest ideas in computer science, often improves performance and sometimes improves availability [1, 3]. Previous uses of caching have
focused on *data content*. It is the presence of a local copy of data that reduces
access latency and masks server or network failures. This position paper puts
forth the idea that it can sometimes be useful to merely *cache knowledge sufficient to recognize valid data*. In other words, we do not have a local copy of a
data item, but possess a substitute that allows us to verify the content of that item
if it is offered to us by an untrusted source. We refer to this concept as *caching
trust*.

Mobile computing is a champion application domain for this concept. Wearable and handheld computers are constantly under pressure to be smaller and
lighter. However, the potential volume of data that is accessible to such devices
over a wireless network keeps growing. Something has to give. In this case, it is
the assumption that all data of potential interest can be *hoarded* on the mobile
client [1, 2, 6]. In other words, such clients have to be prepared to cope with
cache misses during normal use. If they are able to cache trust, then any untrusted site in the fixed infrastructure can be used to stage data for servicing
cache misses—one does not have to go back to a distant server, nor does one
have to compromise security. The following scenario explores this in more detail.

---

1 This contribution originally appeared as an article in *Operating Systems Review*, vol.
35, no. 4, October 2000.

Example scenario

An engineer with a wearable computer has to visit a distant site for troubleshooting. Because of limited client cache capacity, it is impossible for him to hoard all the repair manuals and proprietary company documents he may require at the site. He therefore has to be prepared to cope with cache misses while on site. Unfortunately, that site only has occasional connectivity via a satellite link to the servers at home. Further, satellite communications are restricted to off-peak hours to reduce cost; at other times, the site is effectively disconnected.

At the remote site there is excellent, high-bandwidth short-range wireless coverage. There are also many machines with ample disk capacity available for temporary use by the engineer. It would be convenient to use one of these machines as a surrogate server, staging data in bulk from the real servers to the surrogate so that cache misses can be serviced efficiently on site. Unfortunately, security is lax at the remote site. The engineer cannot be confident that the surrogate will not be tampered with. Under these circumstances, how can the engineer be assured that the data he accesses at the remote site is indeed authentic?

Integrity and privacy

A common trust model is to assume that servers are physically secure and trusted, and that the client-server communication channel is encrypted for privacy. Staging data at an untrusted surrogate hurts both integrity and privacy. The challenge is to preserve these properties even when the surrogate is physically compromised. This can be accomplished either using private or public key encryption. For brevity, the discussion below focuses on a private key approach. The corresponding public key approach is easy to derive.

Integrity is the easier of the two security properties to preserve. We envision an approach in which the user hoards the fingerprints (such as MD5 checksums [5]) of all files of potential interest directly from the server before leaving on his trip. Since fingerprints are much smaller than file contents, this is only a small burden on the disk capacity of the client. When a cache miss occurs at the remote site, the corresponding data is fetched from the surrogate and its fingerprint is computed by the client; the data is accepted only if the computed and cached fingerprints match.

The problem becomes more complex if data can change at the server after the user leaves home. In that case, the user needs to obtain fresh fingerprints. This requires a trusted channel from client to server, but a low-bandwidth modem link may suffice. A public key approach would be simpler in this regard, since digitally signed updates can be sent over an untrusted channel.

It is simple to extend this idea to privacy. In addition to a fingerprint, the client also hoards a per-file private encryption key. The server encrypts each file before staging it on the surrogate. To handle a cache miss at the remote site, the client fetches the data from the surrogate, decrypts it, verifies its fingerprint and then uses the data. The volume of cached keys can be reduced by using a single private encryption key for all files, at the price of total exposure if that key is broken.

This solution to the privacy problem is not fully satisfactory. It is not possible to ensure purging of staged data from the surrogate because it lies outside the administrative domain of the client and server. With enough time and effort, the keys of staged files can be broken and their contents revealed. The keys can be chosen to be strong enough that breaking them will take much longer than the expected duration of surrogate use. However, it is not feasible to guarantee the privacy of staged data indefinitely. This approach may therefore be restricted to situations where privacy is not an issue, or where there is a well-defined time bound on privacy of information.

Status and plans

We are in the early stages[2] of building a system that uses the idea of caching trust. Our work is being done in the context of the Aura Project at Carnegie Mellon, a new research initiative whose theme is "distraction-free, ubiquitous computing." Support for nomadic data access in Aura uses the Coda File System as a back end. Coda was recently extended to exploit surrogates for efficient update propagation over low-bandwidth networks [4]. We now plan to further extend the system to exploit surrogates for servicing cache misses, as described here. An important implementation question we hope to answer is whether the support for using surrogates securely can be fully encapsulated in a user-level proxy that runs on a Coda client, avoiding changes to Coda itself.

From a broader perspective, opportunistic exploitation of remote infrastructure is key to the long-term success of mobile computing. Unfortunately, security concerns loom large in such architectures. Caching trust may prove to be an important enabling technology for these architectures. The idea is particularly relevant to secure coprocessors and smartcards because their limited storage capacity may be adequate for caching trust but not data content.

Acknowledgements

This research was supported by the National Science Foundation (NSF) under grant number CCR-9901696, and the Defense Advanced Research Projects Agency (DARPA) via the Office of Naval Research (ONR) under contract number N66001-99-2-8918. Additional support was provided by IBM. The views

---

2   Editor's note: This status report and future plan relates to the time the original paper was written (i.e., summer 2000).

and conclusions contained here are those of the authors and should not be interpreted as necessarily representing the official policies or endorsements, either express or implied, of NSF, DARPA, ONR, IBM, CMU, or the U.S. Government. Discussions with Jason Flinn, Jan Harkes and Adrian Pavlykevych were valuable in developing these ideas.

References

1. KISTLER, J.J., AND SATYANARAYANAN, M., 'Disconnected Operation in the Coda File System,' *ACM Trans. On Computer Systems*, vol. 10, no. 1, February 1992, pp. 1–25.
2. KUENNING, G.H., AND POPEK, G.J., 'Automated hoarding for mobile computers,' *Proc. 16th ACM Symposium on Operating Systems Principles, Operating Systems Review*, vol. 31, no. 5, December 1997, pp. 264–275.
3. LAMPSON, B.W., 'Hints for computer system design,' *Proc. 9th ACM Symposium on Operating Systems Principles, ACM Operating Systems Review*, vol. 15, no. 5, October 1983, pp. 33–48, reprinted in *IEEE Software*, vol. 1, no. 1, January 1984, pp. 11–28.
4. LEE, Y., LEUNG, K.S., AND SATYANARAYANAN, M., 'Operation-based update propagation in a mobile file system,' *Proc. Usenix Annual Technical Conference*, Monterey, CA, USA, June 1999.
5. RIVEST, R., 'The MD5 Message-Digest Algorithm,' Internet RFC 1321.
6. TAIT, C.D., LEI, H., ACHARYA S., AND CHANG, H., 'Intelligent file hoarding for mobile computers,' *Proc. MobiCom '95: First Annual International Conference on Mobile Computing and Networking*, Berkeley, CA, USA, November 1995, 119–125.

37
Least Privilege and More[1]

Fred B. Schneider

Introduction

What today is known as the Principle of Least Privilege was described as a design principle in a paper by Jerry Saltzer and Mike Schroeder [4] first submitted for publication roughly 30 years ago:

> Least privilege: Every program and every user of the system should operate using the least set of privileges necessary to complete the job. Primarily, this principle limits the damage that can result from an accident or error. It also reduces the number of potential interactions among privileged programs to the minimum for correct operation, so that unintentional, unwanted, or improper uses of privilege are less likely to occur. Thus, if a question arises related to misuse of a privilege, the number of programs that must be audited is minimized. Put another way, if a mechanism can provide 'firewalls,' the principle of least privilege provides a rationale for where to install the firewalls. The military security rule of 'need-to-know' is an example of this principle.

The power of this principle comes from leaving unspecified how frequently privileges might change and their granularity. Back in 1972, Roger Needham certainly understood the value of support for dynamic assignments of privileges, writing [3]:

1   Supported in part by AFOSR grant F49620-00-1-0198, Defense Advanced Research Projects Agency (DARPA) and Air Force Research Laboratory Air Force Material Command USAF under Agreement number F30602-99-1-0533, National Science Foundation Grant 9703470, and ONR Grant N00014-01-1-0968. The views and conclusions contained herein are those of the authors and should not be interpreted as necessarily representing the official policies or endorsements, either expressed or implied, of these organizations or the U.S. Government.

Protection regimes are not constant during the life of a process. They may change as the work proceeds, and in a fully general discussion they should be allowed to change arbitrarily. Statements would be allowed, for example, to the effect that certain segments were only accessible if the value standing in a system microsecond clock were prime. In practice one departs from full generality, and limits those circumstances which may give rise to a change of protection regime.

My own interest in the Principle of Least Privilege developed in connection with devising security enforcement mechanisms for systems structured in terms of a base and a set of extensions which augment the functionality of that base. Such extensible systems are prevalent today in mass-market PC software, where we see new hardware being accommodated in Microsoft Windows platforms through "plug and play" and we see Web browsers—hence, the Web itself—supporting new data formats by use of downloaded "helper apps" that extend a browser's functionality.

A misbehaving extension *Ext* has the potential to compromise the base system B it extends. Examples abound: email containing executable attachments, Microsoft Word documents bearing hostile macros, and new browser "helper apps" that are a far cry from being helpful. This situation could be improved if we posit some sort of reference monitor that intercepts all program actions and, according to privileges held by the issuer of the action, blocks those that would be disruptive. However, to make this vision a reality, two technical questions must be solved:

1.   implementing the reference monitor
2.   determining a policy for it to enforce

Regarding (1), my collaborators and I have elsewhere reported success with program rewriters to modify an object program before execution, adding tests that effectively place a fine-grained reference monitor in-line [2]. This paper sketches my current thinking on (2).

What policy to enforce?

Least privilege

Policies consistent with the Principle of Least Privilege depend not only on the code to be executed but also on what job that code is intended to do. For an extension *Ext* and some specification S_{Ext} of a job to be done, we define *Priv(Ext, S_{Ext})* to be the policy that grants the minimum privileges needed for execution of *Ext* to satisfy S_{Ext}. (A policy here is a mapping from system histories to sets of privileges.) As an example, specification S_{Ext} of a spell-checker extension *Ext* for a word processor might specify that misspelled words be flagged in the word processor's open file F; we would then expect *Priv(Ext, S_{Ext})* to be a policy that permits the spell-checker read (but not write) access to F, read (but not write) access to a file containing a spelling dictionary, and read/write access to a file containing user-added spellings for local jargon terms.

It is clear how the base system comes to get an extension Ext, but how does it get $Priv(Ext, Spec_{Ext})$ for use by its reference monitor? Here are two possible approaches:

1. The base system could itself compute $Priv(Ext, Ext)$.
2. The base system could fetch $Priv(Ext, Ext)$ from some site S.

Approach (1) presumes that $Priv(Ext, Spec_{Ext})$ can be computed—a questionable supposition. Implicit in computing $Priv(Ext, Spec_{Ext})$ is establishing that extension Ext satisfies specification $Spec_{Ext}$, and we know that question cannot be decided for general-purpose programming and specification languages. There might exist specialized languages, however, for which $Priv(Ext, Spec_{Ext})$ could be computed; this is a research question that bears closer scrutiny. One might start by restricting consideration to specifications $Spec_{Ext}$ that are safety properties, because the language of specifications now can be restricted to state predicates that hold throughout system execution. The weakest precondition (wp) predicate transformer might then provide a starting point for defining $Priv$ by structural induction on Ext.

Approach (1) also presumes that $Spec_{Ext}$ is known. This, too, is a supposition of dubious practicality. Since extensions are generally downloaded with some expectation of the job they are intended to do, one might suspect that a high-level, task-oriented specification $Spec_{Ext}$ would be known to the initiator and serve as the impetus for the Ext download. But employing such a high-level task-oriented specification does not suffice if Ext involves implementation details that are not obvious for the task and thus have been omitted from $Spec_{Ext}$. For example, recall the spell-checker extension introduced above, which is specified in terms of a single file F. This spell-checker actually also involves accessing two other files (a spelling dictionary and a jargon dictionary) and might in addition even access a backing-store file perhaps over a local network. Such knowledge of implementation details is not going to be available to the initiator of an Ext download and, therefore, would not be included in high-level task-oriented specification $Spec_{Ext}$, though clearly $Priv(Ext, Spec_{Ext})$ would need to include privileges for accessing the spelling dictionary, the jargon dictionary, and the backing store.

If $Spec_{Ext}$ cannot be deduced locally, then perhaps it could be downloaded and checked. Unfortunately, this architecture also has problems. The local checking is really a form of policy review, and policy review is a hard problem whenever the policy being checked is complicated. A specification $Spec_{Ext}$ that involves internal details is going to be complicated and thus difficult for a human to understand. The alternative to policy review is simply to trust the source of $Spec_{Ext}$. But, then, why not simply trust the source of Ext to provide a safe extension and dispense with reference monitoring altogether?

For approach (2) to be workable, either S must be trusted or the base system must itself have some means to check whether what it has fetched equals $Priv(Ext, Spec_{Ext})$. The latter is unworkable for the reasons argued above. Regarding the former, an obvious question is whether trusting S to provide $Priv(Ext, _{Ext})$ could be materially different from trusting S to provide a safe implementation of Ext.

And more

At least for the time being, then, it seems as though obtaining $Priv(Ext, _{Ext})$ for use by a reference monitor associated with the base of an extensible system is infeasible, and an alternative must be sought. So the policies we are now investigating seek to prevent extensions from subverting a base system or, equivalently, seek to prevent any extension from violating the assumptions underlying the design and implementation of that base. Such assumptions include the following:

- Characteristics of the programming model employed for building the base, such as properties of underlying system abstractions and language-level abstractions. For example, the separate address spaces usually accorded to process abstractions bring guarantees about integrity of storage; and type systems in modern programming languages, like Java and C#, bring guarantees about how certain variables can be used.
- Invariants that the base maintains about state. For example, a complicated linked-list data structure might be characterized by an invariant stating which nodes are reachable from each other; each routine to manipulate the data structure is then designed (i) to work correctly if that invariant holds prior to execution and (ii) upon termination, to leave the data structure in a state satisfying the invariant.

Provided these assumptions can be expressed as safety properties—and most can—then they can be enforced by use of in-line reference monitoring. Prior to execution, each extension is rewritten by adding checks that ensure no action the extension performs will violate any assumption required by the base system.

Notice that in this alternative to $Priv(Ext, _{Ext})$, a single policy is being employed, independent of extension Ext. The problems of deciding what specification $_{Ext}$ to use with a given extension Ext is thus eliminated. But the use of a single policy for all extensions implies that the policy being enforced might not be as restrictive as it could be (thereby admitting attacks) or might be too restrictive (thereby ruling out execution of certain extensions). And there is thus some flexibility in formulating a policy for a given base.

Some final comments

The articulation of abstractions and principles is an important facet of doing research in computing systems. An implementation is certainly one way to demonstrate the utility of a new systems abstraction or principle, with system performance a sensible figure of merit. However, some abstractions are useful even though they cannot be implemented. Belady's optimal page replacement policy [1], which involves predicting future memory references and therefore is unrealizable in practice, is one example. The Principle of Least Privilege might be another, offering value primarily as a benchmark against which to compare policies that are being enforced—when compared with $Priv(Ext, \, _{Ext})$, a deployed policy would be considered inferior if it either admits additional attacks or excludes certain classes of extensions.

The classical approach to computer security—address space isolation associated with processes—would seem a good place to start in a comparison of security policies for extensible systems. It isn't. The context switches required on modern processors for communication and synchronization between separate processes make it impractical to have fine-grained interaction between a base implemented as one process and an extension as another. Without the possibility of such fine-grained interaction, the set of functions that can be implemented as extensions becomes quite limited.

But with in-lined reference monitors, different programs can be isolated from each other without incurring the high cost of context switches. In fact, many forms of fine-grained access control that are not practical with traditional reference monitors become practical with in-line reference monitors. Another concern now confronts us, though: how best to exploit the flexibility. To make progress here, not only must we learn the art of writing policies but we must also develop the mathematical tools for analyzing them. Collections of weak policies are likely to provide workable defenses for broad sets of extensions, for example. Weak policies might well be easier for humans to understand, too. Exactly how these advantages trade with the "security" $Priv(Ext, \, _{Ext})$ provides is the ultimate question. For the present, however, it seems that practical protection for extensible systems is most easily obtained using policies that grant more privileges than would $Priv(Ext, \, _{Ext})$—the least privilege and more.

Acknowledgements

Helpful comments on a preliminary draft of this paper were provided by Lorenzo Alvisi, Butler Lampson, Greg Morrisett, Andrew Myers, and Mike Schroeder.

References

1. BELADY, L.A., 'A study of replacement algorithms in a virtual storage computer,' *IBM Systems Journal*, vol. 5, no. 2, 1966, pp. 78–101.
2. ERLINGSSON, U., AND SCHNEIDER, F.B., 'SASI enforcement of security policies: a retrospective,' *Proc. of the New Security Paradigms Workshop*, Caledon Hills, Ontario, Canada, September 1999, ACM, pp. 87–95.

3.   NEEDHAM, R.M., 'Protection systems and protection implementations,' *Proc. of the 1972 Fall Joint Computer Conference*, AFIPS Conf. Proc., vol. 41, pt. 1, pp. 571–578.

4.   SALTZER, J.H., AND SCHROEDER, M.D., 'The protection of information in computer systems,' *Proc. of the IEEE*, vol. 63, no. 9, September 1975, pp. 1278–1308.

38
Using Sharing to Simplify System Management

Michael D. Schroeder

The cost of ownership for many computer systems in non-home environments is dominated by ongoing system management. This paper addresses the management issues around storage-intensive systems that serve network-attached clients, particularly file servers, mail and calendaring servers, and database servers. The paper begins by describing a three-layer structure for large server systems that is often employed where availability and scale considerations require the use of multiple computers to implement a single service. It then contrasts a system organization called the uniserver model, in which the permanent state is partitioned among the application servers, with an organization called the multiserver model, in which the permanent state is shared among all the application servers. Reviewing the relative advantages and disadvantages of the two models suggests using a multiserver as a uniserver. The sharing from the multiserver model makes a system easier to manage than a uniserver. But if dynamic sharing is avoided in normal operation, as in a uniserver, then the combined system avoids many of the drawbacks of both models.

Three-layer systems

A useful structure for a multi-computer system that maintains a significant permanent state and has network-attached clients is to organize the hardware components into three layers by function.

At the bottom is the storage subsystem, consisting of large numbers of disks and their controllers. These days the storage subsystem is usually interconnected with a storage area network, such as Fibre Channel, to which all the computers are also attached. In the middle layer are the computer systems that implement the service: file servers, mail servers, or database servers. At the top layer are the computer systems that front the system to the network. They collect client requests from the network and distribute them to the middle-layer computers.

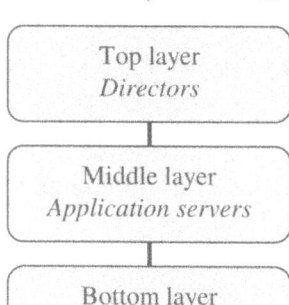

These top-layer computers can be simple directors that pass requests directly to the middle layer, or they can be web servers that implement the visible interface and formulate the needed middle-layer requests.

The bottom-layer storage subsystem is usually responsible for reliably storing the permanent state, although in some systems the middle layer participates too. Reliability is achieved by using data-redundancy techniques such as RAID, as well as by replicating the controllers and network components. Data is usually backed up to offline media. In addition, if the bottom layer provides storage virtualization, then it can do things like load balancing to improve performance. This possibility is discussed later.

The three-layer system organization can be used in two different ways: uniserver or multiserver. With the uniserver model, each middle-layer server acts on a unique partition of the permanent state of the system that is stored by the bottom layer. With the multiserver model, each middle-layer server can act on all of that permanent state. These two models have different strengths and weaknesses.

The uniserver model

Today, the most common organization for dividing the work among the middle-layer servers is to partition the permanent state of the system among them. I call this organization with partitioned state the uniserver model. For example, in a file system, different sub-trees of the naming hierarchy will be implemented by different file servers in the middle layer; in an email system, different sets of user accounts will be implemented by different mail servers; in a database system, different tables of the database will be implemented by different database servers.

The top-layer directors understand the partitioning scheme and direct each request to the middle-layer server that "owns" the permanent storage needed to answer it. Sometimes a request needs to be divided into several pieces, each of which is directed to a different server, and the results combined in order to respond to the client, although atomicity is usually not provided for requests that span multiple servers

As the patterns of client requests evolve and as the system state grows, it is sometimes necessary to redistribute the state among the middle-layer servers and add new ones to maintain good performance. Available tools can detect load-pattern changes and overloaded servers, suggest optimal partitioning of the state, and reorganize the storage layers to achieve good performance.

Another reason for changing the distribution pattern is the failure of a middle-layer server. If high availability is a goal, then the system will be provisioned with extra standby servers to take over from failed servers. Failover requires detecting the failure, detaching the associated permanent state from the failed server, attaching it to a standby server, starting the standby server with the transferred state, and cleaning up any unfinished business found in that state. The top-level directors are then told to direct requests to the new server.

There is some global shared state in a uniserver system: the list of application servers and the characterization of the partitions of the data they each serve. This global state needs to change when the partitioning is changed and when failover occurs, but it changes infrequently and it is small.

The uniserver organization is sometimes called the shared-nothing approach because middle-level servers share no permanent state. The partitions of the permanent state are attached to one middle-level server at a time. The shared-nothing approach was once mandatory, since there were no storage interconnects that allowed disks to be accessed by more than one computer at a time. But even though this constraint has been removed by the march of technology, people continue to claim the enduring value of the shared-nothing approach. The shared-nothing model is used widely in commercial products. For example, Microsoft's SQL, Exchange, or NTFS servers deployed on Microsoft Cluster Server [5] are examples of this organization. I use the term "uniserver" instead of "shared-nothing" because uniserver contrasts better with its alternative, the multiserver model, discussed below.

The multiserver model

An alternative to the uniserver model for three-layer systems is the multiserver model. In this approach all middle-layer servers in a system can operate on all the permanent state contained in the bottom-layer storage subsystem. For example, with a multiserver file system a single (large) hierarchical name space is served by all servers in the middle layer. Any of the servers can operate on any folder or file. Over the last ten years or so, progress in storage area networks, systems area networks, and local area networks has made shared access to storage affordable and scalable with good performance. With the multiserver model the top-layer director function is still required in order to do load balancing and avoid failed servers. In the case of a multiserver, however, the directors can make dynamic decisions that are not completely dictated by data location.[1]

The multiserver model makes extra demands on the implementation of the middle-layer servers. In particular, they need to coordinate their access to the permanent state. Coordination is usually done using a global locking service that allows middle-layer servers to set locks on portions of the permanent state. A lock prevents conflicting access from other servers. Choosing the best granularity for the locking, e.g., per folder, per file, or per byte range in the case of a file service, depends on the pattern of expected client requests. The need to coordinate also complicates the management of data caches in the servers.

A multiserver system is expanded by attaching a new middle-layer server to the storage subsystem, updating the membership list so that the top-layer directors know about the new server, and letting the new server initialize itself by reading from the permanent state.

Failure of a middle-layer server can be covered by directing requests to another server, because all servers can operate on all parts of the permanent state. When servers encounter locks still held by the failed server, they must take a special action to recover the lock and complete or abort the operations it protected. This is similar to cleaning up the unfinished business of a failed server when doing failover for a uniserver system. In both cases the new server reads and acts on the operation log written by the failed server.

Multiserver systems have been around for some time. An early successful example was the DEC VAX/VMS cluster [1], which provides a multiserver file system. The Rdb/VMS data base implemented on such a cluster was the TPC-A performance champion of its time [4]. More recently the Frangipani global-cluster file-system prototype [6] has demonstrated good performance and automatic operation using these techniques.

Arguments in favor of uniservers

Uniserver systems realize several benefits directly from their organization. By having each partition of the permanent data under control of a single server, undesirable interactions among the servers are minimized. Each server has a free hand in managing and caching that data and in accessing the permanent state

---

1   For both uniserver and multiserver systems it is possible to put the director function in a clerk module in the clients. The clerk module retrieves configuration information directly from the middle-level servers and uses it to send each client request directly to the appropriate server. With this structure the top-layer directors are bypassed. Clerk modules work best when clients are modest in number and well-connected to the server system. For large-scale systems with many distant clients, it is best to have the director run on top-layer servers of the system, as described here.

without the interference of other servers. Lack of interference can lead to good performance. An application server is "near" its data, in the sense that the connection from the data storage subsystem to the server for the associated partition doesn't need to branch. When a server crashes it cannot affect the operation of other servers or other partitions. This lack of unwanted interaction contributes to system stability. Finally, failover is an activity confined to the chosen standby server, without system-wide repercussions other than temporary unavailability of data from the affected permanent state.

Arguments against uniservers

The partitioning of the permanent state that characterizes the uniserver organization generates some problems. Perhaps most important is that maintaining optimal partitioning is a management burden in operating such a system. Growth in the load, changes in the access patterns, and growth of the permanent state require repartitioning the system. Such repartitioning can involve copying the data. Repartitioning can be time intensive and can take the system entirely or partially offline. In typical implementations failover is slow: getting the standby server up to speed from scratch can take minutes. Addressing this problem by having a hot standby mitigates some of the simplicity and non-interference advantages mentioned earlier.

Arguments in favor of multiservers

Multiserver systems also have their benefits. Requests can be dynamically distributed according to load. Requests to read-only hot spots in the data, for example, can be satisfied from multiple middle-level servers in parallel without any pre-positioning of the data. The needed data would find its way from the shared storage subsystem into the caches of all the servers, where it could be accessed rapidly at each, increasing throughput of the overall system. Recovery from the failure of a middle-level server can be fast because all other servers are automatically "hot." Repartitioning the permanent state is never necessary since all servers can access all of the permanent state. The result is that management overhead for such a system is low and there are no lengthy outages for reconfiguration.

Arguments against multiservers

Problems with the multiserver organization include interference between servers needing temporary exclusive access to the same data. Such lock conflicts can result in unpredictable performance. Also, implementing the global lock service as a high-performance, scalable, distributed program is complex. With multiserver systems, failures can impact the operation of all other servers as they recover the locks held by the failed server and take over the load. Another negative for the multiserver organization is that many existing commercial file servers, mail servers, and database servers are not designed to share access to their permanent data. While there is general ignorance about how hard fixing this would be, it clearly would be a major development task. Finally, the storage subsystem has to be able to deliver all of the permanent state to all servers with good performance, a requirement that has been difficult to achieve.

Using a multiserver as a uniserver

It seems possible to combine the advantages of the uniserver and multiserver models and lose most of drawbacks. The idea is to use the top-layer directors and distribution tables from a uniserver system on a multiserver system with the same permanent state. The uniserver directors will route requests in a pattern that prevents the multiservers from sharing items from the permanent data, even though they could share. Under this scheme, at system start-up or reconfiguration there would be an initial flurry of activity at the global locking service while each application server collects the locks it needs as requests come in. There would never be contention for these locks, since the directors are implementing the same routing decisions that they would for the uniserver system having a partitioned permanent state. Eventually lock requests would largely stop occurring as each server obtained all the locks it needed. The steady state would be characterized by a background level of lock renewals without contention. The performance concerns surrounding contention in a multiserver system would not surface with this scheme.

But have we gained any of the advantages of multiservers? I think we have. Repartitioning, scaling, and failover can happen faster and with less management intervention or service disruption in a multiserver system. Consider each in turn.

Repartitioning

As with a uniserver system, monitoring tools watch for signs that repartitioning is needed. In addition to server load, lock contention is a good telltale. For the multiserver, however, repartitioning is accomplished by changing only the routing pattern implemented by the top-layer director computers. No changes in the organization of the storage subsystem are required. As the middle-layer servers start seeing requests that require access to new parts of the permanent state they obtain the corresponding locks and fulfil the requests. The previous lock holders release their claims because of these requests for contending locks from other servers. After some interval, locking service activity would drop to a background level again. The system continues offering service while the reconfiguration is stabilizing, perhaps with some small loss of performance due to increased locking traffic.

Scaling

An added middle-layer server attaches itself to the permanent storage of the system and internalizes the meta-data it needs to commence operation. All of the state needed is available to the new server either in the shared storage subsystem or in the membership list and locking service. The membership list for the system is updated to record the new server and the distributors adjust the routing algorithm to allow the new server to operate on a virtual partition of the permanent state. Again, no management intervention is required other than policy direction as appropriate. The system continues to provide service during scaling.

Failover

A failure of a middle-layer server is detected by monitoring mechanisms that are largely similar in the uniserver and multiserver cases. Once detected, the multiserver system adjusts the routing decisions made by the top-layer distributor computers to effectively assign the portion of the permanent data associated with the failed application server to one or more other servers. In the multiserver case, as with the uniserver case, there can be standby servers waiting to receive the load. Lock redistribution follows until the locking service activity quiesces in the new state. When acquiring broken locks abandoned by a failed server, a new server inspects the operations log of the failed server, available from the storage subsystem, to determine the cleanup actions required.

In summary, use of the multiserver organization, but with directors that minimize or eliminate actual sharing among active middle-layer servers, can substantially reduce the cost of management for such systems without much impact on system performance, reliability, or cost.

More on the storage subsystem

As described so far, the bottom-layer storage subsystem is a collection of disks, controllers, and network components with the property that all middle-layer servers can access all disks. Storage reliability is achieved by the use of redundancy within the storage subsystem. This black-box model of the storage subsystem is appropriate for discussing the distinction between uniserver and multiserver systems. Achieving minimum-intervention management and good performance for the overall system, however, may demand additional functionality from the storage subsystem. The extra features are equally useful in uniserver and multiserver systems. In particular, it may be useful for the storage subsystem to implement load balancing, incremental growth, and failover on its own. The key technique for adding these features is storage virtualization, in which the storage subsystem implements one or more virtual storage volumes that are addressed like very large disks. A mapping from the blocks of the virtual volume to the physical storage hides the redundancy scheme and the distribution of the data among controllers and disks.

With a volume virtualization scheme, failed disks and controllers can be replaced and new disks and controllers added on demand. The only change the middle-layer servers see is that the virtual volumes can change size. Automatic algorithms operating in the background copy data among the attached disks to achieve capacity and load balance and to restore the desired level of data redundancy. No management intervention is required. Operator intervention is required to replace or add hardware, but not to configure it. The Petal storage-management system [3] is one example of this kind of storage virtualization.

A shared storage subsystem with volume virtualization clearly would be an asset to a uniserver system as well as a multiserver system and would mitigate some of the management burden associated with uniserver systems.

Discussion

The multiserver organization requires distributed systems software in addition to shared physical access to the storage subsystem. Over the last ten years considerable progress has been made on this software technology. There now are good algorithms for the global state management needed to maintain the system membership list. Perhaps the best algorithms are those in the Paxos family [2]. A global locking service built using leases and depending on server operation logs for lock recovery, as in the Frangipani example, can have good performance and scaling characteristics. This design is a simplification of the traditional distributed lock manager [7]. Because a partitioned multiserver system operates in a way that minimizes or eliminates dynamic sharing, the locking service and the coordination mechanisms for the server data caches are not stressed.

The distinction between uniserver and multiserver systems focuses on two ends of a spectrum of implementations. Many of the ideas I have associated with multiservers can be applied in some form to uniservers. For example, in a uniserver using standby servers for failover, the idea of hot standbys can be pushed to the point where the standby server is tracking the active server, operation by operation, so that its internal state is almost complete and up-to-date when the failover occurs. This can make failover faster. In this case the experienced system designer will be wary, however, since we would be adding a special purpose mechanism used only to support the unusual case of failover, whereas the similar machinery in a multiserver would be part of the base functionality of the system and thus more likely to be correct.

Summary

In this paper I have argued that sharing is a good organizational technique for a multi-computer server system, especially if the system is configured so that sharing is not on the critical path of high-volume operations. The sharing mechanisms can make the inevitable system transitions caused by reconfiguration, failure, and growth fit more seamlessly into system operation, minimizing the management attention required to perform them. A system organization that combines the good features of the uniserver and multiserver models has the potential to realize this goal.

Acknowledgements

These ideas have benefited from discussions with my colleagues Kurt Friedrich, Jim Gray, Chandu Thekkath, and Chad Verbowski. In addition Ulfar Erlingsson, Andrew Herbert, Michael Isard, Bill Laing, Butler Lampson, Roy Levin, Fred Schneider, Leslie Schroeder, Chuck Thacker, and Lidong Zhou made useful suggestions.

References

1. KRONENBERG, N., LEVY, H., AND STECKER, W., 'VAXClusters: a closely-coupled distributed system,' *ACM Trans. on Computer Systems,* vol. 4 no. 2, May 1986, pp. 130–146.
2. LAMPORT, L., 'The part-time parliament,' *ACM Trans. on Computer Systems*, vol. 16 no. 2, May 1998, pp. 133–169.
3. LEE, E., AND THEKKATH, C., 'Petal: distributed virtual disks,' *Proc. 7th International Conference on Architectural Support for Programming Languages and Operating Systems, ASPLOS-VII*, ACM, October 1996, pp. 84–92.
4. LOMET, DAVID, ET. AL, *How the Rdb/VMS data sharing system became fast*, Digital Equipment Corporation Cambridge Research Lab report CRL 92/4, May 1992.
5. MICROSOFT, Windows server 2003: server cluster architecture. Available as: http://www.microsoft.com/windowsserver2003/docs/ServerClustersArchitecture.doc
6. THEKKATH, C., MANN, T., AND LEE, E., 'Frangipani: a scalable distributed file system,' *Proc. 16th ACM Symposium on Operating Systems Principles*, ACM, October 1997, pp. 224–237.
7. SNAMAN, W., JR., AND THIEL, D., 'The VAX/VMS distributed lock manager,' *Digital Technical Journal,* vol. 1 no. 5, Sept 1987, pp. 29–44.

39

An RSA-Related Number-Theoretic Surprise

Gustavus J. Simmons

It is a folklore result that factoring an RSA modulus $n = pq$ given the Euler function $\phi(n)$ only requires the extraction of a single square root. There does not appear to be a correspondingly simple algebraic formula to factor n directly given the universal exponent $\lambda(n)$. If $\phi(n)$ could be calculated from $\lambda(n)$, then n could be factored directly, but $\lambda(n)$, compared to $\phi(n)$, can be as small as $2\lambda(n)$, or as large as $\text{Int}[\sqrt{(n/2)}]\,\lambda(n)$, depending on the choice of the primes p and q. The surprising result presented here is that in spite of this enormous range of possible values for $\lambda(n)$, only a single division is required to calculate $\phi(n)$ from $\lambda(n)$ for any RSA modulus.

Introduction

In the first few years after the discovery of the RSA crypto algorithm, several schemes were proposed that can best be described as common modulus protocols in which a central keying authority (CKA) chose the primes p and q and then calculated pairs of exponents e_i and d_i for each of the subscribers/users to the system. The reason for considering such schemes was that at the time it was very difficult and very slow to carry out modular exponentiations with numbers of the size required for the modulus to be infeasible to factor. By using a common modulus, it was possible for the CKA to do pre-computations that could then be used by all of the subscribers to speed up the encryption/decryption computations. Subsequent advances in both computational algorithms and VLSI chips rendered these considerations moot. Before this happened, though, such systems were shown to be cryptographically insecure by Simmons [1], who gave a probabilistic algorithm that could almost certainly factor n given any multiple of $\lambda(n)$, and by DeLaurentis [1], who gave a deterministic algorithm (valid if the extended Riemann hypothesis holds) to calculate the matching secret key for any public key under the same conditions. Since $e_i d_i \equiv 1 \bmod \lambda(n)$, these two results meant that any subscriber to a common modulus system could compute the secret key for any other subscriber, making such a system totally insecure.

The problem of factoring n given a multiple of $\lambda(n)$ led naturally to considering the special case of factoring n given $\lambda(n) = [(p-1), (q-1)]$, since it is a folklore result that given the Euler function $\varphi(n) = (p-1)(q-1) = n - p - q + 1$, factoring n only requires the extraction of a single square root. If $n = pq$, $p > q$, then

$$p = \tfrac{1}{2}(S + \sqrt{(S^2 - 4n)}) \text{ and } q = \tfrac{1}{2}(S - \sqrt{(S^2 - 4n)})$$

where S is defined by $S = n - \varphi(n) + 1$.

$\lambda(n) = [(p-1), (q-1)]$ always divides $\varphi(n) = (p-1)(q-1)$, but the quotient $r = \varphi(n)/\lambda(n)$ can be as small as 2 or as large as $\mathrm{Int}[\sqrt{(n/2)}]$. In fact, for appropriate choices of the primes p and q, r can be forced to assume any even integer value in this range.

Consider a special case in which the extreme values of r are realized. Let p, q_1, and q_2 be three primes of the form: $p = 2m + 1$, $q_1 = 4m + 1$ and $q_2 = 4m - 1$. For a prime triple of this form:

$$n_1 = 8m^2 + 6m + 1, \; n_2 = 8m^2 + 2m - 1, \quad \varphi(n_1) = 8m^2$$
$$\text{and } \varphi(n_2) = 8m^2 - 4m,$$

so that the two pairs of values are asymptotically the same size.

$$\varphi(n_2)/\varphi(n_1) = 1 - 1/2m \text{ and } n_2/n_1 = 1 - 1/(2m + \tfrac{1}{2}),$$
$$\text{while } r_2 = \varphi(n_2)/\lambda(n_2) = 2 \text{ and } r_1 = \varphi(n_1)/\lambda(n_1) = 2m.$$

For example, let the prime triple be 331, 661, and 659,

$$\text{then } \varphi(n_1) = 660, \text{ while } \varphi(n_2) = 108{,}570.$$

The problem is to compute the factors of n, one of which is common to both n_1 and n_2 and the other pair of which differ only by 2, using values of $\varphi(n)$ that differ by a factor of $m - \tfrac{1}{2}$. Unlike the case for $\varphi(n)$, no simple algebraic formula is known to do this.

Observation[1]

Given three integers $1 < a < b < c$, where $a \mid b$ and $a \nmid c$, define k to be the least integer satisfying $ka > c - b$. Then b/a is one of the k integers in the interval $((c/a) - k, (c/a))$.

Theorem

For any RSA modulus, $\varphi(n)/\lambda(n)$ is the unique even integer in the interval $(n/\varphi(n) - 2, n/\varphi(n))$

---

1   This is a generalization of a special case first observed by Peter Landrock.

Proof

We show that for an RSA modulus $\lambda(n) = a$, $\varphi(n) = b$, $n = c$ satisfy the conditions of the observation and that $k = 2$ in this case.

Since $[x,y] \mid xy$ for all x and y, the first condition is trivially satisfied.

If $\lambda(n) = [(p-1),(q-1)]$, with $p > q$, divides $n = pq$, then $p - 1$ must be q and $q - 1$ must be 1, i.e., $p = 3$ and $q = 2$.

Since this is not a possible RSA modulus pair of primes, $\lambda(n) \nmid n$ for any RSA modulus and the second condition of the observation is satisfied.

To show that $k = 2$, first note that for the example given above,
$$\lambda(n_1) = 4m < 6m + 1 = n - \lambda(n_1),$$ so that $k > 1$.

We next show that for all $n = pq$,
$$2\lambda(n) > n - \varphi(n)$$
$$2[(p-1),(q-1)] > n - \varphi(n) = n - n + p + q - 1$$
$$[(p-1),(q-1)] > \tfrac{1}{2}((p-1) + (q-1)) + \tfrac{1}{2}$$

But for all $x > y$, $[x,y] \geq \tfrac{1}{2}(x + y) + \tfrac{1}{2}$, with equality only at $x = 2$, $y = 1$; the case already dismissed in the consideration of $\lambda(n)$ dividing n. Therefore, $k = 2$, as was to be shown.

To complete the proof, we have only to observe that since p and q are both odd primes, $\varphi(n)/\lambda(n)$ is necessarily an even integer.

Reference

1. DeLaurentis, J. M., 'A further weakness in the common modulus protocol for the RSA cryptoalgorithm,' *Cryptologia*, vol. 8, 1984, pp. 253–259.

40
Application-Private Networks

Jonathan M. Smith

Introduction

The design space for network architectures can be conveniently described as a 3-tuple of *<Application requirements, Protocol elements, Network conditions>*. *Application requirements* can range from reliability and small-message inter-arrival delay to communications secrecy. *Protocol elements* include acknowledgements and error-correcting codes, timers, and a variety of cryptographic transformations. *Network conditions* include delay, delay variance, loss rates, bit error rates (BERs), topology, and available bandwidths. For any given triple, and in particular for a choice of application and requirements, we make assumptions about operating conditions, and protocol elements selected to meet the application requirements under these conditions.

Two examples, the telephone network and the Internet, are useful in understanding this architectural framework. The telephone network in its purest form is engineered [1] to deliver a band-limited audio channel appropriate for interactive voice telecommunications. The application requirements, then, include the ability to deliver about 3000 Hz of audio, with some limits on delay and audible impairments. These requirements have been met in the telephony architecture by using a call set-up protocol of considerable complexity to establish a point-to-point channel for carrying a voice stream. Link, multiplexing, switching, and capacity engineering are voice-centric.

The Internet design, requiring interoperation across a variety of networks and operating conditions, and intended to service many applications, must choose protocols that can tolerate an extremely wide variety of network conditions. Thus, the basic IP transport service is a minimal datagram service, response to network dynamics such as topology changes is provided by dynamic routing, and other application requirements (ordering, reliability, etc.) are provided by end-to-end overlay protocols, such as the Transmission Control Protocol, TCP.

If we contrast the Internet architecture with the telephony network architecture, TCP/IP is intended to be agnostic with respect to applications, and adapts to a large (but not all-encompassing) range of network conditions with its choice of protocol elements. To optimize the placement of protocol functions in the architecture (rather than for a specific requirement), the "end-to-end" design notion pushes functions to the end-points, eliminating redundant implementation and giving application designers the widest range of options for use of the basic network service.

These two examples illustrate the design space and tradeoffs made amongst its "dimensions." Neither architecture is ideal. For example the attempt to remove many dynamics in network conditions within the call makes the telephony architecture limited in its ability to efficiently handle applications with dynamics very different than that of voice. Likewise, the approach to dealing with many applications and network conditions in the IP architecture has forced engineering tradeoffs, such as substantial over-provisioning (to control delay jitter) to support applications such as voice and video.

Automated optimal-network engineering

An ideal network architecture, within the constraints of our design space, would have the property that at any given time, the application requirements and network conditions would result in the best known selection and placement of protocol elements. For example, if network-condition dynamics result in a variable BER, as in a mobile wireless context, the protocol architecture might be adjusted to inject forward error correction (FEC) to move TCP/IP into an operating regime where its protocol element selections result in meeting application requirements. While limited instances of such techniques have been demonstrated experimentally [4], the ideal system would *automate* [6] such responses, under control of high-level models of application requirements.

A great deal of detail is masked by the design-space abstraction presented in the Introduction, but the basic point is not to be lost: for any specified application requirements (including preferences, weights, etc.) and network conditions (we will discuss how information about such network conditions might be made available using the "Knowledge Plane" proposed by David Clark [3] in the next section), one or more equivalent selections of protocol elements can be made which closely meet the application requirements. As this process is fundamentally driven by application requirements, we call such networks *Application-Private Networks*, or *APNets*. The basic design process for an APNet, for a particular application, would result in a protocol architecture optimized for that application's performance, with protocol elements selected in concert with any techniques, such as time-division multiplexing, needed to limit the range of network conditions for these selections. The resulting network architecture is colloquially called a "stovepipe."

An excellent example design from the space-systems domain is the "Remote Agent" [6] architecture used in NASA's Deep Space One (DS1) mission, where many of the challenges are similar to those of network engineering, such as multiple timescales, unplanned events, and overall "mission goals." In the NASA system, very high-level models are used to drive a planning system; current conditions are fed into a system with a limited time horizon to drive specific actions such as recovery, reconfiguration, and reprogramming in the face of system conditions such as failed sensors and actuators.

The challenge in the more general case is large-scale sharing. That is, stovepipe design is economically inefficient, inhibits adaptation and reuse, and makes interoperability with other applications, as well as sharing of facilities, difficult. Further, it makes unfounded assumptions for the general case, where conflicting goals between users are common. The advent of programmability in many network components, such as network processors, software radios, and extensible routers, permits the configuration of such components to be *virtualized*. That is, the component behaviour can support multiple application-driven specializations. The problem is not easy, but is conceptually within reach [6], as demonstrated by the DS1 experiments we have discussed. An abstraction is given in Figure 1a, where application requirements (specified, perhaps, as in the next section) induce behaviors at various logical levels in a network, from host to link.

This process will take place repeatedly according to changes in network conditions. The reconfiguration process must be safe, network knowledge must be available to both the protocol element selection and programmable component configuration processes, and the network knowledge must be trusted, to deal with accidental and malicious failures.

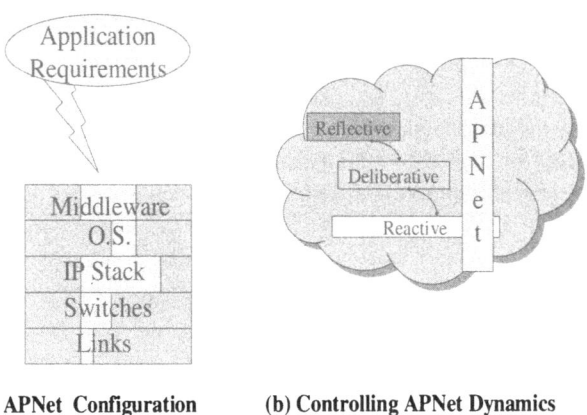

(a) APNet Configuration   (b) Controlling APNet Dynamics

Figure 1: APNets

Among the interesting technical questions to be resolved are issues of security, stability, and degree of extensibility for the architecture as a whole. To touch just briefly on these issues, the degrees of extensibility might include those possible from a machine-learning algorithm in optimization of protocol selections, they might include addition of new protocol elements as they are discovered, or they might include wholesale changes of the control architecture itself. Stability issues include overreactions, damping, and convergence of distributed control schemes. Prototyping and experiments can identify the appropriate adaptation rates for various timescales, ranging from the immediate to relatively long-term, which some researchers have categorized as *reactive, deliberative,* and *reflective* —Figure 1b illustrates how these adaptation timescales might affect the dynamics of *APNet* instances. Security concerns, in addition to the trust of network condition data, include the risk of subtle denial-of-service attacks on a complex infrastructure, data privacy, authorization for code loading, provenance of aggregated data, and finally, the technically difficult issue of what the telephony industry politely refers to as "feature interaction."

Trust architecture for network knowledge

The interaction between the knowledge plane and APNets is important, and if network knowledge is to be widely used, it will be named. Much knowledge will be represented syntactically as strings of the form *<name>=<value>*, e.g., "bandwidth=64K." This scheme has been widely adopted, in contexts from scripting languages to WWW "cookies," and is readily translated to locally convenient representations. An example of such a use of a variable is the TERM variable used to configure terminal handling in some operating systems in concert with a database of information about terminal capabilities. In an APNet, the host operating system might, using the variables specified by the application, configure schedulers, networking stacks, and choose network adapters.

The string representation enables use of *trust management* technology [2] such as the KeyNote system [5], which represents *assertions* as credentials with *authorizers, licensees,* and *conditions.* Public-key technologies are used to build the web of trust, and a compliance checking process is used to test requested actions against the credentials. Consider public keys for rmn and jms77, where jms77's key is the licensee, rmn's key is the authorizer, conditions are

```
$file_owner="rmn" && $filename="/home/rmn/[^/]*"
&& $hostname = "ouse.cl.cam.ac.uk" -> "true"
```

and the signature is with rmn's key. Then jms77 is authorized by rmn to access files in rmn's home directory on a particular host at the University of Cambridge.

This architecture provides capability-like [8] control of resources and robust delegation of authority in spite of distributed control through its use of cryptography to authenticate and authorize remote operations [7], and has many other desirable features. Complete explication would require more space, but among the desirable properties of credentials and a trusted knowledge plane for advanced applications are data provenance, support for micro-payment systems of various flavors, authorization for network control, code-loading, resource allocation, and digital-rights management.

Conclusion

Application-Private Networks extend the range of dynamics for protocol architectures by dynamically selecting protocol elements to meet application requirements in the face of dynamic conditions. Such a network architecture is not only desirable, it is technically achievable within the next decade. A broad range of new network uses would thereby be enabled.

References

1. *Engineering and operations in the Bell System* (2nd ed.), AT&T Bell Laboratories, Murray Hill, NJ, 1983, ISBN 0-932764-04-5.
2. BLAZE, M., FEIGENBAUM, J., AND LACY, J., 'Decentralized trust management,' *Proc. 17th IEEE Symposium on Security and Privacy*, 1996, pp. 164–173.
3. CLARK, D., 'A new vision for network architecture,' private communication, September 2002.
4. HADZIC, I.,'Applying reconfigurable computing to reconfigurable networks,' Ph.D. Thesis, Department of Electrical Engineering, University of Pennsylvania, 1999.
5. KEROMYTIS, A., IOANNIDIS, S., GREENWALD, M., AND SMITH, J., 'The Strongman architecture,' *Proc. 3rd DARPA Information Survivability Conference and Exposition (DISCEX III)*, April 2003, Washington, DC, pp. 178–188.
6. MUSCETTOLA, N., NAYAK, P., PELL B., AND WILLIAMS, B.C., 'Remote agent: to boldly go where no AI system has gone before," *Artificial Intelligence*, vol. 103, no.1–2, pp. 5–48.
7. NEEDHAM, R.M., AND SCHROEDER, M.D., 'Using encryption for authentication in large networks," *Comm. ACM*, vol. 21, no.12, 1978, pp. 993–999.
8. NEEDHAM, R.M., AND WALKER, R.D.H., 'The Cambridge CAP computer and its protection system,' in *Proc. 6th Symposium on Operating Systems Principles*, November 1977, pp. 1–10.

41
Using the CORAL System to Discover Attacks on Security Protocols

Graham Steel, Alan Bundy, Ewen Denney

Introduction

Inductive theorem provers are frequently employed in the verification of programs, algorithms, and protocols. Programs and algorithms often contain bugs, and protocols may be flawed, causing the proof attempt to fail. However, it can be hard to interpret a failed proof attempt: it may be that some additional lemmas need to be proved or a generalisation made. In this situation, a tool which can not only detect an incorrect conjecture, but also supply a counterexample in order to allow the user to identify the bug or flaw, is potentially very valuable. Here we describe such a tool, CORAL, based on a previously under-exploited feature of proof by consistency. Proof by consistency is a technique for automating inductive proofs in first-order logic. Originally developed to prove correct theorems, this technique has the property of being refutation complete, i.e., it is able to refute in finite time conjectures which are inconsistent with the set of hypotheses. Recently, Comon and Nieuwenhuis have drawn together and extended previous research to show how it may be more generally applied [4]. CORAL is the first full implementation of this method.

We have applied CORAL to the analysis of cryptographic security protocols. Paulson has shown how these can be modelled inductively in higher-order logic [16]. By devising a suitable first-order version of Paulson's formalism, we are able to automatically refute incorrect security conjectures and exhibit the corresponding attacks. The flexibility of the inductive formalism allows us to analyse group protocols, and we have discovered new attacks on such a protocol (the Asokan-Ginzboorg protocol for ad-hoc Bluetooth networks [2]) using CORAL.

In the rest of the paper, we first briefly look at the background to the problem of refuting incorrect conjectures and the formal analysis of security protocols. Then we outline the Comon-Nieuwenhuis method. We describe the operation of CORAL and then show how it can be applied to the problem of protocol analysis. Finally, we describe some possible further work, including some other possible applications for CORAL, and draw some conclusions.

Background

The refutation of incorrect inductive conjectures has been studied before, e.g., by Protzen [17], Reif [18], and Ahrendt [1]. Ahrendt's method works by constructing a set of clauses to send to a model generation prover and is restricted to free datatypes. Protzen's technique progressively instantiates terms in the formula to be checked, using the recursive definitions of the function symbols involved. It finds many small counterexamples. Rief's method instantiates the formula with constructor terms and uses simplifier rules in the prover KIV to evaluate truth or falsehood. His method is a marked improvement on Protzen's, but is too naïve for a situation like protocol checking, where it is not obvious what combination of constructor terms constitutes a possible exchange of messages.

Proof by consistency

Proof by consistency was originally conceived by Musser [14] as a method for proving inductive theorems by using a modified Knuth-Bendix completion procedure. It was developed by various authors, [8, 10, 6], for the next fifteen years (see [20] for the story), but interest waned, as it seemed too hard to scale the technique up to proving larger conjectures. However, later versions of the technique did have the property of being refutation complete, that is, able to spot false conjectures in finite time.

The Comon-Nieuwenhuis method

Comon and Nieuwenhuis [4] have shown that the previous techniques for proof by consistency can be generalised to the production of a first-order axiomatisation A of the minimal Herbrand model such that $A \cup E \cup C$ is consistent if and only if C is an inductive consequence of E. With A satisfying the properties they define as a Normal I-Axiomatisation, inductive proofs can be reduced to first-order consistency problems and so can be solved by any saturation based theorem prover. There is not room here to give a full formal account of the theory, but informally, a proof attempt involves two parts: in one, we pursue a fair induction derivation. This is a restricted kind of saturation, where we need only consider overlaps between axioms and conjectures. In the second part, every clause in the induction derivation is checked for consistency against the I-Axiomatisation. If any consistency check fails, then the conjecture is incorrect. If they all succeed, and the induction derivation procedure terminates, the theorem is proved. Comon and Nieuwenhuis have shown refutation completeness for this system, i.e., any incorrect conjecture will be refuted in finite time, even if the search for an induction derivation is non-terminating.

Cryptographic security protocols

Cryptographic protocols are used in distributed systems to allow agents to communicate securely. They were first proposed by Needham and Schroeder [15]. Assumed to be present in the system is a spy, who can see all the traffic in the network and may send malicious messages in order to try to impersonate users and gain access to secrets.

Although security protocols are usually quite short, typically 2–5 messages, they often have subtle flaws in them that may not be discovered for many years. Researchers have applied various formal techniques to the problem to try to find attacks on faulty protocols and to prove correct protocols secure. These approaches include belief logics such as the so-called BAN logic [3], state machines [5, 11], model checking [12], and inductive theorem proving [16]. Each approach has its advantages and disadvantages. For example, the BAN logic is attractively simple and has found some protocol flaws, though in other cases found flawed protocols correct. The model-checking approach can find flaws very quickly, but can only be applied to finite (and typically very small) instances of the protocol. This means that if no attack is found, there may still be an attack upon a larger instance. Modern state-machine approaches [13, 19] can also find and exhibit attacks quickly, but require the user to choose and prove lemmas in order to reduce the problem to a tractable finite search space. The inductive method deals directly with the infinite-state problem and assumes an arbitrary number of protocol participants, but proofs are tricky and require days or weeks of expert effort. If a proof breaks down, there have previously been no automated facilities for the detection of an attack.

Implementation

Figure 1 illustrates the operation of CORAL, built on the SPASS theorem prover [23]. The induction derivation, using the Comon-Nieuwenhuis method as described above, is pursued by the modified SPASS prover on the right of the diagram. As each clause is derived, it is passed to the refutation control script on the left, which launches a standard SPASS prover to do the check against the I-Axiomatisation. The parallel architecture allows us to obtain a refutation in cases where the induction derivation does not terminate, as well as allowing us to split the process across multiple machines in the case of a large problem. Experiments with the system show good performance on a variety of incorrect conjectures from the literature and our on own examples [21].

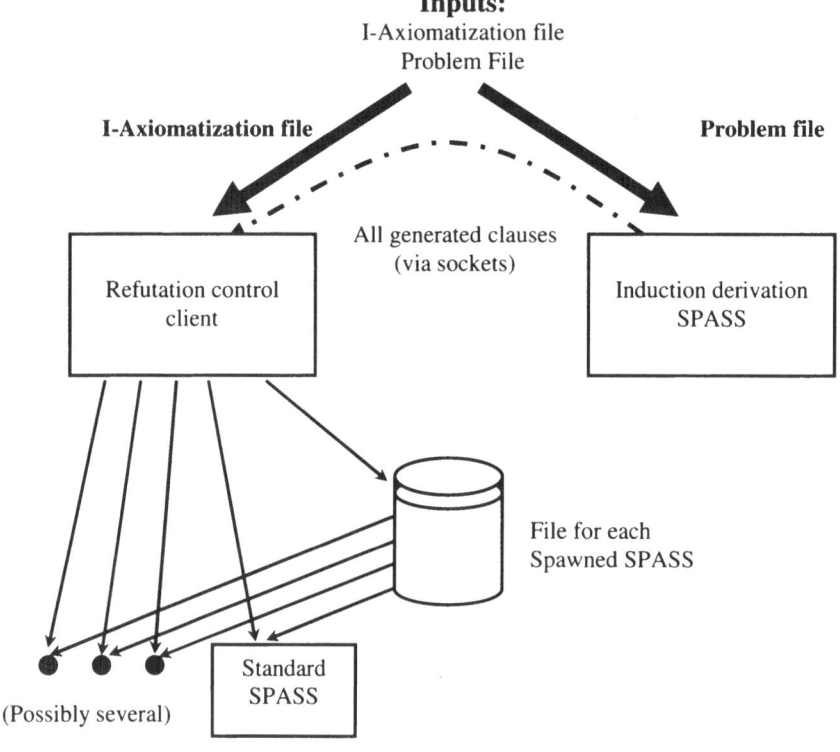

Figure 1: CORAL system operation

Application to cryptographic security protocols

Paulson's inductive approach has been used to verify properties of several protocols [16]. Protocols are formalised in typed higher-order logic as the set of all
possible traces. Properties of the security protocol can be proved by induction on
traces. However, as Paulson observed, a failed proof state can be difficult to interpret. Even an expert user will be unsure as to whether it is the proof attempt or
the conjecture that is at fault. By applying our counterexample finder to these
problems, we can automatically detect and present attacks when they exist. The
use of an inductive model also allows us to consider protocols involving an arbitrary number of participants in a single round, e.g., conference-key protocols.
Paulson's formalism is in higher-order logic. However, no 'fundamentally'
higher-order concepts are used—in particular, there is no unification of functional objects. Objects have types, and sets and lists are used. All this can be
modelled in first-order logic. The security protocol problem has been modelled
in first-order logic before, e.g., by Weidenbach [24]. He used a two-agent model,

with fixed roles for participants, and just one available session key and nonce (a nonce is a unique identifying number), and so could not detect certain kinds of parallel session attacks described above. Like Paulson's, our model allows an indeterminate and unbounded number of agents to participate, playing either role and using an arbitrary number of fresh nonces and keys. Details of the model are in our earlier paper [21], but we will highlight now some recent developments.

We have modified our formalism slightly to make attacks easier to find. The idea is to prune out branches of the search space that cannot lead to an attack, or branches which represent a less succinct expression of a state already reached. For example, we merged together the formulae allowing the spy to send a fake message with those for the standard protocol, so that the spy can only send messages which look like a part of the real protocol. Sending anything else cannot fool any honest participants, since they only respond to correctly formed messages. We also have a reduction rule which prunes out clauses which represent states where the spy has sent two messages in a row. The spy can't gain anything from doing this, so by chopping off these branches we make the search problem more tractable.

With these improvements CORAL has rediscovered a number of known attacks, including the well known ones on the Needham-Schroeder public-key and Neuman-Stubblebine shared-key protocols. It can also find the attack on the simplified Otway-Rees protocol, an attack which requires an honest agent to generate two fresh nonces and to play the role of both the initiator and the responder. Recently, CORAL found two new attacks on the Asokan-Ginzboorg protocol for establishing a secure session key in an ad-hoc Bluetooth network [2]. Details of the attacks and a description of how we modelled this group protocol in a general way without restricting to a small fixed instance are in a forthcoming paper [22].

Further work

Future work will include testing the CORAL system on more group-key protocols. As CORAL is built on SPASS, a theorem prover capable of equational reasoning, we should be able to reason about some simple algebraic properties of the cryptosystems underlying protocols, such as Diffie-Helman type operations. In particular, Asokan and Ginzboorg have proposed a second version of their protocol that uses these kinds of operations, which would be an ideal candidate for future investigation.

There has been a proliferation of protocol analysis tools in recent years, and in the longer term we don't intend to try and compete with others for speed of attack finding or by analysing an enormous corpus of protocols. Rather, we intend to try to exploit the flexibility of our system as a general tool for inductive counterexample finding and apply it to some other security problems. One idea is to use the system to model security problems at a higher level. We could model a company's computer network as a system of local networks and servers, firewalls, etc., all with formally defined behaviour, and examine how interactions in the presence of intruders might lead to exploitable vulnerabilities. To deal with larger problems like this, we might need to enhance SPASS to exploit domain knowledge a little more. Two possible ideas we intend to explore are a user-defined strategy that can vary as the proof proceeds and a critics mechanism [9] to suggest pruning lemmas. In theory, CORAL can also show security properties of protocols to be correct when there are no attacks to be found. However, to make this work in practice would require some considerable work. The formulae to be proved are significantly larger than the kinds of examples that have been proved by proof by consistency in the past. The critics mechanism for suggesting lemmas could help with this.

Conclusions

We have presented CORAL, our system for refuting incorrect inductive conjectures, and have shown how it can be applied to the problem of finding attacks on faulty security protocols. Our formalism is similar to Paulson's, which allows us to deal directly with protocols involving an arbitrary number of participants and nonces, and with principals playing multiple roles. CORAL has discovered a number of known attacks, and some new attacks on a group-key protocol. In the longer term, we hope to apply the system to other, related security problems and exploit its ability to do equational reasoning in order to analyse some crytpoanalytic properties of protocols. (This paper is a shortened and updated version of [21].)

References

1. AHRENDT, W., 'Deductive search for errors in free data type specifications using model generation,' in *CADE-18, 18th International Conference on Automated Deduction*, 2002.
2. ASOKAN, N., AND GINZBOORG, P., 'Key agreement in ad-hoc networks,' *Computer Communications*, vol. 23, no. 17, 2000, pp. 1627–1637.
3. BURROWS, M., ABADI, M., AND NEEDHAM, R., 'A logic of authentication,' *ACM Trans. on Computer Systems*, vol. 8, no. 1, February 1990, pp. 18–36.
4. COMON, H., AND NIEUWENHUIS, R., 'Induction = I-Axiomatization + First-Order Consistency,' *Information and Computation*, vol. 159, no. 1–2, May/June 2000, pp. 151–186.
5. DOLEV, D., AND YAO, A., 'On the security of public key protocols,' *IEEE Trans. in Information Theory*, vol. 2, no. 29, March 1983, pp. 198–208.
6. GANZINGER, H., AND STUBER, J., 'Inductive theorem proving by consistency for first-order clauses,' in Rusinowitch, M. and Rémy, J.J., (eds.), *Proc. 3rd International*

Workshop on Conditional Term Rewriting Systems, Pont-à-Mousson, France, Springer, LNCS vol. 656, pp. 226–241.

7. GANZINGER, H., (ED.), *Automated deduction, CADE-16: 16th International Conference on Automated Deduction*, Trento, Italy, July 1999, Lecture Notes in Artificial Intelligence 1632, Springer-Verlag.

8. HUET, G., AND HULLOT, J., 'Proofs by induction in equational theories with constructors,' *J. of Computer Systems and System Sciences*, vol. 25, no. 2, 1982, pp. 239–266.

9. IRELAND, A., 'Productive use of failure in inductive proof,' *J. of Automated Reasoning*, vol. 16, no. 1–2, 1996, pp. 79–11.

10. JOUANNAUD, J.-P., AND KOUNALIS, E., 'Proof by induction in equational theories without constructors,' *Information and Computation*, vol. 82, no. 1, 1989, pp. 1–33.

11. KEMMERER, R., MEADOWS, C., AND MILLEN, J., 'Three systems for cryptographic protocol analysis,' *J. of Cryptology*, vol. 7, 1994, pp. 79–130.

12. LOWE, G., 'Breaking and fixing the Needham Schroeder public-key protocol using FDR,' in *Proc. TACAS*, LNCS 1055, Springer Verlag, 1996, pp. 147–166.

13. MEADOWS, C., 'The NRL protocol analyzer: An overview,' *J. of Logic Programming*, vol. 26, no. 2, pp. 113–131, 1996.

14. MUSSER, D., 'On proving inductive properties of abstract data types,' *Proc. 7th ACM Symp. on Principles of Programming Languages*, 1980, pp. 154–162.

15. NEEDHAM, R.M., AND SCHROEDER, M.D., 'Using encryption for authentication in large networks of computers,' *Comm. ACM*, vol. 21, no. 12, December 1978, pp. 993–999.

16. PAULSON, L.C., 'The inductive approach to verifying cryptographic protocols,' *J. of Computer Security*, vol. 6, 1998, pp. 85–128.

17. PROTZEN, M., 'Disproving conjectures,' in Kapur, D., ed., *CADE-11: 11th Conf. on Automated Deduction*, Saratoga Springs, NY, June 1992. Springer, Lecture Notes in Artificial Intelligence 607, pp. 340–354.

18. REIF, W., SCHELLHORN, G., AND THUMS, A., 'Flaw detection in formal specifications,' in *IJCAR'01*, 2001, pp. 642–657.

19. SONG, D., 'Athena: A new efficient automatic checker for security protocol analysis,' *Proc. 12th IEEE Computer Security Foundations Workshop*, 1999.

20. STEEL, G., 'Proof by consistency: A literature survey,' March 1999.
http://homepages.inf.ed.ac.uk/s9808756/papers/lit-survey.ps.gz

21. STEEL, G., BUNDY, A., AND DENNEY, E., 'Finding counterexamples to inductive conjectures and discovering security protocol attacks,' *Proc. of the Foundations of Computer Security Workshop*, 2002, pp. 49–58; also in *Proc. of the Verify '02 Workshop*. Also available as Informatics Research Report EDI-INF-RR-0141.

22. STEEL, G., BUNDY, A., AND MAIDL, M., 'Attacking the Asokan-Ginzboorg protocol for key distribution in an ad-hoc Bluetooth network using CORAL,' to appear in *Proceedings of FORTE 2003* (work in progress papers).

23. WEIDENBACH, C., ET AL., 'System description: SPASS version 1.0.0,' in Ganzinger [7], pp. 378–382.

24. WEIDENBACH, C., 'Towards an automatic analysis of security protocols in first-order logic,' in Ganzinger [7], pp. 314–328.

42
On the Role of Binding and Rate Adaptation in Packet Networks

David Tennenhouse

An ongoing debate within the network research community concerns the degree to which packet switching, especially that which is IP-based, can and should subsume other types of networks, e.g., those based on circuit switching.

In this short paper, I discuss four aspects of this debate that have long been of concern to me as a network researcher:

- The tendency of network architects to focus on the "core" of the network, which is its least interesting architectural component.
- The common misconception that statistical multiplexing is the fundamental advantage of packet switching.
- The proposal that late binding and rate adaption are the essential architectural advantages of packet switching.
- The observation that it is the properties of key interfaces, rather than the network internals, that are most deserving of our attention.

While much of what follows will be very familiar to software and systems researchers, these concepts do not seem to be as well accepted within the networking community.

The "core" is architecturally irrelevant

Much of the recent discussion has been focused on the degree to which IP, and packet switching in general, will directly support the underlying transport infrastructure, sometimes referred to as the "core," or "cross-connect," of national scale multi-service networks. While some would argue that it can and should, others conclude that "the core of the network will use optical circuit switching as a platform for multiple services," [1].

I find the question of packet vs. circuit operation of the underlying cross-connect rather tedious for these reasons:

- The topology of the physical media comprising the core is relatively simple and rigid. For example, in the United States, the national scale "core" has on the order of hundreds of nodes.

- The statistical properties of the highly aggregated, or "groomed," cross-connect channels will be relatively predictable and slow to evolve. Since the time constants involved are quite lengthy, relative to the round-trip times within the core, the choice of packet vs. circuit cross-connect is a moot point.

But isn't statistical multiplexing the essence of packet switching?

The focus on the behavior of the core suggests that there is a deep misunderstanding as to the essential merits of packet networks in general, and the Internet in particular. Molinero-Fernandez et al. [1]—and many others in the network research community—ground their reasoning in the following premise:

> From the early days of computer networking, it has been well known that packet switching makes efficient use of scarce link bandwidth. With packet switching, statistical multiplexing allows link bandwidth to be shared...

While the above position is widely held, I find the frequent and very loose generality with which it is applied disconcerting. In particular, the importance and relationship of the words "scarce" and "statistical" are almost always disregarded—as are the time constants involved. Both circuit- and packet-switched networks take advantage of statistical multiplexing, with the only real distinction being the time constants.[1] Per-packet statistical multiplexing is of marginal utility if the traffic is steady over long periods and/or the bandwidth is continuously exhausted. The same is true at the other extreme, i.e., when bandwidth is not scarce as a consequence of over-provisioning.

Packet multiplexing is beneficial within a limited range of statistical patterns and scarcities, typically observed near the edge of the network. It can be highly advantageous at "early multiplexing" points, where modest numbers of relatively dynamic flows are multiplexed into larger aggregates. At these points the bandwidth available to the aggregate may well be scarce relative to the statistical properties of the individual tributaries.

At switching points deep within the core of a national scale multi-service infrastructure, the traffic on each channel is derived from the aggregation of vast numbers of flows. These highly aggregated cross-connect channels will be statistically "smoother," and this has a huge impact on the nature of bandwidth scarci-

---

1   Circuit switched telephony has long relied on statistical properties of call attempts, call duration, etc. Interestingly enough, the signaling system used to setup calls is, itself, a packet-switched network.

ties at the switching points and the potential of any architecture to respond to them.

- Many types of core scarcities can be anticipated months in advance and dealt with through provisioning.
- Large-scale unanticipated scarcities, such as those arising from simultaneous failures and/or coordinated surges in demand, will force any architecture into a "degradation" mode, whose desired behavior will be more a matter of public policy than architectural finesse.
- Most intermittent scarcities falling between the above extremes will have sufficiently long time constants that the distinction between circuit and packet switching may not be relevant. Although some have suggested that IP traffic might be clumped or correlated, recent measurements [2] suggest that channels within the core experience relatively small and predictable delays over the time constants of interest.

Dynamic binding and rate adaptation: the real essence of packet switching

So what, then, is the architectural advantage of packet switching? While I concede the importance of statistical multiplexing at moderate aggregation levels, I have never believed it to be the architectural imperative.[2] I suggest that the real "magic" of packet switching, especially with respect to the operation of multiservice networks, lies in two properties: late binding and rate adaptation.

Binding

Packet-based interfaces multiplex a very large number of logical channels onto a "bearer" channel. In the case of IP, there is a separate logical channel for each unique <source address, source port, destination address, destination port, protocol type> tuple.[3] On any given link, this IP channel space is very sparsely populated, i.e., the vast majority of the logical channels are unused. The bindings for those that are used is highly dynamic: for the most part, the application(s)—and therefore the properties of the traffic—associated with a logical channel are determined at run time; and the bindings between a logical channel and the underlying capacity of the bearer channel are determined on a packet by packet basis. The latter aspect by itself might be construed as "statistical multiplexing." How-

---

2 On this specific issue, I must admit to having reached an impasse with many distinguished experts, most notably my friend and mentor Robert Kahn.

3 As evidenced by NAT, these tuples are only unique at the interface points. Also, there is a slight simplification here, owing to the semantics associated with multicast addresses and some protocol types.

ever, the combination of the two degrees of binding freedom, within the context of a vast logical channel space, is a broader architectural feature that allows IP-based interfaces to function as a "universal solvent"[4] enabling multi-service interfaces.

Rate adaption

This property of packet switching, typically realized through the use of elastic buffers of some sort, allows applications at an endpoint, whose network point of attachment operates at one rate, to communicate with peers whose points of attachment may operate at arbitrarily different rates—many orders of magnitude different in the case of a modem-attached client vs. a data center server. Rate adaptation, over an enormous dynamic range, is one of the most significant advantages of packet switching and its key "trump card" with respect to both multi-service networking and the Internet's ability to absorb rapid innovation, e.g., by ensuring that faster nodes and links seamlessly inter-operate with the embedded base.

Rate adaptation is particularly advantageous in closed-loop scenarios where the traffic patterns of individual packet flows can be dynamically shaped in response to changing network and endpoint conditions. In the case of TCP/IP, rate adaption is enhanced through the combination of lower-layer queues (the elastic buffers) and the TCP layer end-to-end control mechanism, which ensures that the long-term flow of packets is matched to the capacity of the endpoints and of all of the intervening queues along the path. In the simple case of a human user accessing data via a Web browser, TCP feedback controls the flow of data during each transaction, and an outer feedback loop, closed by the human user, governs the overall rate of request submission, i.e., as response time deteriorates, the rate at which new requests are submitted to the system declines.

Unfortunately, some types of "real-time" traffic, especially legacy sample streams derived from the physical world around us,[5] are not readily amenable to feedback-based shaping. Nonetheless, these sources of traffic still benefit from the architectural advantages of rate adaptation. Furthermore, the highly predictable statistical properties of the traffic in question (which are determined by the sampling and compression mechanisms used) may amplify the task of dimensioning the packet network appropriately.

---

4   I am indebted to my colleague Vint Cerf for this wonderful metaphor.
5   Which can not easily be "slowed down."

It's the interfaces that count

Returning to the underlying question, the degree to which IP can be the basis of national-scale multi-service networks, one must first identify the key points at which this question should be considered. That is, if the "core" of a future multi-service infrastructure isn't of architectural interest, then what is? An important step towards answering this question may be to view IP not so much as the basis for a homogeneous soup-to-nuts[6] infrastructure, but as the common protocol "stack" used at a few key classes of interoperability points. Ethernet presents a useful, though limited, analogy here. At one stage, the term Ethernet referred to the design of an entire LAN. Today, what really matters is a few core architectural concepts and their embodiment at the interoperability points. The fact that many different technologies, including wireless, are now used to realize these concepts is of little importance. All that matters at the individual endpoints is that the NIC driver presents an interface that approximates that of the original standard.

Given this perspective, there would appear to be three distinct classes of IP interfaces to be considered:

- The interfaces to individual client nodes and the "early" multiplexing points at which client traffic is multiplexed onto larger aggregates.
- Interfaces (at or near edges) that are very highly multiplexed, i.e., that support large numbers of active logical channels. In contrast to its initial implementation, today's Internet is highly asymmetric with a small fraction of the nodes (e.g., Akamai sites, MSN, Google, etc.) terminating a large fraction of the flows.
- Interfaces that bridge peer Internet service providers. Although the initial architecture envisaged a "catanet," formed through the concatenation of independently operated networks, today's Internet supports a significant degree of service-provider diversity, i.e., core networks operating in parallel with each other.

In a multi-service environment, is it feasible for all three types of interfaces to be IP-based? Independent of whether or not IP is the *best* way to structure those interfaces, do we see any *fundamental* limits to the "absorption" of new types of traffic at those interface points? If there are merely impediments (vs. fundamental limits), then are they of sufficient economic importance to fund the emergence of an alternative interoperable stack in the near future?

Although IP may have some unsightly warts, I am hard pressed to find any of them to be fundamental or even so serious as to create a high enough barrier to offset the power of incremental refinement fuelled by the investment engine driving IP. The continued growth of Voice over IP, especially within increasingly cost-conscious enterprises, is but one example of that engine at work.

---

6   More precisely, edge through core.

The interesting question, then, may be not whether IP *can* continue to absorb new classes of traffic, but how features "around" these three classes of interfaces, and related aspects of the protocol suite, might evolve and/or become increasingly specialized to improve the ability of IP-based networks to absorb new types of services:

- Can the "early multiplexing points" of the Internet be engineered and/or mutate sufficiently to absorb new types of traffic/media at the edges of the network? My best guess is that it can and, for the most economically relevant traffic, will. As an alternative to some of the complex QoS schemes under consideration today, one could easily imagine all of the traffic at these interfaces falling into one of two distinct classes, each of whose handling could be independently provisioned and routed: traffic that is amenable to shaping through feedback and traffic whose statistical properties are highly predictable.[7]

- What opportunities for specialization exist at the heavily multiplexed interfaces? This is an especially tantalizing question, since there may be a considerable degree of homogeneity with respect to the types of services carried on the logical channels of these interfaces.

- Are there obvious specializations that would simplify the implementation of peering interfaces, which are very high volume ingress/egress points? What mechanisms can be introduced to support cross-provider implementation of policy-based requirements, such as the prioritization of traffic during civil emergencies? Can virtual circuit techniques, such as MPLS, simplify the processing at these interfaces and/or improve their robustness to failures, e.g., by making it easier to simultaneously re-route large aggregates? Notwithstanding the feasibility of retaining an IP-based approach, might the relatively small numbers and high value of these interfaces be sufficient to support enhanced architectural diversity at these points?

Summary

In this note I have attempted to identify some of the key architectural advantages of packet-based network interfaces. Could we have arrived at a slightly better architectural solution with a different packet-based protocol suite? Probably. Does it matter? I think not. Does that mean IP is the end of the road for network research? Of course not!

---

7   Additional distinctions may be useful *within* the endpoints, e.g., to distinguish foreground and background activities.

References

1. MOLINERO-FENANDEZ, P., MCKEOWN, N., AND ZHANG. H., 'Is IP going to take over the world (of communications)?' *HotNets '02,* Princeton NJ, October 2002.
2. PAPAGIANNAKI, K., MOON, S., FRALEIGH, C., THIRAN, P., TOBAGI, F., AND DIOT, C., 'Analysis of measured single-hop from an operational backbone network,' *IEEE Infocom,* New York, NY, June 2002.

43
Technologies for Portable Computing: Outlook and Limitations

Chuck Thacker

The last few years have produced a proliferation of new portable computing devices. We now see a wide variety of personal digital assistants, digital cameras, digital media players, tablet PCs, and wireless phones. Many of the technologies employed in these devices have improved as predicted by Moore's Law,[1] but some are more mature and improve much more slowly. In this paper, I will examine the current state of the art in power and cooling technology, processors, displays, nonvolatile storage, and wireless networking in an attempt to understand the possible directions for portable devices over the next few years. I also discuss the characteristics of several devices that have employed leading-edge technologies.

Power and cooling

Supplying the necessary power and removing the resulting heat has been the largest problem in portable-device design. Currently, all portable computing devices are operated from batteries, with the vast majority employing rechargeable cells. Over the last decade, battery technology has improved somewhat, from the early nickel cadmium cells to nickel metal hydride to lithium ion, but the energy density available from a modern lithium ion battery is only about 120 watt-hours per kilogram, and this has not improved significantly in the past three years. For low-duty cycle devices such as mobile phones or PDAs, which dissipate only a few milliwatts when idle, lithium ion batteries provide several days of use between charges at an acceptable weight. For more demanding applications such as laptops, battery life is typically much less than a working day, which requires that the user carry a charger or extra batteries.

---

1   Gordon Moore, Intel chairman, said in 1965 that transistor densities would double every 18 months for the foreseeable future. Thirty-five years later, this "law" still holds, and is expected to do so until the end of the decade.

The primary technology that may improve this situation is fuel cells. Hydrogen fuel cells have been used in military and space applications for decades, but these devices are complex, expensive, and operate at high temperatures. Two new variants, the proton exchange membrane (PEM) [1] and direct liquid-methanol (DLM) cells, use methanol as the fuel and operate at room temperature. These devices provide energy densities somewhat higher than lithium-ion cells and can be refueled from cartridges. A number of research laboratories and companies are exploring this technology, but products are likely to be two to five years away.

Practical cooling alternatives include passive techniques that distribute the heat generated by the electronics to the device's case and active cooling using fans. The former solution is quite limited in the amount of heat that can be removed successfully—the Microsoft tablet PC, for example, dissipates a peak power of about 14 watts, and even though the heat is spread fairly uniformly over the rear surface of the device, the case can become uncomfortably warm. Fortunately, peak performance is rarely needed by today's applications,[2] so this situation is infrequently encountered.

The use of fans is typical in both the largest and smallest portable computers. Today's large laptops make use of desktop-class x86 CPUs, which must be actively cooled. Although the smaller devices make use of lower-powered processors, their radically reduced surface area makes passive cooling impractical.

Processors

While "traditional" laptop computers have chosen to employ desktop-class x86 processors in spite of their high power and stringent cooling requirements, both recent "thin and light" laptops and smaller devices with new form factors have opted for lower powered but slower processors.

For devices that run Windows XP, x86 compatibility is mandatory. Until recently, the primary sources for low-power x86 CPUs were Transmeta and National Semiconductor. Transmeta uses a combination of interpretation and dynamic compilation which they call "code morphing" to run x86 programs on a VLIW core that is considerably simpler than a typical x86. The results of the compilation are held in a region of the system's RAM that the CPU reserves to itself. While this technique works well for applications (e.g., audio and video codecs) that contain loops, starting an application involves interpreting the code, which makes the CPU appear slower than it actually is. Transmeta processors draw between 1.5 and 8 watts, depending on load.

National Semiconductor has approached the low-power market with its Geode family of x86 processors. The Geode GX2 operates between 200 and 333

---

2   Although the use of speech recognition and other energy-intensive user-interface techniques may worsen this situation in the future.

MHz, and dissipates a maximum of 5 watts, with "typical" power between 0.8 and 1.4 watts. Intel has recently responded to competitive threats with its Banias processor, but details of its power consumption are still sketchy.

For devices that do not need to run Windows XP, several energy-efficient options are available. Intel's XScale processor (PXA 250), based on the DEC StrongArm, operates at 400 MHz, while dissipating 750 mW. The AMD Alchemy Au1100, a MIPS-architecture machine, operates at 500 MHz and dissipates 500 mW. These devices are considerably more energy-efficient than an x86 of comparable performance because of their simpler structure and an emphasis on efficiency rather than maximum clock rate.

Dynamic voltage and frequency scaling have also proven valuable in reducing CPU power. These schemes[3] reduce the clock rate and the supply voltage during periods of light computational load. Since dynamic device power is linear in clock frequency and quadratic in supply voltage, small changes can have dramatic effects (~3×) on device power.

One problem that may limit the achievable power reduction in future processors is leakage current. As device sizes become smaller and supply voltages decrease, static leakage current becomes an increasing fraction of the device current. A substantial amount of architectural research is underway to mitigate this problem by gating clocks and powering down entire functional units when they are not needed.

Displays

Today, liquid crystals are the only choice for portable displays. LCDs have undergone intense development to reduce their cost and increase their size, but there has been little progress on increasing the robustness and brightness of LCD panels. Display breakage is still an almost inevitable result of dropping a laptop, and few laptops can be used outdoors due to their low brightness. Some pocket PCs have employed transflective displays with front rather than back lights to make outdoor use possible, but these devices suffer from extremely poor contrast ratios, which makes reading quite difficult.

The display subsystem and its backlight consume about half the power drawn by a modern "thin and light" laptop, or about 5 watts. This power is to a large extent proportional to the area of the display, so it is much less in smaller devices.

From a battery-life perspective, an unfortunate trend is that graphical user interfaces are making increasing use of 3-D effects and animation. This increases

---

3   Called "speed step" by Intel and "long run" by Transmeta.

the power consumed by the system's graphics controller substantially, similar to the way in which speech recognition and other real-time tasks increase the power demands on the CPU.

The most likely replacement for LCDs is a display based on organic light-emitting diodes (OLEDs). The necessary organic polymers have existed for several years, but there has been relatively slow progress in turning these materials into commercially viable displays. The leading manufacturers of these materials are Cambridge Display Technologies (CDT) [2] and Kodak [3]. The latter has recently entered a partnership with Sanyo to exploit their materials.

OLED panels are likely to be brighter and have a larger viewing angle than LEDs for a given power level, and can potentially be much more robust, since they do not need to be transparent and can be fabricated on a metal substrate. Unfortunately, the electronics associated with each pixel are more complex than in an LCD. In LCDs, a single transistor serves to set the voltage of each pixel, which acts as a capacitor. This is similar to the arrangement in a single-transistor DRAM cell. In an OLED, each pixel must include circuitry to provide a varying level of current through each diode during the entire frame time. This requires at least two transistors—one to do the multiplexing and one to do voltage-to-current conversion. These devices, as in a thin-film-transistor LCD, must be fabricated on a glass substrate, and doing it at acceptable yields has eluded manufacturers. Although CDT initially (1998) predicted commercial OLED panels in 2001, most manufacturers are now indicating that the devices will not be competitive with LCDs until 2005.

Nonvolatile storage

Disk storage has exceeded Moore's law in density increase for the past few years. The current state-of-the-art disk for portable devices is a Toshiba 1.8" drive that is the size of a credit card, has a capacity of 20 Gbytes, an areal density of 22.4 Gbits/in^2, and consumes only 1.4 watts. These devices are intriguing, as they enable portable devices that contain *all* of the digital state for a single user. Allowing users to make their state available on any of the computers with which they normally interact might be an attractive alternative to the complex synchronization and copying that is the norm today.

Ultimately, experts believe that magnetic disk density will soon be limited by the "super paramagnetic limit," at which individual domains can be switched by thermal noise. Current estimates for this density are on the order of 100 Gbits/in^2, which corresponds to 80×80 nanometer bits.

A number of companies are exploring the use of microelectronic-mechanical systems (MEMS) to overcome magnetic density limitations. Researchers at IBM [4], for example, have demonstrated their ability to record and read data at a terabyte per square inch, using a heated atomic-force microscopy (AFM) probe to melt nanometer-scale pits in a polymer medium. Hewlett-Packard and a small startup company called Nanochip [5] are both building similar devices.

All of these devices are similar in that they move either the probes or the medium in x and y using actuators that are fabricated using normal semiconductor processing. IBM uses electromagnetic actuators, HP uses electrostatic motors, and Nanochip uses a technique that exploits the thermal expansion of heated wires. Because the devices have a large number of probes, the required motion is small—on the order of 100 μm. The medium (in the IBM device) or the probe array (in the Nanochip device) is supported by springs that are fabricated at the same time as the actuators. The Nanochip device is shown in Figures 1 and 2. It consists of sixteen independently moveable sub-arrays, each with sixteen probes.

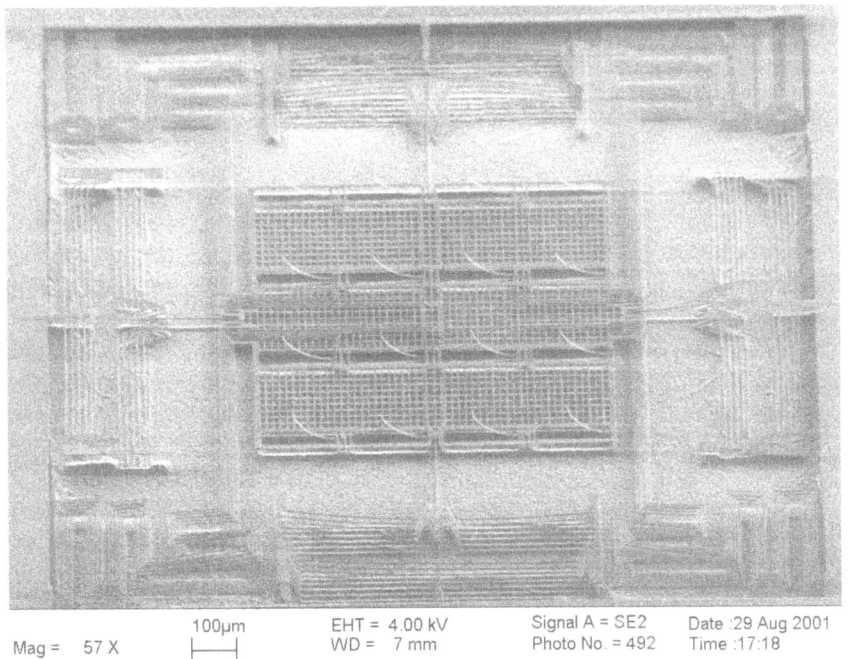

| Mag = 57 X | 100μm | EHT = 4.00 kV | Signal A = SE2 | Date :29 Aug 2001 |
| | | WD = 7 mm | Photo No. = 492 | Time :17:18 |

Figure 1: One of the sixteen Nanochip sub-arrays, showing four actuators and sixteen cantilevered probes.

The IBM device has a low read/write bandwidth (~20 kbits/second per probe), so it must operate hundreds of probes in parallel to provide bandwidth competitive to that of a magnetic disk. This led to their choice of a moving medium and stationary probes. The large number of simultaneously-operating probes also requires the fabrication of on-chip multiplexing electronics. The Nanochip device, which uses a different recording medium that supports higher bandwidth, does not require on-chip active devices.

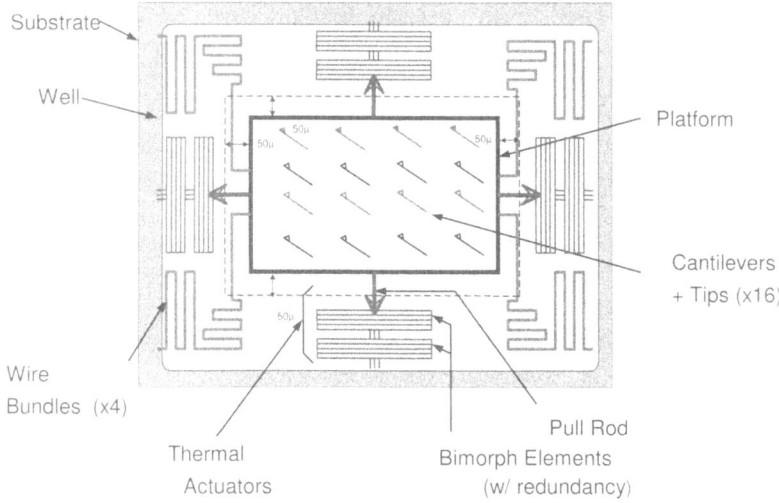

Figure 2: The Nanochip device in schematic form

While MEMS devices can be built in fabrication facilities that are well behind the state of the art, they are still not expected to be competitive in per-bit cost with magnetic disks. The primary competitor that most MEMS manufacturers hope to displace initially is flash ROM. Flash ROM cells are intrinsically smaller than DRAM cells, and since less stringent testing is required,[4] the devices should be cheaper than DRAM, which is now priced at about twenty cents per megabyte. To date, these price levels have not been achieved, perhaps because of lower volumes and lack of sufficient fabrication capacity

Ultimately, MEMS storage devices might replace disks in applications that do not require huge capacity, or in applications in which their low power and complete silence are important. The companies developing MEMS storage anticipate having products available in from two to four years.

Networking

For portable devices, there is an expectation (largely fueled by the popular press) that wireless networking will improve at a pace similar to the improvement in CPU performance. This seems implausible for several reasons. First, increased transistor density in radios doesn't translate into higher performance, as it does

---

4   Flash cells may be erased and rewritten a limited number of times, so error correction is needed for reliability. Manufacturers exploit this by shipping parts with a small fraction of bad bits.

in a CPU, but only into reduced cost. Second, the available spectrum is finite, and increased per-connection bandwidth uses more of it. Spectrum use is regulated by local law and international treaty, and current users have resisted attempts to displace their services.

Improvements in coding have improved the bandwidth efficiency of radio channels, but these improvements are rapidly approaching their limit. One proposal to mitigate these limits is to use the spectrum at ~50 GHz. These frequencies are strongly absorbed by atmospheric oxygen, so very small cells will be needed for ubiquitous coverage. Providing the necessary wired infrastructure will be costly, and it is unclear that users will be willing to pay for it.

For a given cell size, there is also a direct trade-off between power and bandwidth. Current 802.11b radio cards draw approximately 1 watt. Better protocols and better designs can improve this a bit, and the superior modulation used by 802.11g promises a fourfold bandwidth improvement, but these improvements require a smaller cell size.

Example systems

Several companies are developing systems designed primarily for small size and energy efficiency. Figures 3 and 4 show two recent examples, the Tiquit Eighty-Three [6] and a wallet-sized system from OQO Corporation [7].

Figure 3: The Tiqit Eighty Three Computer. This device provides a keyboard, a joystick and a stylus for user interaction.

Both are full Windows XP machines, with 256 MB of DRAM, 20 Gbyte hard disks, and color VGA (480 × 640) displays. The Tiqit device uses a 300 MHz National Geode processor and is fanless. The somewhat smaller OQO device uses a 1GHzTransmeta CPU and requires a fan.

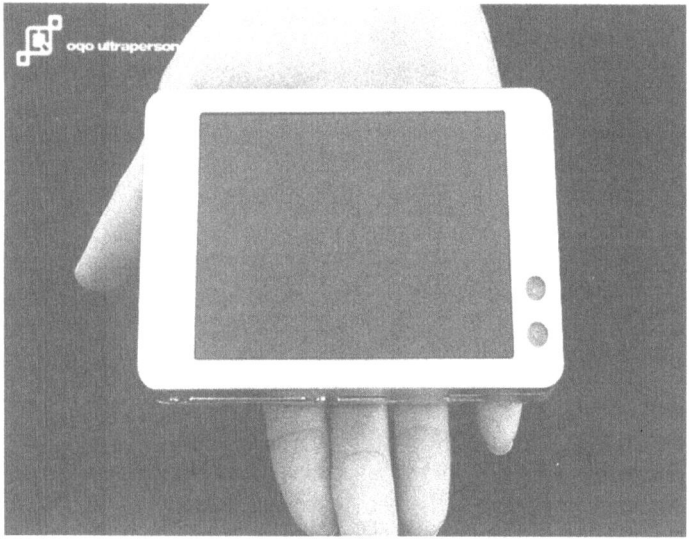

Figure 4: The OQO Ultra Portable Computer.

A number of other devices that combine the functions of a PDA and mobile phone are also appearing in the market. It will be interesting to see whether these devices become popular, since the user interfaces needed for phones and PDAs are quite different. Although carrying a single device is appealing, finding a single form factor that can serve both purposes might be difficult.

Conclusions

The goal of providing a portable, truly personal computer that can provide all the computing, communication, and storage needs of a single user has not yet been achieved, although it seems clear that the underlying technologies needed are very nearly adequate today.

The existence of such devices will pose new challenges for software developers: How can we build new user interfaces that provide acceptable levels of interaction with a very small display? How can we provide an easy-to-use user authentication system that protects the user's data if the device is lost or stolen, or that makes a stolen device unusable? How should these devices interact with the larger world of computing of which they are only a small part?

Providing software and services for these devices will provide new opportunities for innovation in many areas of computing.

References

1   http://www.sciencenews.org/20020907/bob10.asp
2   http://www.cdtltd.co.uk
3   http://www.kodak.com/US/en/corp/display/whatsNew.jhtml
4   VETTIGER, P., ET AL., 'The 'Millipede'—nanotechnology entering data storage,' *IEEE Trans. Nanotechnol.*, vol. 1, no. 1, 2002, pp. 39–55.
5   http://www.nanochip.com
6   http://www.tiquit.com
7   http://www.oqo.com

44
Multiple Alternative Voting

David Wheeler

This paper was the result of discussions with Roger Needham in April 1983. The University of Cambridge was intending to introduce single transferable voting for official ballots, and did so, even though this method has the defects discussed below. More generally, since then electronic voting has become a public policy issue. It is evident that there are more complexities about this, both in principle and in practice, than many may suppose (see, e.g., Mercuri [1]). What follows is an early note on some pertinent problems. Voting is also widely used, for many different technical purposes, in computing systems, and the note implicitly also draws attention to the need for care in the choice of algorithms in these technological contexts.

STV and MAV in brief

The single-transferable-vote system (STV) suffers from one major fault. As it is a single-vote system, it uses the second and remaining choices of a voter in an algorithmic but arbitrary way when more than one vacancy is being filled. This fault can be eliminated with an alternative strategy, multiple alternative voting (MAV), while retaining the advantages of STV. (The two methods are identical when there is a single vacancy.)

In MAV, each voter gives a preference list for the candidates, just as for STV. If there are V vacancies, then one vote is counted for each of the first V preferences of each elector. The candidate with the lowest vote is eliminated from all the preferences and the count repeated until only V candidates remain.

The problems with single transferable voting

The major objection to the STV system is that the second and higher preferences are used in an arbitrary way. That is to say, the voter does not know if or how his preferences are to be used. This arises because the method uses a quota, the minimum number of votes needed to elect a candidate. If the first preference is part of an exact quota, the voter's later choices are unused. This is reasonable for a single vacancy, but not for multiple vacancies, where surplus preferences are reassigned without voter control.

Example

Assume 303 voters filling 3 vacancies from 5 candidates, namely A, B, C, D, E. Assume the votes are cast as follows:

> 76 voters list A, D, E
> 76 voters list B, D, E, C
> 76 voters list C, D, E, B
> 75 voters list D, E, A

With STV, calculation of the quota = 303/4 + 1 = 76. Thus A, B, and C are elected.

Multiple alternative voting

Now consider another strategy, multiple alternative voting. To calculate MAV, suppose the votes cast are these:

	A	B	C	D	E
vote sums	151	76	76	303	303

Use the tie rule and delete, say, B from the ballots. Thus 76 fourth preferences for C are used, giving the following voter sums:

A	B	C	D	E
151	0	152	303	303

Thus D, E, and C are elected. If no one cast fourth preferences, then D, E, and A are elected.

Given the illustrative voting figures and all the preferences, one would expect D and E to be elected and an extra one from A, B or C. However, STV gives A, B and C, and not D or E at all, because it only considers first preferences, with its arbitrary quota. How does an STV voter indicate he wishes to select three candidates with about the same weight? He cannot, because he is at the mercy of the arbitrary quota.

The example just given shows how the MAV strategy is more nearly in accord with what the electors might expect, and how the information from them is used more effectively.

The average elector would expect his first V preferences to be used if he filled them in. He would expect that if a candidate of his were defeated, then his next preference would be used. He would not expect that the use of his preferences would depend on the arbitrary quota.

A few might expect that a single vote would carry more power than if it were split among V candidates. However, this is really a matter of philosophy, and the system is simpler if we arrange that when voters use less than V votes, their votes do not carry greater than unit weight. This means also that when preferences run out for a voter because his early preferences have been rejected, his residual votes do not carry more than unit weight.

In no case yet found does the MAV result appear to be further from what can be claimed to be the voters' intentions and expectation than the STV system in any of its forms. When there is a single candidate, the two systems will give identical results unless the tie arrangements are different.

We now give a more detailed description of the MAV system.

MAV in detail

Voter's ballot form

This consists of a list of candidates, preferably in random order. Each item in the list consists of the candidate's name followed by a box or space for an integer.

Voter's instructions

Mark your first preference with 1 in the box of the candidate you prefer. Mark your second preference with 2 in the box of your second choice. And so on. If fewer than the number of vacancies are filled in, then the empties are taken as abstentions and the effectiveness of the earlier votes is unchanged.

Counting rules

Assume there are V vacancies. The first V unrejected candidates on each voter's list are each given one vote. If V or fewer candidates have non-zero vote sums, these are elected, otherwise the candidate with the least vote sum is rejected and the count is repeated.

Ambiguities are resolved by rejecting the candidate with the least number of first preference votes, then, if still unresolved, using the second, third, etc., preferences. The ambiguities remaining are resolved by algorithmically tossing a coin so that it cannot be "forced." For example, one such rule is to divide the total number of votes by the number of choices to be made and use the remainder to select the candidate to be rejected.

Printed results

First give the sums for each candidate, i.e., the number of votes for candidate A with mark 1, the number of votes for candidate A with mark 2, and so on. Then add the number of votes transferred from the rejected candidate to each of these sums. This is repeated until the final sums for the elected candidates can be given. (One null candidate should be included to simplify the treatment of null votes.)

The above suffices for the simple system. However a number of extra points arise.

Printed list of voters

Should a list of those who have voted be published? It can help in detecting fraud.

Printed lists of votes cast

This can be done anonymously if every ballot paper has a unique reference number by the side of each candidate. A list can be published for each candidate and mark. The list contains the reference numbers of each vote cast for that candidate and the mark. Only the user of the ballot paper and the central counting procedure (probably a computer in this case) know the unique reference number. Thus each voter can assure himself that his vote has finished in the correct count.

Secure counting can be done with separate authenticated programs and computers. There exist a number of precautions to take, but these are known to many people.

Remote voting

If ballot papers can be sent securely to the recipients, then it is easy for a computer to arrange that the random candidate permutation is different for each ballot paper or is uniformly distributed among the ballot papers. The list of contents of the boxes on the paper, together with the voter identification number, is returned as the vote. This also prevents alphabetical bias in the voting.

Li Gong has pointed out that if the identification number is wrong, it is possible to arrange the printing and response such that the vote has been apparently cast but does not contribute to the totals. Thus the buyer of a vote has no guarantee of his purchase, so that postal or online voting can be made about as secure as a voting booth.

Counting methods

If done by computer, there is little point in shortcuts, and a simple MAV program can be verified and checked much more easily than an STV program. If the number of votes is small, say less than 100, the work is relatively simple and quick. Where the number of votes is large and manual methods are used, then repeated scanning can be almost eliminated by having $(C + 1)^V$ separate piles during the first scan. Each pile corresponds to one possible sequence of the first V preferences. Then only the rejected candidates' piles need to be referred to again. Where C is large, this process can be modified easily. For example, if some candidates are likely to attract few votes, their piles can be combined.

Compared with the counting required for STV, the counting at the first stage for MAV is more onerous, as V times as many votes are handled. However, the subsequent counting movements are likely to be fewer.

If all the intermediate sums are not printed, then some further shortcuts are possible. For example, when the low counts cannot affect the result, there is no point in transferring them.

Reference

1   MERCURI, R., 'A better ballot box,' *IEEE Spectrum*, October 2002, pp. 46–50.

45
The Semiotics of Umbrellas

John Wilkes

It's always more fun to tilt at an appropriately sized windmill—and agreeing on which windmill to tilt at often makes the difference between success and failure in research. What I offer here is a humble suggestion for some vocabulary with which to discuss windmill tilting, in the hope that the endeavor will be more productive for all concerned if the beast can better be identified, named, and communicated about.

Once upon a time, I found myself engaged in a discussion with a colleague on the relative merits of prototyping a piece of software. That conversation proved unfruitful: as we later discovered, we had very different ideas about what was meant by the term "prototype". One of us was convinced that the only prototype of value would have to be a first-cut of the software that could be shipped as a product, after some engineering had been "applied" to it. The other was equally adamant that prototypes were merely vehicles to get across an idea—a way to sell a proposal, and perhaps either to demonstrate that it did something useful, or to determine if it did. We parted company, each mystified at the other's intransigence.

Some time later, having become older, if not wiser, I and a new team of people that I was privileged to work with decided that this was all simply a confusion over vocabulary, and that banning the "p-word" would serve us all well. Indeed it has, but we never really found a satisfactory replacement for it that we could remember from one day to the next.

Then, a couple of years ago, something clicked after one of those interminable discussions about "what should we do next". The images shown here emerged (a little soggy) the following morning during my shower. Just for fun, I've reproduced my first scribbles of them—illegibilities and all, together with their definitions, and a few related thoughts.

Research nugget: a coherent unit of research work, and typically the result of a small(ish) research project; maybe as little as a person-month's work, maybe as much as a dozen or so. Often achievable by a person or three. Good ones can result in nice technical papers. Connotations of gold mining are not unintentional.

Testbed: a vehicle for obtaining research results as rapidly and efficiently as possible. The purpose of a testbed is to develop, nurture, and support one or more research nuggets—nothing more. Although a testbed may be (too often is) pressed into service in other roles, such as showing off the research work, this mixing of
purposes is best viewed for what it is: a distraction. The evaluation criterion for a testbed is the ease with which research can be performed. (To help get this across, in a UNIX-centric culture, we used to say, "If MS-DOS works better, use it!")

Vision: a description of some goal, a result that a project is trying to achieve: an "end state" in the consultant's jargon. I've found it helpful to separate out the vision from the research. The research (at least in my world) is best thought of as supporting or enabling a vision. Indeed, it often comes about by working backwards: "What in that vision can't we do today?"

Visions are helpful in justifying work: explaining "what it all means" and why we want to go there. Good visions seem to be contentious and attractive; bad ones vacuous, or simply dull. Visions are good vehicles for teasing out subjective notions of "value" from possible participants in, or customers of, a piece of work: if a vision doesn't catch people's imagination, the work to achieve it is unlikely to be pursued with enthusiasm.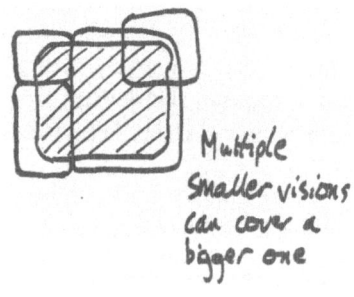

It's usually helpful if there is a common vision, since that means people who subscribe to it agree on the goal. But associated with the one larger vision, it's also common to have multiple, smaller-scale or smaller-scope visions. Ideally (!) the smaller visions complement one another, and can be seen as contributing to the bigger one.

Showcase: a tool used to demonstrate some or all of (1) a vision, (2) research work, and/or (3) that a team is making progress. A showcase that's an executable piece of code is sometimes called a demonstrator. Other forms include published papers, mocked-up user interfaces, storyboards, and presentations (preferably with attractive animations) claiming magnificent things.

The test for a good showcase is that it makes visible what the excitement is all about and focuses attention on the accomplishments, rather than on the effort required to achieve them. Unfortunately, this seems to mean that it's quite hard to build good showcases for operating systems, middleware, or anything that hides or reduces work.

In some cases, a testbed may be usable in (or even as) a showcase. But these two roles are different, and suggestions to "economize" in this form should usually be treated with skepticism: it's all too easy to end up with an unconvincing showcase that is inconvenient to do research in.

Most research nuggets can fruitfully fit into one or more showcases. Indeed, it's often a useful idea to think through how the research will be demonstrated before too much effort is put into doing it!

Showcases can readily complement one another: a larger vision may best be described and demonstrated in pieces, especially early on, although it's often helpful if there's a "core" showcase being aimed for, and some of my colleagues have reported that mocking up such a showcase is often all that it takes to sell a key idea.

Umbrella projects: a grouping or coalescing "wrapper" that ties together a set of other activities into a common theme. Like the p-word, the "umbrella" concept often seems to cause confusion. Indeed, I've heard it used to describe a vision, a single large project, and a politically correct shield for continuing business as usual (especially after inputs of the form "It is now a corporate mandate that all projects must ..."). More useful, perhaps, are the relatively benign forms described here.

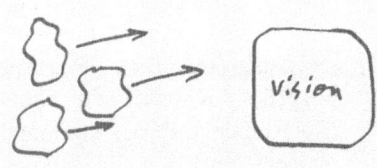

Flying in formation: Here, there is a set of research nuggets that share a common vision, but the ties between the pieces of work that go into the nuggets are relatively weak, and it's unlikely that a single, coherent showcase can be put together.

Compared to the next alternative, the lack of a single showcase can greatly reduce the amount of integration work required, but it still may be possible to spin (sorry: present) all the research as conforming to a single coherent vision.

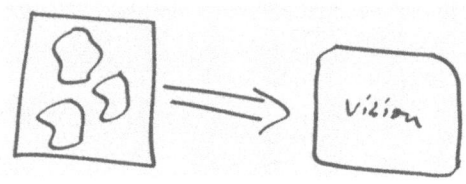

A unifying showcase: this is closer to the "single large project" model. A single showcase is used to tie together the individual pieces of research and demonstrate them and their inter-relationships.

A unifying showcase is usually significantly more work to get set up— especially for the first few nuggets—but can present a correspondingly more compelling façade. In my experience, getting one of these unifying showcases agreed to is a black art. It requires somebody to have the courage of their convictions (and a silver tongue) to persuade others of the viability, utility, and excitement of the associated vision. It can be done. I wish it were done more often. The (slightly) greater ability to pull this off is one of the few distinguishing factors associated with a top-notch industrial research establishment, as compared to an academic one.

If effective, such a unifying showcase has the advantage of achieving higher impact than a single research nugget can manage by itself. The obvious disadvantages are the relatively high risk ("What if we pick the wrong problem?"), exacerbated by the fear of putting too many eggs in one basket; the difficulty of reaching a common understanding of the goal ("What about this other interesting side issue?"); and the potentially high integration cost of the showcase artifact, which now becomes more of an industrial-strength vehicle than a research tool per se.

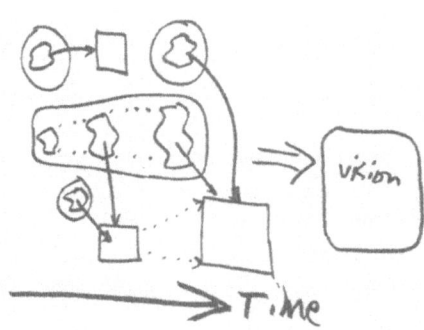

In practice, of course, nothing is as simple as this exposition suggests, as the (deliberately rather muddled) diagram to the left attempts to illustrate. Real-life projects mix and match approaches and techniques, in response to all sorts of outside and internal pressures, requests, and ideas. Research nuggets, testbeds, and showcases come and go—or morph into new ones as understanding, interest, and opportunity allow.

Most projects end up with a mixed bag of assorted testbeds, supporting a set of research nuggets that contribute to different showcases at different times. But good projects seem to retain at least a thread of a common vision—even if parts of it may be submerged temporarily and new elements appear.

I've found that attempting to tease out the different roles and assumptions of each piece is still a beneficial activity. Recursion is often useful in this exercise: what looks to be a research nugget (or vision, etc.) can often be sub-divided, and the same analysis applied to each piece.

Over the past couple of years, these ideas have seemed to resonate with my colleagues, and they have proven useful as a way to communicate ideas for structuring and focusing some of our work. One day, perhaps, they might help us approach the scale of effects and impact achieved by the apparently effortless, *laissez faire* project-management processes that the Computer Laboratory used in the heyday of the Cambridge Distributed System. We can but dream.

46
Computers for Specialized Application Areas

Maurice Wilkes

With the end of CMOS looming ahead—although there is still a significant way to go—it is natural that people should begin to search for innovative computing devices that would be very fast on certain specific problems, even if they were not capable of running a general work load. The economic viability of these devices would depend on finding what is known as a "killer" application, that is, an application of such importance that it would by itself justify the financial investment.

The first of these approaches that I heard about was DNA computing. In nature, a DNA molecule has the role of storing genetic information. However, there is no reason way an artificially synthesised DNA molecule should not be used to represent information of a very different kind. In spite of long continued effort, it was not found possible to identify a killer application, and in consequence, DNA computing has dropped out of the picture as far as high-performance computing is concerned.

Quantum computing is now attracting great interest. A form of universality can be claimed for a quantum computer, but this is a theoretical claim only. Only applications that could efficiently exploit the special quantum features would run at super-speed. Others would run at a snail's pace. A quantum computer would not, therefore, be capable of running a general workload in the way that a PC or a workstation can. For this reason, I am inclined to think that the old-fashioned (analogue) computers, such as the differential analyser, provide a better operational model for quantum computing than the modern PC or workstation does.

The principal application being talked about as a killer application for a quantum computer is the factorisation of large numbers, an operation of importance in code breaking. However, there may be others.

The physics behind the quantum computer is in the early stages of development, and the practical problems of making a working quantum computer have hardly been explored. In spite of the great public interest that has been aroused, it is clear to me that practical applications in the computer field are so far away that developments should be left for the time being exclusively in the hands of the physicists. It is hard to see any present justification for the computer industry investing more than token sums in quantum computing.

However, it is interesting to speculate on what would happen if a quantum computer that would enable very large numbers to be factorised easily were ever developed. This is a subject on which I would much like to have heard Roger Needham's views. The use of encryption algorithms, based on numbers that are hard to factorise, has become so pervasive throughout the computer field that an "industry" may be said to have grown up around it. Would the effect of the quantum computer be to destabilize that industry, with widespread repercussions? What alternative means of encryption could be used instead?

In my view, it is through its impact on computer security that quantum computing, if it ever comes, might have a major impact on the computing world. Even if other killer applications were to emerge and were to become of great importance in their respective specialized areas, they would be of small importance for the computer field as a whole.

Computer Security?

The Royal Society Clifford Paterson Lecture, 2002

Roger Needham[1]

Abstract

The technical aspects of computer security have fascinated researchers (including the author) for decades. It is, however, beginning to appear that the challenging problems are to do with people, rather than with mathematics or electronics.

Historical development

Computer security as a topic is about forty years old. Before then computers were used sequentially by different users, each user being presented with a *tabula rasa* which was restored at the end of the user's session. Computers did not, in general, maintain on-line state in the form of files and other forms of persistent data over long periods for many users.

When this changed security became an issue. Who or what could legitimately access particular files? How could one be sure that the actions of a program running on behalf of one user did not alter or corrupt the behaviour of another user's program? Could a malicious user subvert the entire system so that it did nothing useful for anyone? How did we know that a user was who he purported to be? These were burning system design questions in the 1960s and into the 1970s. Characteristically one was talking about a single computer with many users. It was accordingly possible to incorporate protection mechanisms into the hardware design of the machine, and to arrange that while a particular user's program was running the hardware could be so set up as to make it physically impossible for unauthorized access from the user's program to other programs and data to

---

1 This was Roger's last public lecture, given on 14th November 2002. It was published in the *Philosophical Transactions of the Royal Society, Series A*, vol. 361, 2003, pp. 1549–1555. The editors are grateful to the Royal Society for permission to reproduce this paper.

occur. Nevertheless the systems of that time were in fact not very secure. When calls were made by a user program to the operating system the arguments presented to them often needed validation, but either the validation software was incorrect, or, more insidiously, it proved possible to change the value of an argument after it had been checked but before it was used.

At about the time when single system security was such that one could say with the classically cynical American engineer "That's good enough for Government work" the rules suddenly changed. The invention of local area and wide area networks in the 1970s meant that related computations did not always happen in the same machine or might be spread over several machines. It was no longer possible to use physical means to prevent unauthorized access, since data passed from one place to another on a typically broadcast medium to which numerous other machines were attached. The exposed nature of communication paths made it much harder to pass data designed to authenticate an individual, such as a password.

By one of those coincidences that sometimes solves big problems, at the crucial time cryptographic algorithms became generally available. Earlier cryptography had been an arcane subject practiced by people you didn't want to know about; suddenly, and not entirely to the pleasure of governments, it became a widely practiced and fascinating research topic. By the late 1970s cryptographic techniques were sufficiently well established that it was possible to pass data across a network from A to B in such a way that nobody but B could understand it, and such that if it had been altered in any way B would know; all this without A and B sharing a secret. Additionally these developments gave rise to a wave of new activity in the area that borders between computer science and mathematics; a wave that continues to this day. One can distinguish two strands in this activity. One, in which I have myself worked quite a lot, is to do with protocols for carrying out, in distributed systems, such tasks as user authentication, non-repudiable transactions, program certification, and so on; in general to use known cryptographic techniques correctly. Protocols of this sort are extremely easy to get wrong in subtle ways, and this fact has given rise to a secondary industry of formal methods for exploring protocol correctness. I was lucky enough to be in at the beginning of both these activities.

The other major strand derives from the mathematics of public key cryptography and the believed difficulty of factoring very large numbers and working out some discrete logarithms. People of a much more mathematical turn than I have become extraordinarily agile in putting together algorithms that seem to have security relevance. Why do I say "seem to"? Because in essence what is going on is that we have a set of conditions for some action to be proper, and the mathematics is used to model a test for those conditions. The model may not always be exact. Not only in security is it the case that an ordinary person has a problem and a friendly mathematician solves a neighbouring problem. An example that is of interest here is the electronic book. We have a pretty good idea of the semantics of the paper book. We go and buy it, we can lend it to our spouse or to a friend, we can sell it, we can legitimately copy small bits of it for our own use, and so on. The electronic book is different. It is a device that we own and is convenient for reading text on (whether such things really exist is a different issue). We pay for the digital representation of a book and download it into our device. The publisher of the book has a legitimate interest in the preservation of his intellectual property, and enlists the services of good mathematicians and system designers to make measures to do so. Unfortunately these measures do not have the same semantics as the paper book. I may not be able to lend the electronic book to my spouse without lending her the device even if she has one of her own. I may not be able to copy even small bits of it. The technical solution has not matched the real world need.

Despite all the theoretical progress that has been made, and the very ingenious papers that have been published, systems remain rather insecure. This is not primarily because of bad algorithms or protocols. It is to a substantial extent because of ignoring the human element. Even in the mechanical aspects just outlined, the human element is sometimes crucial. An example is non-repudiation, where the purpose of a protocol is to furnish evidence that will convince an arbitrator that a party attempting to repudiate a transaction did in fact commit to it. The arbitrator is, and has to be, human.

People figure in security in a variety of ways. They may be the users of a system, who need protecting from each other and from whom the system itself needs to be protected. They may be the people who set up security systems; they may be the people who specify lists of access permissions, they may be local security administrators. We shall see how crucial all these people are.

Secrets

All the techniques for authentication depend on the physical inaccessibility of something. People cannot remember elaborate encryption keys, or the codes that characterize their irises, for example. These have to be stored in some object, and the integrity of authentication depends on the integrity of this object. Many objects are quite unsuitable for keeping serious material that should not be disclosed or altered. In particular PCs are unsuitable, and are getting more so as it becomes more usual for home PCs to be connected to the internet all the time. Smart cards are sometimes said be a panacea, with almost magical virtues. But they aren't all that secure, and their contents often get to be used outside the card, where their security is at best problematic. In general it is extremely awkward to run secure systems, and real people typically will not. This was cited, in a recent public debate in the UK, as a reason for it being unnecessary for the Government to take to itself the draconian powers it has to require production of decryption keys in various circumstances. It was said that what the Government needed was a Royal Corps of Hackers, not vast legal powers.

Policies

The security policies of organizations are vast, informal, and incomprehensible. There is no proper notation for saying what the policies are exactly, and they grow up over time. The source of the policies is sometimes what is seen as 'common sense' and sometimes the end effect of legal requirements. As an example of the latter, a corporation has to pay attention to the security of trade secret material because, in the event that some such material is misappropriated, it would be a valid defence in Anglo-Saxon law for the appropriators to say that nothing wrong had happened since the corporation didn't seem to care much anyway. Another instance is the prohibition of certain employees from dealing in a corporation's shares during the period in advance of the announcement of quarterly results. For this prohibition to be effective the results must be kept to as few employees as possible as they are prepared. Then there are policies that come from prudence. In companies that make computers it is, or at any rate was, customary to go to great lengths to conceal future developments from the sales and marketing people. This apparently paradoxical approach was so that the sales folk would not sell things that did not yet exist, generating embarrassment at best and antitrust problems at worst. If you're a manager in Microsoft you have access to salary, bonus, and performance details for those who report through you, but not for those to whom you report (nor, incidentally, yourself). When I was Head of the University Computer Laboratory I signed all purchase orders except that when I was away someone else did, provided that the deputy hadn't raised the order in which case a second deputy was used for separation of duty reasons.

I have given these examples as a miscellaneous collection to show what organizational security policies are really like. In enforcing them we depend on far more than knowing who somebody is. An immediate question is whether, as transactions become steadily more electronic, these rules and practices should be technically enforced or organizationally enforced, as they often are in the paper world. I get the impression that because it is possible to imagine the enforcement being technical then that is often regarded as the ideal goal, and that security engineers should go as far in that direction as they can. In this context I can tell a cautionary tale. In the late 1970s a corporate research lab was experimenting with the 'paperless office'. They devised a system in which documents that looked on screen like well-known company forms such as purchase orders, payment authorizations, expense reports and so forth were passed from one screen to another for successive steps of authorization. Naturally when a manager had signed off on a part of the form subsequent signers could not alter it. This appeared to the researchers to be an obvious requirement. When the system was complete it was tried out in an actual corporate office of the same company. It produced real chaos; almost rigor mortis. In real life forms were altered after signature all the time for entirely good reasons. In the Computer Laboratory, the probability that purchase orders were altered after my signature was not all that high, but it happened often enough that it would be a real pain for me to have to re-sign orders that had been changed from 2000 No. 8 screws to 2000 No. 10 screws, or where a part number had been corrected because the sender noticed it was wrong while putting the order in the envelope.

If we look at my earlier security example, namely backup for me in signing orders, we can glean useful insights. Suppose an order for 10,000 pounds (quite large by the standards of a University Department) had been taken to my first reserve for signature. He would quite probably know whether I was there or not. If not, and if the order was handed to him personally, he would ask the hander whether he'd looked for me. If the order just turned up in his in-tray he would phone my secretary and ask if I was around. If it was a really large order, say for 100,000 pounds, and I had gone to London for the morning to be back by 1500 hours, which fact my secretary would be able to tell him, he would wait. If I was away for a week he probably would not. To enforce all that electronically would be a Big Deal. The reserve would of course have to be authenticated, as would the identity of whoever sent him the order. He would need validated access to my whereabouts and travel plans. Maybe some threshold numbers would have to be incorporated in the program used. When pursuing this sort of line it is very easy to finish up with a requirement to validate an instance of a whole operating system. Indeed, this point is reached very quickly when one tries to protect intellectual property in material to be displayed in an ordinary PC.

My purpose in going into all this is to stress that the more we mechanically enforce rules of ordinary business practice the more metadata we generate, in terms of rules of behaviour, methods of validating data of all sorts, in addition to access control lists, role tables, security libraries, and all the rest of the clutter.

Metadata: the data that describes the data

In a complex set-up, for example a large corporation, someone will ask the question 'Does the ensemble of rules and other metadata actually give effect to the security policy?' A proper interpretation of this would require not only that those actions forbidden by the policy cannot be done but that actions not forbidden by the policy can be done. This soon becomes formidably difficult, and for some access control systems can be mathematically undecidable. Such situations are prone to bizarre errors, as in a case I heard of where the proprietors of a large data system were very proud of their access controls, based on an elaborate security library. It was only as part of an outside investigation that it was noticed that the security library itself was open to write access by anyone! One is strongly pressed to the conclusion that if something can sensibly be enforced by human means it very probably should. Even deciding this is difficult. Essentially human enforcement relies on integrity of people; it is more reasonable to rely on the individual integrity of six senior people in the finance division who are paid a lot than on the individual integrity of five thousand counter clerks who are paid a little.

If we contemplate this conclusion, heretical as it is for a computerist, we can see other good reasons for it. Error in handling metadata is at least as likely to forbid necessary actions as to permit unwanted ones. It is not unusual for a new employee not to be able to do his or her job properly for several weeks because permissions have not been set up. It has happened that the administration of my research lab came to a halt because of an erroneous change to access controls in Redmond, Washington, eight time zones away. Of course when we noticed the problem the person responsible was asleep in bed, and we just had to wait until the next day. This does not matter too much for a research lab, but it would be very damaging for a supermarket or a stockbroker. An extreme case is a military one, where more and more use of computers and data is being made in support of deployed operations. You can't stop a battle while access controls are fixed.

All our experience is that things that should not or even logically cannot happen sometimes do happen, and the more complex the web of technical restraints the more difficult it is likely to be to recover effectively. To illustrate very simply the importance of recovery issues, there is a well-known attack on the Needham-Schroeder authentication protocol [1]. The attack depends on something happening that in the proper course of the protocol should not be able to happen; but the seriousness of the attack comes from the fact that there is no way to recover at all when it has happened. The recovery issue is a very serious one, and compounds the complexity discussed at length above. It is really hard to catalogue, and to find out how to recover from, the things that should not happen but will. If organizational authority can over-ride protocol, then recovery can occur by use of human ingenuity. For example a high-ranking officer can say 'Fire the goddam thing anyway!'

Logging

If we follow this line of thought we can go further. This is where it matters that we are talking about security within an organisation rather than in the world in general. In an organisation there are more ties among the individuals than there are in the outside world; for example soldiers are subject to military discipline, and there is an assumption that employees in general do not want to get fired. To some extent we can exploit this to simplify security matters. Keeping a record of what has been done can be a simple solution to otherwise difficult problems. Here's an example. Anyone can buy a copy of my bank statement from a dubious enquiry agent for some 200 pounds. This is because any teller in the employ of my bank can ask for it, and since the bank is a large one there are enough tellers over all branches that some will be willing to earn a little money on the side. Yet having all the tellers able to have access is in other ways a good thing. The security would be much improved if the act of generating a copy of a statement were recorded in the statement itself, so that when I got my regular monthly printout I could see that a statement was asked for by teller number 3 in the Penzance branch, and I could raise a complaint if I was in Philadelphia at the relevant time. It is not clear to me why banks do not do this, but that is another question. It is worth noting that maintaining logs is often rejected as a security technique on the bogus argument that there is too much log material for anyone to look at. The present case is an example where parallel processing at the level of millions makes light of the volume of stuff. After all, most of us give our bank statements at least a cursory scan.

People

To compound the effects of complexity, humans involved in managing security are fallible, lazy, and uncomprehending. The first applies to all of us, but the other two may seem surprising. I shall now try to explain why they are mentioned here.

Security is a nuisance. It gets in the way, in the manner that a locked door gets in the way even if you have a key to it. Even if you have brought the key with you the door is an obstruction, and is even more so if you have to go back to wherever you left the key. A local security officer has the duty of making sure that the features that make for inconvenience are in place and effective. The life of a local security administrator is much easier, and the administrator much less unpopular with colleagues, if the administrator's job is not done 'properly'. The incentives on the security administrator are thus not very appropriate. I am credibly advised that units in the armed services are particularly adept at simplifying their lives in this sort of way but so are bank branch managers, hospital administrators, and so forth. Wherever there are devolved units that have a certain amount of discretion in the management of their internal affairs, burdensome security will be circumvented.

As much damage cane be done because people are uncomprehending. A well-known story describes two senior bank managers being sent two parts of a cryptographic key to load into a security module. They were sufficiently senior that they didn't care to use keyboards, so they gave the two pieces of paper to the same technician to enter, thus losing the entire purpose of the two parts. They didn't understand why it was supposed to be done the way it was supposed to be done. Another tale, not directly connected with security, concerns a distributed and devolved naming service, that replicated data widely for easy access. For such a system to work it is clearly necessary to have a lot of discipline about the processes of installing new instances so that update messages can be sent to the required places. Local managers simply didn't understand all this, and if one of their instances misbehaved they would simply shoot it and make a new one. Update messages would be directed to the instance that no longer existed, and would be returned undelivered. They would not be delivered to the new instance which soon stopped being current. Confusion reigned. These examples show the results of overestimating the understanding and probably even the intelligence of the local agents. The system was designed by very well educated and well informed people who simply did not think of the contrast between themselves and the people on the ground.

An agenda for research

The conclusion I draw from this in some ways depressing tale is that there is a great scope for research in a number of areas. First, can we find means of expressing security policies such that machine aids may be used to help check whether available technical measures are capable of implementing the policies? It may be impossible, but it would be nice to know. Note that I said 'machine aids.' Researchers working on theorem proving spent a lot of time trying to get fully automatic proof engines, and eventually realised that machine aided proof was much more effective. Second, can we find tools to assist in auditing security data to check for policy compliance? Third, can we find means to express local operating rules so that their rationale is apparent to local operations people, who might therefore take them more seriously? Alternatively, can we find ways to simplify the task of local security administrators so that there is less encouragement for circumvention?

These issues are partly technical and partly managerial. It is greatly to be hoped that the managerial content does not deter computing researchers from tackling them, for their importance is great.

Computing researchers need to climb down from their ivory towers to look at the real world contexts in which their systems will be deployed.

Reference

1. NEEDHAM, R.M., AND SCHROEDER, M.D., 'Using encryption for authentication in large networks of computers,' *Comm. ACM*, vol. 21, no. 12, 1978, pp. 993–999.

Roger Needham: Publications

Compiled by Karen Spärck Jones

With T. Joyce:
'The thesaurus approach to information retrieval,' *American Documentation*, 9 (3), 1958, 192–197; reprinted in *Readings in information retrieval*, ed. K. Spärck Jones and P. Willett, San Francisco, CA: Morgan Kaufmann, 1997.

With M. Masterman and K. Spärck Jones:
'The analogy between mechanical translation and library retrieval,' *Proceedings of the International Conference on Scientific Information* (1958), National Academy of Sciences—National Research Council, Washington, DC, 1959, vol. 2, 917–935.

With A.F. Parker-Rhodes:
'A reduction method for non-arithmetic data, and its application to thesauric translation,' *Information Processing: Proceedings of the International Conference on Information Processing (1959)*, Paris, 1960, 321–327.

With A.F. Parker-Rhodes:
'The theory of clumps,' Cambridge Language Research Unit, Report M.L. 126, 1960.

With A.H.J. Miller and K. Spärck Jones:
'The information retrieval system of the Cambridge Language Research Unit,' Cambridge Language Research Unit, Report M.L. 109, 1960.

'The theory of clumps II,' Cambridge Language Research Unit, Report M.L. 139, 1961.

Research on information retrieval, classification and grouping 1957–1961, Ph.D. thesis, University of Cambridge; Cambridge Language Research Unit, Report M.L. 149, 1961.

'A method for using computers in information classification,' *Information Processing 62: Proceedings of IFIP Congress 1962*, ed. C. Popplewell, Amsterdam: North-Holland, 1963, 284–287.

'Automatic classification for information retrieval,' in *Information retrieval*, ed. Serbanescu, I.B.M. European Education Centre, Blaricum, Holland, 1963.

'Automatic classification for information retrieval,' lectures given at the NATO Advanced Study Institute on Automatic Document Analysis, Venice, 1963; abstracts published as Cambridge Language Research Unit Report M.L. 166, 1963.

'The exploitation of redundancy in programs,' in *The Impact of Users' Needs on the Design of Data Processing Systems*, Conference Proceedings, United Kingdom Automation Council, 1964, 6–7.

With K. Spärck Jones:
'Keywords and clumps,' *Journal of Documentation*, 20 (1), 1964, 5–15.

'Information retrieval,' *Computing science*, Report to the Science Research Council, ed. D. Michie, 1965, 92–94.

'Automatic classification—models and problems,' in *Mathematics and computer science in biology and medicine*, London: Medical Research Council, 1965, 111–114.

'Computer methods for classification and grouping,' in *The use of computers in anthropology*, ed. D. Hymes, The Hague: Mouton, 1965, 345–356.

'Applications of the theory of clumps,' *Mechanical Translation*, 8 (3/4), 1965, 113–127.

'Semantic problems of machine translation,' *Information Processing 65: Proceedings of IFIP Congress 1965*, ed. W. Kalenich, Washington DC: Spartan Books, 1965, vol. 1, 65–69.

'Information retrieval and some cognate computing problems,' in *Advances in programming and non-numerical computation*, ed. L. Fox, London: Pergamon Press, 1966, 201–218.

'The termination of certain iterative processes,' Rand Corporation, Santa Monica, Report RM-5188-PR, 1966.

'Automatic classification in linguistics,' *The Statistician*, 17 (1), 1967, 45–54.

With D.W. Barron, A.G. Fraser, D.F. Hartley, and B. Landy:
'File handling at Cambridge University,' *Proceedings of the 1967 Spring Joint Computer Conference, AFIPS Conference Proceedings*, vol. 30, 1967, 163–167.

With K. Spärck Jones:
'Automatic term classifications and retrieval,' *Information Storage and Retrieval*, 4 (2), 1968, 91–100.

With M.V. Wilkes:
'The design of multiple-access computer systems: part 2,' *Computer Journal*, 10, 1968, 315–320.

With D.F. Hartley and B. Landy:
'The structure of a multiprogramming supervisor,' *Computer Journal*, 11, 1968, 247–255.

'Consoles in the cloisters,' *Datamation*, January 1969.

With D.F. Hartley:
'Operational experience with the Cambridge multiple-access system,' *Computer Science and Technology*, Conference Publication 55, Institution of Electrical Engineers, London, 1969, 255–260.

'Computer operating systems,' in *Encyclopedia of linguistics, computation and control*, ed. A.R. Meetham and R.A. Hudson, London: Pergamon Press, 1969, 57–58.

With D.F. Hartley:
'Theory and practice in operating system design,' *2nd ACM Symposium on Operating System Principles*, Princeton, 1969, New York: ACM, 1969, 8–12.

'Software engineering techniques and operating system design and production' and, with D. Aron, 'Software engineering and computer science,' in *Software engineering techniques*, ed. J. Buxton and B. Randell, NATO Scientific Affairs Committee, NATO, Brussels, 1970, 111–113 and 113–114.

'Handling difficult faults in operating systems,' *3rd ACM Symposium on Operating System Principles*, Stanford, 1971, New York: ACM, 1971, 55–57.

With B. Landy:
'Software engineering techniques used in the development of the Cambridge multiple access system,' *Software—Practice and Experience*, 1 (2), 1971, 167–173.

'Tuning the Titan operating system,' in *Operating systems techniques*, ed. C.A.R. Hoare and R. Perrott, London: Academic Press, 1972, 277–281.

'Protection systems and protection implementations,' *Proceedings of the 1972 Fall Joint Computer Conference*, *AFIPS Conference Proceedings*, vol. 41, 1972,

571–578; reprinted in *The Auerbach Annual, 1972—Best Computer Papers*, ed. I.L. Auerbach, Philadelphia, PA: Auerbach (?), 1972.

'Protection—a current research area in operating systems,' *Proceedings of the International Computing Symposium 1973*, ed. G. Gunter, B. Levrat, and H. Lipps, Amsterdam: North-Holland, 1974, 123–126.

With M.V. Wilkes:
'Domains of protection and the management of processes,' *Computer Journal*, 17 (2), 1974, 117–120; reprinted in *The Auerbach Annual, 1975—Best Computer Papers*, ed. I.L. Auerbach, New York: Petrocelli/Charter, 1975; reprinted in Japanese, 1976.

With R.D.H. Walker:
'Protection and process management in the CAP computer,' *Proceedings of the International Workshop on Protection in Operating Systems*, IRIA, Paris, 1974, 155–160.

'The future of central computing services,' *Proceedings of the 1976 Computing Services Management Conference*, ed. D.H. McClain, Inter University Computing Committee, 1976, 74–76.

Articles in *Encyclopedia of computer science*, ed. A. Ralston and C. Meek, New York: Petrocelli/Charter 1976.

'The CAP project—an interim evaluation' (6th ACM Symposium on Operating System Principles, 1977), *Operating Systems Review*, 11 (5), 1978, 17–22.

With R.D.H. Walker:
'The Cambridge CAP computer and its protection system' (6th ACM Symposium on Computer Operating System Principles, 1977), *Operating Systems Review*, 11 (5), 1978, 1–10.

With A.D. Birrell:
'The CAP filing system' (6th ACM Symposium on Computer Operating System Principles, 1977), *Operating Systems Review*, 11 (5), 1978, 11–16.

With M.D. Schroeder:
'Using encryption for authentication in large networks of computers,' Xerox Palo Alto Research Centre, Report CSL-78-4, 1978; *Communications of the ACM*, 21 (12), 1978, 993–999; reprinted in *Advances in computer security*, ed. R. Turn, Dedham, MA: Artech House, 1988.

With A.D. Birrell:
'An asynchronous garbage collector for the CAP filing system,' *Operating Systems Review*, 12 (2), 1978, 31–33.

With A.D. Birrell:
'Character streams,' *Operating Systems Review*, 12 (3), 1978, 29–31.

With H.C. Lauer:
'On the duality of operating system structures' (Second International Conference on Operating Systems, 1978), *Operating systems: theory and practice*, ed. D. Lanciaux, Amsterdam: North-Holland, 1979, 371–384; reprinted in *Operating Systems Review*, 13 (2), 1979, 3–19.

'Protection' (Advanced Course on Computing Systems Reliability, Newcastle, 1978); in *Computer systems reliability*, ed. T. Anderson and B. Randell, Cambridge: Cambridge University Press, 1979, 264–287.

'Protection—theory and practice,' *Proceedings of the SEAS Anniversary Meeting 1978*, vol. 1, 1978, 80–84.

With M.V. Wilkes:
The CAP computer and its operating system, New York: Elsevier North-Holland, 1979.

'Adding capability access to conventional file servers,' *Operating Systems Review*, 13 (1), 1979, 3–4.

'Systems aspects of the Cambridge Ring' (7th ACM Symposium on Operating System Principles, 1979), *Operating Systems Review*, 13 (5), 1979, 82–85.

With M.V. Wilkes:
'The Cambridge model distributed system,' *Operating Systems Review*, 14 (1), 1980, 21–29.

With A.D. Birrell:
'A universal file server,' *IEEE Transactions on Software Engineering*, vol. SE-6 (5), 1980, 450–453.

With N.H. Garnett:
'An asynchronous garbage collector for the Cambridge file server,' *Operating Systems Review*, 14 (4), 1980, 36–40.

With A.J. Herbert:
'Sequencing computation steps in a network' (8th ACM Symposium on Operating System Principles, 1981), *Operating Systems Review*, 15 (5), 1981, 59–63.

'Design considerations for a processing server,' *Proceedings of the 8th Annual Symposium on Computer Architecture*, 1981, IEEE, 501–504.

'Capabilities and protection' (Proceedings, GI-10, Saarbrücken, 1980), *GI-10. Jahrestagung*, ed. R. Wilhelm, Berlin: Springer-Verlag, 1980, 45–53.

With A.D. Birrell, R. Levin, and M.D. Schroeder:
'Grapevine: an exercise in distributed computing' (presented at the 8th ACM Symposium on Operating Systems Principles, 1981), *Communications of the ACM*, 25, 1982, 260–274; reprinted in Birrell et al., 'Grapevine: two papers and a report,' Xerox Palo Alto Research Centre, Report CSL-83-12, 1983.

With A.J. Herbert:
The Cambridge distributed computing system, Reading, Mass.: Addison-Wesley, 1982.

With M.F. Richardson:
'The Tripos Filing Machine—a front-end to a file server' (9th ACM Symposium on Operating Systems Principles, 1983), *Operating Systems Review*, 17 (5), 1983, 120–128.

With A.J. Herbert and J.G. Mitchell:
'How to connect stable memory to a computer,' *Operating Systems Review* 17 (1), 1983, 16.

With M.D. Schroeder and A.D. Birrell:
'Experience with Grapevine: the growth of a distributed system,' *ACM Transactions on Computer Systems*, 2 (1), 1984, 3–23; reprinted in Birrell et al. 'Grapevine: two papers and a report,' Xerox Palo Alto Research Center, Report CSL-83-12, 1983.

With I.M. Leslie, J.W. Burren, and G.C. Adams:
'The architecture of the Universe network' (SIGCOMM 84 Tutorials and Symposium: Communications Architectures and Protocols), *Computer Communications Review*, 14 (2), 1984, 2–9.

With A.G. Waters, C.G. Adams, and I.M. Leslie:
'The use of broadcast techniques on the Universe network' (SIGCOMM 84 Tutorials and Symposium: Communications Architectures and Protocols), *Computer Communications Review*, 14 (2), 1984, 52–57.

'Fifth generation computing,' in *Information comes of age*, ed. C. Oppenheim, London: Rossendale, 1984, 71–77.

'Protection,' in *Local area networks: an advanced course*, ed. D. Hutchison, J. Mariani and D. Shepherd, Lecture Notes in Computer Science 184, Berlin: Springer, 1985, 261–281.

With M.D. Schroeder and D.K. Gifford:
'A caching file system for a programmer's workstation,' DEC Systems Research Centre, Palo Alto, Report 6; (10th ACM Symposium on Operating Systems Principles, 1985), *Operating Systems Review*, 19 (5), 1985, 25–34.

'Is there anything special about AI?' (Workshop on the Foundations of Artificial Intelligence, 1986), in *The foundations of artificial intelligence: A source book*, ed. D. Partridge and Y. Wilks, Cambridge: Cambridge University Press, 1990, 269–273.

With A.D. Birrell, B.W. Lampson, and M.D. Schroeder:
'A global authentication service without global trust,' *Proceedings of the IEEE Symposium on Security and Privacy*, 1986, 223–230.

With D.L. Tennenhouse, I.M. Leslie, C.A. Adams, J.W. Burren, and C.S. Cooper:
'Exploiting wideband ISDN: the Unison exchange,' *IEEE INFOCOM Conference Proceedings*, San Francisco, 1987, 1018–1026.

With M.D. Schroeder:
'Authentication revisited,' *Operating Systems Review*, 21 (1), 1987, 7.

'The Unison experience,' *Proceedings of the 23rd Annual Convention of the Computer Society of India*, ed. S. Raghavan and S. Venkatasubramanian, New Delhi: Macmillan, 1988, 51–57.

With D.K. Gifford and M.D. Schroeder:
'The Cedar file system,' *Communications of the ACM*, 31 (3), 1988, 288–298; reprinted, in Japanese, in *Bit*, November 1989, 30–50.

With A. Hopper:
'The Cambridge fast ring networking system,' *IEEE Transactions on Computers*, 37 (10), 1988, 1214–1223.

With M. Burrows and M. Abadi:
'Authentication: a practical study of belief and action,' *Proceedings of the 2nd Conference on Theoretical Aspects of Reasoning about Knowledge*, ed. M. Vardi, Los Altos, CA: Morgan Kaufmann, 1988, 325–342.

With M. Burrows:
'Locks in distributed systems—an observation,' *Operating Systems Review* 22 (3), 1988, 44.

With M. Burrows and M. Abadi:
'A logic of authentication,' DEC Systems Research Centre, Palo Alto, Report 39, 1989; *Proceedings of the Royal Society of London*, Series A, 426, 1989, 233–271; reprinted in *Practical cryptography for data internetworks*, ed. W. Stallings, Washington DC: IEEE Computer Society Press, 1996.

With M. Burrows and M. Abadi:
'A logic of authentication' (12th ACM Symposium on Operating System Principles, 1989), *Operating Systems Review*, 23 (5), 1989, 1–13; and *ACM Transactions on Computer Systems*, 8 (1), 1990, 18–36. [Refers to the previous Report 39, etc., version as fuller.]

With T.M.A. Lomas, L. Gong, and J.H. Saltzer:
'Reducing risks from poorly chosen keys' (12th ACM Symposium on Operating System Principles, 1989), *Operating Systems Review*, 23 (5), 1989, 14–18.

'Authentication,' in *Safe and secure computing systems*, ed. T. Anderson, Oxford: Blackwell Scientific, 1989, 189–196.

'Names' and 'Using cryptography for authentication' (Arctic 88; Fingerlakes 89: Advanced Courses on Distributed Systems), in *Distributed systems*, ed. S. Mullender, New York: ACM Press and Addison-Wesley, 1989, 89–101 and 103–116.

With J.M. Bacon and I.M. Leslie:
'Distributed computing with a processor bank,' Technical Report 168, Computer Laboratory, University of Cambridge, 1989.

With M. Burrows and M. Abadi:
'The scope of a logic of authentication,' *Proceedings of the DIMACS Workshop on Distributed Computing and Cryptography* (1989), ed. J. Feigenbaum and M. Merritt, New York: American Mathematical Society, 1991, 119–126.

With A. Herbert:
'Report on the Third European SIGOPS Workshop, "Autonomy or Interdependence in Distributed Systems",' *Operating Systems Review*, 23 (2), 1989, 3–19.

With L. Gong and R. Yahalom:
'Reasoning about belief in cryptographic protocols,' *Proceedings of the 1990 IEEE Symposium on Security and Privacy*, 1990, 234–248.

With M. Burrows and M. Abadi:
'Rejoinder to Nessett,' *Operating Systems Review*, 24 (2), 1990, 39–40.

'Capabilities and security,' *in Security and Persistence: Proceedings of the International Workshop on Computer Architectures to Support Security and Persistence of Information*, ed. J. Rosenberg and J. Keedy, Bremen, Germany, 1990, 1–8.

With M.D. Schroeder and others:
'Autonet: a high-speed, self-configuring local area network using point-to-point links,' DEC Systems Research Centre, Palo Alto, Report 59, 1990; *IEEE Journal on Selected Areas in Communications*, 9 (8), 1991, 1318–1335.

'What next? Some speculations,' in *Operating systems of the 90s and beyond*, ed. A.I. Karshmer and J. Nehmer, Berlin: Springer Verlag, 1991, 220–222.

'Later developments at Cambridge: Titan, CAP, and the Cambridge Ring,' *IEEE Annals of the History of Computing*, 14 (4), 1992, 57–58.

With A. Nakamura:
'An approach to real-time scheduling—but is it really a problem for multimedia?' (NOSSDAV 92), in *Network and Operating System Support for Digital Audio and Video*, ed. P. Venkat Randan, Lecture Notes in Computer Science 712, Berlin: Springer-Verlag, 1992, 32–39.

'Names' and 'Cryptography and secure channels,' in *Distributed systems*, ed. S. Mullender, 2nd ed., Reading, MA: Addison-Wesley, 1993, 315–326 and 531–541.

With M.A. Lomas, L. Gong and J.H. Saltzer:
'Protecting poorly chosen secrets from guessing attacks,' *IEEE Journal on Selected Areas in Communications*, 11 (5), 1993, 648–656. Abraham Award for Best Paper in the Journal for 1993.

'Denial of service,' *Proceedings of the 1st ACM Conference on Communications and Computing Security*, 1993, 151–153.

'Distributed computing,' Guest Editorial, *Computer Bulletin*, 6 (2), 1994, 2.

With M. Abadi:
'Prudent engineering practice for cryptographic protocols,' *Proceedings of the 1994 IEEE Symposium on Security and Privacy*, 1994, 122–136. Outstanding paper award.

'Computers and communications,' *Computer Science and Informatics* (Computer Society of India), 23 (4), 1993, 1–6.

'Denial of service: an example,' expanded version of 1993 paper, *Communications of the ACM* 37 (11), 1994, 42–46.

With M. Abadi:
'Prudent engineering practice for cryptographic protocols,' expanded version of 1994 IEEE Symposium paper, DEC Systems Research Centre, Palo Alto, Report 125, 1994; *IEEE Transactions on Software Engineering*, 22 (1), 1996, 6–15.

With A. Nakamura:
'The dependency protocol for real-time synchronisation,' *RTESA 94, Proceedings of the First International Workshop on Real-Time Computing Systems and Applications*, IEEE, Seoul, 1994.

With D. Wheeler:
'Two cryptographic notes,' Technical Report 355, Computer Laboratory, University of Cambridge, 1994.

With D.J. Wheeler:
'TEA, a tiny encryption algorithm,' *Fast Software Encryption*, 1994, 363–366.

With A. Nakamura:
'The dependency protocol for real-time synchronisation,' *Transactions of the Institute of Electronic, Information and Communication Engineers*, vol. J78-D-I no. 8, 1995, 649–660.

With P.W. Jardetsky and C.J. Sreenan:
'Storage and synchronisation for distributed continuous media,' *Multimedia Systems*, 3 (4), 1995, 151–161.

With R.J. Anderson:
'Programming Satan's computer,' in *Computer science today*, ed. J. van Leeuwen, Lecture Notes in Computer Science 1000, Berlin: Springer, 1995, 426–440.

With R.J. Anderson:
'Robustness principles for public key protocols,' in *Advances in cryptology—CRYPTO 95*, ed. D. Coppersmith, Lecture Notes in Computer Science 963, Berlin: Springer, 1995, 236–247.

'Fast communication and slow computers,' *Twelfth International Conference on Computer Communication*, Seoul, 1995.

'Computers and communications,' in *Computing tomorrow*, ed. I. Wand and R. Milner, Cambridge: Cambridge University Press, 1996, 284–294.

'The changing environment for security protocols,' *IEEE Network*, 11 (3), 1997, 12–15.

'Logic and oversimplification,' *Proceedings of the Thirteenth Annual IEEE Symposium on Logic in Computer Science*, 1998, 2–3.

With R.J. Anderson and others:
'A new family of authentication protocols,' *Operating Systems Review*, 32 (4), 1998, 9–20.

With R.J. Anderson and A. Shamir:
'The steganographic file system,' in *Information hiding* (Second International Workshop on Information Hiding), ed. D. Aucsmith, Lecture Notes in Computer Science 1525, Berlin: Springer, 1998, 73–84.

'The changing environment' (transcript, with discussion), *Security Protocols*, 7th International Workshop, Cambridge, ed. B. Christianson et al., Lecture Notes in Computer Science 1796, Berlin: Springer, 1999, 1–5.

'The hardware environment,' *Proceedings of the 1999 IEEE Symposium on Security and Privacy*, 1999, 236.

Editor, with K. Spärck Jones and G. Gazdar:
'Computers, language and speech: formal theories and statistical data,' *Philosophical Transactions of the Royal Society of London, Series A, Mathematical, Physical and Engineering Sciences*, vol. 358, no. 1769, 2000, 1225–1431.

With K. Spärck Jones and G. Gazdar:
'Introduction: combining formal theories and statistical data in natural language processing,' 'Computers, language and speech: formal theories and statistical data,' *Philosophical Transactions of the Royal Society of London, Series A, Mathematical, Physical and Engineering Sciences*, vol. 358, no. 1769, 2000, 1225–1238.

'Distributed computing: opportunity, challenge, or misfortune?' in *Millennial perspectives in computer science* (Proceedings of the 1999 Oxford-Microsoft Symposium in honour of Sir Tony Hoare), ed. J. Davies, B. Roscoe, and J. Woodcock, Basingstoke, Hants: Palgrave, 2000, 283–287.

'Mobile computing versus immobile security' (transcript), *Security Protocols*, 9th International Workshop, Cambridge, ed. B. Christianson et al., Lecture Notes in Computer Science 2467, Berlin: Springer, 2001, 1–3.

'Security—a technical problem or a people problem?' *Proceedings, Information Security Summit*, Prague: Tate International, 2001, 7–9.

'Donald Watts Davies CBE,' *Biographical Memoirs of Fellows of the Royal Society*, 48, 2002, 87–96.

'Computer security?' *Philosophical Transactions of the Royal Society, Series A, Mathematical, Physical and Engineering Sciences*, 361, 2003, 1549–1555.